Social Mobility in China

Social Mobility in China

*Status Careers
Among the Gentry
in a Chinese
Community*

Yung-Teh Chow

Chou, Jung-te

Atherton Press / New York
1966

Introduction

This book is a splendid contribution to the scientific literature on social stratification and mobility and more specifically to the sociology of pre-Communist China; done shortly before the Communist take-over, it is the result of several years of intensive study of the Chinese gentry and the larger society of the cities and rural areas of a county in Yunnan Province. Although the products of field research, the author's analyses and theoretical discussions give the work a broad interest and significance that make it far more than an ethnographic report and place it securely in the general literature of sociology and social anthropology.

The case study was the principal field method used. Richly documented throughout, it was applied to forty-seven gentry (extended) families and to the careers of 1,200 individuals in their many genealogical and social connections. Although the social areas stretch widely in time and space, the book provides an intimate picture of the individuals, the families, and the status groups in Chinese social life. Some of the excerpts from the biographies read like dramatic episodes from contemporary novels. Although the author is admirably detached and presents his evidence accordingly, the reader senses the impending breakdown of the old moral order; he soon clearly discerns that the conditions had been established there for a subsequent new revolutionary social order, Communist or whatever.

In the 1940s, the Institute for Census Research of the National Tsing Hua University set up the Kunyang Research Station under the direction of Dr. Chow. The research was conducted with the aid of several assistants, most of it during the Japanese War but some of it as late as 1948. The latter part was carried on by a resident assistant in Kunyang. A census was taken of the population in Kunyang County by the Institute, making it possible for Chow to place his biographies and his intensive study of the gentry in the larger social perspective of the county itself. Through interviews and personal acquaintance the fieldworkers established a biographical directory that covered all the prominent gentry members, including those of one subgroup, the government officials. In the family case studies, the genealogies and lineages were traced back for at least five generations, thus allowing us to see the persistence and transition of status forms, mobility practices, and behavior over a long period of time.

Three status groups are first delineated: the numerous peasants at the bottom of this agricultural society, the small gentry class, and the very small group of officials, the latter temporarily the resident local agents of the outside central government but for most purposes a subgroup of the gentry class, separate from the local gentry.

The members of officialdom in Kunyang County and elsewhere in China occupied such lofty positions that they were not ordinarily approachable by the peasantry; consequently the gentry acted as intermediaries between them and the peasants. The outward appearance of an official was also exceedingly forbidding to the ordinary peasant. His elegant uniforms, silk gowns, and awe-inspiring titles removed him from any approach by the lowly peasant. The members of officialdom, unlike the native gentry, were outsiders, but many members of the native gentry had served elsewhere as officials and had returned to Kunyang to live the superior life of the upper class.

The position of officialdom is well described in the testimony of one magistrate, who declared that he and his staff could not go "directly to the people"—that the members of the gentry, the educated people, "are the leaders of the masses and control public opinion." "One cannot get rid of them," the magistrate continued, "in fact, if the magistrate does not cooperate with them [the gentry] completely, he cannot do anything and will be in danger of losing his secure place."

The peasantry was the lowest level in society. Most peasants were engaged in some kind of agricultural labor from which they received very small incomes; a considerable proportion lived in misery and poverty. Of 10,000 households studied in Kunyang, only a small percentage was ranked in the upper-tenure group, about 37%. The overwhelming majority were peasants. These peasants were graded at several levels. The middle land-owning level, which did its own work and did not employ others, composed 47% of the households. Forty-four per cent were at still lower levels, and these two general classes together made up more than 90% of all the agricultural groups. (The lowest 44% were the ones characterized as living in "miserable poverty.")

When the census of peasant households was taken, 64% had no members with any education and were graded as "illiterate households." They were the ones most dependent upon gentry members to act as intermediaries with the powerful outside officials who ruled the area for the central government. The lowest status level was thus itself graded, and there was a struggle for mobility from lower to higher peasant grades. At the top of this level, efforts were made through the generations to push families out of the peasant class into the lower levels of the gentry.

The gentry, the primary subject of this book, consisted of the local families of power and prestige; in a secondary sense, the families of the officials who were posted temporarily from the outside were also in this class. Although gentry status adhered to scholars, retired officials, and those with education, the core of the gentry class was the large land owners and, secondarily, the wealthy merchants. These agriculturists did not cultivate their own land; they depended upon peasantry under the tenant system. Other families in the gentry class included such professional men as doctors, professors, and others engaged in higher education. The emphasis upon education, traditional or Western, was very great.

Money was accumulated by the gentry and officials through rampant corruption; money given to the gentry by peasants was viewed as gifts for favors the givers sought from the recipients.

The gentry was also graded along several dimensions; members enjoyed long or short occupancy of high positions, were large or small owners of land, possessed great or little wealth. They were further divided into a prestige hierarchy based on the increased territorial participation and renown of the family in the village, the larger district, the county, or the province, in an ascending order of significance.

Both in ideal and in fact, the gentry family was extended rather than nuclear. Ordinarily it was composed of a number of interrelated nuclear families, families of brothers, fathers, and sons. The individual in such an extended family had his own place and opportunity for achievement. He could go to the outside world and there gain renown and wealth, but upon his return his achievements would contribute to the increased glory of the family, which in turn would give him increased prestige and power. The primary goal of this striving individual or of his nuclear family was the strengthening and raising of the extended family's status within the hierarchy of the gentry.

Many families of the gentry had held their positions for centuries; some had become known as "scholar families" or as families of high military renown. It was therefore the duty of the generations to pass on the traditions of the family so that its glory would be maintained through the coming generations.

The son was in a particularly difficult situation. If his family was well down in the status hierarchy, it was his duty to attempt to achieve higher position and thereby to bring his parents and those kindred around them up to his own. If he belonged to a family with great prestige, his task was to rise within the family profession and to maintain or increase the prestige of the extended family group. But given the chaos of the rapidly changing society of the country at that time, this achievement could be very difficult, for it was no longer the charted mobility route of traditional China.

Although the gentry had top status in an open class system in which various forms of mobility were possible, Chow's genealogical records, which trace the movements of families through time, demonstrate that what may appear to have been the movement of one individual or family into higher status may have taken several generations of slow movement upward, generations of accumulating wealth and increased position. Furthermore, the position of the parvenu, judged by the evidence, was not an easy one; it took time for him to learn how to display his wealth in elaborate *rites de passage* and other ceremonies, as well as to purchase and furnish the kind of great house in which the gentry members lived. Etiquette itself was a matter of expensive training.

The traditional occupational ranking in China ideally placed the scholar at the top, the farmer next, then the artisan, and, at the bottom, the merchant. But in fact, the money power of the merchant contributed greatly to the high actual ranking he received. Many members of the scholarly gentry were silent partners in commercial enterprises. Furthermore, at least from the period of the Japanese War, the money makers promoted themselves to higher positions, perhaps illegitimately, but no more so than had some of the political and military officials.

Chow gives considerable attention to the different modes of mobility. Obviously, any particular family might use several. The author takes each family's primary method and studies the rise of individuals and generations using this method. The principal kinds of mobility he discusses involve schooling, medical practice, the army, the government, commerce, upward marriage, and insurrection and revolution.

Perhaps the most honored and most honorable road for advancement into the higher gentry was higher education and scholarly activity. Medical practice was respected, as was the route through governmental activity. Under the old system the local schools, particularly their lower branches, were easily accessible to all, providing a family had the necessary income; and even for some of the less wealthy, they were accessible if the parents were willing to make the necessary sacrifices. In this system, the mobile man went to a private school for ten years; he could live at home, and at the end of that time, with a little luck and some talent, he could move into an official position. In the new Western system, college was necessary, and the time required was sixteen years; most important, it was necessary for the aspirant to go away to an urban center for his advanced education. This shift not only involved learning a new way of life but also was far more expensive, to the point that many of the well-to-do could not afford to send their sons to the high levels necessary to educate the new men most acceptable to the new China. Furthermore, the old scholar with his elegant gown had come to be mildly derogated, and the man in Western clothes was the kind of man most likely to achieve high position.

The most advantageously placed student was he who left China for Europe, Japan, or the United States to take higher degrees. The result of all this change is clear: The mobility routes were rapidly closed to a considerable portion of the gentry, as well as to the wealthier peasants. Many sons could not compete for high achievement in the scholarly channels of mobility previously available to them.

During the latter years of the Republic, when traditional Chinese culture was still important, marriage was closely related to scholarly achievement for those who aspired to higher positions. The ideal was "equality of gates and doors" between intermarrying families, meaning, of course, equality of status. The result often was a nice trading of kinds of status; for example, a young man from a wealthy family might be contracted to marry a young woman whose family was politically powerful. This nicety of fit was not always attained, however, for differing values might be involved. For example, a poor and pious young man might be viewed as the right kind of husband for the daughter of a wealthy merchant of high position. The young man who came from this low position with a family of reputation for piety and good character would thus rise in status. There are such instances in Chow's records. Accumulation of wealth through trading, mining, manufacture, and other methods was still one of the principal means by which men could rise. Wealth, after all, can be translated into other kinds of highly valued social objects and social activities.

As the system became more disorganized, the influence of the military became very great. The political route, linked to military advancement, was often used; the civil war offered great opportunity for the aspiring soldier. During this same period, a large percentage of rural and small-town males emigrated; the registration of migration shows that about 73% of these emigrants enlisted in the army. Officers and soldiers usually came from different backgrounds, the former from the middle and upper gentry, the latter from the peasantry. In either case, economic gain was the principal motive. Military advancement could be rapid and sometimes easy. Quick success often attended a man's becoming an officer and a gentleman. The military academy was free, and many took this route.

A few of the lowly peasants rose to great height and prestige. Some aspiring military men attached themselves to men of position and, as proteges, advanced rapidly to positions that paid them well. These parvenus were not the only men who rose via the military route. The renowned old military families continued to supply young men who advanced through traditional military channels.

To any student of American social class, Chow's findings can easily be compared with those based on mobility among our own elites. It is clear that we have both birth and mobile elites. The Chinese too had their old elites, far older of course than ours, and their mobile elites, some of whom had come directly from the peasantry and from the lower grades of the gentry. The problems besetting the Chinese mobile man were quite similar to those facing our own. The man who came out of the peasantry in China had to change his way of life completely. As a matter of fact, he had to change even more than rising Americans do, because, in effect, his new education changed his culture from an all Chinese to a partly Western one. The birth elite might follow the traditional pattern, but its young men also had to move out from the shadows of their fathers to find their own sunlight.

The open class system of China, with the gentry at the top, which permitted entry from the grades and statuses below, changed from fluidity to disorganization during the period of dissolution. The revolution came not because of the rigidity of the class system or the bureaucracy; rather, it came as China entered the world system and changed from a traditional to an innovating society in which the old class system could not, or did not, work. This dissolution resulted in the Communist revolution.

It is easy now to say that the system failed because of moral corruption or technological failure or a variety of other reasons and that the new Communism was successful because it was morally impeccable, had a strong ideological system, or adopted the technology of the new scientific society. All these observations may be true, but the inferences are too facile. It is quite possible that the old society might have undergone rapid change, as others have, that would have enabled China to adjust to the new world conditions without a Communist revolution. In either case, the gentry Dr. Chow has studied could not have been today what it then was. Too much was needed that could not be supplied by the old and new gentry.

Preface
and
Acknowledgments

This book tests a conceptual framework of social mobility and the methods of empirical research associated with it; it also studies status system and mobility in a Chinese county. Originally the former objective was the main one, but without a community to provide the necessary social laboratory it would have been extremely difficult to analyze the aspects and processes of social mobility and to formulate any useful generalizations about it. Of course, the book makes no pretense of being a comprehensive survey of Chinese social history for the period under investigation. The coverage is restricted to the subject matter related to social mobility.

Since Pitirim Sorokin published his *Social Mobility* in 1927, there has been no other comprehensive study in that field of sociology. (D. V. Glass, *Social Mobility in Britain,* New York, 1954, p. 5, note 1.) Although its most valuable contribution was analytical, it ranged too far and too wide in time and space, perhaps, to induce confidence in some of the author's sweeping generalizations. It raised many pertinent questions concerning contemporary society where the admitted paucity of existing research indicated the need for further inquiry. (Milton M. Gordon, *Social Class in American*

Sociology, Durham, N. C., 1958, p. 62.) Indeed, every sociological concept remains tentative until it is tested or illustrated empirically.

A preliminary draft of this study was written in 1955. It was revised during 1956–1957 and used as my doctoral dissertation at The University of Chicago. Since then the entire manuscript has been substantially revised.

It is with the greatest respect and warmest affection that I wish to make special acknowledgments to a number of persons for their generous assistance in the collection and analysis of the data and to several institutions for their financial support. It goes without saying that any significant study in a discipline like sociology is by no means a product of individual work but is essentially a social enterprise. Because my academic training and research took place in both China and the United States, this study is actually a convergence of biculture and a product of marginal man. In every instance in which thought has been borrowed consciously from any sociologist or scholar, I have tried to give credit. In some rare cases, if I have unconsciously incorporated the thought of another as though it were my own and do not name the sources, probably because it seemed pedantic to refer to resources of common knowledge, I am nevertheless grateful to him. In any case, the selected bibliography should be considered as an integral part of the book.

First of all, I should like to express my appreciation to Messrs. Yang Chan and Tu Lien-yüan for their participation in this study at its inception and for their able and skilled field investigation, which supplied invaluable research evidence. I am grateful to all my former colleagues at the Kunyang Research Station of the Institute for Census Research, National Tsing Hua University, and to many Kunyang friends, informants, and members of the gentry itself for giving me the immeasurable benefit of their information. It is a great pleasure to present a study of a group of persons who have shaped, preserved, and given distinctive color to the social system. In order to protect the anonymity of the subjects, however, all the personal and village names in the life histories of the gentry families are fictitious. All the personal names have been written as the Chinese write them: with the surname first, except for the scholars who have written in English and have recorded their names with the surname in terminal position.

Then, to Professors Ta Chen and Quentin Pan, I owe not only my initial training in sociology but also my interest in the empirical study of social mobility. Their instructions have been the deep sources of my research inspiration. During the entire writing of this work, I have drawn upon Professor W. Lloyd Warner for a sustained supply of personal encouragement and paternal understanding of the difficulties besetting a newcomer in this country. In addition to his introduction to this book, his guidance and direction have been most helpful in making the present research a reality. Professor Everett C. Hughes and the late Professor R. Richard Wohl were kind enough to offer many perceptive criticisms of an earlier draft of the study. Their advice has constantly been taken into consideration. My special tribute should be paid to Professor William L. Holland, who has given his sympathetic patronage to the development of this study and has furnished counsel as needed through the years. The late Bruno Lasker and Professor John K. Fairbank offered many fertile ideas when the work was in its various stages of advancement. The impact of their penetrating comments may be found in many parts of my writing. I am profoundly grateful to Professor Pitirim A. Sorokin, the late Professor Robert Redfield, and Mrs. Margaret Park Redfield for their friendly interest and their most valuable suggestions. Another debt of gratitude I owe to two friends of mine, Dr. Shu-ching Lee and the late Dr. Ju-shu Pan, for their frequently stimulating discussions of the source material. My appreciation is due to Dr. J. W. Smurr for his careful reading of the entire manuscript and fruitful help in improving its English throughout. Mr. Thomas Callahan, Dr. Peter Kong-min New, and Dr. Emmit V. Mittlebeeler read parts of the manuscript and helped shape and polish its style. For their invaluable assistance both the author and the readers should be grateful.

Furthermore, acknowledgment should be made to my alma mater, National Tsing Hua University, for a scholarship that enabled me to undertake advanced study in the United States and to The University of Chicago for a fellowship under which the analysis of data was completed. The preparation of the manuscript for publication was made possible by a grant-in-aid from the Wenner-Gren Foundation for Anthropological Research, Inc. I am particularly grateful to the late President Yi-chi Mei of National Tsing Hua University and the late Dr. Paul Fejos of the Wenner-Gren Foundation for their kindness and encouragement.

Finally, Dr. Robert A. LeVine and Miss Marlene Mandel deserve special thanks for their editorial suggestions. Special acknowledgment is made of the courtesy of The University of Chicago Press for permission to reprint excerpts from the six copyrighted life histories in *China's Gentry,* Copyright © 1953 by The University of Chicago Press, and to The Institute for Census Research of National Tsing Hua University for permission to use its unpublished statistical data, which were prepared under the supervision of Professor Shih-kuang Tai. My thanks are also due to Miss Barbara Olstad for having helped me with typing and proofreading.

Indeed, without the magnanimous assistance, counsel, and support of all these teachers, mentors, friends, colleagues, and academic institutions, my study would not have been accomplished. Much as I owe to all this scholastic grace and material aid, I claim any errors, or any shortcomings, or any unsound views the readers may find in the exposition as my own.

YUNG-TEH CHOW

Moorhead, Minnesota
May, 1965

Contents

———— ►◄►◄◄ ————

Tables
and
Illustrations

TABLES

ILLUSTRATIONS

1

Scope and Methods

This book presents a study of social stratification and mobility in traditional Chinese society through the analysis of social statistics and life histories drawn from one Chinese county, with special reference to its gentry. The gentry, *shên-shih,* was a kind of ruling class, to which considerable sociological attention has been directed.

The gentry was also sometimes referred to as *shih ta-fu,* or "scholar-official." Actually the gentry, although closely linked with the group of scholar-officials, should be distinguished from it. The term *shih ta-fu* was derived from the literature of Chou Dynasty (1122–256 B.C.). A common designation in Chou literature for members of the upper class was *chün-tzŭ* or "rulers' sons." Originally this term was primarily indicative of good birth, but later, under Confucian influence, it acquired a strong moral coloration in a manner very similar to the English "gentleman." The lowest group among *chün-tzŭ* was known as *shih,* which was perhaps roughly comparable in status to the knights of medieval Europe. All these aristocrats, regardless of whether or not they bore titles of nobility, differed from the rest of the population in that they maintained family genealogies and the ancestral cult, performed no agricultural or artisan labor, did not engage in trade, and lived according to an elaborate but (in earliest times) unwritten code of ceremonial and etiquette known as

1

li (variously rendered as "rites," "ceremonies," "traditional mores," "customary morality," and so forth). These *li*, which took the place of any fixed code of law, were designed to cover all the major activities of life and required much time to learn. On the military side, they remind us in some ways of the chivalric code of European knighthood. Warfare was waged more for prestige than to gain loot or territory: one was not to resort to unfair stratagems or push one's victory too far. When not engaged in warfare, these aristocrats amused themselves by feasting, hunting, and engaging in such games as archery contests. To a greater extent than their medieval European counterparts, however, they seem also to have been seriously interested in the administrative affairs of peace. Many were well-educated men who, at diplomatic assemblies or court gatherings, could buttress their arguments with appropriate quotations from ancient literature like the *Book of Odes*.[1] *Shih ta-fu*, although they were at the bottom of the hierarchy of the ruling class, were still part of that class. At that time the gap between the commoners and the aristocrats was great. Social mobility from one class to the other virtually did not exist. A common man could become a noble no more easily than a woman could change to a man.[2]

Having conquered the last of the opposing states in 221 B.C., the King of Ch'in adopted for himself the grandiose title of *Shih Huang-ti*, "First Sovereign Emperor." He abolished feudalism and saw to it that the Ch'in Empire (221–206 B.C.) was without an acre of land of investiture (*feng*). Although certain noble titles were retained, they were honorary only and had no territorial significance. The empire was divided into forty-two *chun* or commanderies. Each commandery was governed by a centrally appointed triumvirate of administrator, military governor, and overseer and was subdivided into an indeterminate number of *hsien* or prefectures, governed by prefects. Consequently, the administrative power lay in the hands of the centrally appointed bureaucracy, which under Emperor Ai (6–1 B.C.) of the Han Dynasty (206 B.C.–A.D. 222) amounted to 130,285 officials, who were paid in cash or grain rather than in land (though much of their capital was invested in land). Thus was created the vitally important official gentry class, which in most later periods was the effective ruling group in China and which, though it tended to be self-perpetuating as a status group, never achieved individual hereditary rights in the government posts it held. The orthodox ideology of this group was Confucianism.[3]

During the later dynasties the gentry's position and qualifications became formalized through the imperial examination system. The acquisition of title, grade, degree, or official rank automatically made the holder a member of the *shên-shih* group. Titles, grades, and degrees were meant to indicate the holders' educational standings. Official rank was generally conferred only upon people who had proof of such standing. Educational grades and degrees were obtained by passing government examinations, which was the formal way of proving educational qualification. Those who became members of the gentry through examinations may therefore be called the "regular" group. Educational titles could, however, be purchased. Although those who bought such titles were usually literate and had some education, they were not required to give proof of educational qualifications. Such members of the gentry may be called the "irregular" group.[4]

Of these two groups, the "regulars" were, then, those who had passed the government examinations. The educational grade for gentry status was *shêng-yüan*, which was gained by passing a series of these examinations. The term *shêng-yüan* is best rendered as "government student." It described students of the district and prefectural schools. *Shêng* literally means "students," and *yüan* means "a definite number." The whole term referred to a definite number of students admitted through examinations to each district or prefectural school. These *shêng-yüan* could strive for advancement through participation in higher examinations for the degree of *chü-jen,* graduate of the provincial examinations, and the degree of *chin-shih,* graduate of the metropolitan examinations. Some of the *shêng-yüan* who had not succeeded in the higher examinations but whose higher scholastic standings were recognized were granted the academic title of *kung-shêng,* "imperial student." The *chin-shih, chü-jen,* and *kung-shêng* had risen above the *shêng-yüan.* Together with the many who remained *shêng-yüan,* they formed this most important section of the gentry qualified through academic rating, the group we have called "regular." From the holders of the higher academic degrees, the *chin-shih, chü-jen,* and *kung-shêng,* government officials were selected. Indeed, the earning of such degrees was the regular way to officialdom. As officials, these men entered government service and carried out functions for the government, but at the same time they remained members of the gentry of their home areas, and their official rank increased their prestige among the gentry.[5]

The other way of becoming a member of the gentry was through the purchase of an academic title. This title was that of *chien-shêng,* student of the Imperial College. Most *chien-shêng,* with very few exceptions, did not actually move to the capital to study in the Imperial College. For them the title was important. It admitted them to gentry status and privileges and was an opening for further advancement and official positions. Moreover, the title of *kung-shêng,* mentioned in the first group, was sometimes attained not through examination but through purchase. Those who purchased academic titles could then purchase official rank or position. Indeed, the academic title and the official rank or position were often purchased together. The "irregular" route could lead only to the lower offices, but such official rank, even though "irregularly" obtained, raised the holder's position as a member of the gentry. Furthermore, if one acquired gentry status by purchasing an academic title, one could still become a "regular" gentry member later through participating in the higher examinations for the *chü-jen* and *chin-shih* degrees. If a person passed these examinations, he was then considered a "regular" member of the gentry. Some candidates bought the *chien-shêng* title simply to gain speedier admission to the higher examinations.[6]

Among the gentry were also those who had gained their positions by acquiring military titles, grades, degrees, or official ranks. There was in the examination system a special section of military examinations leading to the academic grades and degrees of military *shêng-yüan* (*wu shêng-yüan*), military *chü-jen* (*wu chü-jen*), and military *chin-shih* (*wu chin-shih*). The holders of higher military degrees could become military officers. Men of military education could also buy the academic title of *chien-shêng* and from there move to military office. The majority of the officers of the Chinese government army, however, rose from the ranks. These men had not been of the gentry first, but the official rank thus obtained gave them gentry status. These military men from the ranks, who were a much smaller and less influential group within the gentry, were an exception to the general rule of educational qualification, as they had gained their gentry status without having first obtained academic titles, grades, or degrees.[7]

In traditional China the officials were no longer relatives or members of the emperor's own family but were employees appointed by the government. To be born into a gentry family did not necessarily ensure that one would become a scholar or an official. The appointment could be obtained only through one's own efforts, especially after the establishment, in the middle of the seventh century, of the nation-wide competitive imperial examination system, through which the dynamic government selected an intellectual elite, even of obscure origin, once every three years. The incentive for upward social mobility in this system was remarkable.

After the breakdown of feudalism there was another important change. The throne became the object of capture by the strong, by the seekers after power. Under feudalism, in which political power was distributed to relatives and kin, anyone not born into a noble family was a common man who had no chance of reaching the throne, of touching, or even of seeing, the divine paraphernalia of monarchy. But, after feudalism went, it was theoretically possible for anyone to become emperor. Political power thus became an object of struggle. This point is illustrated by the story of the historian Ssŭ-ma Ch'ien of Hsiang Yü, who, during the Ch'in Dynasty, while watching an imperial procession, said to his friend, "This I can seize." After that time the struggle for political power never ceased. "Those who emerged victorious in this struggle became emperors; the defeated became bandits," so to speak.[8]

Members of the gentry might be scholars or active or retired high officials. The traditional gentry was clearly defined by the qualification of having passed at least the lowest grade of the imperial examinations, which gave a man the privilege of entering county and provincial government offices and seeing officials—and thus gave him power as an intermediary between government and the common people. In the Republican period, after the abolition of the imperial examination system and the discarding of Confucianism as the orthodoxy of the state, the old Confucian scholars with imperial examination degrees or grades were rapidly eliminated from officialdom through senility and displacement by officials emerging from the new educational system. The new officials did not restrict their contacts with the people to the scholars; their visitors included rich merchants with little formal education and at times even notorious elements. Public influence and wealth, instead of formal scholastic success, became the criteria of judging those who could approach the government officials directly on private or community affairs. Big landlords and local politicos took the place of the old-style scholars as intermediaries between the government and the people under the Republican political order, which did not, however, change the traditional dichotomy between the ruler and the ruled. The new group that had risen in the old gentry's place was thus much less ideologically homogeneous in composition and less well defined in status.[9] In any case, these people had no real political power in shaping policies and might not even have had any direct connection with politics whatever, yet they tended to have influence in government and to be immune from political exploitation. With wealth and good political connections they enjoyed high prestige in the district. And the more frightening the ruler, the more valuable was the gentry's protection from above. In such circumstances it was difficult to survive except by attaching oneself to some important family.

When this historical and theoretical analysis is applied to the actual functioning of community-level society, two points must be clarified. First, after the downfall of the Manchu government in 1911, the emperor no longer existed. His place was taken over by the warlords. Each warlord occupied one or more provinces. He maintained his own army and taxation and had absolute power in his own area. The central government nominally ruled the entire country, but it could represent the whole country only in such matters as foreign affairs.

Second, "officialdom" and "gentry" were but two different names for the same class of persons on a supracommunity level. During their periods of official tenure bureaucrats were absent from their home communities. In their official positions they represented the government, in contradistinction to all groups of society, and were in this capacity not regarded as part of the gentry. But they still remained part of the gentry in their home areas, whether they actually were at home or were exerting their influence in distant places. The gentry was therefore close to officialdom, and this proximity gave its position a special political importance. Whether functioning as members of a social group or serving as officials of the state, gentry members derived their authority from their educational qualifications as shown in their degrees. Whether in or out of office, the gentry was thus an essential part of the bureaucratic system.[10] But in a community like a county, this group differentiated itself into two subgroups for two reasons: First, the magistrate was an agent of provincial government. During his term of office he had certain power in the territory under his rule. A member of the native gentry could impose his influence on him only behind the scenes. Second, in a semi-independent province like Yunnan, the magistrate was usually a native of Yunnan but not of the county under his authority. I was informed that prior to 1945 there had not been a single magistrate who was native to Kunyang in the history of that county. In a county the magistrate and his company were rulers who came from other places and, in a certain sense, became a "they group" to the gentry of the area, who had a certain degree of community patriotism. Although the magistrate was called *fu-mu kuan,* "parent-official," which meant that, of various officials, the magistrate was closest to the life of the people, it was impossible for him to be familiar with the local conditions and people because the term of office was usually only about two years. Consequently, in spite of the fact that the officials and the gentry were "two sides of a coin" on the national level, in the community the officials and the gentry were in fact two subgroups in the status system.

THE RESEARCH PROBLEM

This work is concerned with social mobility—the social mobility of individuals, families, and a status group in a community. It is focused on the study of social status and social mobility of the Chinese gentry. The study has three parts:

First, we shall examine the status system of Chinese society in general and the social functions of the gentry. There were two major classes in the Chinese society of the 1940s, the peasantry and the gentry. But in a county like Kunyang, the magistrate and his company belonged to one group, and the gentry of Kunyang belonged to another group. In the status system each group had its appropriate social position and definite social functions. The gentry formed an indispensable part of the local government and had molded itself into what Max Weber has termed a "status group"—a group with identical ideology, honor, and privileges.[11] It played a series of social roles.

Second, we shall investigate the social characteristics of the gentry. Closely connected with the conception of social structure is the conception of "social personality" as the position occupied by a human being in a social structure. The human being is involved in a complex of social relationships and therefore the object of study for the sociologist. We shall analyze such social characteristics of the gentry as the "style of life," literacy and aspirations, the family pattern, the display of prestige, and the social structure of the gentry.

Third, we shall inquire into the social mobility of the gentry. The gentry originated among the peasantry. Its families became prominent through a process of upward social mobility. A number of questions are raised: How could a common farmer become a member of the gentry? What were the motives and goals of upward mobility? What were the routes of upward mobility into the gentry for individuals and families? What were the types and processes of upward mobility? What were the various forms of social mobility?

The history of the gentry in Chinese social life is analogous to a play in which the status system is the stage, members of the gentry are the characters, and social mobility is the plot, a comedy or a tragedy. All three elements constitute an integrated whole. Similarly, the place of the gentry in the status system, the gentry's social personality, and the pattern of social mobility are viewed as functionally interdependent in the totality of social life. They have an inner coherence and cannot be understood separately.

China was a densely populated country. In the rural areas there were too many hands for the available jobs, and labor was therefore cheap. Farm implements were simple: Those of importance were the plow, hoe, and sickle; consequently, work was actually toil. It was therefore quite natural for those who could afford to live without earning their livings by physical exertion to regard this emancipation from toil with pride. A leisure class emerged. It lived on the rents collected from its tenants. The rate of rent was generally as high as 50 or 60% of the chief crop, rice. The tenants rented farms from the landlords and worked the land. They might work the whole year and not earn their livings, especially if it was a bad year. They had to accept any terms dictated by the privileged because of a limited supply of land and because, apart from farming, other occupations were seldom available. Many people possessed no land and therefore had to find other means to earn bare livings. They became casual laborers, mercenary soldiers, gangsters, and bandits. According to a Chinese expression, they were "people who tie their cooking stoves to their feet."[12]

The gentry class, being emancipated from toil, could pursue high culture if so inclined. The difficulty of the Chinese written language had prevented the laboring class from attaining classical literacy. Only those who could spend years of leisure in study could hope to master the Chinese classics; by mastering these classics they became better informed of the traditional moral teachings. A society ruled mainly by tradition gives high prestige to those who have access to classical teachings. The propertied class therefore became also the prestige class. The elegant long gown symbolized perfectly both the Chinese leisure class and high culture.[13]

The gentry constituted an indispensable part of the local government and acted as a medium between the populace and the government. It became a kind of buffer between the government and the common people. It collected taxes for the government and palliated some of the official abuses for the peasantry. In the peasant community its members were the local elite, the upholders of convention, and the numerous tentacles of the great power hierarchy. In the whole country, they provided most of the nation's brains, leadership, and organizing ability, and they were the main vehicle of transmission of the national culture.

The continuous domination of the peasantry by the gentry had been maintained through centuries by the single fact that the officials had been chosen from the Confucian scholars in the past and from the school graduates after the establishment of a modern educational system, and these men were chiefly recruited from the wealthy families. The processes depended on the different types of upward mobility. Generally, it was through education that the people found opportunity to rise into officialdom. It usually took several generations for a farmer-peasant to climb. A poor but ambitious peasant might climb up the social hierarchy within a lifetime through such channels as mercenary soldiering, but these shortcuts were the most hazardous and uncertain routes.

THE SETTING

In order to undertake this study, I selected Kunyang Hsien (Kunyang County) in the province of Yunnan as a social laboratory. During the years of the Japanese War, I served as a research associate at the Institute for Census Research of National Tsing Hua University, which had been moved from Peiping (now Peking) to Kunming, the capital of Yunnan. The Institute was established in Chengkung in January, 1939 under the direction of Dr. Ta Chen. After one year and a half, the Kunyang Research Station of the Institute was also set up. I took charge of the Research Station from May, 1943 to June, 1946, as a successor to Ru-chiang Su, another research associate of the institute, when he left for the United States.

The counties in China were classified into three groups according to geographical location, size of population, and socioeconomic conditions. Kunyang was a third-class county. It was located in the middle of Yunnan, sixty kilometers south of Kunming, bordering Kunming Lake and connected with Kunming by steamboat. There were two important motor roads. One went to the East and connected with Chinning (fifteen kilometers), Chengkung (forty kilometers) and Kunming (sixty kilometers). Another went to the South and connected with Yüchi. The distance from Kunyang to Yüchi is thirty kilometers. Two buses ran back and forth every day.

The temperature of Kunyang is almost uniform through the

year, varying from 11.8° C. (53.2° F.) in January to 22.8° C. (72° F.) in August. The annual rainfall averages 978.5 mm., concentrated in the four months of June, July, August, and September. During the monsoon season, the rain often pours down and inundates the fields. But when the dry season arrives, the sky is clear, and the sun shines almost every day. The lack of water and moisture frequently arrests the normal growth of food crops and plants. Winters rarely bring daytime freezing temperatures.

Kunyang is in the Kunming plateau, 1,896 meters above sea level. The County contains lowlands of considerable size and is fairly well irrigated, especially along Kunming Lake. For centuries this region has been devoted to agriculture, and to this day it is considered generally typical of the agricultural regions in the Southwest. Both extensive and intensive farming are the prevailing methods of cultivation and have shown little modification during the last few hundred years. In the plain the chief agricultural products are rice, wheat, corn, sorghum, soybeans, barley, tea, and tobacco. On the hillsides, potatoes, wheat, buckwheat, and beans are produced. Fruits include peaches, pears, apricots, and oranges. In years of plenty the production of rice is sufficient to feed the local population for about six months of the year, and other food crops have to make good the deficiency. In years of poor harvest, the shortage in food is seriously felt by the local inhabitants.[14]

The reasons for low production at the time of our study were inefficiency of farm labor, the small size of farms, poor management, and antiquated farm implements. During the previous half-century or more, little improvement had been made in the hoe, the buffalo cart, the grain thresher, and the simple device for carrying water from the river to the field for irrigation.[15]

The Yunnan highlands are moderately well supplied with mineral assets. In western Kunyang iron ore provided the basis for a small wartime blast furnace and steel industry at Ma Chieh Tzŭ on the western outskirts of Kunming. Reserves are large, but mining methods were primitive, and transportation was costly. Hydroelectricity was available in great amounts at Shih Lung Dam in northern Kunyang.

The Kunyang Hsien included 259 villages and had a territory of 775.3 square kilometers. It was divided into eight districts, seven *hsiang* or rural areas and one *chên* or urban area. Each *hsiang* had a chief called *hsiang-chang,* and the chief of the *chên* was called *chên-chang.* Each *hsiang* or *chên* included from six to fifteen *pao,* and each *pao* had a head called *pao-chang.* Each *pao* included from six to fifteen *chia*, and each *chia* had a head named *chia-chang*. Each *chia* included from six to fifteen households, and each household had a head named *hu-chang*.* The figures are shown in Table 1.

Table 1. *The Distribution of Hsiang, Chên, Pao, Chia, and Households, Kunyang, 1940*

Hsiang or Chên	Pao	Chia	Households[a]
Chung-Ho Chên	15	176	2,372
Chung-Pao Hsiang	6	59	616
Ho-Hsi Hsiang	15	123	1,241
Ping-Ting Hsiang	11	119	1,728
Pao-Shan Hsiang	10	127	1,253
Jen-Teh Hsiang	6	86	1,183
Nei-Tien Hsiang	11	113	1,162
Chiu-Tu Hsiang	12	118	1,213
Total	86	921	10,768

Source: The county government of Kunyang.

[a] The household figures of the *pao-chia* were used by the government as a basis for sharing provincial taxes and labor conscriptions. In order to decrease the share of taxation, the head of the *pao* office discounted the extremely poor families. The household figures of the *pao-chia* were therefore usually smaller than the actual numbers. (According to the census taken on March 1, 1942, by the Institute for Census Research, there were 11,220 households. The difference between the two figures is 452 households.)

According to the census data collected by the Institute on March 1, 1942, there was a *de jure* population of 69,231 in Kunyang Hsien. In the northwestern area of Kunyang lived 12,923 Lolos, or 18.7% of the total population, and 471 Min-chia, or .7% of the total. Each of these two ethnic groups had its own language, culture, and history.[16] Among the Lolos, 11,750 or 90.9% lived in the two northwestern mountainous districts, Nei Tien Hsiang and Chiu Tu Hsiang.

* The *pao-chia* system, under which ten households, whose members were held to be mutually responsible for one another's behavior, were grouped in a *chia*, ten *chia* forming a *pao*, was first instituted in 1069–1070 by the famous statesman Wang An-shih. The Nationalist government reinstituted the system in 1932 in the province of Kiangsi in order to register and organize the people more effectively against the Communists. As the system had been much criticized for the arbitrariness of its organization, the practice in Yunnan became more flexible as to the number of units. During the years of the Japanese War, the system was converted into the lowest government administrative organ to carry out urgently needed taxation, conscriptions, and other affairs.

There were 641 Moslems of an ethnic group of Turkic origin in the northern area.

Among the total population of 69,231, 30,035 or 44.2% were classified as nonworking population and 39,196 or 55.8% as working population, the latter defined as twelve years old or over and gainfully employed. Kunyang was still pre-eminently agricultural. Farming by the natives occupied 85.8% of the total working population of both sexes, 76.6% of the males and 95.8% of the females. Manufacturing, mining, commerce, communication, and transportation constituted only 7.4% of the total working population for both sexes. The details are shown in Table 2.

Table 2. *Gainfully Employed Natives of Kunyang by Sex and Occupation, 1942*

Industry and occupation	Both sexes		Males		Females	
	Number	Per-centage	Number	Per-centage	Number	Per-centage
Agriculture	33,627	85.8	15,692	76.6	17,935	95.8
Mining	49	0.1	47	0.2	2	0.0
Manufacturing	1,765	4.5	1,508	7.4	257	1.4
Commerce	760	1.9	440	2.1	320	1.7
Supplying necessities of life	211	0.5	153	0.7	58	0.3
Communication and transportation	366	0.9	342	1.7	24	0.1
Public service	1,722	4.4	1,719	8.4	3	0.0
Liberal professions	336	0.9	272	1.3	64	0.3
Personal service	200	0.5	160	0.8	40	0.2
Unknown	160	0.4	145	0.7	15	0.1
Total	39,196	99.9	20,478	99.9	18,718	99.9

Source: The Institute for Census Research, National Tsing Hua University, "Experimental Population Census and Vital Registration in Kunming Lake Region, Yunnan Province." Kunming: Committee on Experimental Census and Vital Registration for Kunming Lake Region, 1944, pp. 322–9, Table 8.

Illiteracy in Kunyang was unusually high, and the peasants as a rule knew very little about sanitation. In the ordinary homes the rooms were generally dark and rarely admitted the sun's rays. Doctors of the traditional style, in whom the peasants normally had confidence, hardly ever gave effective medicine to the sick people. In the peasant families, small incomes prevented them from calling doctors of modern training, who usually resided in the city, and the death rates were therefore excessively high. According to vital statistics registered by the Institute, the average crude death rate for the two years from August, 1943, to July, 1945, was 46.3. It was more than four times higher than that of the United States (10.6 for 1939–1944).[17]

The infant mortality rate is generally considered a very good index of living conditions in any population group—the lower the infant mortality rate, the better the level of living—as well as a good indication of the general health conditions prevailing in a population. The average infant mortality rate in Kunyang for the two years between August, 1943, and July, 1945, was 281.9 per 1,000 live births. It was more than six times higher than that of the United States (46 for 1938–1942) and much higher than that of both India (159) and Chile (214) for 1938–1942.[18] As a consequence, even the crude birth rate in Kunyang was as high as 47.5 for the same period, the natural increase rate being only 1.2 because of the high crude death rate (46.3).

During the war with Japan, several hundred thousand Chinese fled to Yunnan from the invaded areas near the coast. Many were businessmen and professional people from Peiping, Tientsin, Shanghai, Nanking, and Canton, and they brought with them new capital, new skills, and new ideas. A nationalist regiment of artillery was moved to Kunyang. Several factories—a munitions factory, an optical factory, a cement factory, and a paper factory—were also moved into the district. The immigrants to Kunyang and the emigrants from it were, however, about equal in numbers. Kunyang's agricultural status was apparently little affected by the influx of coastal Chinese, and it maintained a relatively lower population density of 89.3 persons per square kilometer than those of the neighboring counties and urban communities like Chinning (129), Chengkung (127.4), Kunming Hsien (125.8), and Kunming City (10,340.1).[19]

Kunyang was a community in which world influence was felt in a limited way. While the traditional way of life still remained, many other traditional traits had either totally disappeared or had been fundamentally altered by gradual or radical changes. As was traditional, the interest of the family group remained among the leading social values. It had five essential features: emphasis on the father-son relationship; family pride; encouragement of the extended family; the ancestral cult; and common ownership of family property. The group cohesion of the *tsu,* or "common descent group," had disappeared, however. The lineage had no more judiciary power, such as had traditionally been recognized by the state for the purpose of preventing and punishing both mutual aggression within the group and aggression against other people in the community. It no longer assumed collective legal responsibility toward the government for its members.[20]

At times religion is a significant social force warranting serious attention. One of the items of our census concerned the religion of the people. Every person twenty years old or over was asked, "Do you have any religion?" If his answer was affirmative, he was asked, "What is your religion?" According to the results of the census, 38,930 out of 69,231 natives of Kunyang, or 57.1% of the total, were twenty or over. Of this group, 16,920 or 43.5% had no religion, 10,142 persons or 26.1% were Animists; 5,507 persons or 14.1% professed Buddhism; and 5,296 persons or 13.6% followed the ancestral cult. Although we witnessed the persistent influence of religion upon the life of the people, a notable event of the modern China had undoubtedly been the trend toward secularization, which had weakened the influence of religion in many strategic aspects of Chinese social life and had particularly affected the views of the modern Chinese intellectuals, with whom social and political leadership rested.[21] The details of the religions of the Kunyang natives are shown in Table 3.

The Sino-Japanese War accelerated social change. The most devastating effects upon the fabric of Chinese society came from runaway inflation. Although prices in Yunnan steadily increased after the outbreak of the war, violent upward turns started with the discontinuance of service on the Yunnan-Indochina railway in September, 1941, and with the closing of the Burma Road to international trade in the spring of 1942. The general tendency of price behavior, according to an index of retail prices for twenty articles—rice, flour, corn, soybeans, pork, salt, lard, brown sugar, cloth, vegetable oil, charcoal, firewood, tea, liquor, tobacco, and so on—surveyed in the Lung Chieh, or Dragon Market, of Chengkung and compiled by the Section of Statistics, the Institute for Census Research, is shown in Table 4.

Prices reached their peak in August, 1945, and then after V-J Day dropped violently by more than 50%. After a short period of going up and down month by month, prices started on an upward curve again when the civil war between the Nationalists and the

Table 3. *The Religions of the Kunyang Natives, Aged 20 and Over, 1942*

	Both Sexes		Males		Females	
Religions	Number	Per-centage	Number	Per-centage	Number	Per-centage
No religion	16,920	43.46	9,692	51.66	7,228	35.84
Ancestral cult	5,296	13.60	2,994	15.96	2,302	11.41
Animism	10,142	26.05	4,295	22.89	5,847	28.99
Buddhism	5,507	14.14	1,274	6.79	4,233	20.99
Taoism	202	0.52	120	0.64	82	0.41
Mohammedan-ism	641	1.65	301	1.60	340	1.69
Catholicism	3	0.01	1	0.01	2	0.01
Protestantism	6	0.02	2	0.01	4	0.02
Others	213	0.55	83	0.44	130	0.64
Total	38,930	100.00	18,762	100.00	20,168	100.00

Source: Institute for Census Research, National Tsing Hua University, "Experimental Population Census and Vital Registration in Kunming Lake Region, Yunnan Province." Kunming: Committee on Experimental Census and Vital Registration for Kunming Lake Region, 1944, p. 321, Table 7.

Table 4. *Index of Retail Prices, Chengkung, 1940–1946 (Base: January, 1937, as 100)*

Year—January Only	Index of Retail Prices
1940	503.97
1941	896.40
1942	2,890.75
1943	13,231.02
1944	38,363.56
1945	145,566.56
1946	366,820.25

Source: The Institute for Census Research, National Tsing Hua University, "A Report on the Registration of Vital Statistics in Chengkung and Kunyang, Yunnan Province" (mimeographed), 1946, pp. 66–7, Table 9.

Communists (who had formed a united front to resist Japanese aggression during the war) broke out. The price upheaval month by month between June, 1945, and May, 1946, is shown in Table 5.

Table 5. Index of Retail Prices, by Month, Chengkung, June,
1945–May, 1946 (Base: January, 1937, as 100)

Month	Index of Retail Price
1945	
June	547,327.98
July	623,143.57
August	642,488.24
September	318,984.11
October	362,619.37
November	444,384.39
December	411,063.96
1946	
January	366,820.25
February	359,892.42
March	389,048.02
April	360,217.58
May	364,366.47

Source: Institute for Census Research, National Tsing Hua University, "A Report on the Registration of Vital Statistics in Chengkung and Kunyang, Yunnan Province" (mimeographed), 1946, p. 67, Table 9.

The inflation caused many social, economic, and political effects, which had far-reaching consequences in the form of social change. It stimulated widespread corruption and incompetence in the government. The fast erosion of real income and the lags in salary adjustments and payments often reduced the remuneration of government employees during wartime to only about 10% of their prewar salaries. During those years a monthly salary equivalent to thirty United States dollars for a teacher or military or civilian employee would have been considered very high. A private in the army often received less than one United States dollar a month. Such incredibly low remuneration created a new depressed class and accounted in large measure for the low morale and the corruption among government employees and military personnel.[22] When the inflation reached its peak, the unpopularity of the Nationalist government began to pyramid. The prevalent leftist intellectual leanings paved the way for ultimate Communist victory.

The inflation affected not only the well-to-do salaried class but also the peasants. As earnings did not increase as fast as prices, the ordinary peasant found it difficult to make ends meet. The economic position of the farmers was less satisfactory during the war than before it. According to a study of peasant life in Kunyang made by Ru-Chiang Su, among 506 peasant families, 61.1%, the majority being small landowners and tenants, were worse off during the war; 23.7%, mostly big landowners, did better; 15.2%, largely middle landowners, maintained the same socioeconomic status before and during the war. Many farmers were borrowing in order to relieve hardships. According to the study, 310 out of 506 peasant families, or 61.3% of the total, most of them tenants and small landowners, were reported to be in debt.[23]

While the meager incomes and possessions of hundreds and thousands of peasant families and members of the salaried class were dissipated under the intensification of inflation, the process facilitated the accumulation of wealth through speculation (often in the form of gold and foreign assets) for a small privileged group. The absence of progressive taxation on income and profits made it possible for these speculators and profiteers to become legal owners of such windfalls. Widespread antigovernment sentiments among the people reflected social injustice.

The *hsien* was not only a unit of administration but also a well-integrated community that possessed a political, economic, and cultural center; it was a "working whole" of the social life and the proper unit of sample for studying social status and mobility. Although there were Lolos in the population, the Chinese culture and traditions were dominant. The war had certainly taught the Chinese people to be more nation-conscious by breaking down provincial barriers and by eliminating some bigoted ethnocentrism. The people of foreign provinces came into Yunnan with their own social formations, however. They had reserved for themselves a special position in Yunnan and were not geared to the social life of the larger community. They were treated mainly as distinguished guests and did not affect the local social life as a whole; they are therefore not included in this study. A county was suitable as a field of research because the number of its gentry was sufficient for making a scientific analysis of this group in Chinese social life.

THE METHODS

In order to study the gentry, I have chosen life histories as the main body of data. In regard to the use of life histories as sociological material, I share the opinion of Thomas and Znaniecki:

We are safe in saying that personal life-records, as complete as possible, constitute the *perfect* type of sociological material, and that if social science has to use other materials at all it is only because of the practical difficulty of obtaining at the moment a sufficient number of such records to cover the totality of sociological problems, and of the enormous amount of work demanded for an adequate analysis of all the personal materials necessary to characterize the life of a social group.[24]

The personal life history constitutes the perfect type of sociological material because fundamentally it is the product of an individual's adaptation to the social environment of his community. No person can be understood in terms of himself alone. The individual can never escape the influence of social framework and the controls of a particular community. His activity is regulated and defined by the society. The life history is an account of how a person is added to a social group and becomes an active member capable of meeting the traditional and conventional expectations of his society. It shows how his attitudes, sentiments, and aspirations are influenced by the social heritage as transmitted to him through the behavior of other persons. Consequently, the life history is the medium through which institutions and practices find external expression. It makes the picture of institutions and practices real and intimate, because its subject has actually grown up in the community and experienced its social life. The stories of social, economic, and political activities can well be told through the careers of prominent men.

The main source materials for this study are forty-seven life histories of Chinese gentry families,[25] which I collected during the years 1943–1946. Supplementary information was received from my assistant, Mr. Yang Chan, with whom I maintained close communication until the end of 1948. The life histories include those of scholars, active and retired officials, rich merchants, landlords, and others. Among these subjects not all had climbed successfully upward. Some of them had stopped at certain stages, while others had reverted to obscurity. The data also include both brief mentions and more detailed accounts of the lives of more than 1,200 persons.

Each of the main life histories deals comprehensively with all the accessible and important aspects of its subject's career. As the social and economic unit was based on the family rather than on the individual, the life histories that I collected are actually the case histories of mobile families. Each case history includes at least five generations, though, for the remote generations, it may cover only single episodes or fragments of their careers. The life histories are therefore familistic and genealogical.

One of the central problems of sociology is the way in which a society assures its own continuity from generation to generation. The stability and continuity of the social system are maintained by the transmission of social norms and cultural patterns from the adults to the young through the socialization process. Social mobility does not always run its course in a single generation. The men I saw moving into the gentry from the peasantry did indeed make the long jump in their own careers, but most men reached their final high and powerful positions only as the result of continuous efforts by several generations. The succession of generations introduces a distinct category of social mobility, in which comparisons must be made between father and son, rather than between successive states of the individual career.

Social mobility, on the other hand, involves a certain inter-generational discontinuity in which the young do not grow up simply as replicas of their forebears. It is possible to examine the deep and continuing trends of change in Chinese society by comparing the generation of the 1940s with an earlier one. The changing states of mind and manners of life between the older and younger generations are revealed in the life histories.

It is obvious that the life histories of the gentry have limited significance unless they are placed in perspective against the whole population of the community. A census of the population of Kunyang was taken by the Institute on March 1, 1942, in cooperation with the Ministry of the Interior, the Yunnan Provincial Government, and the Economic Council of Yunnan.[26] The census schedule included the following items: name; relationship with the head of the household; habitual residence; place of birth; sex; age and date of birth; marital status; education; religion; occupation and occupational status (if the occupation of the head of household was agriculture, three more questions about the tenure of farmland were asked); and physical or mental deformity. After census-taking, vital registration including births, deaths, marriages, and migrations ensued in four of the eight districts of the County. The statistics of the gentry families may therefore be singled out for comparison with those of the whole population, and many such characteristics of the gentry as family size, education, occupation, land ownership, and life chances can be shown by means of contrast.

In obtaining the information for designating members of the gentry in the community, I was aided by my six junior staff members in the Kunyang Research Station. All of them were natives of Kunyang. I called them together to discuss the research project, and then, through a process of matching and consensus, we worked out a list of members of the gentry who were well known and recognized by the people. For a further check on the accuracy of the list, I used the official invitation lists for the important meetings or formal parties held by the local government. As the criterion of eligibility for people who attended the meetings or parties included a certain social status, these invitations were marks of dignity for those invited. As a result, our list covered all the prominent gentry of the community. These people generally held or had held responsible positions or had established reputations for unusual accomplishment. They constituted a *de facto* social group recognized by the people themselves.[27]

Once we had selected the gentry sample, we could assume that we were dealing with a group that had experienced upward social mobility. Our list of names was a preselected sample of successful men. In order to study downward mobility, we also collected the life histories of several notorious opium smokers whose forebears only one or two generations before had been great names. The men of downward social mobility were less easily observed, as in the ancient poem that reads, "When the flowers come into bloom, they are easily to be seen; when the flowers are out of bloom, they are difficult to be found." A social phenomenon is much like the phenomena of nature. Those who sank to the bottom of society were lost in loneliness and poverty. They were frustrated and withdrawn. Their careers were often hidden or disguised because they felt ashamed.

In collecting these life histories I was helped by my two junior staff members, Messrs. Yang Chan and Tu Lien-yuan. Both were natives of Kunyang and had been graduated from Provincial Kunhwa Senior Middle School in Kunming. Before joining the Kunyang Research Station as research assistants, both Mr. Yang and Mr. Tu had been schoolteachers for several years in the community. Mr. Yang had also served in the army as a first lieutenant for one year. Before they took up this task, both had been enumerators of census and supervisors of vital registration. They were trained to undertake social surveys and to handle simple statistics by the Institute. Both were seriously interested in human situations. They not only had intimate knowledge of the county but also possessed considerable experience and great skill in field work. Above all, they were not only able to furnish information but also willing to do so. Mr. Yang assisted me from the beginning to the end. After the University was moved back to Peiping in 1946, he continued to collect data for two more years on my personal financial subsidies.

As the main body of the material for the study was the forty-seven life histories of the Chinese gentry families, the intensive interview became the most important field method. The crucial point for field work was that the fieldworker fully understand the significance of the study and devote initiative and ingenuity to his work, because our interview demanded great depth and range of inquiry into the respondent's most intimate life and the underlying realities of the social situation being examined. We began a pilot study and collected only twelve life histories; then we used these few case histories as a basis for discussion, analysis, and criticism. After we felt confident enough about the contents and the operations, we proceeded on a full scale. As interviewing was an arduous task and required special training and skill, our experience and methods proved valuable.

Generally, the fieldworkers labored five days in the field to collect data and five days at home to write reports. After a case history was finished, it was handed to me for review. If more material was needed, it would be gathered right away. There was no definite assignment. In work of that sort, it was necessary to keep up the morale and interest of the fieldworker. The interview proceeded in an easy and natural fashion. The fieldworker, in approximating himself to the position of a participant, was often stimulated to a better effort. He always tried to adopt a positive attitude toward his scientific problem.

We felt that a good fieldworker should be active, alert, patient, and dogged. He should not be shy or timid. He should be intelligent, humorous, and unwearied by his task of obtaining reliable material. As the role of the fieldworker was changed according to the context in which he found himself, the job demanded extreme flexibility in his personality.

During the period of field work, the interviewer often visited teahouses, wine restaurants, opium dens, and gambling houses to look for clues to what was going on in the community because these places were the clearinghouses for political gossip and public opinion. In such situations he was expected to join the conversation but never to argue or to antagonize anyone. His manner was to be gentle and easygoing; his words were not to offend other people. Whether the talk was right or wrong, he was to listen attentively. When the speakers stopped, he was immediately to pay for tea or opium for them and veer to another topic.

Each case history could involve two kinds of investigation: direct and indirect. These two methods were to be mutually complementary. The data collected from direct investigation with the subject were usually very general and abstract. He would tell only his good deeds and would not reveal his wrong actions. Furthermore, some persons liked to boast of themselves and "spoof" the interviewer, the interviewee wishing to convey how heroic he was, how he had struggled, and how he had struck out. If the interviewer were careless, he would surely be cheated. The interviewer therefore had to use his reports as a basis for gathering more data through the method of indirect investigation with the subject's relatives, friends, rivals, and opponents. Although the subject's enemies usually exposed only his weak points and ill behavior, his good friends and relatives usually candidly mentioned both his strong and weak points, both his virtues and misconduct. The materials from these three different sources had to be compared one with another. If several reports about the same event were contradictory, we used our own judgment to distinguish the true from the false. Our data were recorded in the form of oral statements.

For this kind of research, we could not always tell the interviewee frankly that we were investigating his case history, because he would then wonder, "What does he investigate my case history for?" Many of our best interviews took place when the subject under investigation was unaware of being studied. Otherwise, his response would have been either refusal or apathy. If his attitude was apathetic, it was still easy to cope with him. Our approach had to be slow and mild. Our speech had to be polite and agreeable. Our conversation had to start with his good aspects. If he talked about his glorious past, we would admire and praise him. Our respect would make him happy. If he mentioned his miserable experiences, we would sympathize with him, even share his tears. Thus he would feel that we were on his side and would tell us what he carefully kept in his mind. If he talked too much and brought up unimportant matters, we would interrupt with consolation, sympathy, or encouragement. Then we would raise another point and let him talk freely. In this way, we could gather the most valuable material and would be welcome for our second and third interviews.

If our request for an interview was rejected at the very beginning, our method of approach had to be different. We would try first to remove the "resistance"—that is, the fears or doubts—without rushing the subject. We would wait for some other day and look for an appropriate time "to break the ice." Many times the approach had to be indirect. The interviewer would meet the subject through his good friends in order to become acquainted and find out his temperament. It was important never to antagonize him; on the contrary, we would drink with him, gamble with him, or smoke opium with him, according to his appetite. If he had faith in us, it was easy to interview him. Nevertheless we could never let him know our motives for collecting his case history.

The fieldworker had to be deliberate about his interview. He needed to be quick-thinking and able to exploit the moment when an opportunity developed during the interview. The interview situation would be informal and friendly. Whenever we met someone who was related to one of our subjects, we would initiate the greeting and approach him with a quick smile. An easygoing man was best. Even if he ignored us the first time, we could still salute him politely. Wherever we went, we would pay attention to all kinds of gossip. We would quietly ask what people were talking about. We always kept our purpose in mind. "Keeping your purpose in mind" is the first rule for a good fieldworker.

The fieldworker needed to plan his interview in advance. Where could he collect what kind of material? How should he proceed to gather the material? In order to obtain inside information, sometimes he had to steal, to spy, to bluff, to cheat, and to counterfeit. He had to play these tricks expertly, for otherwise he would have forfeited other people's faith in him.

Furthermore, a good fieldworker was never to feel frustrated. If after meeting some difficulty, he were immediately to feel disappointed or seek an easy way around it, the fruit of his field work would certainly have been of limited value. The greater the difficulty in collecting the data, the higher would be the value and significance of the case history.

It was necessary for a fieldworker to have broad associations. He had to make friends with people in all walks of life, whether they were persons of good or bad reputation, high or low social status. These people were his eyes and ears. A fieldworker had to be able to take things both seriously and lightly, to emulate either a mature scholar or an enthusiastic youth. He needed to inspire confidence if he was to lead an adequate interview. Our association with the Institute of the University greatly aided our acceptance because it identified us as responsible and respectable persons.

When we went out for field work, we not only had to prepare

to meet all kinds of difficulty but also had to have sufficient expense money. For fruitful field work, spending money was unavoidable. An invitation to have tea, a drink, or dinner was very common in these circumstances. It was impossible "to catch fish with empty hands." Sometimes we spent a great deal of money for very little return in our field work. If we had not been generous in spending money, it would have been difficult to do field work. Field work called for not only time, energy, and intelligence but also ample funds.

A Chinese proverb says, "Unless you do not do a thing, no matter how secret, it will be known." The problem was that we had to find the right way to acquire the data. Where could we find the "right way"? After we had found it, how should we proceed? How could we make the interviewee talk freely and tell us the whole story without any reservation? The answers depended on our abilities and techniques. An inexperienced fieldworker can gather only superficial material and will find interviewing tedious work. In short, a skillful fieldworker must be very patient, able to laugh off humiliations and overcome all sorts of difficulty. The following examples are taken from Mr. Yang's field notebook:

Chairman Wang

Chairman Wang's case history was easily collected, in comparison with others, because he was an old man, a well-known scholar, and had done nothing immoral in his life. If you wanted to extol his fame, he would be very happy. In principle, he would not reject your interview. In fact, however, he would not give you much cooperation.

He usually played mah-jongg every evening. Even if you accompanied him the whole night, you could not ask questions in the presence of other people. He went to bed about five o'clock in the morning and slept until two o'clock in the afternoon. After getting up, he would have to take care of his official business.

He did not talk much. Occasionally, even if he said something, he talked very slowly. Later, because I went to his home every day to ask for material, he gave me a biography dictated by himself and written down by his youngest son, Wen Hua. It was a cliche essay and gave few details. He accepted our suggestions and revised it. I acquired much material from his former schoolmates and especially from Chairman Wang's assistant for fifteen years. The case history as a whole was still unsatisfactory until I got a chance for a direct interview.

One day, when he went back to his home village from the city of Kunyang, I accidentally met him at Chun Shu Ying, a market town of Nei Tien Hsiang. He was in a good mood that day and talked a great deal about his life. He asked me to play mah-jongg with him. In order to collect more material, I accepted his invitation and accompanied him to play mah-jongg that evening.

Commander Chu

I had a great deal of trouble interviewing Commander Chu. He was a prestigious retired officer and always showed off his superiority. When I visited him at first, his nephew came out to greet me and asked me to wait outside of his house. I waited for two hours and he never returned. When I visited him the second time, his servant came out to meet me and told me to wait in front of the gate. He went back and released a watch dog to scare me away. But I waited for another hour until he came back to tell me, "Commander Chu is busy." When I visited him the third time, I went with his nephew. He bade me to wait in the sitting room and went upstairs to notify Commander Chu. After murmuring for a while, he came back and told me, "Commander Chu is not at home," although I had seen him returning home before I came. I could only gather some material from his younger brother, his nephew, his friends, and former colleagues.

Fortunately, Commander Chu was a candidate for Representative to the National Assembly* for the Democratic Socialist Party in Kunyang and campaigned hard for his election. One day when the Kunyang Association of Veteran Officers was first organized, he gave a long speech for more than two hours during the meeting. He gave a detailed account of his career, his deeds, his political ideals, and his personal experience and appealed to all the officers of the association to vote for him. I was elected as a secretary of the association and took notes of his whole speech. Thus, I finished his case history.

Chief Chang

One day I visited Chief Chang. As soon as I entered the door of his house, he haughtily asked me, "What do you want to come to my home for?" I respectfully replied: "I specially come to visit

* The National Assembly was to elect the national president and vice-president.

you, because you are one of the prominent people in Kunyang. I admire your character, career, and virtues." He answered, "Humph!" and immediately walked away. However, his mother was very polite, and asked me, "What do you want to ask him?" I talked with his mother for a while and left with a feeling of annoyance.

The next time, I went to his home with Vice-Chairman Loh's son to visit his mother. She was Chang's aunt. This time the circumstances were quite different. I gathered from her a good deal of material about Chang's father and grandfather.

Later Chief Chang started to campaign for the Chairman of the Citizen's Political Council of Kunyang. So I visited him as the Chairman of the Kunyang Association of Education and talked with him about the election. He was very pleased and told me a great deal about his history and views. Since then I have visited him several other times for gathering supplementary material.

Chief Ku

Ku Hsiang Chang, Chief of Pao Shan Hsiang, was a man puffed up with conceit and pride. He was cautious and suspicious and rarely revealed his innermost thoughts and feelings. As I knew his father, and once we had had dinner together, I started my interview with the parent. I visited his home with two packages of delicacies. His father welcomed me enthusiastically. I stayed at their home for one day and night and gathered material under the pretext of a friendly visit.

After a few days I visited Mr. Ku personally. When I went to his district government, he showed off his status as a district chief and absolutely ignored me. I was a little bit frightened. I flattered him and addressed him as "Hsiang Chang!" He only replied, "Ai!" I tried to ask him some questions, but he would not sit down for three minutes. I fawned over him, and he walked away. However, I discovered that he had a hobby of playing mah-jongg. When he played mah-jongg, he was very talkative. I played mah-jongg with him and invited him to visit a wine restaurant and on other occasions tea-houses. For several days I could collect only superficial material.

One day I invited him to visit a wine restaurant. I ordered four dishes and half a *ching,* or catty, of distilled wine. After we finished up the wine, he demanded to have more. I asked him, "How much can you drink?" He replied, "Drink as much as you can, nobody should quit." After drinking for a while, his conversation became a little repetitive. I knew that his consumption was almost up to his capacity and that my opportunity had come. The Chinese proverb says, "People, after taking liquor, reveal the truth." As I knew he had reached his limit and felt it was not the right place for an interview, I helped him to walk back to his residence. He lay on his bed and was in high spirits. I only had to mention some points, and he would talk continuously and freely. Although I was gathering valuable material, I pretended to have gotten drunk. When finally he fell asleep, I had finished his case history.

Tang Sheng-kuang

Tang Sheng-kuang's life history represents a case of downward mobility. He was something of a ne'er-do-well and wandered to all the places every day. Usually he talked much, but he never got into serious discussions. You could hear his voice either in a teahouse or in a wine restaurant. He submerged himself in alcohol, opium, and gambling. In order to gather the material of his case history, I slept two nights with him. I do not know how many times I invited him to visit wine restaurants and opium dens. I played mah-jongg with him and treated him as a good friend of mine. Hence he told me how he had enjoyed himself when he was young and what he did when he became poor. He told me his thoughts, feelings, recollections, and sentiments in detail. Although I spent much time and money for this case history, the result was very satisfactory.

Liu Tsung-tao

Liu Tsung-tao is an old friend of mine. Yet I spent a great deal of time collecting his life history. His home was in a village which is about fifty kilometers west of the walled city of Kunyang. Not only was the transportation difficult, but the region was filled with bandits. Above all, he rarely stayed at home.

During my first visit I did not have a chance to see him at all, although I stayed there for two weeks. I inquired of many people and nobody knew his whereabouts. I sent two letters to his home and received no reply. I was told that he had not been home for more than two months. Fortunately, I had taught in an elementary school there for two years. I knew most of the prominent persons in the area, and all the people with whom I talked had a good impression of him. When I mentioned his name, all of them admired his talent, bravery, thoughtfulness, sense of justice, and his concern with common people. You could hear people talking about him everywhere. One of Liu's former colleagues told me of Liu's personality in great detail.

When I visited him the second time, I had written him and received a letter expressing "hearty welcome." When I arrived at his home, he felt honored by my visit, because I came from so far away. After I explained my purpose in visiting him, he was very cooperative. He talked with me for two nights and let me read his diaries. I got all the data that I wanted and felt that, "although tilling the soil is hard work, the harvest is fortunately abundant."

In investigating the subjects we used an interview guide, the items of which included the geographical conditions of the subject's home village; social and economic background; families (great-grandparents, grandparents, parents, brothers, sisters, important relatives, wife and children, and others); childhood; boyhood; adulthood; marriage; careers, paying special attention to the subject's extraordinary experiences and vital decisions with far-reaching consequences; readings, speeches, documents, deeds, aspirations, recreation and so on; the criticisms of others on the subject. In addition to the subject himself, all the subject's family, neighbors, former teachers, schoolmates, colleagues, friends, rivals, relatives, lineage members, and servants who knew him well and were accessible were interviewed.

Having resided in Kunyang for more than three years, I had acquired much firsthand information about this community. Because of my position in the University, I had the advantage of personal contact with most members of the gentry and was often a guest of their families. The local government was very courteous to us and supplied us with whatever material we asked for. And above all, I was often invited to attend the most important meetings and the formal parties held by the local government. At the same time, in order to return our thanks and accentuate our friendship with the top-ranking officials and the gentry, we held a dinner party in their honor once a year. It was only through the aid and cooperation of all these people that I was able to collect the data presented in this study.

In his remarks on historical material and the use of local gazetteers for community studies, Morton H. Fried has pointed out:

It is almost mandatory for a community study to begin by referring to the size of the local population and sketching in a few historical facts. The range of the use of historical materials has been great but the most intensive use of such data in the available Chinese community studies falls short of the potential of such an approach.[28]

There was a local gazetteer in Kunyang. The old gazetteer had been published about forty years previously. The new one was then in the editorial process. We did not find either of any use to us. The old gazetteer, for example, described the population of Kunyang in the following way: "It was most populous under the regime of Chien Lung in the Ch'ing dynasty. Since that time it has never increased for more than two hundred years." It gave not a single figure of population. Though one should not make a sweeping generalization, it is doubtful how valuable local gazetteers are for scientific study.

During the field investigations, we tried to pay special attention to psychological factors. We stressed the emotional impact of transitional points in the life careers and in the descriptions of personalities. We were concerned with the problem of values and sanctions as reflections of psychic processes. We tried to explore what drove or led the men to success. But we had not used psychological testing for collecting the material about personality types, owing to my inadequate preparation in psychological testing techniques, which have been proved fruitful elsewhere. For example, Warner and Abegglen used the Thematic Apperception Test to study American business leaders and demonstrated it successfully.[29]

Inasmuch as every facet of the study, the research design, the observations, the collection of material, and the analysis of data, was systematically guided by a valid concept, it is necessary here to discuss the term "social mobility." According to Sorokin:

By social mobility is understood any transition of an individual or social object or value—anything that has been created or modified by human activity—from one social position to another. There are two principal types of social mobility, *horizontal* and *vertical*. By horizontal social mobility or shifting, is meant the transition of an individual or social object from one social group to another situated on the same level. Transitions of individuals, as from the Baptist to the Methodist religious group, from one citizenship to another, from one family (as a husband or wife) to another by divorce and remarriage, from one factory to another in the same occupational status, are all instances of social mobility. So too are transitions of social objects, the radio, automobile, fashion, Communism, Darwin's theory, within the same social stratum, as from Iowa to California, or from any one place to another. In all these cases, "shifting" may take place without any noticeable change of the social position of an individual or social object in the vertical direction. By *vertical* social mobility is meant the relations involved in a transition of an individual (or a social object) from one social stratum to another. According to the direction of the transition there are two types of vertical social mobility: *ascending* and *descending,* or *social climbing* and *social sinking.*[30]

In order to clarify the concept of social mobility, two points should be mentioned: First, it is more fruitful and methodologically more correct to distinguish social mobility from social or cultural change, to restrict the concept of social mobility to the shifting in social position of an individual or a group, and to conceive the transition of "social object or value" as an effect of social mobility. Second, it is essential to distinguish between migration and social mobility. In most cases, changes in social position are connected with changes of residence, but they may be "horizontal" as well as "vertical." A "horizontal" movement in geographical space is not, as such, a "social phenomenon," and it is not necessarily identical with a change in social position. The question whether a certain change of social position means a horizontal or a vertical movement and, in the second case, whether it means ascending or sinking, can evidently be decided only in relation to a given system of social stratification.[31]

Theory, implicit or explicit, is basic to knowledge and even to perception. The method followed in presenting the material was designed to be factual and "inferential." I have chosen to let the facts speak for themselves with a minimum of discussion. The data have been arranged within a framework that is based on the theory of structure and function. It was assumed that individual human beings are connected by a definite set of social relations into an integrated whole. There is an orderliness within social phenomena. The analysis of social mobility is mainly institutional.

Although case study has been thought of as a kind of qualitative analysis, the analysis of a large number of case histories relies upon statistical procedures. Of the various devices employed in assembling my data, the most important was the "social personality card." Each of the gentry families was represented by an index card. The card was designed to give us such general information as name, place of birth, change of residence, age of first marriage, education, occupation, social status, and kinship for each generation. The card therefore amounted to a brief resume of the principal items of the life history and served as an important technique for classificatory analysis.

THE STUDY IN HISTORICAL PERSPECTIVE

In the investigation of a great and complex society like that of China, the community study method has a special value. It enables us to view, more or less in totality, a specific and functioning body of people that recognizes its own integration.[32] There are some significant aspects of social life that can be captured only if that life is viewed at close range. There are some qualities that stand out only in the relationships among persons living in intimate groups. There are institutions that exist only in the local world, and there are processes of social interaction that cannot be found except in a specific cultural milieu in which individuals interact as persons rather than as functionaries.[33] Communities make up the "grass roots" of social life. In a community we can directly apprehend something about the people's ways of thinking and feeling that are characteristic of the human race under certain particular circumstances. Community study, by the nature of its smaller scale and greater compactness, is thus able to mirror the richness of social life in a rounded fashion, in comparison with which scientific enterprises on a large scale appear segmental, fragmentary, and remote. The facts and insights of community study, therefore, may well be important in qualifying more inclusive social propositions and also indispensable for the establishment and the testing of general scientific propositions about human nature and the social order.

The community-study approach in China started in the 1920s. So far eighteen works have been produced that can be classified, by and large, as community studies. The number is not large, but we must note that the first one, Daniel H. Kulp II's *Country Life in South China* (New York, 1925), is separated by more than a decade from the next two, Hsiao-tung Fei's *Peasant Life in China* (London, 1939), and Ta Chen's *Emigrant Communities in South China* (New York, 1939). Thereafter they become more frequent: C. P. Fitzgerald, *The Tower of Five Glories* (London, 1941); Fei and Chih-I Chang, *Earthbound China* (Chicago, 1945); Francis L. K. Hsu, *Under the Ancestors' Shadow* (New York, 1948); Martin C. Yang, *A Chinese Village* (New York, 1945); Lin Yueh-hwa, *The Golden Wing* (London, 1948); Hsu, *Religion, Science and Human Crisis* (London, 1952); Morton H. Fried, *Fabric of Chinese Society* (New York, 1953); Sidney D. Gamble, *Ting Hsien, A North Chinese Rural Community* (New York, 1954); C. K. Yang, *A Chinese Village in Early Communist Transition* (Cambridge, Mass., 1959); Isabel and David Crook, *Revolution in a Chinese Village: Ten Mile Inn* (London, 1959); Lin, *The Lolo of Liang Shan (Liang Shan I-chia)* (translated by Ju-shu Pan and edited by Wu-chi Liu, New Haven, Connecticut, 1961); Gamble, *North China Villages* (Berkeley, 1963); Cornelius Osgood, *Village Life in Old China* (New York, 1963); W. R. Geddes, *Peasant Life in Communist China* (Ithaca, 1963); and Jan Myrdal, *Report from a Chinese Village* (New York, 1965). Although this list does not pretend to be exhaustive,[34] it includes all the book-length community studies available in English. It is noteworthy that contributions in the field of Chinese community studies are preponderantly from the hands of Chinese social scientists.

The study of the Lolo by Lin Yueh-hwa, as is clear from the title of the book, was not a study of a Chinese community. The works of C. P. Fitzgerald and F. L. K. Hsu, especially of the former, may also be regarded by some as not properly studies of Chinese communities because the majority of the population in each case was Min-chia. The Min-chia are the descendants of a people centered in Yunnan whose linguistic and cultural background, though similar to the Chinese, shows many differences. The Min-chia speak a Sino-Tibetan language, one that has undergone a massive onslaught from Chinese, at least in its vocabulary. The last major politically independent stand of these people was in the thirteenth century, when the Mongols reduced Nan-chao. Despite the long period that has elapsed since that event and despite evidences of a long history of the diffusion of Chinese traits in Nan-chao prior to its political collapse, the Min-chia retain a distinct language and numerous cultural traits that set them apart. Fitzgerald, in his study, was acutely conscious of the Min-chia deviation from Chinese norms; Hsu, on the other hand, minimized the differences and proceeded to analyze "West Town" as if it were fully representative of Chinese culture and subject only to such reservations as would be made for any other locality. Regardless of their different points of view, however, we list both of these studies of the Min-chia among Chinese community studies because, to state it broadly, the highly acculturated Min-chia represent an important, though in many senses peripheral, point on the continuum that is Chinese culture.[35]

During the 1930s China was swept by social surveys. Among them, the work done at Ting Hsien, a county located in the North China Plain, in cooperation with the Mass Education Movement, was by far the most comprehensive and substantial. Gamble's studies represent the monumental works of that period. The field work was directed by Franklin C. H. Lee, and the resulting three volumes were published in Chinese. It is a pity that readers of English should have had to wait for several decades to see a translated counterpart of those Chinese volumes.

Social-survey workers are often satisfied with a hodgepodge of raw and unconnected materials on many divergent subjects without a thesis. A community study is scientific only when the community is reported with reference to some conceptual framework. The field study is designed to test the theory. Gamble's works were not done in the light of a sociological perspective; Lee and Gamble would probably argue, however, that they were interested only in the presentation of numerical and descriptive accounts in an objective and precise manner, leaving to others the tasks of generalization and conceptualization.[36]

In dealing with Chinese communities we can hardly ignore cultural traits correlating with differences of socioeconomic class status. It is surprising, however, how frequently such an obvious pitfall has caught students in the past. Among the community studies we have cited, Kulp, though making a rough breakdown of the population into three classes based upon wealth, failed except in the most obvious matters to cite differences in behavior or attitudes correlating with the class division he had made. Francis L. K. Hsu, whose book also failed to make distinctions based on class except in such obvious cases as the distribution of concubinage, was specific on the matter:

> Some time ago I came to appreciate a difference in social behavior between the wealthier households and the poorer ones in some parts of China. The wealthier and more scholarly tended to adhere much more than the poor to the socially upheld big-family ideal; this apparently explains the larger households among the rich as a whole as contrasted with the poor as a whole.
>
> Using this difference as a springboard, I proceeded to analyze the culture of West Town. It is here that an answer may be found to the long-puzzling problem—based not so much upon a difference in social behavior between the rich and the poor as upon different consequences of the same social behavior because of economic and status differences.[37]

Disregarding the tautological "explanation" Hsu gave for the distribution of large families, it must be noted that his findings seem at odds with those reported in *Earthbound China, Fabric of Chinese Society,* and *A Chinese Village in Early Communist Transition.* Furthermore, the simple distinction between rich and poor on which Hsu relied is not synonymous with class.[38]

Martin Yang's work shows remarkable affinities in this respect with that of Francis Hsu. Yang, however, was dealing with a much smaller population (about 720 as against about 8,000) and with an almost totally agricultural unit, whereas Hsu dealt with a market town with more than 250 shops, some of which represented large investments of capital, and a well-developed system of cloth manufacture. Fei expressed himself most clearly on class-oriented cultural differences in contexts other than his community studies,[39] and his work always showed awareness of this factor. Yang, however, explicitly rejected the problem by asserting that there were no permanently fixed social classes in their village and no large landlords in the whole area. Because the cycle of a family's economic rise and fall was common to all, no family regarded another as significantly different from itself and the inequality of income did not seriously threaten the sense of village solidarity.[40]

In dealing with Chinese social structure, Fei and Chang gave more detailed descriptions of peasant life and discussed the problems of the gentry. A comprehensive inquiry of the generic character of the gentry in Chinese social life from the point of view of social status and social mobility comparable to the present study has never been made, however.

As to social status, other than the peasantry and the gentry several newly rising groups are significant but have never been subjected to empirical study. After the Opium War of 1839–1842, the Western merchants reached the Chinese coast in the van of naval forces. Those who served as compradors for the Western establishments in the trade-port cities had generally been persons of humble stock. Some of their offspring became wealthy and powerful. Another group was formed by those who had been forced out of the overpopulated and destitute farming villages. Taking advantage of administrative intricacies and conflicting interests, the underworld had flourished since the end of the nineteenth century and had achieved a formidable organization. This group, backed by financial strength and alien interests, rose to power during the national revolution of 1927. As the members of these two groups had been born in a social milieu of foreign-dominated and lucrative concessions in the trade-port cities, vacuums of culture, they had set themselves free from the moral and ethical standards of both China and the West. Many were "converted" to Christianity. In struggling for money and power, these groups resorted to any means to achieve their ends.[41] Furthermore, for comparison, the Chinese Communist elite should be studied. Perhaps "Kunyang in Transition" would be in order.

The study of social status and social mobility in China is still a new field. Most students who are interested in this subject have been impressed by the imperial examination system as an avenue of upward mobility.[42] This system served to recruit the talented and intelligent administrators for the empire and therefore inspired the West to develop its modern civil-service examination system.[43]

Some other students adhere to a different point of view about the imperial examination system. They find that some "fresh blood" may have been absorbed from the lower strata of society by means of the examination system but that the system had been greatly discounted by the *yin* prerogative, especially under such dynasties of conquest as the Liao, Chin, Yuan, and Ch'ing. *Yin* means "shade, shelter; to protect." The son of an official who entered the civil service through the *yin* privilege was indeed, thanks to his father's position, "protected" against the hardships and pitfalls of the regular examinations.[44] As the *yin* privilege elevated the recipient directly into officialdom, an extensive application of this system would certainly have seriously affected the functioning of the examination system as an avenue of upward mobility.

It is important to make a candid and scientific appraisal of the functioning of the civil-examination system as an avenue of upward social mobility. How many men who were recruited into governmental service through the examination system had no official background whatever? How "democratic" was the examination system?

In order to answer these questions, E. A. Kracke, Jr., made a study with the examination lists of *chin-shih* for the years 1148 and 1256. The numbers of men were 330 for the list of 1148 and 601 for 1256. The lists gave each man's name, his legal residence, and the names and academic and official careers of his father, grandfather, and great-grandfather. After analyzing the material, Kracke reached two conclusions: The first is that there was a high proportion of men with no apparent official family tradition whatever (56.3% for 1148 and 57.9% for 1256). The second is that there was a remarkable similarity in the social composition of the two academic classes, separated in time by more than a century.[45]

A full discussion of the significance of these figures would have to touch upon many phases of the changing institutional, political, social, economic, and ideological scene over a period of many centuries. It must suffice here to say that the two extant Sung lists give scanty information on candidates' family histories. Furthermore, Kracke's two examination lists are the results of "the successive work of several hands during the Sung and Yuan periods,"[46] and he had no way to check the family backgrounds of the men with the original sources, one by one. Additionally, as in Sung times there was no formal degree lower than *chin-shih,* the holders of lower degrees and equivalent ranks in the Ming and Ch'ing periods offer in some ways a better comparison with the Sung doctoral degrees. The proportion of new men as a whole is significantly greater among lower-degree holders in the later periods than among the doctoral-degree holders of the same periods.[47] As Kracke himself emphasized, "an answer to these questions in quantitative terms must remain tentative for the present."[48] Nor can we believe in the reliability of such a high proportion, without further evidence.

Ping-ti Ho's study was based on, among other things, lists of successful candidates for civil-service examinations of the Ming (1364–1644) and Ch'ing (1644–1911) periods. After analyzing forty-two Ming and Ch'ing *chin-shih* lists, which give information on the backgrounds of more than 10,000 cases, Ho found that "as the examination system became the most important channel for the selection of officials toward the middle of the fifteenth century, between 40 and 50 per cent of the candidates came from families which may be regarded as humble."[49] I should like to point out that in the Ming and Ch'ing periods the *chin-shih* degree was then the highest honor attainable. One who came from a humble family and could win it had really made a "big jump." It was highly honored because only a few could make the grade. Ho himself indicates in the same article "that over a long period of relative political and social stability people of lower status would almost inevitably suffer increasing disadvantages in the competition against their social superiors, especially since circumstances in the early period had been abnormally favorable to the lowly."

There is another study made by Quentin Pan and Hsiao-tung Fei.[50] It may be suitable to compare it with the samplings of Kracke and Ho because they are of the same nature. Pan and Fei collected 915 prints of the examination papers of the *kung-shêng,** *chü-jen,* and *chin-shih* during the Ch'ing Dynasty. The custom was that, after receiving the degree, each of the *kung-shêng, chü-jen,* and *chin-shih* would print his examination paper for distribution among his relatives and friends. The examination papers for *kung-shêng* and *chü-jen*

---

* *Kung-shêng,* "imperial students," were selected from district or prefecture colleges for presentation at the capital, theoretically to study in the Imperial College.

were printed with black ink, and the examination papers of *chin-shih* were printed with cinnabar. Of the 915 examination papers 506 were printed during the reign of Kuang-hsü (1875–1901), 128 under T'ung-chih (1862–1874), 86 under Tao-kuang (1821–1850), 80 under Hsien-feng (1851–1861), 26 under Chia-ch'ing (1796–1820), 13 under Ch'ien-lung (1736–1795), 8 under K'ang-hsi (1662–1722), and 14 in other periods. Although the examination papers were collected in Peiping, the geographical distribution of the authors included nineteen provinces plus Taiwan and the army. Of the 915 authors, 187 came from the Province of Chili including Shun-t'ien-fu, the metropolitan prefecture; 113 from the Province of Kiang-su; 104 from Anhwei; 57 from Shansi; 51 from Honan; 47 from Fukien; 42 from Hupeh; 28 from Kiangsi; 22 from Kwang-tung; 20 from Kewichow; 15 from Hunan; 14 from Szechwan; 12 from Shensi; 11 from Yunnan; 11 from Kwangsi; 4 from Kansu; 2 from Feng-t'ien; 1 from Taiwan; and 12 from the army.

Each of the examination papers includes an essay with the name of the supervising official of the examination and the grade and remarks given by the official for the paper. The foreword of each paper includes the author's background, which consists of two parts: his teachers and academic friends; his family background, including his patrilineal forebears for the previous five generations, his matrilineal forebears back to his mother's grandfather, his wife, and the husbands of his great-aunts, aunts, and sisters. The academic and official careers of the author's previous five ancestors (father, grandfather, great-grandfather, great-great-grandfather, and great-great-great-grandfather) were listed in minute detail. The results of the analysis of these family backgrounds are shown in Table 6.

The figures in Table 6 indicate that 66.56% of the fathers of the 915 *kung-shêng, chü-jen,* and *chin-shih* had official records and that 86.67% of the forebears of the past five generations had official records. Of the 915 authors of the examination papers only 122, or 13.33%, had no official record at all for their forebears of the preceding five generations.

As the source of material of the study of Pan and Fei is first-hand, the conclusion is more reliable than those of Kracke and Ho. If we accept the conclusion of Pan and Fei, the proportion of men who passed the civil examination with nonofficial backgrounds was 13.33%. Although some opportunity did exist for men without advantages to rise through their abilities and diligence, the social avenue

Table 6. Family Backgrounds of the 915 Kung-Shêng, Chü-Jen, and Chin-Shih of the Ch'ing Dynasty

Family Background

Generations	Without official records		With official records		Totals	
	Number	Per-centage	Number	Per-centage	Number	Per-centage
	(1)	(2)	(3)	(4)	(1)+(3)	(2)+(4)
1 generation (father)	306	33.44	609	66.56	915	100
2 generations (father and grandfather)	192	20.98	723	79.02	915	100
3 generations (from father to great-grandfather)	152	16.61	763	83.39	915	100
4 generations (from father to great-great-grandfather)	129	14.09	786	85.91	915	100
5 generations (from father to great-great-great-grand-father)	122	13.33	793	86.67	915	100

Source: The figures are taken from the study by Pan and Fei, and the table was compiled by the present writer.

of the civil-examination system was indeed not very broad for the common people. The advantages were still in favor of those who had prestige and power.

In large measure, these studies of mobility through the examination system may be seen as limited to the problem of elite *recruitment,* rather than as dealing with recruitment and also with later official *advancement.* Without follow-up studies of the later official careers of the men who took the examination path to their initial appointments in the bureaucracy, we shall have an inadequate account of the *over-all* process of intragenerational elite mobility.

Degree holders were often more numerous than the number of available official posts. Securing appointments may have been a much greater obstacle for commoners' sons than for officials' sons.[51]

In order to make this point clear, Robert M. Marsh analyzed a sample of 572 officials drawn from the two-volume biographical dictionary, *Eminent Chinese of the Ch'ing Period,* 1644–1912, edited by Arthur W. Hummel. His data showed that, although 80% of the sons of official families entered officialdom through the examination competition, the other 20%, who did not take the examinations, nevertheless held posts in the top three ranks *much longer* than did commoners' sons who *had* taken the examination path. The official advancement of commoners' sons who did *not* take the examinations more closely approximated that of the sons of official families. The examination competition may not be the significant place to look in studies of mobility. What is needed is the systematic analysis of *alternative* recruitment paths (examinations, purchase, rising through the ranks, military careers) and their influence, along with the influence of other factors, upon official advancement in the bureaucracy as a whole, including officials of all ranks.[52]

If the imperial examination system had definite limitations as a ladder of upward social mobility for commoners, the new educational system established in 1902 under Western impact, with study abroad as its highest stage in fact if not in name, was even narrower as a mobility channel. According to a study made by Y. C. Wang, though study abroad involved heavy expenses that most people could not afford, a notable feature of the movement to study abroad was the steady decline of the proportion of the holders of scholarships and fellowships among Chinese who were following such a program. For example, between 1854 and 1953, there was a total of 20,906 Chinese students in the United States. In 1905, 61% held scholarships; in 1910, 32%; in 1925, 20%; between 1929 and 1935, 19%; and in 1942, only 3%. As grants from nongovernmental sources were insignificant, the decline of government support meant in effect the increase of self-supporting students, that is, the recruitment of the educated elite from the wealthy urban classes in China.[53]

Men educated abroad, particularly those who studied in the United States, had substantial advantages in gaining employment over those who had only Chinese college degrees. Western-educated leaders in China enjoyed a decisive advantage in some fields of employment —notably higher education, central government, and industries under the government's control. Between 1932 and 1947, as many as 71 to 80% of the leading government officials were foreign-educated. While the distribution of various foreign-educated groups followed no fixed pattern, the political opportunities of the Western-educated were better than those of the Japanese-trained men in proportion to their respective numbers in China.[54]

The relationship between merchants and foreign-trained scholars is of special interest. The former had little education themselves, but a large proportion of the Chinese students abroad came from urban business families. Sons of businessmen who were educated abroad had the prestige of "returned students" but possessed little knowledge of their fathers' business and were therefore more apt to become officials, professors, or perhaps lawyers than to become merchants. A study of the members of the Kuomintang Central Executive Committee from 1924 to 1929 reveals that merchants' sons accounted for between 31% and 64% (at different times) of those on whom information was obtainable. This pattern of social mobility is hardly conceivable without the new educational system in China. As a consequence, because the central government was staffed largely by the educated class, the urban orientation of the latter was inevitably reflected in the national policies. The needs of the rural masses were neglected, and political instability ensued. In this way political changes in China were closely related to social changes.[55]

Recently, some quantitative studies of the Chinese gentry and social mobility have been made mainly based on district gazetteers. As pointed out before, although we must be cautious, it is doubtful how valuable the local gazetteer is for scientific study. It is well known that this type of official document has a certain peculiar style and purpose, like stressing morality. For example, one compiler of district gazetteers described his standards as follows:

Local virtuous men are naturally models for scholars and are the first to be recorded in the gazetteers. Loyal, filial, chaste, and righteous examples are useful in the maintenance of moral principles and in encouraging others to follow suit. But only those already officially commended or those who have received insignia are to be included in the gazetteers. Others, if unanimously claimed to be worthy and proof can be definitely traced, are also included.[56]

As the compiler of the district gazetteer had a certain point of view, which he promoted or at least kept in mind, he usually described an ideal and not the actual practice. Conclusions based on such material are thus limited in their validity, if not misleading. Hsu reached this conclusion:

In American life an individual may achieve social prominence in a variety of ways. . . . In China, on the other hand, the path of social ascension has been very narrow. Of 7,359 prominent individuals involved in 5,331 histories from four widely separated districts, only one individual was marked as distinguished due to "wealth through commerce."[57]

Hsu's conclusion gives the impression that "wealth through commerce" can hardly have been an avenue of status mobility in China. His finding is statistically correct but sociologically misleading in view of the fact that even a cursory examination of historical social realities reveals the contrary. The capitalist industrialists, merchants, and money-lenders of the Former Han period (206 B.C.– A.D. 8) not only defied the sumptuary laws by "conspicuous consumption" but traveled with large retinues and were treated almost as social equals by the vassal kings and marquis. They were so formidable a menace to small men and ordinary consumers that they were called by contemporaries *su-feng* or "untitled nobility." Although Sung laws forbade merchants and their families to take the civil examinations, there is definite evidence that many officials and frustrated candidates openly engaged in trade and that not a few members of merchant families managed to pass the national examinations and become officials. During the Mongol period many great *sê-mu* (non-Mongol and non-Chinese peoples from Central Asia and beyond) merchants dominated domestic and international trade and even governmental fiscal administration. The removal of the most serious disabling laws against merchants during Ming and Ch'ing times may be regarded as belated recognition by the state of the increasing power of such groups.[58]

My own data indicate that commerce was one of the important routes of upward social mobility in Chinese society. In the main city of a county the chamber of commerce was usually the most powerful organization. But the Confucian scholar traditionally discriminated against the merchants. "If one did not belong to this *cultured* stratum he did not count."[59] That is why Hsu found that of the 7,359 prominent individuals only one individual had been marked as distinguished due to "wealth through commerce."

In another study by Chung-li Chang, many individuals were not of the gentry at all. But they were recorded for moral principles, for being filially pious, loyal, and chaste. Of 5,473 biographies 32% were classified by Chang as of the "inactive" gentry. These gentry members were not recorded for merit in any of the following eight categorical functions: raising funds for charitable and civic organizations; arbitration; organizing and commanding local defense corps; supervising the financing, construction, and operation of public works; acting as intermediaries between the government and the people; raising funds for governmental expenses; maintaining Confucian institutions; and giving alms to the poor. Compared to those who took an active part in community affairs these men were relatively "inactive" and were therefore so classified. These "inactive" members of the gentry—paradoxically enough—received mention for other reasons, such as being "filial" or in some other way meritorious.[60]

Although the district gazetteer may give us some idea of the prominent people of the gentry, it is not likely to throw any light upon the processes of social mobility or upon the manner in which the gentry as a status group is related to the society. It is particularly unlikely to throw light upon the motives prompting different individuals in what appears to be the same society and exposed to what is regarded as the same culture to behave differently with reference to the norms prevailing in the differentiated groups in which the individual participates. I suggest therefore, without attempting to depreciate the value of documents, that we reconsider the reliability and the validity of the official documents as evidence of social life. Fundamentally, it is a problem of sociological theory and methodology. Acquaintance with sound theories might enable us to bring up more significant questions and contribute to a better understanding of the basic principles. A community study involving interviews is the most, if not the only, effective way to obtain the information required.

NOTES

1. Derk Bodde, "Feudalism in China," in *Feudalism in History*, edited by Rushton Coulborn (Princeton: Princeton University Press, 1956), pp. 59–60.
2. *Cf.* Hsiao-tung Fei, *China's Gentry: Essays in Rural-Urban Relations*, revised and edited by Margaret Park Redfield, with six life-histories of Chinese gentry families by Yung-teh Chow and an introduction by Robert Redfield (Chicago: The University of Chicago Press, 1953), pp. 1–2.
3. Bodde, *op. cit.*, pp. 69–70.
4. Chung-li Chang, *The Chinese Gentry: Studies on Their Role in Nineteenth-Century Chinese Society* (Seattle: University of Washington Press, 1955), p. 3.
5. *Ibid.*, pp. 4–5.
6. *Ibid.*, pp. 5–6.

7. *Ibid.*, p. 6.
8. Fei, *op. cit.*, pp. 18–9.
9. *Cf.* C. K. Yang, *A Chinese Village in Early Communist Transition* (Cambridge: The Technology Press, distributed by Harvard University Press, 1959), pp. 112–5.
10. Franz Michael, "Introduction," in Chang, *op. cit.*, p. xvii.
11. H. H. Gerth and C. Wright Mills (trans. & ed.), *From Max Weber: Essays in Sociology* (New York: Oxford University Press, 1946), p. 434.
12. *Cf.* Kuo-heng Shih, *China Enters the Machine Age: A Study of Labor in Chinese War Industry,* with a supplementary chapter by Ju-kang Tien, edited and translated by Fei and Francis L. K. Hsu (Cambridge: Harvard University Press, 1944), p. 158.
13. *Ibid.*, pp. 158–9.
14. Ta Chen, *Population in Modern China* (Chicago: The University of Chicago Press, 1946), p. 12.
15. *Ibid.*, p. 48.
16. The Lolos and Min-chia were two native peoples who lived in the mountainous regions of southwestern China and had hardly been acculturated or Sinicized.
17. Warren S. Thompson and David T. Lewis, *Population Problems* (5th ed.; New York: McGraw-Hill Book Co., 1965), p. 337, Table 12–1.
18. *Ibid.*, p. 357, Table 12–10.
19. Chen, *op. cit.*, p. 87, Table 12.
20. *Cf.* Hui-chen Wang Liu, *The Traditional Chinese Clan Rules* (Locust Valley: J. J. Augustin Inc., 1959), pp. 1–7.
21. C. K. Yang, *Religion in Chinese Society: A Study of Contemporary Social Functions of Religion and Some of Their Historical Factors* (Berkeley: University of California Press, 1961), p. 341.
22. Shun-hsin Chou, *The Chinese Inflation, 1937–1949* (New York: Columbia University Press, 1963), pp. 244–5.
23. Ru-chiang Su, "A Study of Rural Economy in Kunyang," The Institute for Census Research, National Tsing Hua University (mimeographed), 1943, pp. 110, 116–7.
24. W. I. Thomas and F. Znaniecki, *The Polish Peasant in Europe and America,* 2 vols. (New York: Alfred A. Knopf, Inc., 1927), II, 1832*f.*
25. Six of the forty-seven life histories have previously been published. See Fei, *op. cit.*, pp. 149–287.
26. Chen, *op. cit.*, pp. 10–6.
27. As a point of interest, we may compare Warner's rating techniques combined in the "evaluated participation" (EP) method for stratifying a community and for placing families and individuals at their proper levels in the status system of a community. For details, see W. Lloyd Warner, Marchia Meeker, and Kenneth Eells, *Social Class in America* (Chicago: Science Research Associates, Inc., 1949), pp. 36–9.

28. M. H. Fried, "Community Studies in China," *The Far Eastern Quarterly,* 14 (1954), 32.
29. W. Lloyd Warner and James C. Abegglen, *Big Business Leaders in America* (New York: Harper & Row, Publishers, 1955), Chapters 4, 5, 7, and 8. The Thematic Apperception Test was invented by Professor Henry Murray of Harvard University (see his *Explorations in Personality* [New York: Oxford University Press, Inc., 1938]). It provides evidence and understanding about the organization of the psychic life of the individual, probing beneath the conscious level to the deeper emotional structure of the personality.
30. Pitirim A. Sorokin, *Social and Cultural Mobility* (New York: The Free Press, 1959), p. 133.
31. Rudolf Heberle, "Review of 'Social Mobility' by P. Sorokin," *American Journal of Sociology,* 34 (1928), 220.
32. Fried, *The Fabric of Chinese Society: A Study of the Social Life of a Chinese County Seat* (New York: Frederick A. Praeger, Inc., 1953), p. 2.
33. Louis Wirth, *Community Life and Social Policy,* edited by Elizabeth Wirth Marvick and Albert J. Reiss, Jr. (Chicago: The University of Chicago Press, 1956), p. 182.
34. *Cf.* Fried, "Community Studies in China," p. 18. Ju-k'ang T'ien's *The Chinese of Sarawak: A Study of Social Structure* (London: The London School of Economics and Political Science, 1953) is excluded from the list because the community is not in Chinese territory.
35. *Ibid.,* pp. 19–20.
36. *Cf.* Shu-ching Lee, "Review of 'Ting Hsien: A North China Rural Community' by Sidney D. Gamble," *American Sociological Review,* 19, No. 5 (1954), 642–3.
37. Hsu, *Under the Ancestors' Shadow: Chinese Culture and Personality* (New York: Columbia University Press, 1948), p. 9.
38. Fried, "Community Studies in China," p. 24.
39. Fei, "Peasantry and Gentry: An Interpretation of Chinese Social Structure and Its Changes," *American Journal of Sociology,* 52 (July, 1946), 1–17; and *China's Gentry.*
40. Martin C. Yang, *A Chinese Village, Taitou, Shantung Province* (New York: Columbia University Press, 1945), p. 132.
41. *Cf.* Shu-Ching Lee, "Intelligentsia of China," *American Journal of Sociology,* 52 (1947), 495.
42. See, for example, François Quesnay, *Le despotisme de la Chine,* translated in Lewis A. Maverick, *China, a Model for Europe* (San Antonio, Texas: Paul Anderson Co., 1946), p. 172; E. R. Hughes, *The Invasion of China by the Western World* (London, 1937), p. 132; and S. W. Williams, *The Middle Kingdom,* I (New York, 1899), 562–5.
43. Ssŭ-yü Teng, "Chinese Influence on the Western Examination," *Harvard Journal of Asiatic Studies,* 7 (September, 1943), 267–312.
44. Karl A. Wittfogel, "Public Office in the Liao Dynasty and the

Chinese Examination System," *Harvard Journal of Asiatic Studies,* 10, No. 1 (1947), 13–40.
45. E. A. Kracke, Jr., "Family *vs.* Merit in Chinese Civil Service Examinations under the Empire," *Harvard Journal of Asiatic Studies,* 10, No. 2 (1947), 103–23.
46. *Ibid.*
47. Kracke, "Region, Family, and Individual in the Chinese Examination System," in John K. Fairbank, ed., *Chinese Thought and Institutions* (Chicago: The University of Chicago Press, 1957), p. 266.
48. Kracke, "Family *vs.* Merit."
49. Ping-ti Ho, "Aspects of Social Mobility in China, 1368–1911," *Comparative Studies in Society and History, An International Quarterly,* 1 (June, 1959), 330–59.
50. Quentin Pan and Fei, "The Civil Examination and Social Mobility," *She-hui K'o-hsüeh (The Social Sciences),* 4, No. 1 (1947), 1–21.
51. Robert M. Marsh, *The Mandarins: The Circulation of Elites in China, 1600–1900* (New York: The Free Press, 1961), pp. 82–3.
52. *Ibid.,* pp. 94, 83.
53. Y. C. Wang, "Western Impact and Social Mobility in China," *American Sociological Review,* 25 (December, 1960)), 843–55.
54. *Ibid.*
55. *Ibid.* See also Robert C. North, *Kuomintang and Chinese Communist Elites* (Stanford: Stanford University Press, 1952), p. 65.
56. *P'ing-yüan chou hsü-chih,* introductory *chüan,* cited by Chung-li Chang, *op. cit.,* p. 211, note 2.
57. Hsu, "Social Mobility in China," *American Sociological Review,* 14, No. 6 (1949), 770.
58. Ho, *op. cit.,* pp. 333–4.
59. Gerth and Mills, *op. cit.,* p. 268.
60. Chang, *op. cit.,* pp. 212–3.

2

The Status Structure

A society, much like an organism, has a structure. Individual human beings are connected by a definite set of social relations into an integrated whole. The continuity of structure is maintained by the process of social life, which consists of the activities and interactions of the human beings and of the organized groups into which they are united. We define social life in a community as the functioning of the social structure. The social structure as a whole can be *observed* only in the functioning of various groups or classes.[1]

With these concepts in mind let us begin a systematic investigation of community life in Chinese society *circa* 1943–1948. What was the pattern of the social structure? How did the social structure function? What were the functions of each status group? What were the social roles played by the gentry?

THE STATUS SYSTEM

In front of the East Gate of the City of Kunyang, there was a huge stone tablet placed by "the officials, the gentry, and the masses of people of Kunyang" to commemorate an important reconstruction.[2] "The officials, the gentry, and the masses of people," or *kuan, shên,* and *ming-chung,* indeed, were social strata the people themselves

46

recognized, although the status lines had never crystallized into caste lines. The masses of people were for the most part, of course, peasants. The gentry possessed its prestige and privileges, while the magistrates received the highest esteem in the community.

Traditional Chinese society had two major groups: the peasantry and the gentry. Within each community, the gentry was differentiated into two subgroups—the officials and the local gentry. Each group had its definite functions. Members of officialdom were the agents of the provincial government. They received orders from the provincial government and carried them out. They were the rulers and masters within the territory. They imposed the governmental power upon the people. They were too high up to be approached by the common people. The masses of people were the ruled, who paid taxes to support the government and the ruling class. The gentry, on the other hand, was made up of the families of power and prestige. They had social positions equal to those of officialdom, but they were natives of the community, in this case Kunyang. They were recognized by the people. They acted as a medium between the government and the common people.

Officialdom was the smallest group in the status structure. It consisted of active officials posted from other places. The peasants regarded the government with the terror and dismay of the old days. Government to them was an invincible force, aloof and beyond their control. They had no sense of nearness to it and familiarity with it. Government had become something "far away to heaven," not something the peasants could touch or shake by the hands. They could see only the external trappings, the awe-inspiring uniforms, the silk gowns of the government officials, the men who bore arms before the austere *yamen* gates. Everything about the officials distinguished them from the peasants. They were addressed as "Ta Lao Yeh," "Great Excellency." The top man was the Magistrate. He came to Kunyang with a dozen or so important helpers like the Secretary of the County Government, the head of the Bureau of Policemen, the bodyguards, and the head of the Mailing Division. The Magistrate was appointed by the provincial government, not elected by the people. During my residence in Kunyang, there were two magistrates—Magistrate Chao and Magistrate Huang, both of whom came from other counties. Magistrate Chao had studied in Japan. He had been the head of a division of the Department of Reconstruction of the provincial government of Yunnan and a junior colleague of the director of that department for several years. His

wife and the wife of the Governor were "sworn sisters."* Magistrate
Huang was a university graduate and a student of political science.
His wife was the niece of the Governor's general secretary. We do
not know how these men came to be appointed magistrates, but we
do know how Chairman Wang's eldest son, Wen-hung, obtained his
appointment as magistrate in another county. According to my
informant, he had these qualifications:

> Chairman Wang's eldest son, Wen-hung, studied in a primary school
> in the City of Kunyang. After graduation from primary school, he went
> to Kunming and entered a middle school, and from there he entered the
> Central Political Academy of the Kuomintang in Nanking. Graduated
> from the academy at the age of twenty-eight, he returned to Yunnan
> and served as head of a division in the Department of Finance of the
> provincial government of Yunnan. After one year he went to Japan and
> entered Waseda University in Tokyo, where he received the degree of
> Master of Arts in political science. He was the first to go abroad from
> Kunyang. After returning to China, he served as a secretary in the pro-
> vincial government of Shansi for six years.

In order to obtain his position as magistrate, Wen-hung undertook an extensive campaign.

> He returned to Yunnan during the Japanese War and served as the
> head of a division in the Department of Education of the provincial
> government. After four years he was recommended by the director of
> the Department of Education to the Governor as a candidate for magis-
> trate. For the purpose of approaching the Governor he spent $500,000†
> CNC to send some top officials to the Governor, for entertainment, and
> for gifts to officials. The Governor asked him many questions about his
> qualifications and the careers of both himself and his father. After visiting
> the Governor, he spent a million dollars to buy gifts for the high officials
> of various departments and to invite them to have Western-style dinners.
> Soon after, his appointment as magistrate was announced by the pro-
> vincial government. Later, he spent more than $100,000 CNC on the
> petty officials of the provincial government. Then he received the *certif-
> icate* of appointment. He became Magistrate of the County of Fu Ning.
> After succeeding in his campaign for the position of magistrate, he
> rushed home to ask his father to raise two million dollars to cover his
> expenses in taking over the position of magistrate and for payment of

---

* This phrase describes a kind of nonkin relationship based on a special sort
of interpersonal understanding and embodying intense sentiment and affection.
The related parties took oaths not to betray each other. It had become an
institutionalized social bond between unrelated persons.

† At that time this sum of Chinese National Currency (CNC) was equivalent to about 1,900 silver dollars, or about $950 American, because of inflation.

salaries to faithful helpers. His father sold 20,000 *ching,* or catties,* of iron to meet this need.

My informant continued:

One who wants to be a magistrate must have at least three million dollars for capital. Otherwise he cannot obtain this position. Though Wang Wen-hung spent such a large sum of money in advance, he made back this sum after half a year. "The wool comes from the body of the sheep." If he had spent more money for the position of magistrate, he would have grafted more money from the people to compensate for his expenditures.

Three points in Wen-hung's case are noteworthy: First, he was not a relative of the Governor. The Governor was impressed by the careers of both himself and his father. Chairman Wang had had a remarkable official career, and Wen-hung not only had very good qualifications but he also had adequate experience in governmental administration. He was appointed magistrate to a county far away from Kunyang. Second, as my informant has pointed out, "One who wants to be a magistrate must have at least three million dollars for capital. Otherwise he cannot obtain this position." A talented but poor person had no chance to become a magistrate. Third, as "the wool comes from the body of the sheep," the people would certainly suffer from the exploitation of the officials.

The officials received their incomes in the form of fixed salaries, but the salaries were extremely low. Their main source of income was graft, which was regarded as almost legal, and this practice was a real scourge to the people. One of Wang Wen-hung's helpers during his term as magistrate told me:

Wang Wen-hung is a man who is slow in his actions. He smokes a large quantity of opium. When he was a magistrate, he was very greedy. It seemed to him that this term of magistrate was his only opportunity for making money. If his junior staff member could not help him to get money, the junior member would be despised by him as having no ability. He considered himself so important that even his wife, also a college graduate, could not get along with him. He often quarreled with her. We saw that many attendants of the Magistrate who came to Kunyang made a lot of money. But we who followed him to the county under his regime were so poor that we did not even have enough money for traveling home. After having been in the position of magistrate for two and a half years, Wang Wen-hung was reported to the Governor

* The *ching,* or catty, was equivalent to sixteen *liang,* exactly 1⅓ lb. (604.8 gm.).

for corruption and was dismissed. After dismissal he was forcibly detained in the county by action of the local gentry. After half a year he was released on the condition that he return part of the money that he had received illegally during his term of office.

Wang Wen-hung is not an isolated example. Both Magistrate Chao and Magistrate Huang were reported to the Governor for corruption and dismissed. Furthermore, after being dismissed, Magistrate Chao was forcibly detained in Kunyang by the new Magistrate and the gentry for more than half a year.

The authority of officialdom was ceremoniously demonstrated. When Magistrate Huang came to Kunyang in December, 1943, and took over his position, a ceremony was held in the main hall of the county government. During the performance, which I was invited to attend, the dismissed Magistrate passed the official seals of the county government to the new Magistrate. The officials who attended the ceremony included the two magistrates, an official from the provincial government, Chairman Wang, and others. Chairman Wang of the Citizens' Political Council of the county, made a short speech at the ceremony. He said: "In recent years the taxation has weighed heavily upon the people. I wish Magistrate Huang would ease the burden of the people." After the ceremony was over, Chairman Wang was the first to stand up, and he bowed down upon his knees before the new magistrate. The new magistrate immediately helped him to rise. They bowed to each other. Then Chairman Wang immediately withdrew. The ceremony dramatically symbolized the authority of officialdom and the obedience of the people.

The active and retired officials of Kunyang belonged to the gentry. One who had been a high official, however, always used his official title and was invited to all official functions as well. For example, while I was in Kunyang, the title of respect, Chu Ssŭ Ling Kuan, Commander Chu, was still used by the people, though he had last actually held his position more than thirty years before. Whenever new magistrates or other high officials came to Kunyang, they would still visit him. He was invited to all official functions in the county, and, if there were any important meetings, the Magistrate would ask him to be present. As Commander Chu was a native of Kunyang, he was a member of the local gentry.

The gentry as a status group was larger than was officialdom but much smaller than the peasantry. The members were scholars and active or retired officials. In villages, the gentry members might have been simply the educated landowners or the wealthy merchants.

As they were usually old, respected people, they were called *shên-lao* or "gentry-elders." Theoretically, nongentry family members did not have the status and privileges of gentry if they themselves did not have such qualifications as degrees, grades, titles, or official ranks. But actually, a position or an office would soon be offered to some other extended family members of the high official. Commander Chu's brothers offer a good example.* The family structure and ethics did not permit a son to leave his parents a humble social position when he himself had won social and economic distinction. With the member's achievement of official status, the whole family entered the ranks of the gentry. Holding a position determined not by birth and legal distinctions but by common estimation, the gentry combined the local and popular attachments essential for playing a representative role in dealing with officialdom. Its members were highly respectable people. Education had a high rank in their scale of social values. Furthermore, the gentry was a wealthy group and depended on its wealth for much of its power.

Inconsistencies are, of course, inevitable when a group freely recruits its members from below. Nevertheless, the group concerned is not difficult to identify. Its members may have varied widely in wealth, but, though ragged at its edges, the gentry had a solid core. That core was landowning. The gentry's primary source of income was land that its members owned but did not themselves cultivate. They lived mainly on rents levied upon their tenants. Otherwise, they were professional men—schoolteachers, eminent medical practitioners, and the wealthier merchants—and they had usually received higher education.

The members of the gentry may be viewed, in Max Weber's term, as "amateurs" or "nonprofessional" types of administrative personnel who had certain characteristics: First, by virtue of their economic situations they were able, on a continuous basis, to occupy positions of leadership and authority in a corporate group without remuneration or with remuneration that was merely nominal. This type of "amateur" status rested, in its primary significance, on the essential condition that the individual was able to live *for* politics without living *from* politics; he had to be able to count on a certain level of provision from private sources. Second, regardless of the basis on which the gentry rested, its members occupied positions of social prestige such that, if there had been a formal democratic

* See Chapter 5, Commander Chu's case history.

process, they would probably have been elected to office; they were believed especially well qualified because of their experience and abilities. From a material point of view this form of government is especially cheap, indeed, sometimes completely without cost.[3]

The prestige and power of the gentry came from its co-ordinating position. Members of the gentry always tended to hold strategic positions in the local organizations. Social prestige, however, is different from political power. The local gentry did not possess direct political power. They relied upon the good will and confidence of the magistrate and upon opportunities to do their work, which, of course, might easily be undone by the accession of a new magistrate. As the length of the term for a magistrate was generally two years, they knew very well that there could be no assurance of permanence in any work they might achieve. The executive function of the gentry had only a symbolic or honorary importance, rather than a primarily effective one.

Though the gentry occupied the same position as officialdom in the social hierarchy, it had never organized itself as a group for political power. Its members cooperated with or opposed the magistrate basically for the purpose of guaranteeing their individual interests or the interests of their respective lineages or of the people of their respective localities. They had no sense of political responsibility. The ideal gentleman assumed a passive attitude toward his official position. Chairman Wang's case is typical:

In 1919, 1920, and 1921 Chairman Wang was three times elected to the provincial People's Political Council and appointed inspector of opium suppression of I-men District.

Chairman Wang had then about seventy *kung*[4] of farmland. His income could provide only for the school tuition of his children. Though not rich, he was very happy. His daily life consisted of reading his official correspondence and newspapers at home. If there was a meeting of the provincial People's Political Council, he would go to Kunming to attend it. But he sponsored no particular plan of action. After the meeting, he would return home. In 1921 he was also appointed governor's counselor for bandit suppression. During those years his prestige reached its highest. If he suggested resolutions to the Magistrate, they were accepted without question. The gentry of Kunyang had faith in him. When he had any suggestion for the Magistrate or gentry, he would not care whether it were adopted or not, though his suggestion was usually very important. He would say, "Is he not a superior man who manifests no indignation even though no one takes note of him?" He did not force his influence on anyone. He neither blackmailed the common people nor flattered the high officials, nor did he boast of himself.

In 1936 he was fifty-four years old. He was again elected chairman of the People's Political Council and was appointed a member of the Committee for Opium Suppression. He felt that he was too old to take the responsibility of these positions. Nor as a good fellow did he want to offend anyone. He did not take situations as seriously as others did, but he did everything according to the principles of *p'ai nan chieh fen* (clearing up misunderstandings and settling difficulties for others) and *hsi shih ning jen* (smoothing over matters and pacifying those concerned instead of taking drastic action). He therefore accomplished nothing important for the People's Political Council and the committee.

A perfect gentleman indeed shunned public duty and did not want to remain in his official position for long. Once he had well established his record and influence, however, his honor and prestige would have practical value without an official position. Commander Chu furnishes a case in point:

During the eight years of the Sino-Japanese War, taxes, including the land tax, were very heavy. But Commander Chu did not pay anything. It was said that he believed that the county government would not dare to ask for his taxes. Once a staff member of the Tax Department of the county government stated openly in a finance meeting that I attended that Commander Chu had never paid any taxes. After several days, my assistant told me: "After the meeting, the staff member was reproved for his *faux pas* and warned that Commander Chu would make things difficult for him. In explaining the reason for his father's not paying taxes, Commander Chu's eldest son, Chu Lung, said, 'My father has served the government for so many years that he should not be asked to pay taxes now.' "

Commander Chu had built a public privy at the corner of the main street in the city of Kunyang. A farmer paid 240 catties of rice to him every year for the privilege of using its wastage as fertilizer. The head of the Bureau of Public Sanitation was a comparatively well-trained administrator. He came from Shanghai and later became a friend of mine. He petitioned the Magistrate to move Commander Chu's privy because it was bad for public sanitation. But Commander Chu protested vigorously, saying: "I have a right to build a privy on my own ground. No one can interfere with my property rights." The petition was quashed without question.

Though Commander Chu was a retired official, he refused to pay any taxes and defied the Bureau of Public Sanitation's attempt to move his privy. He certainly believed that, as a gentleman and retired official, he was entitled to special privilege.

Upward social mobility also brought into power new groups who were ambitious, energetic, and schooled in fishing in troubled waters. Chief Chang, of the Section of Civil Affairs of the county government, may be taken as such a type:

As he had suffered a great deal and taken enough beatings, Chang had learned much about how to act toward others in order to get on in the world. Chang saw clearly that, if a man wanted to ascend in the social scale, he should be an opportunist and do everything possible to gain the approval of society and that his words and actions should conform to the psychology of the gentry and educated younger generation of the community. Besides, he should be generally sociable and make friends with various kinds of influential people. Chang himself followed these principles and gradually won the confidence of the public.

When he was thirty-four, Chief Chang was appointed director of the Bureau of Reconstruction of the county government to succeed Director Tai. He was happy in his success and promotion. Promotion meant prosperity. He was ordered to complete two highways, from Kunyang to Yüchi and from Kunyang to Chinning, which had been half done by his predecessor. He selected the workers and supervisors himself and sent a petition to the provincial government to ask for an appropriation of money. The provincial government promised to give ten cents a day for each worker. He, however, withheld the appropriation money from the workers and kept 4,000 silver dollars for himself.

The highways were to be paved with basalt. This kind of stone should have been mined by stonecutters from a region fifteen kilometers away. Expenses were to be paid by the Department of Reconstruction of the provincial government. But he told the workers to pave the highways with stones that could be gathered from the mountains nearby and to mix in only a little basalt. He received a sum of 6,000 silver dollars from the provincial government for further expenses. He "squeezed" this amount of money, too, and with it built his house.

Chu Lung's case shows how *he* fished in troubled waters:

In 1943 a complaint was made by the local gentry to the provincial government against the corruption of the Magistrate of Kunyang. Chu Lung felt that it was an opportunity to exercise his influence. He had printed in the Kunming newspapers the statements of a number of people attesting to the honesty of the Magistrate and presented a petition to the provincial government to hold off judgment on him. Successful in his enterprise, Chu Lung was appointed by the Magistrate to be head of the Department of Military Affairs of the county government. As the Magistrate was, like himself, an opium-smoker, he and Chu Lung became fast friends.

After Chu Lung became head of the Department of Military Affairs, the temporary taxes of every family were suddenly increased. If a farmer of some means did not send a conscripted son exactly at the appointed time, he would be arrested and put in jail. But if the farmer used bribery, his son would be free from conscription. Sometimes Chu Lung led many policemen to the village at night to "shanghai" able-bodied men for the army. He often snatched the only sons of rich people for purposes of extortion.

Once the guards of the Governor sent an officer to Kunyang to catch a soldier who had escaped. This officer was Chu Lung's schoolmate. Chu Lung therefore acted as go-between for the officer and the family of the soldier. This time he received $30,000 [1,062 silver dollars]. Soon after he was reappointed to the position of *chên chang*, chief of the urban district government, because his grafting as head of the Department of Military Affairs was discovered. But the new position gave him a good opportunity for grafting also. When the New Eighteenth Division sent officers to Kunyang to conscript soldiers in August, 1943, the number of able-bodied men from Nei Tien Hsiang was not up to the quota. Chu Lung led a group of militia in the seizure of two men in Pao Shan Hsiang to make up for his quota and received $50,000 [1,770 silver dollars] from the *hsiang* for this venture. Local citizens reported to him that a Mr. Lee, who had three brothers, should be conscripted, but Mr. Lee evaded conscription by giving Chu Lung two cartons of American cigarettes* and $50,000.

Both Chief Chang and Chu Lung were brought into power through upward mobility. They were energetic and ambitious.

The peasantry may be viewed as both a factor in production and an important group in the power structure. It occupied the lowest rank in the power hierarchy. Though the peasants were in the overwhelming majority, they were the weakest and most unprotected.

Most of the peasants did manual labor and had very low incomes. According to the census taken by the Institute for Census Research in 1942, there were altogether 11,220 households[5] in Kunyang. In a survey of the occupation of the head of household, 10,362, or 92.35% of the total, were reported engaged in agriculture. The distribution of tenure groups among peasant households is shown in Table 7.

Landlords whose main occupations were not agricultural are not included in the table of peasant households. For example, Chairman Wang's occupation was public service; therefore, even though he was also a landlord, he is not included in the table. The upper landowners were those who had no other occupation than owning large amounts of land; they owned animals and implements and did general farm work, though at the same time they hired laborers. Most of them either lent or leased out parts of their holdings or both. The middle landowners possessed land, owned animals and implements, and engaged in farm work, without hiring or rarely hiring other laborers. The lower landowners had small pieces of land, owned some of the

* American cigarettes were bought from American soldiers, rather than from the market, and were comparatively expensive and difficult to obtain for common people.

Table 7. *Tenure Groups among Peasant Households in Kunyang, 1942*

Peasant Households

Tenure Groups	*Number*	*Percentage*
Upper landowner	310	2.99
Middle landowner	4,903	47.32
Lower landowner	3,435	33.15
Tenant	959	9.25
Hired laborer	151	1.46
Unknown	604	5.83
Total	10,362	100.00

Source: The Institute for Census Research, National Tsing Hua University, 'A Report on the Population Census of Kunming Lake Region, Yunnan," Appendix, 10(B) (unpublished).

necessary implements, but hired themselves out for other work as well as their own. The tenants worked on farms rented from landlords. The hired laborers possessed no land, owned no animals or implements, and earned their livings solely by selling their own labor. About 44% of the peasant households were those of lower landowners, tenants, and hired laborers, and they lived in miserable poverty. A sampling of 506 peasant households was studied by Ru-chiang Su. The average sizes of farms held by the peasant households of various tenure groups are shown in Table 8.

Table 8 shows that the average size of farm held by the upper landowner was 60.59 *kung;* by a middle landowner, 27.56 *kung;* by a lower landowner, 29.06 *kung;* and by a tenant, 12.48 *kung.* The total percentage of the households of lower landowners and tenants was 58.1. The households of the lower landowners and tenants suffered from excessive taxes and rents, from usury, and from acute shortage of land.

The peasants generally had little formal schooling. Our 1942 census indicated that, among the 11,220 households, 7,219 total 64.34% were "illiterate households"—households in which no member had had any formal schooling. There were 8,783 children of school age, 4,615 boys and 4,168 girls between six and twelve years old. According to law, all children of those ages were to be compelled to attend school. Actually, only 2,423, or 27.58% of the total number of children of school age, 2,047 or 44.36% of the boys and 376 or 9.02% of the girls, did attend school. Among the population of

Table 8. Tenure Groups among 506 Peasant Households and
the Sizes of Their Farms, 1943

Tenure Groups	Number of Households		Total Farms of Each Group		Average Size (in *Kung*) of Farm for Each Household
	Number (1)	Per-centage (2)	*Number* (3)	Per-centage (4)	(3)÷(1)
Upper landowner	19	3.8	1,151.3	7.9	60.59
Middle landowner	193	38.1	5,319.0	36.4	27.56
Lower landowner	269	53.1	7,817.7	53.6	29.06
Tenant	25	5.0	312.0	2.1	12.48
Total	506	100.0	14,600.0	100.0	28.85

Source: Ru-chiang Su, "A Study of Rural Economy in the County of Kunyang," The Institute for Census Research, National Tsing Hua University, 1943 (mimeographed).

69,231 persons, 34,334 males and 34,897 females, only 10,305 or 14.89% of the total population (9,623 or 26.98% of the total males and 1,039 or 2.98% of the total females) had attended school.

There was social mobility for the poor peasants through various channels like the army, secret societies, illegal trade, and even robbery. If one were capable and lucky enough, he might climb up and suddenly become a landlord, though the general situation for the peasants did not offer strong incentives to personal accomplishment and improvement. Standards of honesty were generally low. The peasant group was the one most prey to lack of legal protection, and at the same time it probably had least respect for law and justice. The case history of the late Sun Chung-fa, Sun P'ei-hsüeh's grandfather, typifies the upstart peasant family that had suffered for several generations and had suddenly climbed to landowning and usury.

Sun P'ei-hsüeh, a declining landlord, was born in 1921 in a village named Chin Shan Ts'un of Chung Pao Hsiang. The village was situated at the foot of a hill by the side of the highway from Kunyang to Yüchi and was about five kilometers south of the walled city of Kunyang. Before the highway was built, the village had been a stop for the people coming to and from Yüchi. It was a busy village, especially when it was a market day for the city.

According to our census taken on March 1, 1942, the village had thirty-one families and 179 inhabitants. All the villagers were farmers except a few living on driving wagons. Most were poor and illiterate. Only a few could read and write.

Sun P'ei-hsüeh's great-great-grandfather, Shu-huang, had been a farm laborer. Though he was diligent and frugal all his life, when he died, he left only five *kung* of farmland and a hut to his son. P'ei-hsüeh's great-grandfather, Ta-kiang, had also been a farm laborer. He had often been threatened with starvation as a boy. Yet he was honest and self-possessed. He often said, "If one's mind is level and easy, heaven will eventually give him a way out." P'ei-hsüeh's grandfather, Chung-fa, had been an only son and a very clever boy. His father loved him very much and often played with him. Though the family was poor, Chung-fa led an easy life in his boyhood.

Chung-fa was married at eighteen. After the arranged marriage, he and his wife came to love each other, but their life together was difficult, for they had only eight *kung* of farmland. Chung-fa's wife was extremely shrewd and capable. She would get an idea, it was said, by simply "dropping her head" or "knitting her eyebrows." When Chung-fa was thirty-five years old, his parents died in succession. In order to arrange his parents' funerals, he not only spent all his savings but also went deeply into debt. A poor man was despised even by his close relatives and intimate friends. There was a bitterness too deep for tears.

One evening seven ox-dealers came to his humble cottage to ask for the night's lodging. At first he was very sympathetic toward them and let them stay as they asked. After they had eaten and washed, the ox-dealers talked with him for a while. He was very friendly toward them. When Chung-fa inquired about their business, they told him frankly what they were engaged in. They talked much, for they were elated at their luck and prosperity.

After they went to bed, Chung-fa and his wife were in a mixed state of excitement and fear. They did not know what they should do. They thought that, if they could get a large sum of money, they could escape their impoverished circumstances. The rest of their lives would be better. They rationalized to themselves that "a man will not fear death, when he is in a desperate situation; that hunger is the gateway to theft" [a Chinese proverbial saying]. A plan to murder the ox-dealers for their money formed in their minds. But still, they knew that it was no easy matter to do away with seven men.

Chung-fa and his wife argued back and forth for quite a while. Finally they decided to take action in the dead of night. Each was to kill two of the seven ox-dealers while all slept. After that, even if the remaining three men awoke and began fighting, they could easily cope with them. Resolved, they quietly crept into the room with sharp knives in their hands. They killed all the sleeping men in only about twenty minutes.

After killing them, they still had many things to do. First, they hurriedly buried the seven bodies behind the staircase and piled hay and firewood over the spot. Then they washed away the blood stains in the room. Finally, they buried their loot in a safe place. They were busy for the whole night. In order to cloak his crime, Chung-fa went to the mountains the next morning, carrying across his shoulder a staff and a pair of baskets, on the pretext that he was collecting fertilizer. On his return home, the baskets were conspicuously covered up, and he later explained this display by saying that he had unearthed a large sum of money in the mountains and had been hiding it from thieves. His sudden rise in society thus went unsuspected for a time.

At first Chung-fa and his wife dared not actively purchase farmland. They dispersed part of their money by lending it. If anyone wanted to borrow money from them, he had to pledge his farmland for security, the loan going at the monthly interest of 5%. If the debtor could not repay the money at the set date, he had to change his contract and would then pay on the interest incorporated with the capital at the same 5%. Some of their debtors repaid the capital but could not afford to pay the interest at the same time. Chung-fa and his wife would then refuse to return the mortgage. Furthermore, after one or two years, they would deny that the debtor had repaid the loan if the debtor had trusted them and had not asked for a receipt. Many people who had borrowed money from them were later ruined by them. In the meantime, Chung-fa's wife often took advantage of demanding payment to extort free meals. She would go to a debtor's home in the early morning and ask him to repay the loan at once. Otherwise, she would grow angry and threaten to foreclose. The debtor could ask her to defer the loan, however, if he invited her to have a good meal. Soon everybody caught on to her real intention. After that, when she went to someone's home to ask about the loan, she would be immediately invited to dine. She would go to one family in the morning and to another in the afternoon. Rarely did she eat at home. Chung-fa bought 113 *kung* of farmland in the neighboring villages and another thirty-five *kung* in other *hsiang* or districts in the next few years. He also built two large houses of seven rooms each. He thus became a prominent landlord in the area.

After Chung-fa became a prominent landlord, some people admired him and said that he had been destined to be wealthy by fate. Some people wondered that he had obtained a windfall yet could not tell the source. Most of the people believed he had unearthed the money in the mountain, as he wanted them to believe. As a Chinese proverb says, however, "Unless you do not do a thing, no matter how secret, it will be known." One of Chung-fa's lineage members, a neighbor, had seen the seven ox-dealers entering his house that fatal evening. Later the neighbor came to hate Chung-fa's snobbishness and revealed what he had seen. [My assistant told me that he had checked the story with Chung-fa's wife. As it was an event of forty years earlier, she felt safe in confiding it to him. By that time Chung-fa had been dead twenty years. Chung-fa's wife died in 1947 at eighty-one years of age.]

Chung-fa's case history represents a long jump in upward

mobility. He was originally a very poor peasant, but, in a few years, he became a well-known landlord in the district.

The peasantry had long supported the state and the ruling class with a great part of the product of its labor. The peasants were poor and illiterate. The gentry, on the other hand, was formed of families of power and wealth. They had leisure and could devote themselves to formal education. This distinction had given China a bifurcated social structure. It must be remembered, however, that this social structure had not been frozen into a caste system. There was social mobility, which brought energetic persons from the lower classes into upper status.

THE POWER STRUCTURE IN THE STATUS SYSTEM

Under the rule of absolute government, the people have only duties without rights. An official can be checked only by a superior one. The official, backed by political power, has the highest esteem in the community.

In the bureaucratic type of system, the office hierarchy and the levels of graded authority are based on a firmly ordered system of super- and subordination. There is supervision of the lower offices by the higher ones. Such a system offers the people the opportunity of appealing the decisions of a lower office to its superior authority in a definitely regulated manner. As the gentry in China was better informed than was the peasantry, its members knew how to take, and certainly did take, advantage of such an opportunity. It was not uncommon for a member of the family or a relative or a friend of a certain member of the gentry to become a superior official, and the local gentry in effect gained the upper hand over officialdom. The officials were therefore sometimes vexed by rivalry in the local gentry. Major Chang was a case in point.

In 1945, Major Chang was the *aide-de-camp* of the division commander, who was at the same time vice-commander of the garrison troops in Kunming, the capital of the Province of Yunnan. (The Commander was the eldest son of the Governor.) After Major Chang was appointed to his position, he became one of the most powerful men in Kunyang. He was usually in Kunming and seldom visited Kunyang. On one of the occasions he returned home because his own village was carrying on a legal dispute with a neighboring village called Miao Lin Ts'un over the ownership of a nearby reservoir. Mr. Yü, the head of the Judiciary Department of the county government, had received a bribe from Miao Lin Ts'un and had decreed that the reservoir belonged to that village. Major Chang was angered by his verdict and decided to take reprisal against him. He led a group of twenty able-bodied men of his own lineage and beat Mr. Yü almost to death. After beating him, Major Chang went to the county government to explain the matter to the Magistrate. The Magistrate reversed the original verdict and gave another decision in favor of Major Chang's village. From that time on the people of his village were grateful to Major Chang for the benefit of irrigation. Whenever Major Chang came home, the people of his village would hold a lavish banquet in his honor. [My assistant told me that, despite the bribery, the reservoir was legally owned by Miao Lin Ts'un. The people of Major Chang's village simply took advantage of his power to occupy the reservoir.]

Major Chang's case indicates that, if an order was unacceptable, the gentry, who had social equality with officials, could call upon the district official to discuss the matter. If no agreement resulted from these negotiations, the gentry would be inclined to have friends and relatives in the large city take the matter up with the higher levels of the bureaucracy, in time, perhaps, working up to the very top. Eventually, an agreement of some sort would be reached, the central government would change the original order, and things would settle down again.[6] Commander Chu's case serves as an illustration:

Commander Chu was a candidate for representative in the National Assembly for the Democratic Socialist Party in Kunyang. He was anxious to be elected. Before election day, he sent many agents to the country to campaign for him. But he was defeated by a magistrate who had been put up as a candidate by the Nationalist Party. Commander Chu was very unhappy at his failure and went to Kunming to ask his friends to arrange for him to have the seat. Because he was so very well known, the headquarters of the Nationalist Party in Nanking telegraphed the Nationalist Party in Kunyang to ask the newly elected man to vacate his position in favor of Commander Chu, who flew to Nanking to attend the Assembly.

Nevertheless, officialdom and the local gentry generally acted in concert and maintained fairly smooth relationships, for the former desired to strengthen its hand as ruler by the aid of the gentry, while the latter aimed at influence through alliance with authority. For example, the relationship between Magistrate Ho and Chief Chang was typical:

Chief Chang cultivated a close friendship with Magistrate Ho. For the Magistrate's birthday Chief Chang suggested to the gentry that it present him with a eulogistic scroll along with gifts in honor of his virtuous administration. As a result, Magistrate Ho liked Chief Chang very much and often invited him to his bedroom to teach him the music to various verses. When Magistrate Ho was dismissed by the provincial government, Chief Chang also suggested that the gentry build a pavilion in his honor.

As he was a good friend to the Magistrate and the Magistrate agreed with his opinions and respected his requests, Chang took advantage of his position to take many bribes.

Sometimes members of officialdom and the gentry had ill feelings and became opponents. In that case, the local officials had a political weapon with which to protect themselves. On the other hand, as the gentry members included candidates for official positions and had relatives in higher government offices, they did not fear the officials' "squeeze." Tensions were thus attributable to various causes. First, the magistrate and his helpers were outside masters. Community feeling was easily aroused against "outside invaders." Second, there was a certain confusion of status between the officials and the local gentry because a member of the gentry might consider himself socially superior to the official who was at the moment dominant. Third, the officials often gave formal and impersonal treatment when individual, personalized consideration was sought by the gentry. Fourth, the local gentry was usually divided into several factions. The magistrate might play one faction against another by sending a staff member to talk to members of the gentry individually and thereby to separate them into rival cliques. Such tensions often resulted in the people's accusing the Magistrate to the Governor. A sensational case follows:

In 1943 the people of Kunyang complained of Magistrate Chao's corruption and inefficiency. Chief Chang felt that it would be advantageous to back the people's complaints to the government. He solicited the aid of Wu Li-shih, or Chairman Wu (of the Chamber of Commerce of Kunyang), Liao Ko-chang (head of the Department of Military Affairs), Ting Chên-chang (head of a district government), and others to suggest that the Citizens' Political Council hold a meeting. In the meeting a special committee to accuse the Magistrate was organized. Chairman Wu, Liao Ko-chang, Ting Chên-chang, and Chief Chang himself were elected by the committee as the representatives. They went to Kunming for this purpose.

The task was not easy, because Mrs. Chao, the wife of the Magistrate, and the Governor's wife were "sworn sisters." Mrs. Chao went to Kunming for help. At that time the gentry of Kunyang was divided into three groups: One, the leader of which was Chang, was against Magistrate Chao; the second group, the leader of which was the eldest son of Commander Chu, was in favor of Magistrate Chao; the third group, the leader of which was the third son of Chairman Wang, was neutral. It was

therefore difficult to predict which side would win the struggle to overthrow Magistrate Chao.

In this crisis Chief Chang used desperate measures. He was advised
by his nephew, who was *aide-de-camp* to the division commander, to offer
a bribe of half a million dollars to the eldest son of the governor. As
he was a very good friend of ex-Magistrate Ho, who was then the
general secretary of the Provincial Administrators Training School, he
asked Mr. Ho to help him write the petitions. He also published the facts
of Magistrate Chao's corruption in the newspapers in Kunming and
distributed handbills in Kunyang and Kunming to enlist favorable public
opinion. After four months he attained his goal, and Magistrate Chao
was dismissed.

During Chief Chang's stay in Kunming for the purpose of accusing
Magistrate Chao, his position in the county became insecure. He did not
dare go home for fear of reprisals until Magistrate Chao was dismissed
and a new magistrate appointed. When the newly appointed Magistrate
came to the county to take over the position, Chief Chang and the other
representatives of the Committee to Accuse Magistrate Chao followed
him back to Kunyang.

After their return to Kunyang, two events occurred. One was street
fighting between groups of supporters and enemies of Magistrate Chao;
the other was that the Committee to Accuse Magistrate Chao was renamed "The Committee for Settling Magistrate Chao's Accounts and
Debts." Magistrate Chao was detained in Kunyang by the new Magistrate
and the Committee.

The expense of bringing charges against Magistrate Chao was
$1,002,000 [equivalent to 4,600 silver dollars]. The money was advanced
by Chairman Wu, Liao Ko-chang, and Mr. Chang himself.

After several joint meetings of the Committee for Settling Magistrate Chao's Accounts and Debts and the Citizens' Political Council, a
preliminary report was published. It stated that Magistrate Chao had
taken more than 400 *shih** of government rice for himself. Other items
of Magistrate Chao's corruption were still under discussion.

Once when I talked with the new Magistrate about the local
administration, I asked him why the gentry often complained of him
to the Governor and why it did not cooperate with him. The Magistrate explained:

As most of the people are illiterate and unorganized, the Magistrate
and his few staff members cannot go directly to the people. There is a
wide gap between the government and the public. The members of the
gentry are generally educated people. They are the leaders of the masses
and control public opinion. This group includes the rich merchants, educated landlords, scholar-literati, retired officials, and the families of the
active high officials. They are most keen in their interests and are politically minded. Even though the Magistrate does not want any contact

* In Kunyang a *shih* was equivalent to 800 catties.

with them, they insist upon having contacts with the Magistrate. One cannot get rid of them. In fact, if a magistrate does not cooperate with them completely, he cannot do anything and will be in danger of losing his secure place. Furthermore, some institutions, like the Committee to Finance the County, must legally be joint organizations of the county government and the gentry. If a magistrate wants to do something, he must have money. Thus, he has to cooperate with the gentry.

As the Magistrate cannot get rid of the gentry, he must try to cooperate with it. And as the Magistrate has to cooperate with it, the gentry gets to know most of the secrets of the Magistrate. If they want to report any corruption to the provincial government, it is relatively easy to gather the evidence. Furthermore, as most of them belong to the propertied class, they can advance the money for the expenses involved in such an action. As most members of the gentry are retired officials or belong to families of active high officials, they have much influence in the provincial government.

As the gentry are most keen in their political interests and are often divided into different groups, they readily take advantage of their opportunities to bring charges against the Magistrate as part of their struggle for prestige and power.

The gentry cooperate with the Magistrate for its own interests because the status of the gentry depends on its association with the government. But when the situations run counter to its interests, it will be against the Magistrate under the guise of protecting the interests of the people and their native place.

Generally speaking, cooperation between the government and the gentry enabled both to manage civil affairs more efficiently than they could have done had they acted independently. On the widest scale, this situation corresponded to a symbiotic interdependence or interaction.

The attitude of the ordinary peasant to officials who had maltreated him and robbed him at every turn was naturally one of hostility, but he displayed a similar outlook and distrust toward all who were not of his class, a reflection of the cold contempt with which he was himself usually treated by society. It was a common occurrence for even a minor official or business employee to treat the peasants like tramps, while the peasants used "Old Gentleman" or "Sir" to address them. It was by way of retaliation for such treatment, therefore, that the peasants were so suspicious even of friendly townspeople settling in the country, were so ready to blackmail and cheat them and so unresponsive to all their well-meant approaches. There was a kind of fog of misunderstanding between them that prevented each from seeing the other's good points. Each belonged to a different world.

If a peasant was involved in trouble, a lawsuit for example, the only way to clear himself was to bribe the proper official through some member of the gentry. Bribery was rampant among both officialdom and the gentry, though its forms may have been different. As officialdom was remote from the ordinary peasant, bribery was usually indirect and impersonal, through the hands of the gentry, while in the gentry it was usually conducted by direct and personal offer.

For many centuries China had been ruled by bureaucracy subject to no popular control. The gentry thus served as an intermediate agency between the government and the populace. In the village the members of the gentry were the only persons who could deal with the new ways of the city. They could speak Mandarin and could read and write. They knew how to meet and negotiate with officials from the towns and cities. The peasants had to rely on the gentry for protection against encroachment from the officials. When an ordinary peasant was in trouble, he went to one of the local gentry members to ask for help. And as the social distance between the officials and the populace was very great, the peasants did not have faith in the government. It was impossible for the government to win the cooperation of the people. Only the gentry could bridge the gap. As the gentry wanted gratitude and wanted its power and prestige to be recognized, it was willing to assume this responsibility.

Owing to their strategic position in the power structure and their social roles, members of the gentry had acquired certain codes of professional ethics. They preached the doctrine of order, that everyone should behave according to, and be satisfied by, the position he occupied in the social structure. They said, "To the contented, even poverty and obscurity bring happiness" (an ancient saying). If some people were to revolt against the ruler and disturb the social order, the gentry would fight against them. It was a social responsibility. A privileged class itself, it had an interest in maintaining order and security. The case history of Captain Yang is an illustration.

"Yang Tui-chang," or Captain Yang—the captain of a company on investigation—was born in the village Da Ma Ts'un. Because of the short distance from the village to the city of Kunyang, and the fertility of land, most of the villagers engaged in truck gardening. On the land they grew cabbage, squash, turnip, leek, and eggplant. As the village produced much kohlrabi, it was nicknamed P'ien Lan Ts'un (Kohlrabi Village). The vegetables were sold to the city dwellers and in other nearby markets. The villagers had more cash money than they needed. There were many loafers, opium smokers, gamblers, and even thieves among the villagers. The people of this village were well known for their wantonness and lawlessness.

Captain Yang's grandfather, Yang Hou-hsi, was a hard-working farmer. Captain Yang's father, Yang Keng-ju, was spoiled by his parents from boyhood. When he was ten years old, he was already cruel, violent, and mischievous. When he was thirty years old, he lost a great deal of money gambling. Since he had no way to repay his debts, he went to Kuo Chiu as a tin miner. After one year, however, he returned home, penniless.

When Captain Yang was born, the economic condition of his family was bad. Hence, he had no opportunity to enter school. Ever since he was a boy, he was crafty, bold, and witty. He spent his time swearing, teasing, plotting, and fighting against boys whom he did not like.

In 1918, when Captain Yang was sixteen, he voluntarily enlisted in the army. After five years he was promoted to sergeant. Unfortunately, his troop suffered defeat at the border of Szechuan and Yunnan. He left the army and returned home.

One day in December, 1928, Captain Yang's cousin came to tell him that his cousin had been insulted by a young man. His cousin usually earned his living by bringing persons or transporting goods with his horse to and from Yüchi and Kunyang. This time a young man hired his horse to go from Yüchi to Kunyang. When the young man arrived in Kunyang, he discovered that his overcoat was lost. The young man not only refused to pay for hiring the horse but also asked Captain Yang's cousin to return his overcoat. After hearing this, Captain Yang left the teashop immediately and hurried to the East Gate of the city to find the young man. When he saw him, Captain Yang boxed his ears and knocked him down. He took off his overcoat and threw it to the young man, saying: "Son-of-a-bitch! Is this overcoat yours? You take it. Are you the only one to have an overcoat? You must wipe your eyes." He turned his back and walked away. The young man stood up and ran after him to offer an explanation, but he did not pay any attention to it.

This young man was the nephew of Colonel Chen in Kunming. After returning to Kunming, the young man told his uncle of the beating by Captain Yang. Colonel Chen was so angry that he sent two sergeants and a group of soldiers with his nephew to Kunyang for revenge. After arriving at Kunyang, they looked for Captain Yang everywhere. At last someone pointed him out in a teashop, so that when the two sergeants entered the teashop, they immediately aimed their pistols at him. Captain Yang pretended that he was not Captain Yang and stood up to leave. When he walked to the door, the young man, who was waiting outside, shouted: "He is the man we want! He is the man we want!" Captain Yang was seized by the soldiers who guarded the door. They wanted to bind his arms behind his back, but Captain Yang said submissively that he would go anywhere and that there was no need to tie up his hands. At that time one of the Captain's good friends, who was also an army sergeant and was drinking tea with him, saw that there might be a misunderstanding and tried to see if he could help. He was also seized by the soldiers, who then searched Captain Yang and his friend for arms. When they discovered no arms, they did not tie their hands, but both were held by men on each side and were compelled to walk down the street.

The soldiers wanted to shoot Captain Yang. Fortunately, it was a market day and some spectators said: "There are too many people here. You had better shoot him outside the north gate of the city." At this critical moment Captain Yang was in great anxiety. He felt that the most important thing was to save his life. The Chinese proverb said: "One who starts first is stronger." Captain Yang complained that his shoelaces were loose and asked the men who held his arms to let him tie them. They found that his complaint was true and let go of one of his hands. Captain Yang bent down, suddenly drew a sharp knife from his stocking, killed the two men, and ran away. Though the other soldiers ran after him, with guns drawn, they could not catch him. He disappeared among the crowd, ran out of the street, and hid in a public toilet. There he took off his gown, threw it into the pit, and walked out. When the soldiers who had run after him and could not find him finally came back, he had already climbed over the city wall and was far away. It was unfortunate that his friend was shot instead of him.

After escaping from the city, Captain Yang hurried home to tell his family of the situation and then went to the home of his sister's father-in-law to hide. After seven days he saw that nothing had happened. But he felt that if he did not join the army he would still be in danger of being arrested. At that time Commander Shu, the commander of a division in Kunming, was on the lookout for a courageous man for his guard. Captain Yang enlisted in the army. Commander Shu was Colonel Chen's superior officer and was informed that Captain Yang had killed the two sergeants under Colonel Chen. Because he wanted to test Captain Yang's courage, Commander Shu purposely asked him if he would like to see Colonel Chen. Captain Yang answered readily: "Yes, Commander. Please give me your visiting card." Then Captain Yang went to meet Colonel Chen with Commander Shu's visiting card. As Captain Yang was carrying out Commander Shu's order, Colonel Chen did not mention his past offense and received him politely.

Captain Yang's younger brother, Yang Pei-liang, was illiterate and an evil man. He also enlisted in the army of Commander Shu through his elder brother's help. He was put in charge of provisions for the army, a lucrative post, because one could "squeeze" money from purchasing supplies. Captain Yang and his brother served in the army for three years. During these years they were in Szechuan and Kwangsi and fought with the enemy dozens of times. Though Captain Yang was noted for his courage and adventurousness, he was selfish and cunning. As Commander Shu had known him for a long time, he gave some money to Captain Yang and his brother to return home, after he was defeated by his enemy in Kwangsi Province. After returning home, Captain Yang and his brother made acquaintance with rascals of various sorts and wasted their money in drinking, gambling, and visiting prostitutes. When they had no more money, they began to rob travelers. Once they killed an ox-dealer and robbed him of all his money.

Captain Yang had thick, black eyebrows, fierce eyes, and a devilish face. He spoke and acted discreetly. When he walked he kept his eyes to the front. You could not know his intentions from his facial expression. It was said that he had assaulted several women and that, when he raped a woman, he held a knife in his mouth so that the woman dared not resist or cry out.

Captain Yang first married at twenty. His wife was tall and wild. She had lost her chastity before her marriage, and this angered her husband. When he was thirty, he took a concubine, who was the daughter of a merchant in Yüchi. Captain Yang gathered more than thirty members of his gang and went to Yüchi to carry her off. When her father discovered where she was, Captain Yang sent some money to him for compensation. The merchant thought that as "the rice has been boiled," even though he could claim back his daughter by appealing to the court, it would not be easy to marry her to another. So the merchant was compelled to marry his daughter to Captain Yang as a concubine.

In 1933 and 1934, bandits were rampant in Kunyang. Captain Yang associated with the gangsters in the neighboring counties of Kunyang. They plundered not only the country but also the city. When they committed robbery in Kunyang, Captain Yang himself would not join the looting openly but secretly arranged the plans for the gang. All the money and goods he received he distributed equally. When they plundered in the other counties, however, Captain Yang would join in. They had a leader in every district. Captain Yang was the leader of Kunyang and was called Ta Ko (Elder Brother) by the members of their secret organization.* He was always followed by several bodyguards.

Captain Yang swaggered through the streets every day. He associated with gangsters of other counties to do various lawless deeds. Captain Yang's men often robbed money and goods from merchants or travelers at the passes between two counties. There was one case of robbery every three or four nights in the city of Kunyang. The rich merchants in the city were extremely afraid of him. They had to stay up all night to watch their property. Captain Yang was noted for his hatred of the rich people. He did not disturb the poor people.

In 1937 Magistrate Ho came to Kunyang. He was immediately in-

* The members of the organization were all sworn brothers. The ranks were decided according to the age and ability of each member. The member of the lower rank had to obey the member of the higher rank. When one member entered the organization, he had to formally swear under the open sky and drink some "chicken's blood—wine." This formality symbolized "blood is thicker than water." Each swore to be responsible for the happiness or misfortune of the others. Each one had to protect every other member and the entire organization. One person was chosen as a leader in every place. When a member arrived in his place, the leader of that place had to be responsible for the member's food and lodging. If a member was not loyal to the organization, he would be dismissed and punished by the other members. They had various gestures and secret language, so they could know each other even if they had not met before. They usually made their living by gambling, robbing, and being hired as assassins.

formed by the gentry that the public order in the county was a matter of great concern. After inquiring about the organization of the gang, Magistrate Ho knew that Captain Yang was the highest leader. He invited Captain Yang to the county government and asked his opinion about the public order of Kunyang. Since the Magistrate praised him highly and begged him earnestly to do so, Captain Yang promised to accept an appointment as captain of the company on investigation.

After taking over this position, Captain Yang appointed all the able robbers under him as members of the company. Indeed, the robberies within the district of Kunyang decreased daily. In the city the cases of robbery disappeared completely. Captain Yang was loyal and grateful to the Magistrate and accompanied him every day. Hence, Magistrate Ho regarded Captain Yang as a reformed man and had faith in him. Captain Yang suddenly became one of the most powerful men in Kunyang. When the families of the gentry had feasts or banquets, he was always invited as an honored guest. The Magistrate and the gentry gave him a eulogy—*ch'u pao an liang* ("getting rid of evil and giving peace to the good"). The richest merchant of Kunyang, Wu Chi-min, took Captain Yang's daughter as a fiancée for his son, because he wanted to receive protection from Captain Yang. When Captain Yang walked in the streets, the common people would bow before him. When he went into a teashop or restaurant, he was greeted with cordiality by the people and the owner of the shop. Captain Yang's father was called Lao Tai Yeh ("Great Excellency"). In a word, Captain Yang had climbed from the bottom to the top of the social hierarchy.

During this period, though he did not plunder, Captain Yang found another way of accumulating wealth under the cover of the company on investigation. He often raided the gambling houses and ordered his men to arrest the gamblers. He also searched the opium houses. If the gamblers or the owners of the opium houses were arrested, they would be fined severely. He got a great deal of money this way, part of which he distributed to his men. Furthermore, he allotted his men at various passes to search the travelers. If opium or guns and bullets were found, all would be confiscated. It was estimated that he got about 10,000 *liang* of opium and more than two hundred pistols in this way. He prepared to use these arms as a foundation to enlarge his power.

Two years later, Captain Yang returned to his old vices. He hated the rich and often sent his men at night to plunder them of their money and goods. Captain Yang would pretend to seek after robbers, but his efforts were naturally in vain. Thieves from the local and other counties would visit Captain Yang first if they wanted to be robbers in Kunyang. If a thief had been allowed the territory by Captain Yang, he would have to divide the money or goods with Captain Yang. Otherwise, if he tried to carry on his business in Kunyang, he would lose his life. Captain Yang acquired a great deal of money. He did not use his money to buy farms but built a large new house. Magistrate Ho was informed many times that Captain Yang plundered in the city, but he did not believe it because there was no evidence. Nevertheless, the Magistrate began to pay attention to this.

In January 1941, Captain Yang secretly opened many gambling houses in the county, while he allotted his men to arrest the gamblers. All the arrested gamblers were fined severely according to their means. In three nights in succession, he got more than $100,000 (equivalent to 11,000 silver dollars). He kept the money for himself. One day, his right-hand man, Fan Piao-meng, wanted to borrow some money. Captain Yang not only refused his request but also scolded him. Henceforth, Fan began to hate him.

One night Captain Yang asked the Magistrate to lend him two ten-round automatics and one hundred bullets. The Magistrate asked him what his purpose was. He answered: "In recent days there have been many cases of plundering in the city. I shall use them for searching and arresting the robbers." The Magistrate had a hard time turning down this request. If he lent him the pistols, it might be harmful; if he did not, he might offend him. At last, the Magistrate made an excuse that the pistols were not at hand and asked Yang to take fifty bullets with him first. The next night Captain Yang took the fifty bullets and went to plunder the family of a rich merchant in the city. The neighbor of the rich merchant was a restaurant owner. Captain Yang ordered some dishes at the restaurant in the daytime for their eating at midnight.

After drinking and eating at midnight, Captain Yang and his men piled the tables and benches on top of each other on the top floor of the restaurant and climbed over to the rich merchant's home. When they began to carry out the goods, however, the rich merchant found them. Captain Yang's brother fired at the merchant's right hand. Hearing the gunshot, the policemen came to arrest the robbers. When they found that it was Captain Yang, they immediately went back. At this time the family of the rich merchant cried and shouted for help. Captain Yang and his men ran away in great haste. Unfortunately, Captain Yang left the fifty bullets behind him at the counter in the merchant's shop. The next morning Captain Yang pretended to gather his men to hunt the robbers. But the rich merchant had reported the case of robbery and the fifty bullets to the county government. The Magistrate was greatly surprised to recognize the bullets he had lent to Captain Yang and became convinced of the truth of the information which the gentry had reported to him.

As the Magistrate was very worried, he appointed a man in his confidence to make secret inquiry if there was anyone who dared to assassinate Captain Yang. The reward was appointment to the position of commanding officer in the county government and $10,000. Information was obtained that Fan Piao-meng had quarreled with Captain Yang, and he was asked to kill Captain Yang. The Magistrate secretly called Fan to the county government and personally asked him to promise to carry out this mission. The Magistrate gave Fan a written order to kill Captain Yang within ten days. After accepting the order, Fan was struck with fear when he saw Captain Yang and dared not execute the scheme. Later Fan asked someone else to carry out the plan. This man, however, was also afraid to act.

Unexpectedly, the Magistrate's nephew told what was being planned to Captain Yang. Captain Yang, with five of his men, each with pistol in hand, went to the Magistrate's bedroom and angrily asked: "It is said that you are asking someone to kill me. Please tell me how have I offended you?" Though his heart was beating rapidly, Magistrate Ho remained calm and said: "No such thing! Captain Yang, please don't believe rumors of this sort. I cannot keep my position without you. I need you so much. How could I do that? You know that I have always treated you kindly. It doesn't matter that I am in the position of magistrate. The feeling between you and me is very important. Please take it easy. In the near future, I will make inquiry as to the source of this rumor." After hearing Magistrate Ho, Captain Yang became calm. The Magistrate also asked him to smoke opium.

As he had had a narrow escape, Magistrate Ho urged Fan Piao-meng to execute their scheme as soon as possible.

After this, though puffed up with pride and feeling that no one dared to kill him in Kunyang, Captain Yang planned to move away. On the morning of January 23, 1941, he picked up his luggage, fed his horse, and was ready to leave his native county. Before setting out, he went to the teashop. This information was reported to the Magistrate. Magistrate Ho thought that, if he did not kill Captain Yang now, it would be like releasing a tiger in the mountains. It would mean trouble in the future. The Magistrate told the head of the Division of Receiving and Sending Public Letters of the county government, Chin Cho-jan, to accompany Captain Yang to the teahouse and to order the assassin to kill Captain Yang at once. Fan Piao-meng let the assassin enter the teashop first. After a while Fan himself came to the teashop, ostensibly to drink tea also. While Captain Yang was walking with Chin Cho-jan and Fan Piao-meng, the assassin suddenly came over with a knife and stabbed Captain Yang several times without warning. Though he was wounded seriously, Captain Yang still tried to get out his pistol to shoot. Fan Piao-meng hurried to Captain Yang and asked: "What happened? Elder Brother, give me the pistol!" Captain Yang thought Fan was coming to help him and gave him the pistol. Fan Piao-meng took the pistol and fired twice at Captain Yang. Captain Yang died.

Hearing of his elder brother's assassination, Yang Pei-liang immediately hurried to the city with a gun in his hand. When he arrived at the south gate, he was advised not to fall into the trap. Thus he returned to his home in haste. The city guard eventually came to the village and encircled Captain Yang's house. They looked for Yang Pei-liang everywhere; but he had escaped from his home before their arrival. The other gangsters fled when they heard that the Magistrate had hired an assassin to kill Captain Yang. One of them, however, was arrested and shot the next day by the county government police.

After the death of Captain Yang, his family was mournful and busy. Because they had been advised to hide their things of value, Captain Yang's wife, concubine, and parents transported their goods to another place. Captain Yang's home became an empty shell of four walls in a short time. When the Magistrate's men came to liquidate Captain Yang's home, they found only some articles of no value. In the evening the family went to the city to claim Captain Yang's corpse. They cried bitterly. Captain Yang's mother cried: "My clever and talented son, I repeatedly warned you to be clear-sighted. But you said that you had nothing to fear." Captain Yang's wife cried: "My brave and martial-looking husband, you were a great hero when you were alive; you must be an evil spirit after your death. You must revenge your death in the next world."

People reacted in various ways to the death of Captain Yang. The gentry and rich merchants considered Captain Yang a troublemaker in Kunyang and felt happy after his death. They said: "If the great thief were not dead, there would be no public order in Kunyang." The peasantry, however, felt that, though he was ill-famed, Captain Yang had never bullied or blackmailed any poor country people, and they sympathized with him and his family. They said: "We admire him because he was a man not afraid of force or oppression."

A schoolteacher commented: "Captain Yang could temporarily indulge himself as he did because he was backed by the force of his underground group. The county government did not attempt to arrest and kill him, because to do so might only result in Captain Yang and his men retiring to the mountains as bandits. However, with the coming of Magistrate Ho, the situation changed. The Magistrate was a very artful official. He adopted a policy of 'pitting one against another' to annihilate the group. Captain Yang and his fellow gangsters fell into the Magistrate's trap. Although the gangsters had organization, they were not well organized—with no common ideology and group interest or consciousness. Though Captain Yang might have tried to take advantage of his position to enlarge his strength, he had no idea of political intrigue." The schoolteacher continued: "After becoming the captain of the company on investigation, if he had changed his former ideology and conduct, Captain Yang might have become a member of gentry forever. But after becoming Captain, he still hated the rich people and did not use his money to buy land. He was in the position of a member of the ruling class, but he still carried on action against it. 'Because of having no secure property, one could not have a stable mind.' [A Mencian saying.] Captain Yang had no firm position. Furthermore, as Captain Yang himself and his ancestors had not been educated, they were not fit for the status of gentry. Captain Yang could not pick up a 'brush' or pen, instead of a sword or gun. Even when Captain Yang was in power, the other members of the gentry and the rich people did not really respect him; they just dared not speak out even though they were angry. These might be the reasons for Captain Yang's discontent with his position as a member of the gentry." In explaining why Captain Yang did not become a social revolutionist, the schoolteacher said: "Though the gangsters and the gentry belong to different classes, they are just the same in that they do not engage in production and are parasitic on the industrious peasantry. The peasants are envious of them for their ease of life. Captain

Yang was a leader of the gangsters and feared by the people. He was not respected, loved, and championed by them. Though sometimes he might appear to be a chivalous knight-errant whose inclination was to defend the weaker and poor groups against the rich and powerful gentry, Captain Yang was actually greedy, unscrupulous, and relentless. He would resort to any means to achieve his ends when he was struggling for money and power. As he did not belong to the peasant group, he could not win the support of the masses. It is true that in the last years before his death, Captain Yang used most of the money which he plundered to buy arms and secretly distributed them to more than five hundred members of his gang, and he might have made some political attempt, because he often said that he wanted to suppress the rich and protest social injustice. Yet, as he himself was illiterate, Captain Yang had no vision of a new society."

Captain Yang's special ability was to fire a gun accurately and to use a sword swiftly. He could meet the greatest dangers with the utmost calmness and get out of the difficulty. The main reason for Captain Yang's failure was his lack of sophistication. Though he was noted as an evil-doer and "unreasonable," he was very kind to the common people.

The consequence of Captain Yang's dissatisfaction with the position he occupied in the social structure was death. The gentry thus maintained the order of the society and fulfilled its social responsibility.

To the peasantry the leading persons were, of course, the landlords. The *nouveaux riches* with little education, however, were not accepted by the gentry and were even swindled and oppressed, though they could wield political power through manipulation of their wealth, as is illustrated by the case history of Sun Chung-fa, the first part of which we presented earlier in this chapter.

Sun Chung-fa's family became richer and richer. His wife bought two houses of four rooms each and a store of four rooms. She leased the two houses to others as operating inns and the store to Chu Erh Lao Yeh, the second elder brother of Commander Chu, for residence. The Chu family was then at the height of its prestige. She leased her store to Chu at a nominal rent and without pledge in order to contract a friendship with him and thus to enhance her own social status. At the same time, she also made acquaintances among the other wealthy and powerful members of the gentry. As a consequence, almost everybody knew her as a rich woman in the city.

Later, the gentry became annoyed by her snobbishness and tried to "squeeze" her. She then changed her area of acquaintanceship from the gentry to governmental officials and thus offended the gentry. Its members said: "You have bribed all the top officials. But sooner or later they will leave. Since the officials will change, how can you bribe so many of them? We are always here to be your opponents."

It had been customary for wedding banquets to last three successive days. When her oldest son married, however, the government had been attempting to reform the custom and had persuaded the people to reduce wedding banquets to one day. She felt that, as she had attended many others' weddings, all of which had had banquets for three successive days, it was her opportunity to reciprocate their hospitality. And, as her family was wealthy and had prestige, it was improper to reduce the banquets to only one day. So she gave a banquet of three days. The gentry immediately reported to the Magistrate that she had broken the governmental order and suggested that she be punished severely as a warning to the people. After a process of bargaining, she was punished by being made to pay for paving the road between Li Chia Ts'un and her own village with blocks of stone. The distance was about one kilometer. It was said that this kind of punishment had never before been heard of. The expense was no difficulty at all for her. The only thing that hurt her was that she "lost face."

After she became an opponent of the gentry, she was involved in lawsuits one after another and failed again and again. Due to her snobbishness and to that fact that she never undertook any philanthropic enterprises, no one sympathized with her when she was in trouble. She failed even when she had an airtight case because no one would be her witness. One case concerned a graveyard.

A geomancer told her that, if she buried Chung-fa's ancestor at the site that he indicated, after ten years her descendants would become military commanders. She also thought the graveyard to be *hao feng-shui*, "good wind and water."[7] But the site was situated a little lower than her own graveyard. So she attempted to buy the piece of land from the owner. The owner, however, also believed that it was a propitious site and refused to sell it to her. As a result, she secretly buried Chung-fa's ancestor there. But the owner insisted that the bones be moved from his graveyard. The governmental officials heard of the affair and urged her to be a plaintiff. She was fooled and lost the case. Consequently, she was ordered to vacate the graveyard and fined a large sum of money.

Chu Erh Lao Yeh immediately took this opportunity to occupy her house, where he and his family resided already, declaring that he had bought her house a long time ago and had paid all the money to her. He thought that she would simply yield to his threats and that he soon would own the house without further ado. On hearing of it, she went to Chu's home to ask his wife about the rumor. Chu's wife confirmed it. Chu's family was then powerful, and nobody dared to offend it. She, however, accused Chu before the county government of occupying her house. After two years the case was still undecided because, on the one hand, the Magistrate was afraid that trouble would ensue from giving a verdict in her favor; on the other hand, as Chu had no evidence that he had bought the house, the Magistrate was reluctant to give a verdict in favor of Chu. As she knew that this case could not be decided in Kunyang, she pressed the government to give a verdict so that she could appeal the case to the court of justice in Kunming. In order to pacify her, the Magistrate held another hearing.

The hearing was held in a packed courtroom. More than 300 spectators were present. Chu Erh Lao Yeh declared before the Magistrate that he had bought the house and paid all the money according to the negotiated price but that she had been slow to sign the bill of sale. Chu's wife repeated the same story. Chung-fa's wife became excited and used her shoes to give Chu's wife a box on the ear, pressing her to show the evidence. The people whispered about the case everywhere, and the Magistrate secretly told Commander Chu to persuade his elder brother to return the house to her. But Chu Erh Lao Yeh insisted on his argument. At last, she appealed the case to the court of justice in Kunming. As Chu Erh Lao Yeh was unknown in Kunming and as Commander Chu did not support him, the verdict was in her favor. She claimed the house. The news of her victory spread like wildfire. She immediately became a heroine in Kunyang.

At the beginning of the case, the people had generally believed that the house would be occupied by Chu. Many people had warned her that "egg and stone should not strike each other." Even her sons had been afraid of Chu and had asked their mother to give up the case. But she was resolute to fight to the end and at long last was victorious. [My assistant made this comment: "Chu Erh Lao Yeh was conquered by her courage and resolution. Though she sacrificed money and suffered a lot of traveling and anxiety, she won the admiration of the other gentry members and the people of Kunyang."]

The cases of Captain Yang and of Chung-fa and his wife illustrate the relationship between a rising peasant and the gentry. In order to achieve a solid position at high levels of society, it was necessary not only to be mobile in job and income but also to re-express this new status in manner of living and social relationships acceptable to every higher social stratum. To arrive at the final and stable high status these men aspired to, they and their families had to be accepted by, and become part of, the community of prestige and power in their society. On the other hand, the gentry had difficulty in accepting and imposing the kinds of reciprocal obligation that close friendship and intimate social contacts imply because the rising peasants' lack of formal education made it impossible for the gentry to accept them as equals. No doubt the accusation of provincialism and boorishness directed to the upstarts was valid.

The gentry was generally socially isolated from the peasants, but, like the peasants, it consisted of natives with relatives, friends, and tenants in the community. Both kin and nonkin relationships served as ties between the gentry and the peasants. The powerful members of the gentry usually had extended families and large lineages, which were organized around biological relationships. They maintained closer ties with one another than with other families in the community. Nonkin ties, however, also served many functions. There were ties that assured production. There were relationships that relieved farm labor shortages and surpluses. There were contacts that were used to broaden the economic areas from which income could be derived or supplemented. There were also nonkin relationships underlying tenancy and many connections that flowed from the existence of a state that made many demands on the farmers. All these kinds of relationship were basic to elementary survival. They preceded relationships that involve religious, educational, or recreational adaptations.[8]

The influence of the gentry ran through the entire sphere of governmental institutions, from the central government down to the village. This power spread within the status system is shown symbolically in Figure 1.

In Figure 1 the circles (solid and dotted) represent the spheres of power. The solid arrows represent the direction of executive power through the subordinate spheres in the bureaucracy. The dotted arrows represent the operation of various kinds of influence. The overlapping of the circles represents the fact that some active officials in the government were members of the gentry and that, at the same time, many members of the gentry were retired officials. The system placed the status of the gentry on a footing equal to that of officialdom. The mechanism for exerting influence from the bottom upward worked through the informal pressure that the gentry exerted upon relatives and friends in officialdom. The top and the bottom thus came together in a network, and it was because of this combination that the total system was a functioning unity.

THE SOCIAL ROLES OF THE GENTRY

Members of the gentry may have competed with one another, but they were intimately identified with the life of the locality and were the visible symbols about which a great part of the community's rituals and traditions centered. They played a leading role in peacetime and were looked to in occasions of crisis. The Chinese gentry know no frontiers; it was the recruiting ground of talent, the natural social sphere of all who had capacity for leadership in the widest meaning of the word. Such men were social statesmen. In addition to special abilities, it seems that there is a more general capability known as "community sense." It is an ability to deal with unusual situations

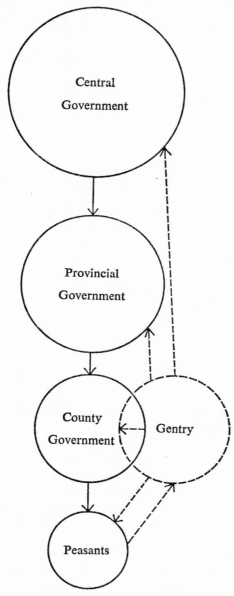

Figure 1. A Schematic Diagram of the Power Structure in the Status System

in the best possible manner and is acquired in the course of experience.

The gentry as a status group was the product of an agrarian society. On a vast continent with bad communication systems, power was centralized in name only, not in fact. In many a peasant village there were only a few landowners and literati, and even fewer used their leisure and knowledge to manage the civil affairs of the community. As most of the peasants were illiterate, the gentry acted as the medium of diffusion of information communicated by the newspapers and official documents and fed community conversation with matters of gossip; its members were thus the directors of public opinion.

The villagers were not joiners. Most of them belonged to the same lineage. The village provided certain organizations in which membership was based on age, sex, and marital status. They were natural divisions of the population for the expression of piety (ancestor worship), prestige, and security. In such a lineage village jealousy between families might exist, but there was little room for snobbery. Nevertheless, the recognized dignity of the long gown shielded the gentry from too great familiarity with the peasantry. The gentry took charge of the village for its children and secured for itself those higher and more specialized services that the villagers could not manage to achieve. The social system became more elaborate through the necessity for carrying out the requisite functions and had therefore been favorable to the appearance of a privileged class. The gentry became the most important group, the group that ran the community.

Many roles were played by the gentry. The most important was that of social leader, organizing the defense of the community, settling the everyday disputes of the people, showing concern for the livelihood of the populace, imposing norms and ideals upon the people of the community, and finally looking after wedding and funeral arrangements. We shall elaborate on these roles one by one in the following pages.

First, members of the gentry served as social leaders and representatives of the community. The village gentry was neither hereditary, appointed, nor elected. One of its most important functions was to interpret local needs, to formulate definite programs, and to assume leadership in taking appropriate measures. Its members had to be men of wide information and sound judgment who could see the technical problems in the whole setting. They had to be courteous, kindly, and solicitous, and, because of their roles, they were naturally very sensitive to these characteristics in anyone else. They had to distinguish themselves from the rest of the people by considerable knowledge of law and social affairs, by means of which they secured popular confidence in their abilities. They had also to have traveled to some extent and to have met different kinds of people, to have developed the assurance that they would be able to grasp any new situation. They thus became especially responsible for the fates of their fellows and for the integrity of their community. Insofar as they controlled the collective forces of the community, their leadership became a source of social prestige. A member of the village gentry was therefore a social leader largely because he was recognized, trusted, admired, respected, and obeyed by the common people. The case history of Wang Chu-tung illustrates this point:

Chairman Wang's grandfather, Wang Chu-tung, was the elder of two brothers. He began to study when he was eight but left school at eleven. He could make calculations, record accounts, and write letters and other documents.

After leaving school, he did nothing but hunt and practice weight-lifting. He was tall and strong and with his strength beat everybody in his native place. He passed the military examination of the county when he was twenty-four and received the degree of *wu hsiu ts'ai* [a colloquial term for *shêng-yüan*], becoming a graduate of the prefecture examinations in military arts.

He wanted to become an officer very badly. He felt that there was no future in living at home and decided to serve as a private in the army. He studied military science diligently and worked very skillfully, was honest and obedient to his superiors, and, after three years, was promoted to the rank of second lieutenant.

During those years he found, however, that the officers were unfair to their junior staff members and that life in the army was corrupt. Sometimes one who had no "pull" with the high officers would work faithfully yet be reprimanded for no good reason. On the other hand, one who had a "special" background would have an easy time and be promoted quite rapidly. Furthermore, Chu-tung was upright in attending to public duties and therefore could not get along with his colleagues, who liked to gamble or to visit houses of prostitution. He became disillusioned and left the army.

After leaving the army, he went back home and engaged in farming and mining. Because he was respected by the villagers, he was elected to be a manager of the public affairs of the village. He often settled or mediated quarrels for the people and helped to avenge the wrongs of others. The strong dared not bully the weak, and the village was peaceful. If there were any lawsuits or calamities of any sort, or any illness, he was always the first to try to help solve the difficulties. He promoted such improvements in the village as paving roads, constructing bridges, and building temples. Anything he undertook to do, he would see through to the end. The people said after his death, "He ate the rice of only one family; yet he wisely governed the affairs of one thousand families."

Another typical case history is that of Captain Yang's great-grandfather:

Captain Yang's great-grandfather, Yang Ping-kan, was an able, clever, tall, strong, and shrewd man. Though he was illiterate, he spoke distinctly and eloquently. He was engaged in agriculture and had ninety-five *kung* of farmland and a house of seven rooms. He was then the richest man in the village.

Yang Ping-kan went to the city every day and liked to meddle in other men's affairs. When anyone had a misfortune, he would go and console him; when anyone had good luck, he would go and congratulate him. He would look after wedding or funeral arrangements by mortgaging a house or selling a farm. If there was some problem, as someone's ox's or horse's eating another's soybeans or rice in the field and thus causing a quarrel, he would try to mediate the affair. When he mediated quarrels for people, he would convince both sides of the rights and wrongs of the issue. He thus won the confidence of the people. After he had mediated a quarrel, the people would invite him to have a meal as reward. He liked to drink wine.

As a member of the gentry won the confidence of the people, he would be elected as a representative when it was necessary. Director Shen of Ping Ting Hsiang is a good example:

During the Japanese War, several factories were moved into Ping Ting Hsiang. Most of the workers came from the coast provinces. Because of the differences in dialects and customs between these workers and the local people, there were many misunderstandings, often resulting in fights. Furthermore, the workers gambled and encouraged prostitution. The public order was greatly disturbed. The local people complained of all these things to higher authority but dared not themselves interfere. One day Director Shen came upon a gang of workers beating a merchant. He stepped in to stop it. In the process, he was insulted by them. He immediately gathered all the able-bodied men of the *hsiang* and held a public meeting at the *hsiang* government. In the meeting he urged everyone to arm himself with tools, clubs, and stones. Having persuaded the citizens, he led them to fight with the workers. The workers were frightened and hid. The incident was reported to the manager of the munitions factory, who immediately requested that the people send a representative to the factory to mediate the dispute. Director Shen was elected representative.

He visited the manager of the munitions factory and requested him to gather the workers, and then he gave a speech. As the workers felt that his speech was impartial and thoroughly in the right, they quickly changed their arrogant attitude to a more agreeable one and assumed civil responsibility. The manager of the factory felt that Director Shen was a real leader of the locality and that his ability would be useful in future negotiations with the people. The manager therefore appointed him as a staff member of his factory.

After one year, the county government of Kunyang and the factory collectively organized a corps for maintaining public order. Director Shen acted as a representative of the county government and was re-appointed head of the corps. He was paid half by the county government and half by the factory. When there was a meeting he would speak as a representative of the local people. He analyzed the merits and defects of both the people and the workers. He investigated the reasons for the conflict between them and prevented the conflict accordingly.

The functions of the gentry were not limited to the sphere of a village. They could be enlarged to encompass a whole district, a county, or a province. A member of the gentry might be popular in a district, a county, or a province. The following case history of Liu Tsung-tao demonstrates how a member of the gentry became a leader of a *hsiang* or district:

After four years Liu Tsung-tao was graduated from the normal school in the City of Kunyang. Before graduation, he had gone to Kunming to compete in the graduating examination given by the Department of Education of the provincial government of Yunnan. He had stayed in Kunming for ten days.

After returning home, Tsung-tao became a schoolteacher in an elementary school in a market town. After a year he went to Kunming to attend the elementary schoolteachers' advanced practice class during summer vacation.

During the year of teaching, Tsung-tao visited the *chu** officials very often. He thus became friends with the head of the district government and with the local gentry. His ability, knowledge, sense of responsibility, and politeness were highly appreciated by them.

In 1938, when he came back from Kunming, Liu Tsung-tao was immediately asked by the chief of the *chu* government to become a staff assistant. He felt much more interested in administrative work than in teaching. He was prudent and energetic, enthusiastic and upright. Little by little he became an outstanding figure in the district.

Though he won the faith of the people and of many members of the gentry, he stirred up the jealousies of the other staff members. He often openly criticized their corruption and their lack of responsibility, and he thus gained many enemies among his colleagues. At last he was compelled to resign his position. The intrigues of the local administration impressed him deeply.

After leaving the *chu* government, Liu Tsung-tao won the warm

* Before 1940 the county of Kunyang was divided into five *chu*. After that year, with the reintroduction of the *pao-chia* system, Kunyang was divided into eight *hsiang-chên,* seven *hsiang* and one *chên.*

sympathy of many common people and gentry members. He bravely stood out and told the people what he would do for their benefit and for his native place. Simultaneously, the provincial government ordered the Magistrate to do away with the system of *chu* government and enlarge the original *hsiang-chên* instead. When Liu Tsung-tao found that public opinion was on his side, he took advantage of the opportunity to urge the people to present a petition to the county government. The Magistrate, finding that the area of the district was too large and that there were bandits in that *chu,* promised to divide it into two *hsiang* for convenience in administration. The eastern part was named Nei Tien Hsiang and the western part Chiu Tu Hsiang. Liu Tsung-tao was chosen as the chief of the Chiu Tu Hsiang.

After he was appointed chief of the *hsiang,* Liu Tsung-tao immediately set up the machinery for the district administrative office. He decided that his staff members should include both able youths and older men of the gentry class. The former would be responsible for action and the latter for supervision. He found the most important principles to be honesty and justice. First of all, the government should avoid doing harm to the people. Then the government should try to do some welfare work for the district. He had no desire for wealth but only for a good reputation. He often said, "The superior man searches after truth, not after food" [a Confucian saying].

Liu Tsung-tao himself was an able youth. Both his character and his deeds were admired by the gentry and the people. After the establishment of the *hsiang,* taxes were suddenly decreased. The government became the center of activity for the people of the district. They knew what the government had done and would continue to do. Furthermore, Tsung-tao asked his staff members to make public the government expenses once a month. He himself did not charge any fees. If he received any orders from the county government, he explained them to the people. As a consequence, the condition of Chiu Tu Hsiang was much better than that of Nei Tien Hsiang.

After putting the affairs of the *hsiang* in order, Liu Tsung-tao turned his attention to popular education. There had formerly been a central elementary school under the *chu* government. After the *chu* was divided into two *hsiang,* Chiu Tu Hsiang had no central elementary school. Furthermore, there were no junior primary schools in most of the villages. He ordered every *pao* to have a junior primary school and the head of the *pao* to be responsible for the compulsory education program. After one year the number of students was greatly increased. Then he suggested the establishment of a separate central elementary school for his own *hsiang.* Because of transportation difficulties, it was more convenient for the students.

Liu Tsung-tao's most outstanding achievement was the suppression of bandits. Bandits had been so common that people were being looted or killed almost daily. People dared not walk freely in the daytime and could not sleep tranquilly at night. Then Liu Tsung-tao secretly befriended some of the rascally element. He often invited bandits to drink wine and asked them about their operations. At last he organized some of them as a corps for bandit prevention and asked their leaders to be corps officers. He divided the *hsiang* into three districts and distributed the districts to different leaders and organized still another group under his own command. He often led his corps in fights with the remaining bandits. Because of his bravery and strategy, he was very much feared. Hearing of his determination to be rid of them, the bandits fled. He thus kept public order in the whole *hsiang* and won the admiration and support of all the people.

From these case histories, we can see how the gentry played the roles of social leader and representative of villages or districts. Its members became social leaders largely because they were recognized, trusted, admired, respected, and obeyed by the common people.

The defense of a community against enemies is an important function in any organized society. In China a rural community was easily invaded, and there were no policemen in the country. The village gentry and its henchmen held the police power, a second function of the gentry. They served as "ears" and "eyes" for the government. Especially when a new and difficult situation necessitated collective action, it often happened that a retired officer was asked to assume this kind of leadership and not only to make a plan for others but also to direct its execution. The case history of Commander Chu is representative:

Commander Chu felt that the only way to correct the bad impression made by his family on the local people was to be of service to the people. He tried to do something for his native place when the opportunity came to him. The political situation in Yunnan was then in chaos. Each of a number of warlords occupied a part of the province and carried on warlike preparations. During the civil war that followed there was a group of soldiers who came one day to Kunyang and plundered the people. The officer of the troop demanded of the Magistrate and the gentry 50,000 *tael* [a Chinese unit of money roughly equivalent to one and a half Chinese silver dollars] of silver. Commander Chu bravely argued with the officer. He told him about the poor economic condition of the county and said emphatically, "If you can find 50,000 *tael* within this county seat, I will be glad to have all of my property confiscated." The officer was convinced, and he dropped his claim and after two days moved his troops to another place.

This act was not the only good deed Commander Chu performed. At another time a company of soldiers was coming to Kunyang as vanguard of an army. The soldiers were stationed outside the East Gate of the city, having been sent to investigate the condition of Kunyang to see if it could support their whole army. After several days Commander Chu led a group of volunteers to inquire about their business. He warned them not to stay at Kunyang. The soldiers refused to listen to him. He then ordered the militia to encircle them. Consequently, the company of troops fled away that very night.

When the Japanese army attacked Kweichow, the county was ordered to organize a volunteer group. Commander Chu was appointed commander of the group and his son, Chu Lung, vice-commander of a company. After the surrender of Japan the group was dissolved.

Here is another example:

Commander Chu's father, Chu Kan, had a great deal of strength and beat everyone in boxing and fencing. He could raise a square stone of sixty *ching* with one hand. He passed the civil-service examination of the county at twenty-six and passed the examination of the province and received the degree of *Wu Chü Jen* at twenty-nine. Then he was chosen by the gentry and appointed by the Magistrate to be captain of the county guard. He collected a group of volunteers and trained them daily in the use of sword and spear. He was adventurous and brave.

During the period of 1847–1872 an uprising of Lolos spread widely throughout Yunnan. Kunyang did not escape. Chu Kan led his group of volunteers to resist the enemy at Kunming Lake. He was unfortunately wounded in the leg by a bullet from the enemy and fell from his boat into the lake. He was rescued at once and escorted back home, where the local people showed him great respect and where he was visited by the Magistrate personally. After two months his leg healed. The medical costs were, of course, paid by the local government.

The case history of Commander Chu clearly shows that the gentry played the role of defender of a community against enemies. It not only made a plan for the people but also directed its execution.

A third striking function of the gentry was to settle the everyday disputes of the people. Many quarrels led quickly to complaints before the gentry. Formal actions and litigations were often undertaken only after mediation had failed. The homes of the gentry practically became the public offices of the community.

There was no lawyer in the village. The peasants were illiterate and did not know how to write proper petitions or how to send them to the proper quarter. Furthermore, the cost of litigation and the terrifying delay in the judicial proceedings, which so often inflated the costs, had placed normal judicial representation beyond the reach of the peasant families. Countless stories and proverbs had discouraged poor peasants from submitting their cases to the legal machinery. A particular member of the gentry was often respected by the people of the district for his fair-mindedness and might often act as judge for the disputing parties. Except for serious criminal acts like murder, most of the disputes were not settled by law. Even if a member of the gentry failed to produce a settlement and the plaintiff referred his case to the civil court, the disputing parties would still look to the gentry for advice and encouragement because its members were not only familiar with legal matters but were also on good terms with the local officials.

The gentry's capacity for settling disputes was related to social status. As a responsible member of the gentry would wish to retain his reputation for impartiality, he could not allow his personal inclination to override his judgment. If some member of the gentry tried to conduct a lawsuit and to exploit the peasants, he was labeled *lieh shên,* an "evil gentleman," a term of great opprobrium.

The method of mediation was to strike an average. The spirit of conciliation was compromise. The principles of intercession were "clearing up misunderstandings and settling difficulties for others" and "smoothing over matters and pacifying people instead of taking drastic action." The object of dealing with a case was not to distinguish right from wrong but to work out a solution that would be accepted with a minimum of furor. The tactful, wise arbitrator had to try to reconcile the disputants as smoothly as possible and to avoid the crude, harsh, inhuman, and impartial verdict of the upright judge. Persuasion took the place of authority. There would thus be no great public loss of face for either party.

When there was a serious conflict, particularly between two village dignitaries, a member of the gentry had to act as a go-between unofficially in order to accommodate the conflicting claims of the involved parties. Though each one might try to take his side of the story to the gentry at the first opportunity, a man's standing depended partly upon the gentry's belief that he had been conducting himself properly.

As the settlement of disputes became one of the most important functions of the gentry, social justice was much more important than was legal power in protecting the weak against violence of any sort. A powerful member of the gentry became the first door of appeal for people who had disputes. The case history of Chu Hsin is an illustration:

After Chu Hsin, Commander Chu's younger brother, called "Sze Lao Yeh," or the Fourth Excellency of the Chu family, assumed the position of head of the Bureau of Finance of the county government at Kunyang, he became the most powerful individual among the gentry of the county. He controlled not only finance but also education, reconstruction, and other public affairs. If he did not agree to a plan, it would not

be carried out. People involved in lawsuits would necessarily ask him
for help. If the lawsuit was not serious he would settle it by himself.
If it were difficult to solve, he would discuss it with the Magistrate and
indicate the side he favored. The Magistrate had to agree with his opinion. The other side lost its lawsuit, even though it might have had an
airtight case. Before he would promise to settle the lawsuit, both sides
had to agree to accept his decision. If the case did not involve his relatives
or friends, he would settle it justly. It was said, therefore, that he was
t'ou tao yamen.*

In 1944 every *hsiang* government was ordered to organize a
committee for mediating disputes. There were five or seven members
on each committee. Virtuous members of the gentry were invited
to be members. The system of mediating disputes was thus institutionalized. The following thumbnail sketch depicts a typical member
of the Committee for Mediating Disputes:

Li Yin-tang of Ho Hsi Hsiang was fifty-four years old in 1945. He
had studied ten years in a private school when he was young. He had
120 *kung* of farmland. He was a man of morality and respected by the
people of his village.
Because of his well-known kindness and impartiality, he was elected
as a member of the Committee for Mediating Disputes in Ho Hsi Hsiang.
He was enthusiastic about this honorary office. He felt that he should
live up to the title he had won and that he should show his records to
the people. His policy of mediating disputes was "to turn great affairs
into small; small affairs into nothing." He often told the disputants:
"At present the officials are greedy. When you refer your case to the
legal court, you are not fighting for justice, but are simply squandering
your money. To become angry means to damage your wealth." No
matter how serious the case, Li would try his best to break through any
deadlock and patiently to reconcile the disputants.

From the cases of Chu Hsin and Li Yin-tang, we can see that the
settlement of everyday disputes for the people was a striking role of
the gentry. It fulfilled the functions of both lawyers and judges in the
village. Their object in dealing with a case, however, was not to distinguish right from wrong but to work out a solution that would be
accepted by the involved parties.

Fourth, the gentry as a status group was expected to be concerned with such problems of the community as famine, charities,
and epidemics. The problem with which the gentry was most concerned was irrigation. An illustration will clarify this point:

When Chief Chang was thirty-four, Magistrate Chen came to Kun-

---

* *T'ou tao* means "first step." As both lawsuits and public affairs were first
settled and approved by him, his office was the first resort.

yang. Chief Chang visited him very often as the people's political representative. He described the general situation at Kunyang to the Magistrate and told him how drought harmed the crops of the county. He suggested to the Magistrate that a dam be built at the foot of Sung Shan (Mount Sung) to collect the water for irrigating the farms west of the city and that the owners of the farms south and east of the city be taxed so that a twenty-horsepower water pump could be bought. The problem of drought in the area near the city would thus be solved completely. In this way, he won the confidence of the Magistrate and was appointed director of the Bureau of Reconstruction of the county government.

Mr. Chien's case furnishes another illustration:

Mr. Chien, the representative of Kunyang on the Provincial Citizens' Political Council of Yunnan, intended to buy a water pump with his private capital to use the water of Kunming Lake to irrigate the farms of Ho Hsi Hsiang. He planned that a fee should be charged per *mow* [equivalent to 666 square meters] for the use of water during the whole year. He felt that not only could he make a profit but also the production of the farms could be guaranteed. His plan was not realized, however, mainly because the charge on water was prohibitive for the poor peasant and labor saved by the machine had not yet found any other productive use.

One irrigation project of much earlier days was realized:

When Mr. Wu's father assumed the headship of the Bureau of Finance of the county government, he was extraordinarily enthusiastic about the constructive affairs of the locality, especially the irrigation system. His notable achievement was to dig out a wide ditch to lead the water from a pass in the mountain in Jen Teh Hsiang. The water of this pass originally flowed in Jen Teh Hsiang but was of no use to that region. Mr. Wu gathered the peasants of the ten villages that could use the water for irrigation to dig the ditch. The Bureau of Reconstruction of the county government gave the workers one meal a day. There were 300 workers working daily under his direction and supervision. The ditch was three *chang* [a *chang* is equivalent to about eight feet] in depth and ten *chang* in length. As a result, all the peasants of the ten villages gained the benefit of the irrigation. The people of the whole county admired him for his great service.

These examples clearly show that the gentry was concerned with problems of the community, especially irrigation.

Such service should not be considered different from other services of the bureaucracy because the men involved in these roles were administrators. There was no problem of technical qualification. The most important talent was that for organizing the people to undertake the work with crude and simple tools. The gentry, however, was not to blame for the peasants' crude tools. Technical change was conditioned by the class structure of a society; it could not be produced or accepted by the people without corresponding change in the structure of society. For example, Commander Chu took part of his money to buy a machine for husking rice and to build a factory of six rooms. The machine husked rice in the daytime and supplied electricity for the city at night. He and several hired technical workers managed his factory, which began to operate in 1931. Though he encouraged the people to use electric lights, many people feared having anything to do with him and dared not use them. At the same time not enough electricity was produced to give much light. So the business was suspended and in 1935 was terminated.

A fifth vital function of the gentry was to impose norms and ideals upon the members of the community. In Chinese society, *shên-shih,* or "gentleman," was the name for "man as he should be." It was a collective and social ideal. The gentry was a group that had selected a code and standard of conduct most conducive to prosperous and pleasant social relations. It was decisive for the development of loyalty and *esprit de corps.*

Members of the gentry generally had more education than did any of the peasants and consequently were not only more literate but also had very different mental outlooks. They were supposed to have uplifted spirits and a distinctive character or quality. Chairman Wang conformed to this type. In answering my question why Chairman Wang had the highest prestige, my informant explained:

> Why has Chairman Wang had the highest prestige among the gentry for more than twenty years? There are several reasons: In the first place, he has very good qualifications. As he is a *hsiu ts'ai* of the Ch'ing Dynasty, he is able to compose various classical literary pieces, such as couplets, birthday scrolls, elegiac prayers, and so on, which are still necessary for social intercourse. But he is not only a Confucian scholar; he also was graduated from the provincial normal school. Among the older generation of the gentry, nobody was better qualified than he. His age and virtuous behavior were also recognized.
>
> Second, his children have added to his prestige. His first son has been a student in Japan and is working in the provincial government; his second son is in the United States; his third son is the principal of a primary school in his native district and the head of the *hsiang;* his fourth son is studying at the National Southwest Associated University in Kunming. As scholars are traditionally respected by the people, his family is regarded as most promising.
>
> Third, when he was thirty-four years old, his prestige was increased by a particular incident. Many members of the gentry were jealous of

him and anxious to involve him in some crime. It happened that a merchant was killed by bandits in his native district. Chairman Wang's enemies accused him of associating secretly with the bandits and even of being the main criminal in this affair. Furthermore, he was accused of being a dictator in local affairs and of being corrupt. As a result, he was put in jail. Though his friends knew that he was innocent, no one tried to help him. But he himself was very calm and strong. He insisted that "when the water is shallow, the stones will appear." At last, the real facts came to light. "Pure gold stands one more test." Though he was not actually involved in this crime, he was impressed so deeply by what happened to him that he acted even more carefully than before. He felt that the ways of the world were difficult and dangerous. Today he is still an honest and upright man. He is neither proud nor mean before his superiors nor contemptuous and insulting to his inferiors. He is now sixty-four years old and has served the government for about thirty years, yet he is not known as wealthy.

Fourth, as he is old and lacks the energy to do heavy work, he is not averse to inviting the able and strong youths to help him. He is quite careful of others' self-esteem. He always goes personally to a man's residence to make the request. The one requested cannot refuse him because of respect for his age. He trusts his junior staff members and allows them to take responsibility for their acts. For example, in 1940 he was appointed the head of the Department of Education of the county government. Then, in addition, in 1942 he was also appointed principal of the normal school and junior middle school of the county. At the same time he was appointed chairman of the Mobilizing Committee for the War Resistance against Japan. It seemed impossible for one person to do these three jobs. But he did them easily. He chose Mr. Chen as his right-hand man in the Department of Education, asked Mr. Yuan to be dean in charge of the school, and requested Mr. Lu to be general secretary to the Committee. He himself acted only as their adviser and attended important meetings. When there were more immediate decisions to be made, the men in charge went to his home to ask advice. The county Magistrate liked him because he never wanted to create trouble.

When Chairman Wang failed to fulfill the expectations of the populace, the people were very disappointed, and his prestige was greatly lowered.

In 1943, owing to the emergency of war, the Citizens' Political Council was organized. Wang was elected chairman. During those years the administration was inefficient, the Magistrate of the county was very corrupt, the officials—especially the officials charged with overseeing conscription and tax-collection—were greedy, and the heads of *hsiang* or *chên* and *pao* exploited the people by every means at their command. The people naturally hoped that Chairman Wang would come out strongly for the impeachment of these corrupt officials. Unfortunately, he was old and did not perceive their malfeasance. Then, too, some of the members of the Citizens' Political Council cooperated with the Magistrate in "squeezing" money. Chairman Wang not only refused to join the people in accusing the Magistrate to the provincial government but, when the Magistrate was dismissed, also wrote a eulogistic scroll to present to him and saw him off when he left the county. As a consequence, Wang's prestige was greatly lowered. If he had retired earlier, it would have been better for his reputation; in that case, the people would not have rebelled against his authority. Certainly, he himself recognized the situation. He said: "I am too old to do anything important. I have become a useless man." Regrettably, as he was not rich, he could not retire to enjoy his old age.

The life history of Chairman Wang proves that the gentry imposed norms and ideals upon the common people of the community. The gentry was expected to furnish a high standard of conduct for the common people. It had to live up to the norms and conventions. Those who could not fulfill the expectations of the people would lose prestige.

Finally, the Chinese gentry, especially the gentry of the older generations, played a role in family rituals. Its members played an important part in giving names to infants and looking after wedding arrangements or funeral ceremonies. It was as though they had charisma. For example, K'ung Chin-shih had often been invited to direct funeral ceremonies. My informant told me:

K'ung Chin-shih received the degree of *chin-shih* during the Ch'ing Dynasty. As his father had also been a *chin-shih*, his family had been well known as *shuang chin-shih*, "*chin-shih* in pairs." Because of his fame, almost all the rich and important families of the community request K'ung Chin-shih as the director of funeral ceremonies.[9] If he is invited, on the evening before the funeral day the family of the deceased must prepare a banquet for his reward. When the banquet is sent to K'ung's home, two musicians must be hired to lead the procession and play musical instruments. The *hsiao-tzŭ*, or "filial son" should follow the procession to his home and personally make the request. On the funeral day, the *hsiao-tzŭ* should go to his home with two musicians playing musical instruments to request him again. After the ceremony, the *hsiao-tzŭ* should personally escort him back home. The rewards usually include two *ching* of pork and a jar of wine. Sometimes money can be offered instead. The amount of money depends on the economic condition of the family. If the family lives far away from his home, a sedan chair must be provided. He is now eighty-four years old [in 1945] and still healthy. Many families therefore still ask him to be a director of funeral ceremonies.

The case of K'ung Chin-shih gives us a good illustration of how the gentry looked after the wedding and funeral arrangements for the people. They were proficient in ritual and had charisma.

It is noteworthy that the gentry tried to introduce modern technical advancement to the rural community. Chief Chang suggested to the Magistrate that the owners of the farms south and east of the city be taxed so that a twenty-horsepower water pump could be bought. Mr. Chien also intended to buy a water pump with his private capital to use the water of Kunming Lake to irrigate the farms of Ho Hsi Hsiang. He planned that a fee should be charged per *mow* for the regulation of water during the whole year. Their plans were not realized, however. Furthermore, Commander Chu bought a motor and established a factory for husking rice. At night the motor generated electricity, and he encouraged the people in the city to use electric lights, but they dared not use it, lest they be exploited. The business was eventually terminated. Modern industrialization requires not merely modern machinery and modern engineering but also modern political and social organization.

In former times, the tentacles of the central power had stopped at the *hsien* or county. When the magistrate carried out the order of the provincial government, he sent an agent to the village to transmit it. The agent himself was a conscript from the village. He enjoyed no prestige in his own community. In practice, he was only a messenger of the magistrate. The government order passed unofficially from the hand of the agent to a member of the village gentry, usually the leading one, who occupied no official position in the government constitution. The order then would be announced and discussed in the village teashops. All those present might participate. No vote would be taken, but the village gentleman would decide according to the public opinion as well as to his own sense of appropriateness whether or not the order should be followed. If the decision was in the negative, the agent would be sent back to the magistrate without achieving anything. He would have to assume all the responsibility for the failure in executing the order and would be punished with beating. The village notable, however, would call on the magistrate or ask some of the town gentry to call on the magistrate for negotiation. As the gentry had connections with the power hierarchy, the magistrate had to consider its suggestions and modify his order.[10]

Ever since the introduction of the *hsiang-chên* and *pao-chia* systems in Kunyang in 1940, the political track had been brought from the top down to every household, and many functions of the gentry had been taken over by the government. For example, settling the everyday disputes for the people had been a notable function of the gentry. As the *hsiang* or *chên* government was ordered to organize a committee for mediating disputes for the people, this function was actually taken away from the gentry by the government. Furthermore, the village school had traditionally been maintained by the gentry. According to the new law the *pao-chang* was concurrently president of the *pao* hall, principal of the primary school, and head of the civil defense corps, while the schoolteacher was concurrently a clerk of the *pao* hall. Actually, most of the *pao-chang* had not the slightest idea of the Chinese written language, which necessitated appointing assistants to handle the official letters. The position of the *pao-chang* was equivalent to that of the agent in the former administrative system, although the *pao-chang* legally had the right to keep the public funds and to manage local affairs. The respectable people of the community were usually unwilling to take the job of *pao-chang*. A respectable schoolteacher, if he wished to preserve his status, could not accept a place in the system that would make him lower in status and subject to orders from those whose status was lower than his. As a consequence, the number of village schools rapidly decreased. For example, Pao Shan Hsiang included thirty-four villages. It had eleven junior primary schools before 1940. On the average, every three villages had a junior primary school. But after the introduction of the *pao-chia* system, the number of junior primary schools in Pao Shan Hsiang decreased to nine in 1943 and to four in 1945. The process by which the gentry relinquished its basic function implies not merely voluntary surrender and failure of will power but also the existence of pressure from the objective political and social situations that resulted in inactivity and flagging will. It implies not only *giving up* but also *taking away*.

In short, the gentry operated well when it fulfilled its basic functions of promoting the welfare of the people. But the group proved unadaptable to the new needs brought by the impact of industrialization, with its agricultural mechanization and Western social values.

NOTES

1. A. R. Radcliffe-Brown, *Structure and Function in Primitive Society: Essays and Address* (New York: The Free Press, 1952), pp. 178–81.
2. The county seat of Kunyang is situated about five kilometers south of Kunming Lake. A canal, which connects the city and the lake, was dug out about fifty years ago to facilitate transportation, but it was narrow and shallow and thus could only accommodate sampans or sailing vessels. Because there was a steamboat running between

Kunming and Kunyang on Kunming Lake, transportation capacity was, however, greatly increased. The canal became a very important route. In order to meet the need for a larger waterway, the Magistrate and the gentry proposed to dredge and dike the canal in 1935 so that large boats could reach the East Gate of the city. At the same time, a new wharf was also built. After the project was successfully completed, a stone tablet was subscribed to mark the reconstruction.

3. Max Weber, *The Theory of Social and Economic Organization*, translated by A. M. Henderson and Talcott Parsons (New York: Oxford University Press, Inc., 1947), pp. 413–4.

4. In Kunyang the size of a farm was expressed in terms of the *kung*, the amount of land that could be worked by one laborer in one day. The standard *mow* of 666 square meters was roughly the equivalent of 2.6 *kung*. For further discussion of this point, see Hsiao-tung Fei and Chih-i Chang, *Earthbound China: A Study of Rural Economy in Yunnan* (Chicago: The University of Chicago Press, 1945), pp. 28–30.

5. According to the then current Chinese concept, the family (*chia* or *chia-ting*) was the economic family, a unit consisting of members related to one another by blood, marriage, or adoption and having a common budget and common property. Both the members staying together and those temporarily absent were included. The family often coincided with the household (*hu*)—in the lower classes, for example—but the two terms were not identical. Slaves, servants, boarders, even relatives staying temporarily with the family were members of the household but not of the family. After family divisions, parents and children, brothers and other relatives ceased to be members of the same family. See Olga Lang, *Chinese Family and Society* (New Haven: Yale University Press, 1946), p. 13.

6. Fei, *China's Gentry: Essays in Rural-Urban Relations*, revised and edited by Margaret Park Redfield, with six life-histories of Chinese gentry families by Yung-teh Chow and an introduction by Robert Redfield (Chicago: The University of Chicago Press, 1953), p. 83.

7. *Feng-shui*, or geomancy, is based on the assumptions that the *Wu-Hsing* (Five Planets), the *Pah-Kwa* (Eight Diagrams), the directions of surrounding objects, and the physical configuration of the landscape have influence on a grave and in turn on the prosperity or misfortune of the descendants of the deceased.

8. Morton H. Fried, *Fabric of Chinese Society: A Study of the Social Life of a Chinese County Seat* (New York: Frederick A. Praeger, Inc., 1953), p. 100.

9. The funeral ceremony was one of the most important family ceremonies, and its procedures were very complex. The descendants had to wear certain kinds of dress. The definite periods of mourning, certain funeral writings, poems or prose, the titles, words, type of writing, color of the paper, and so forth were all strictly chosen. If there was anything wrong, the family would be disgraced in the

community. The best scholar of the community was therefore invited to direct the ceremony.

10. Fei, "Peasantry and Gentry: An Interpretation of Chinese Social Structure and Its Changes," *American Journal of Sociology,* 52 (July, 1946), 1–17.

3

The Social Characteristics of the Gentry

In the previous chapter we described the persistence of the status system, the mechanism that maintained the network of social relations, and the social roles of the gentry. We cannot study persons except in terms of social structure. Simultaneously, however, we cannot study social structure except in terms of the persons who are the units of which it is composed. Closely connected with the conception of social structure is the conception of "social personality" as the position occupied by a human being in a social structure, the complex formed by all his social relations with others. We shall analyze the social and cultural behavior of the gentry under the headings of "style of life," literacy and aspirations, families of the gentry, the display of prestige, and the social structure of the gentry.

THE "STYLE OF LIFE"[1]

The first requirement for a status group is status unity. By "status unity" we mean that the members of a certain status group can be set off clearly from those of other status groups. The most general and effective method of drawing dividing lines is the possession of a common mode of life.

The gentry as a status group had an organized system of behavior patterns by which the activities and interrelations of individuals were controlled. The system could find expression in the physical world only through the medium of the individuals who composed the group; without the system the group would have remained simply a group of individuals incapable of functioning as a whole.

In order to gain and hold esteem, it was not sufficient for the gentry to possess merely wealth or power. As Veblen has pointed out, wealth or power must be put in evidence, for esteem is awarded only on evidence. And not only does the evidence of wealth serve to impress one's importance on others and to keep their sense of his importance alive and alert, but it is also of scarcely less use in building up and preserving one's own self-esteem. In all but the lowest stages of culture the normally constituted man is comforted and upheld in his self-respect by "decent surroundings" and by exemption from "menial offices."[2] The gentry's incomes were enough for adequate clothing, sufficient nutrition, decent housing, and the education of their children. The whole pattern of its family life seems to have been an attempt to live up to the standards set by its ambitions and perhaps controlled by the standards of wealthy relatives. Members of the gentry were generous to one another, emulous of virtue as they understood it, kind to their children, filial to their parents, and by no means harsh to women. The expressions on their faces were generally humane, and many of them were attractive. These outward and visible signs connoted inward and invisible graces. Their assured, curt voices, their proud carriage, their handsome manners, their elegant, abstruse language all showed that they belonged to a distinguished group.

It is but natural that the clothing of the gentry should have differed from that of the peasants. The "long gown" was the typical symbol of rank and prestige. It gave members of the gentry a large part of their social personality. Through their clothing they identified themselves, and the common people recognized them. The elegant "long gown" expressed not only a man's life of contentment but also his sense of status and prestige. It also made plain to all observers that the wearer was not engaged in any kind of productive labor. As Veblen has indicated, the pleasing effect of neat and spotless garments is chiefly, if not altogether, due to their carrying the suggestion of leisure—exemption from personal contact with industrial processes of any kind.[3]

The conspicuous difference in costume between the older and younger generations of the gentry is well known. Members of the younger generation, who gave up the long gown, had different tastes.

They considered the old fashion rustic and unsuitable. They wore student uniforms or Western suits. The older generation experienced difficulty in changing and adhered to the long gown. Nevertheless, there was no notable loss in prestige or authority for the gentry of the older generation.

The peasants in the community usually took two meals a day, one at about nine o'clock in the morning and another at about five in the afternoon. Besides these regular meals, members of the gentry had two extra meals at noon and night.

The magnificent house was considered a great mark of eminence and success in the village world. The gentry therefore became very conscious of the social significance of housing. The most massive and best-built houses in the villages and towns were always the households of the gentry. These houses were built of stones, burned bricks and tiles, lime, and good grades of wood. The newly built houses were in both Chinese and Western architectural styles and were as impressive inside as outside. Each member of the gentry boasted his pleasant guest room, his study, his little front garden, his collection of paintings, and his calligraphy written by noted scholars of the province. The rooms had glass windows and were stocked with mirrors, phonographs, sofas, and foreign beds. The beds had sheets, imported blankets, bedspreads, foreign-style pillows, and curtains. These homes were kept clean and in order.

Members of the gentry had attained a high standard of living in the community. They were usually free not only of work but also of running their homes. The household tasks were performed by maidservants. The masters were faced with the burdensome problem of passing time, for which there was no constructive use in the villages or towns. The popularity of conversation over glasses of pale tea at home, visiting teahouses or wine restaurants, playing mah-jongg in hospitable friends' homes, and indulging the habit of opium-smoking adequately contributed to their enjoyment of leisure.

Among the gentry members themselves, there were still some differences of degree. The lives of Confucian scholars were simpler and more old-fashioned. Chairman Wang's is an excellent example:

Chairman Wang was accustomed to living a simple life. He generally wore a long gown of a dark color, a pair of homemade cloth shoes, and a cap. When he was invited to join a party or attend a formal meeting, he would put on a jacket. Several of his teeth, however, were inlaid with gold, which was then coming into fashion in the county. He smoked tobacco in a long thin bamboo pipe. When he rented a house in the city, all his furniture was made of wood in the old fashion. Hanging on the walls were several couplets written by noted scholars of the province. In the court were a couple of pots of orchids, which symbolized the scholarly character. We often saw in his hall one or two pretty birds that he had caught in his native place and that he kept in a cage.

Chairman Wang's meals were very simple. His favorite pastime was playing mah-jongg. He played with several intimate friends almost every night. He went to bed very late. He was happy that all his sons could live independently. He often said, "Some people leave their sons a full chest of gold; I leave my sons only the ancient classics."

Vice-Chairman Loh of the Citizens' Political Council of the county was a physician. His life was as simple as that of Chairman Wang.

Vice-Chairman Loh's life was very regular. He got up daily at about twelve o'clock. He then took two eggs stewed with brown sugar for his breakfast. Lunch he took at one o'clock. He paid close attention to nutrition. Cabbage, spinach, bean-curd starch, arrowhead, and lotus root were his favorite foods. He never ate uncooked or hard or cold food. After taking his lunch, he would go upstairs and would lie on his bed to rest about fifteen minutes. He would smoke opium and drink tea for a while. Then he would come to the hall to cure his patients. He usually went to bed around ten o'clock at night. If he needed some service, he did not call but tapped the upstairs floor with his long thin bamboo pipe. His family would immediately go upstairs to take care of him. He was carefully attended by his wife and concubine. Loh's tobacco was prepared daily by his wife. He drank wine but never beyond his capacity. Because he took special care of his health, Loh's complexion looked fresh and florid though he was in his old age. His carefully trimmed long beard was elegant and beautiful. As he had peculiar habits, he could not go to another's home for more than a short while. If somebody out of town wanted to invite him to cure an illness, the patient had to provide a sedan chair for him.

Usually Loh stayed at home all day. When he had nothing to do, he would read books or practice calligraphy or enjoy his garden. He never worried. He often said: "Human life is short. We should enjoy ourselves. Worry is useless." If he saw some good painting or handwriting that he liked, he would be elated. He liked beautiful flowers very much, and all the flowers and shrubs in his garden were planted by himself. When the flowers were in bloom, Loh would put a pot on the counter of his shop for display. He especially like peonies. He often said that the peony was the queen of flowers. When one of them came into bloom, he would decorate it with a piece of red silk in celebration because he considered it a good omen. He disliked luxuriously dressed men and women. He thought the world had gone to the devil. He liked to visit attractive scenic spots or sites of *hao feng-shui*.

While the lives of Confucian scholars were simple and old-fashioned, the lives of merchants and military men were more urban, fashionable, and luxurious. Chief Ting's case is an illustration of the merchant's life:

Once I visited Chief Ting, a rich merchant, at his home. His house was very large and clean. In the court there were many pots of flowers. Scrolls of painting and calligraphy were hung on the walls in the hall and study room. The tables and chairs were made of rosewood. In the hall several hams and salted ducks were hung from the ceiling.

Ting usually went to bed very late and got up about nine o'clock in the morning. After he got up, his daughter would carry him water to wash his face. His food included fish, pork, ham, egg, salted duck, various vegetables, and rice. His clothes were made of wool of foreign manufacture. He carried a fountain pen that had been imported from the United States and wore a wristwatch and a pair of leather shoes. He also had an overcoat in the Western style. His bed had a wool blanket and satin bedclothes, and in his bedroom there was a radio. When he was at home, he would listen every night to the current market reports. Everyone who saw these things would praise him highly.

Ting went to Kunming four or five times a month on business. Sometimes he invited several intimate friends to his home to play mahjongg, though he himself did not join them. Because he had been very often sick in recent years, he started to smoke opium, thinking that opium would cure the sickness.

Commander Chu's life was about the same as that of Chief Ting. He had houses in both Kunming and Kunyang.

After retiring from the army, Chu bought a house of four rooms for his residence in Kunming. Though at times he stayed in Kunyang, most of his time was spent in Kunming.

Commander Chu built a two-story house in the City of Kunyang. The house was built in both Western and Chinese architectural styles. Around the house were a large flower garden and orchard encircled by a wall. Furnishings included a sofa, a foreign bed, and a phonograph, objects seldom seen in the community.

Commander Chu smoked opium but did not drink wine. He went to the movie theater once or twice a month in Kunming. He liked to visit well-known spots of beautiful scenery. When he felt lonely at home, he would play records to pass the time. He usually wore a silk long gown of bright color.

The gentry constituted a status group and had a common heritage of customs and traditions, which played a great part in social life and control. A young man fresh out of school who did not have the habits of smoking, drinking, and gambling would soon acquire them. Chairman Wang's youngest son, Wen-hua, was typical:

Wen-hua was graduated from the teachers college of Southwest

Associated University in Kunming when he was twenty-six. He was shy, gentle, and reserved. Before, he would not smoke, drink, or gamble. After he became the principal of the normal school and the junior middle school of the county, he felt that it was necessary to be sociable. He began to smoke cigarettes, drink wine, and play mah-jongg. He would go to bed late and get up late, like an old man.

Members of the gentry "lived in clover" and nourished their health. They valued longevity. They used their leisure in various ways. Their way of life, their pattern of living, was one that all the young men in the community wanted to have. It seems that the life of the gentry class stressed the notions of human understanding, high-mindedness, detachment from life, absence of triviality and vulgarity. But if its members had any philosophy of life, it was "an idle philosophy born of an idle life."[4]

LITERACY AND ASPIRATIONS

The gentry generally furnished the intellectual leaders of the community, and learning had always been regarded as a primary duty and a mark of distinction for this class. The materials its members read can be analyzed under six headings: classics and histories; stories and novels; works on social techniques, religions, medicine, geomancy, and physiognomy; current books; and newspapers and magazines.

The old-fashioned scholars were essentially students of the classics of the Confucianist school and dynastic histories. In a predominantly peasant society the literati constituted the only articulate group and held the reins of government in their hands. They exercised power on the basis of Confucianism, which, broadly speaking, consisted of an elaborate body of ethical doctrine dealing with man-to-man relationships. It emphasized harmony rather than competition. Harmony was to be achieved through self-abnegation and consideration for others. The conduct of man toward his fellow man was governed by explicit rules prescribed on the basis of relative status. A man was to be filial to his parents, loyal to his prince, respectful to his superiors, and authoritative but kind to his subordinates. The idea of obligation was ingrained in the minds of all. The individual could not exist apart from the whole. The idea of the whole and the emphasis on the hierarchy of status combined to assign to the family a place of paramount importance in man's life. The supreme obligation of a man toward his family was not to give them wealth and power but to reflect on them the honor that he could achieve by the strictest conformity to Confucian ethics.[5]

Traditionally, the main gateway to gentry status had been through the civil-service examination. Studies for these examinations were limited to a few classics. In order to pass, a candidate had literally to know the classics by heart and to understand their meanings in an exhaustive manner. This education in itself constituted a process of indoctrination. It ensured a homogeneity of outlook among the literati and imbued them with a sense of mission toward the masses and indeed toward all humanity. A strong sense of propriety and of *noblesse oblige* characterized the Chinese literati, and it was this sense that enabled Confucian society to last for so many centuries.[6]

The second category of reading material was stories and novels. There were about a dozen such books that were widely read. The Confucian scholars did not include them in the domain of their more "solid" scholarship; these books became the reading of men who were not sufficiently well educated to compete in the civil examinations but wanted some reading matter for entertainment within their ability to understand. Although these men were not well acquainted with the classics, their minds were often sharpened by the fantastic subtlety and complexity of these enormously long novels to a higher degree than those of men who constantly drilled themselves in Confucian moral principles. The case history of Mr. Yao's father, Yao Kuang-tsu, is suggestive on this point:

After the division of his family, Mr. Yao's grandfather, Yao Tao-sung, had sixteen *kung* of farmland and a house with two rooms. Tao-sung tried his best to send his only son, Kuang-tsu, to school, though the economic condition of their family was not very good. Kuang-tsu started to study at the age of seven. He had a good memory, studied at school very hard, and made fast progress. Unfortunately, he had to quit at twelve and hired himself out to a landowner as a cattle tender. His yearly wage was forty catties of rice, two suits of clothes, one pair of shoes, and a cap. He was clever and industrious, and his master liked him very much. He usually tended his cattle on the hill with a young companion. His companion recognized more characters than he and liked to read novels: *The Romance of the Three Kingdoms, All Men Are Brothers, The Romance of the Feudal States, The Record of a Journey to the West,* and so forth. Kuang-tsu thus had an opportunity to learn from his companion. After several years, he had read many such books himself, and his mind was gradually enlightened. He talked elegantly.

When he was twenty-two years old, Kuang-tsu felt that he had no future as a farm laborer and that a man should be ambitious if he wanted to be prominent. He solicited eight friends to go to Kwangsi Province to join the army voluntarily to fight against the Manchu government. He was ingenious and eloquent. He often told stories, which he had read in the popular novels, when he and his colleagues were off duty. His stories often amused his colleagues or encouraged them to forget fatigue, difficulties, and danger. He was therefore liked by his superior officers and promoted to captain in a few years. After eight years, he resigned his post and came home with honor and prosperity.

Although many men who were not formally educated acquired some intellectual cultivation through these popular stories and novels, they were not considered really educated by the Confucian scholars. The children of the solid gentry were usually discouraged from reading these books.

The most popular novel in the community was *San Kuo Chih Yen I* (*The Romance of the Three Kingdoms*), attributed to Lo Kuan-chung. It is an historical novel based upon the wars of the Three Kingdoms, which were fought at the beginning of the third century A.D. It consists of many stirring scenes of warfare, of maneuvers by skillful generals, and of Homeric deeds by blood-stained warriors. Armies and fleets of countless thousands are from time to time annihilated by one side or another—all in an easy and fascinating style, which makes the book a constant joy to old and young alike.[7]

The next most popular novel was *Shui Hu Ch'uan* (*All Men Are Brothers*), written in colloquial language by Shih Nai-an. It deals with the exploits of a band of generous noble robbers during the early twelfth century. Some of the characters are historical, and the setting (Shantung) is geographically accurate. The episodes related were derived from popular traditions. They tell how men of many sorts, fleeing from the oppression of government and the ruling class, came to "Liang Shan" to band themselves together and how they lived by defying the government and preying upon the rich people and officials.[8]

The third widely read book, *Lieh Kuo Ch'uan* (*The Romance of the Feudal States*), written by an anonymous author, is an historical novel dealing with the exciting times of the Warring States and covering the period between the eighth century B.C. and the union of China under the First Emperor. It is a genuine history, not a mere novel.[9]

The fourth popular book was *Liao Chai Chih I* (*The Ghost and Love Stories in a Studio*), written by Pu Sung-lin (1640–1715). It comprises 431 stories. The author achieved a degree of realism in treating the supernatural and wrote in a simple and elegant style that vitalizes the flimsiest and most hackneyed plots.[10]

The fifth prominent novel, *Hung Lou Meng,* conveniently but erroneously known as *The Dream of the Red Chamber,* written by Tsao Hsüen-chin, is the work touching the highest point of development reached by the Chinese novel. As a panorama of Chinese social life, in which almost every imaginable feature is submitted in turn to the reader, the *Hung Lou Meng* is altogether without a rival. Reduced to its simplest terms, it is an original and effective love story, written for the most part in an easy, almost colloquial style, full of humorous and pathetic episodes of everyday human life and interspersed with short poems of high literary finish. The opening chapters, which are intended to form a link between the world of spirits and the world of mortals, belong to the supernatural; after that the story runs smoothly along, always, however, overshadowed by the presence of spiritual influences.[11]

The last popularly read novel was *Hsi Yu Chi (The Record of a Journey to the West),* which was the work of a known writer, Wu Chen-en (c. 1500–1580). Instead of treating realistically the adventures of popular heroes, it presents allegorically the exploits of supernatural agents. The basis for the plot is the seventh-century pilgrimage of the Buddhist priest Hsüan-tsang to India to obtain sacred texts. Hsüan-tsang's own record of his journey is an important firsthand description of Central Asia and India in his day; his biography by a contemporary provided an inspiring description of a brave and devout man prepared to face any danger to accomplish his mission. The novel introduces Hsüan-tsang as such a character and then confronts him with obstacles beyond the power of any mortal man to surmount. But if his opponents have become supernatural, his guides and assistants are also superhuman. A fabulous stone monkey, invulnerable and endowed with infinite resourcefulness, is the chief agent whereby Hsüan-tsang reaches his goal—not simply a far-off country, but the "West Paradise"—and the monkey is the real protagonist, leaving Hsüan-tsang a minor role necessary to the plot but of secondary interest in its development. The style is naive, appropriate to a fairy tale, but *Journey to the West* is not primarily a story for children. The allegorical pilgrimage is reminiscent of that of Bunyan, but there is in addition a strong undercurrent of satire that makes *Journey to the West* an acute criticism of society and bureaucracy.[12] Other novels were less pretentious than those mentioned but also popular.

The books about social techniques accented the proper forms

of social behavior and emphasized how to write a good letter. The classics of Buddhism, medicine, geomancy, and physiognomy stressed man's struggle against fate.

The current books were mainly fictional but of the realistic type. The novels, essays, and *tsa-kan* (random thoughts) of Lu Hsün and the novels of Pa Chin were the most popular. Lu Hsün (pseudonym of Chou Shu-jen) was born in Shaohsiang, Chekiang Province, in 1881 and died in Shanghai in 1936. A prolific writer, he published *The Outcry* (1923) and *Wandering* (1926), two volumes of such short novels as "A Madman's Diary," "K'ung I-chi," "Medicine," "My Native Place," "Benediction," "Soap," and "Divorce." His most famous work was "The True Story of Ah Q." Its immense success was due mainly to its recognition of the hero as the embodiment of national disease and of the "silent soul of the people." Ah Q was a village lout of the lowest economic status who lived at the time when the Ch'ing Dynasty was about to topple. Repeated humiliations had taught him to pretend to "spiritual victory" when bullied, and to bully the physically weaker whenever they came across his path. As most villagers were better off and stronger, Ah Q had perforce to live in a slap-happy world of self-deception. He cheered himself up under whatever distressing circumstances and assumed an air of superiority in the face of manifest defeat. To Chinese readers this trait of character, reminiscent of recent history, gave a fresh satiric perspective to their country's pathetic stance among the bullying and more powerful nations.[13] Most of his sixteen volumes of essays, including *Hot Air* and *The Grave,* attacked backwardness, ignorance, and misgovernment. Lu Hsün was one of the most biting satirists among contemporary Chinese writers. His writing typically reflects the mood and temper of modern China, especially those of young China, toward its ancient culture. He represents the literature of revolt. Behind his work we see a heart-rending spirit of repentance and, best of all, an unquestionable zeal for reform. He was more a warrior than a "literary man." It was his uncompromising, challenging, fighting spirit that so charmed his readers.[14] In the later years of his life, he actually became a champion of the theory of proletarian literature.

Pa Chin (the pen name of Li Fei-kan) born in Chengtu, Szechuan Province, in 1904, was a popular and voluminous writer. He is the author of *Destruction,* a romantic tale about love and hatred. The hero Tu Ta-hsin (Tu Big Heart) was a sensitive child who cried over dead chickens and was early bereaved of his mother. In a season of famine, he saw human misery in all its grimness: In the field outside of the city huge pits were dug. Those who died of starvation were tossed pell-mell into the pits, like so many maggots. As he grew older, Big Heart fell in love with a girl cousin who, submissive to parental authority, finally married someone else. Some years later, after he had moved to Shanghai to engage in revolutionary activities, he again met this girl. Now an unhappy widow, she entreated his forgiveness and love, but Big Heart was too embittered to care. With a flourish he dismissed her and said, "No, I can no longer love you. I no longer have that heart of love. This heart is no longer capable of loving or being loved." Far from being unable to love, of course, Big Heart was now dedicated to the love of the suffering masses. He was poet, pamphleteer, leader of a labor union, and editor of its magazine. He lived by the proposition that "whoever builds his own happiness on the suffering of other people shall be destroyed." His *Love Trilogy—Fog, Rain,* and *Lightning—*together with a short interlude called *Thunder,* which precedes *Lightning,* describes the dilemma of love versus duty. On the one hand, it is noble to relinquish romantic love, the last infirmity of the bourgeois mind, for the pursuit of a more arduous ideal; on the other, it is perhaps even more thrilling to find the solace and beauty of love in the very context of revolution. What could bring greater personal satisfaction than to face the firing squad with the girl one loves and to die together for the sacred cause? His stories of noble humanitarianism, intellectual debates, romantic entanglements, and revolutionary conspiracies spoke directly to the youthful readers' hearts.[15] His other ambitious trilogy entitled *Turbulent Currents* includes *The Family, Spring,* and *Autumn.* These stories portray the darkness of traditional Chinese society, the dissatisfaction of petty-bourgeois intellectuals, their confusion, their distress, their wavering, and their vacillation after the defeat of the revolution in 1927. His works, especially *The Family,* were widely read by the young people and exercised a considerable influence on them.

Revolutionary books and magazines like the *Democratic Weekly* (with contributions by university professors) brought the currents of thought that gave the gentry's rural life some of its distinctiveness, in strange contrast to the intellectual stagnation of the peasantry. On the whole, the modern intellectuals can be said to have inherited the importance of the literati in the old society. The fact is not surprising when we remember that the masses in China remained illiterate. The older gentry members, however, were still conservative. They believed in ghosts, divination, geomancy, fortune-telling, and the old calendar.

The newspapers of Kunming came daily to Kunyang through steamship, bus, and mail.

What do we find as we go through the books that the gentry read? We find that there were none on the social and natural sciences and none on great divergent schools of philosophy.

What were the life goals, visions, objectives, and ideals of the gentry? These questions can easily be answered by reference to the status system described in the last chapter. The gentry had a core of ideals and values that were compatible with the status system. The gentry's aspirations were constructed around the effort to maintain its prestige in the community with minimum challenge. How to build its prestige, how to maintain its prestige, and how to enhance its prestige were the central themes of the gentry. It was this goal that actuated the gentry and in a large measure controlled its members' careers. Within the socially approved framework and under the impetus of glorifying his family and ancestors, the individual exhibited a strong drive toward success. As it was education that led to knowledge and consequently to official position, education became a driving goal among gentry families. This goal was expressed by gentlemen in their educational ambitions for their children. The following quotations show not only the ideals of the gentry but also the different levels of their aspirations.

Liu Tsung-tao, a middle landowner, was thirty-six years old in 1946 and had two sons and one daughter. His elder son was nine years old and was studying in an elementary school. The second son was four years old and the daughter one. Liu placed great hope in his children because both sons were very clever. He attempted to have them be graduated from the middle school and become men of high position in his own region. He did not think that he had the wealth to support his daughter's education.

Feng Chia-mi, an educated wealthy landlord, was thirty-eight years old in 1946 and had two sons and two daughters. His elder son was then nine years old and the second son five years old. His elder daughter was seven and the second two. His elder son was studying in an elementary school. Chia-mi intended to let his two sons study in Kunming and be graduated from the University and to have his two daughters be graduated from the middle school.

Although he himself had received only a small amount of education, Chief Ting, a wealthy merchant, intended to have his three daughters complete the middle school and to have his two sons be graduated from the University.

Major Chang intended to let his two sons and one daughter all complete their educations at the University. He planned to have his two sons separately engage in the army and teaching. His family would thus have both power and fame and be respected and admired by the people.

Commander Chu's wife bore no child, but his concubine bore him three sons and two daughters. All the children were very intelligent. His two daughters married; the oldest son, Chu Lung, was graduated at twenty-one from a middle school that had been specially built by the Governor for educating the children of the officials in Kunming. After his graduation, he could not pass the entrance examination into any college, however. His father then sent him to a military academy, but after a month in the academy he ran away because he could not bear the regimentation. The second son, Chu Hu, twenty years old, was studying in a middle school in Kunming. The youngest son, Chu Lin, at fourteen years old, was studying in a primary school. Commander Chu hoped that each of his sons would become a man of distinction.

Chairman Wang's family was well known as a *shu hsiang shih chia,* a "scholar's family." According to census data taken in 1942 by the Institute for Census Research of National Tsing Hua University, among the population of 69,231, there were only six persons who were college students, four persons who had been graduated from college, and three persons who had returned from Japan, France, and the United States. Chairman Wang had four sons—two of them had returned from abroad, one was a college student, and the other had been graduated from a four-year normal school.

These cases highlight two points that are noteworthy: members of the gentry were generally willing to put more investment into the education of their sons than into that of their daughters, although Major Chang made no such discrimination; second, it seems that Major Chang's plan for his sons was typical in the community. Most members of the gentry wanted their sons to be divided between the army and teaching. Their families would thus have both power and prestige and be respected and admired by the people.

Economic conditions and ambition were not the only factors that decided the educational advancement of the children of the gentry. For example, Commander Chu was wealthy and powerful enough to support his children through the highest education. But his eldest son, Chu Lung, did not receive such an education because, after being graduated from a middle school, he could not pass the entrance examination into any college, and after one month in a military academy he ran away. Clearly, in order to receive good educations, the children themselves had to be able and willing to struggle forward. On the other hand, Chairman Wang had only moderate wealth. But his four sons had the highest educations.

It is true that members of the gentry hoped to give as much education as possible to their children. Nevertheless, education was not an end in itself; it was viewed as a stepping stone to obtaining official position of social prestige. Chairman Wang's four sons are cases in point.

Of Chairman Wang's four sons, one, an official of the Kuomintang, was so scandalously corrupt in office that he was dismissed; another became degenerate through opium addiction; the third, though not actually badly behaved, seemed to lack mental and moral fiber; and only the fourth escaped to a scholar's life in America.

THE EXTENDED FAMILIES OF THE GENTRY

The single distinctive goal of the gentry family was to bolster its status in the community. The large or extended family system was accepted as an ideal. The general aim was to have as many male children as possible, which was both a fundamental religious and ethical command and the earnest desire of the gentry. The importance of the family's standing lay in the fact that any member's glory was reflected on the family and therefore any member could trade upon it.

Most members of the gentry did have large or extended families. Among the twenty-six distinguished gentry families well known in the community, seventeen were large families; seven were stem families;[16] only two were nuclear or small families.

Table 9. Sizes of the Twenty-six Upper Gentry Families, Kunyang, 1942

Family Size	Frequency	Family Size	Frequency
5	1	16	1
6	3	18	1
7	1	21	1
8	1	22	1
10	3	23	1
11	6	24	1
12	2	25	1
15	1	30	1
		Total	26

Table 9 indicates that more than one-third of the twenty-six upper gentry families included fifteen or more persons each and that only four families included six or fewer each. The average size of the twenty-six upper gentry families was 13.5. On the other hand, the average family size of the general population was much smaller. Most families were nuclear or stem families, as shown by the 1942 census.

Table 10 shows us that the large or extended family organization was not a general characteristic of the population. Of 11,220 families,

Table 10. Family Size in Kunyang,[a] 1942

Family Size	Number	Percentage	
1	175	1.56	
2	533	4.75	
3	1,268	11.30	
4	1,844	16.44	
5	1,794	15.99	
6	1,543	13.75	
7	1,140	10.16	
8	810	7.22	
9	624	5.56	
10	423	3.77	
11	313	2.79	
12	226	2.01	
13	168	1.50	
14	89	0.79	
15	83	0.74	
16	48	0.43	
17	48	0.43	
18	26	0.23	
19	16	0.14	
20	14	0.13	
21	12	0.11	
22	5	0.04	
23	5	0.04	
24	5	0.04	0.2
25	5	0.04	
29	2	0.02	
30	1	0.01	
Total	11,220	100.00	

Source: The Institute for Census Research, National Tsing Hua University, "A Report on the Population Census of Kunming Lake Region, Yunnan," Appendix, 10(B) (unpublished).

[a] Including those members temporarily absent.

7,157 or 63.79% included six persons or fewer each. There were 10,154 families, or 90.5%, with ten or fewer persons each. At the same time, there were only 270 families, or 2.4%, with fifteen persons or more each. The average family size was 6.17, less than half that of the twenty-six gentry families.

The large or extended family generally included three generations and three nuclear or conjugal families. Among the twenty-six gentry families, three had two generations each; seventeen had three generations each; and six had four generations each. The extended family had, on the average, 3.1 generations.

Table 11 shows that seventeen of the twenty-six upper gentry families included between three and eight nuclear families each. The average was three or four nuclear families each.

Table 11. Nuclear Families among the Twenty-six Upper Gentry Families, Kunyang

Nuclear Families	Gentry Families	Nuclear Families	Gentry Families
1	2	5	1
2	7	6	2
3	8	7	2
4	3	8	1
		Total	26

The gentry family could have a larger size and a more extended organization because members of the gentry could afford to have more children. They had more children because they were married earlier, had concubines, and lost fewer children in death. In order to perpetuate the family line and preserve the family fortune and honor, male descendants were of the utmost importance. The local term for the continuity of family line was the "continuity of the smoke of incense" at the ancestral shrine. The parents' earnest desires for posterity can be seen in their anxiety to see their sons married and in their happiness at having children and grandchildren. The early marrying ages of the gentry members and of their fathers and grandfathers are shown in Table 12.

Table 12 shows that the youngest age at first marriage of the twenty-six gentry members was sixteen years. None was married later than at twenty-two years of age. The average age was 18.2. On the

Table 12. Age at First Marriage of the Twenty-six Upper Gentry Members and Their Fathers and Grandfathers

Age at First Marriage	Gentry Members	Fathers	Grandfathers
15		2	
16	3	2	
17	6	4	7
18	7	6	8
19	5	7	3
20	3	1	1
21	1	1	
22	1	1	1
Unknown		2	6
Total	26	26	26

other hand, the marriage age of the general population was much higher. As Table 13 suggests, the average age at first marriage of the general population in the registered area of Kunyang was 21.2 years, three years later than that of the gentry. Among the 796 married males, there were 229, or 28.8%, whose ages at first marriage had been greater than twenty-two. Many poor peasants even delayed their marriages until they were thirty or forty years old.

Table 13. Ages at First Marriage of the Males in the Four Districts of Kunyang, August, 1943 to January, 1946

Age at First Marriage	Number	Percentage
15–16	115	14.45
17–18	138	17.34
19–20	200	25.13
21–22	114	14.32
23–24	78	9.80
25–29	58	7.29
30–34	31	3.89
35–39	26	3.27
40 and over	36	4.52
Total	796	100.01

Source: The Institute for Census Research, National Tsing Hua University, "A Report on the Registration of Vital Statistics in Chengkung and Kunyang, Yunnan" (unpublished).

When a first child was born, the family would be extremely

happy and would usually throw a party in celebration. Chairman Wang's case is a typical example:

Chairman Wang was born in 1881. Because he was their eldest son, his parents loved him very much. The proverb says, "To have a son early in life is more important than to become rich." When he was a month old, his father gave a dinner party for about 160 people. The guests included grandparents-in-law, relatives, friends, and villagers. The entertainment lasted for three days.

The gentry's desire was *ts'ai ting liang wan,* "that both purse and family should be prosperous." But if parents had had to choose, they would probably have put family ahead of purse. Liu Tsung-tao's family offers an appropriate example:

Liu Tsung-tao was the elder son of Liu Yen-tau. When he was born his father was already thirty-one years old. His father was very happy and loved him very much. Yen-tau often said: "Both family and purse should be prosperous. But family is more important than the purse, because the purse is a *ssŭ pao,* a dead gem, while the family consists of *huo pao,* a living gem." He undertook all the jobs of housekeeping in order to allow his wife rest and time to care for the child.

Another way of acquiring more children was to take a concubine,* although a concubine was sometimes taken for prestige or because of polyerotic desires. Among the twenty-six gentry members, ten had one or two concubines for various reasons: two because their wives had been barren; one because his wife had given birth to only a daughter; one, with two concubines, because his wife had given him only one son; three because, while they had been serving in the army as officers, they had found their illiterate and feet-bound wives no longer adequate; one because his position as magistrate seemed to demand it for status; one because he found his wife incompatible and disliked her. One man took a second wife and a concubine after the death of his first wife, though by that time he already had four adult sons and several grandsons. There was one extreme case: One member of the gentry had five concubines. He was labeled "Hsiao Lo-tzŭ," or "Little Mule."

Gentry members were able to raise more children partly because fewer of their children died. According to our surveys, the infant mortality rate among the gentry families was less than ninety per

* Although the concubine was generally of lower social status than was the first wife and her position in the home therefore inferior, her children counted as equally legitimate with those of the first wife, and no discrimination was made between them.

1,000 live births. On the other hand, it is evident that the infant mortality rate of the general population was higher than that of the gentry. According to the vital statistics registered by the Institute of Census Research, among the 33,874 persons in the registering area, the average infant mortality rate for the two years between August 1943, and July 1945, was 281.9 per 1,000 live births. It was more than three times higher than that of the gentry families. Clearly, economic conditions had a significant effect upon the differential infant mortality rate.

The extended gentry families could include on the average 3.1 generations, because the adults were able to live to old age and become grandparents and great-grandparents. Among the twenty-six gentry families the average age at death was 70.5 for the grandfathers, 67.9 for the grandmothers, 71.4 for the great-grandfathers, and 70.5 for the great-grandmothers.

In large families, the members were distributed among different occupations. Some took up agriculture, some became scholars, and some became merchants. This diversity was one of the reasons why the gentry family was powerful. When a family was dissolved and its common resources divided among the male members, it suffered a serious loss of prestige, and thus members were reluctant to dissolve the family. Mr. Fan's family offers a distinctive case in point:

Mr. Fan's grandfather, Fan Lien-ching, was a merchant and a landowner. He had studied five years in a private school. When he was thirty-five years old, he and his two brothers divided their family property. He received twenty-five *kung* of farmland, 3,000 *liang* or *tael* of silver and a house. He was energetic and experienced in both farming and business. When he was fifty years old, he bought fifty-five *kung* of farmland and built three houses facing the street in the county seat. He had five sons. The third son died in childhood.

Lien-ching's eldest son, Tao-yuan, was a Confucian scholar. His second son, Tao-heng, had studied five years and could write letters and keep accounts. He devoted himself to business. Lien-ching's fourth son, Tao-chen, went into agriculture. He had never been to school. The fifth son, Tao-kao, was engaged in business. He studied four years in a private school. He was good at writing and at figuring with the abacus. All the sons were married, and each had several children. Tao-yuan's two sons and Tao-heng's eldest son also were married, and each had one child. The large family thus consisted of eight conjugal families and four generations. There were altogether twenty-five persons in the family.

It was the eldest son, Tao-yuan, Mr. Fan's father, who was the hero of the large family. He was able, intelligent, and handsome. He had started to study when he was six years old and had often been praised by his teacher. He had received the degree of *Hsiu Ts'ai* at seventeen years of age. After obtaining the degree, he became a teacher and continued to study. He had received the degree of *Chü Jen* at twenty-one and was number two in the class. The official in charge of the examination admired his composition very much. And after Tao-yuan had held his *Chü Jen* for three years, the official was appointed Magistrate of Kunyang and immediately invited Tao-yuan to become his secretary. As the Magistrate had faith in him, the young man became the most powerful member of the gentry in Kunyang. He was called "Tao-yuan Lao Yeh," or "Tao-yuan, His Excellency."

After serving as a secretary for half a year, he was promoted to the head of the Bureau of Finance of the county government. Lien-ching, his father, immediately took this opportunity to enlarge his business. If he happened to be short of funds, he would tell Tao-yuan to give him a few days' advance from the money of the county government. Lien-ching thus established his business reputation. Thereafter, both the Standard Oil Company and Nan-Yang* Brothers Tobacco Company requested him to serve as agent. His house was stocked to the ceiling with kerosene and cigarettes. The merchants of the neighboring counties of Kunyang—Yüchi, Tung-hai, Ho-hsi, O-shan, and Yi-men—all came to Kunyang and purchased goods from him. In the short period of two years, he accumulated a fortune of 500,000 silver dollars and became the most prosperous merchant of Kunyang. In addition to kerosene and cigarettes, he also sold rice, cloth, salt, and soybean oil. On market day, the customers lined up before his three stores. All the members of the family were busy and willing to sell goods, entertain customers, and the like. Tao-yuan became the soul of pride and the pillar of his large family.

In 1917, Tao-yuan went to Kunming to enter the competitive examination for the members of the provincial political council. He was selected and listed as number four. Consequently, he was chosen as a member of the group to be sent to Japan to study. He was quite happy at his success and came back home to ask permission from his parents. His parents felt, however, that they were too old to take care of the household, that Japan was too far away, and that, above all, the working mechanism of the family and the business of the stores were dependent upon his prestige and wide connections with the outside world. They therefore prevented him from going abroad. Eight years after he became secretary to the Magistrate, he had helped his father buy 100 *kung* of farmland and build a house of four rooms. Furthermore, he had bought a piece of land in the city as a site for an ancestral hall.

In 1924, he succeeded in the competitive examination for the Magistrates Training School. After one year's training, he was appointed Magistrate of Tun Chung. But one day in the summer he went for a swim and became sick as he returned home. After a few days of sickness, he died at his post. He was then only forty years old. When the news of his death came, the gentry and the people of Kunyang felt deep regret.

After his death, the glory of the Fan family vanished. There were

---

* Nan-Yang, "South Seas," is the common Chinese expression for all the territories of Southeast Asia.

quarrels among the sisters-in-law. The brothers became openly selfish. The young grew wild and lazy. The old parents lost control, and the family members lost their feeling of *esprit de corps*. A prominent large family was thus divided.

Mr. Fan's family was prosperous and powerful because Fan Lien-ching's four sons were engaged in agriculture, commerce, and public service. All the members of the family were willing to do various kinds of work for the common good. Lien-ching's eldest son, Tao-yuan, a Confucian scholar and head of the Bureau of Finance of the county government, was the center of the family. After the death of Tao-yuan, however, the glory of Fan's family was gone.

The power of the family could also be secured by deliberately organizing the members into two or more branches. One branch would remain in a rural town, close to the family's land and maintain the flow of wealth from this land. The other branch would reside in the county seat or in the provincial capital, filling various government posts and exercising influence on behalf of the family as a whole. Members of such an extended family structure could protect one another. The land-holding branch could support the political position of the city branch with its wealth, and the latter could give political protection to the former.[17] Chairman Wang's family furnishes an excellent example:

Chairman Wang was born in a village about thirty miles west of the county seat of Kunyang. He had four sons. His family was broken into four branches:

In 1913, Chairman Wang served as the principal of the county primary school. In the next year he was also appointed the chairman of the Office of Compulsory Education and the general inspector of county education. For convenience he and his family moved to the county seat. He rented his farms to tenants and went back only once a year to collect the rents. He rented a house in the city. In 1946, Chairman Wang's youngest son, Wen-hua, after being graduated from college in Kunming, went back to Kunyang to join his father. While he had been at college, he had been invited by the Magistrate to return to Kunyang to serve as the principal of the normal school and the junior middle school of the county. But the Magistrate appointed another man, Mr. Lin, as the principal of the school and asked Wen-hua to serve as head of a division in the Tax Department of the county government. Wen-hua was disappointed and thought of going to Kunming to find a job. His father was old, however, and the other boys in the family could not live with him, so he decided he had better stay home to keep his father company. He therefore agreed to assume the position.

Chairman Wang's third son, Wen-chang, after graduation from a normal school, went back to his native place and taught in the primary school and managed his home and farms simultaneously. During those years he became an opium smoker. He would smoke opium the whole night. He went to bed in the early morning and got up around two o'clock in the afternoon. He was lazy and in low spirits. Nevertheless, because of the prestige of his father and brothers, he was respected by the local people and elected a *hsiang chang,* the chief of a district government, and was also the principal of the central primary school of his native district.

Chairman Wang's oldest son, Wen-hung, after graduation from the Central Political Academy of the Kuomintang in Nanking, returned to Yunnan and served as head of a division in the Department of Finance of the provincial government of Yunnan. After one year he went to Japan and entered Waseda University in Tokyo, where he received the degree of Master of Arts. After returning to China, he served as a secretary in the provincial government of Shansi. After six years he returned to Yunnan and served as the head of a division in the provincial government's Department of Education. When he became a magistrate, he rushed home to ask his father to put together two million dollars for his expenses and to pay the salaries of faithful helpers. His father sold 200,000 *ching* of iron to meet this need.

Chairman Wang's second son, Wen-ta, after studying two years at Tsing Hua University in Peiping, left to serve as a member of the Provincial Headquarters Committee of the Nationalist Party of Yunnan. In a year he gained a scholarship to study abroad from the Central Headquarters through a competitive examination among party members. He went to the United States in 1931 and received the degrees of Master of Arts and Doctor of Philosophy. He married an American woman and remained in the United States. Otherwise, he might have set up another branch of his large family in the national capital.

Chairman Wang's family was organized in three branches: one in his native district, where his third son was the chief; one in the county seat, where he himself was the chairman of the Citizens' Political Council and where his youngest son was the principal of the junior normal school and junior middle school of the county; and one in the provincial capital. Chairman Wang's eldest son was head of a division of the Department of Education of the provincial government, and his second son was then in the United States. I suppose that if he had gone back to China, he probably would have settled down in the national capital, because of his educational background. Chairman Wang had the highest prestige among the gentry for more than twenty years. It was certainly not an accident.

Some gentry families were able to maintain their social positions for centuries. Their sons were more likely to follow the same occupational careers as had their fathers. Generation after generation, they built up the eminent traditions of their families, like Chairman

Wang's *shu hsiang shih chia* ("scholar's family") or Commander Chu's *i mên wu jen* ("outstanding military family"). Under these familial traditions, a man was completely submerged in the family organization and was not expected to make his own way. He was only a part of the great system of family life. Children were not trained to develop gradually, but at every turn they were encouraged to imitate and to participate in the ways of the adults, which were, in turn, the ways of the ancestors.[18] Boys were expected to be more self-assertive, to enter officialdom, and to behave as masters, more important than women in their patriarchal culture. Within this framework, a young man was not even held responsible for selecting his own wife. Marriage was the business of his parents. The main purpose of marriage was the procreation of children to perpetuate the family name. The first principle of wedlock was "equal status of two families," while mutual compatibility between husband and wife was left to chance. A son was merely called to take his place in a family already established and to fit himself to carry on the family fortunes and to bring glory upon the ancestors. The expectations and pressures of the family limited the scope of the individual's career to a characteristic pattern.

The continued renown of the gentry family was based on a regular track. Generally, a member of the gentry, unless his prestige was solely dependent on the power of another family member or relative, had been traveling for a period of time. Travel provided him with a sense of a larger and different world from that in which he lived. It gave him self-assurance and faith to establish himself in the community. If he succeeded in the outside world, he would return as the object of envy and emulation and would in every respect enjoy superiority over the "rice-pot-keeping-turtles" who lacked the courage to break away. He came back to his home community at around forty years of age. In the first place, he would carry on the inherited family fortune because his father would be getting too old to retain the responsibility. He had therefore to reinforce the social position of his father. In the second place, he would still have enough time to make use of his prestige and advantages gained outside for the benefit of his home community. According to the traditional expression, he came back home to *fu wu sang tzŭ* "to serve his home community" (*sang* or "mulberry" and *tzŭ* or "catalpa" were two kinds of tree planted near each house to symbolize sentimentally one's own homestead and one's place of origin). In the third place, by that time he should have been helping his own son to make a good start on the social ladder. It was this track that made the transmission of family status from one generation to another possible, in spite of the individual's physical discontinuity. In order to proceed along this track, every generation had to follow the same specific life cycle, and close coordination among three successive generations was essential.

The life cycle worked this way: The boy of the gentry family began to go to school at six or seven years of age. When he had completed the study of *San Tzŭ Ching* (*The Classic of Three Characters*), *Pei Chia Hsing* (*The Hundred Surnames*), the Four Books, and the Five Classics and had mastered the style of composition needed for taking civil examinations, he would be about twenty years old. Between sixteen and twenty-two, he had to be married. Then he would enter a series of competitions in the civil examinations. If he succeeded, he would certainly continue his career and become a member of the upper gentry group, although if he attained only the degree of *hsiu ts'ai,* he would probably be honorable enough in his native place. Even though he could then go no further, he would have to try to find a position in officialdom or to serve as a personal secretary to some official or as a teacher for several years in the outside world. Unless he became a high official, he would probably return home when he was around forty years old. His family prestige, his degree, his ability and experience all would qualify him as a full-fledged member of the gentry.

In order to follow the track, close coordination among the three generations was essential. There were three factors, however, that obstructed effective coordination. The first was that the father might die early. Under such a circumstance, the youth would then have to stay at home to assume the responsibility of his family and would have no opportunity to seek his fortune. As he would lack prestige and essential experience, he could not be highly respected by the local people and could not become a member of the gentry. The second was that the son himself might die in his youth. There would then be a wide gap between the older and younger generations. When the men of the older generation died, the widow and orphans could become the subjects of bullying and oppression by local toughs. Even though the young generation could struggle to rise again, the family power would have declined at least temporarily. The third factor was that one might have no child to continue his family line, which would have been the most serious. There were two ways to help prevent such a thing from happening. They were early marriage and taking a concubine. The last resort of childlessness was adoption. It was the least desirable measure and taken only reluctantly. We do not have any case of it recorded in our data. As the coordination among the three generations usually covered a period of sixty or seventy years, breakdowns were not rare. The life history of Chief Chang's family provides a case in point:

Chang's father, Chang Wei-lung, had had three sons and two daughters, but only one son lived, all the others having died when they were still young. He regretted their deaths deeply and passed away himself at the age of forty-four.

When Chang Wei-lung died, Chief Chang was only twelve, too young to be responsible for the welfare of the family. Wei-lung's wife was by nature very exuberant and willing to do any kind of work. After the death of her children and her husband, however, she became so moody that she was forced to look for distraction in order to forget her troubles. In her depression she took no more interest in the farm, business, or household. After several years her grief lessened, but by that time the economic condition of her family was very bad.

Chief Chang was Wei-lung's last son and was thus especially loved by his parents. In the community one who had no son was pitied. According to custom, one who had no son could not be buried at the cemetery of his ancestors' tomb. He would be despised by the people, because to have no son was considered most shameful. On the other hand, *erh sun man t'ang*, "to have the hall full of children and grandchildren," was rated most highly by the people.

Chief Chang began to study at the age of six. Before then, he had had no opportunity to play with other children, as his parents had overprotected him and would not let him out of their sight. If he wanted something, his parents would always give it to him. Perhaps that was the main source of Chang's headstrong character. When he began to go to school, he liked it not only because of his parents' encouragement but also because of the companionship of the other children. He was clever and had a very good memory from boyhood on.

Wei-lung's early death made more difficult his family's ascent to the position of gentry. The previous few generations of Chang Wei-lung's family had all been illiterate. But Wei-lung, as a graduate of a provincial normal school and as a schoolteacher, had been a qualified gentleman. His methods in the treatment of diseases had made him well known in Kunyang, and gradually this reputation had raised his position to that of gentry. Moreover, he had made friends with men in every walk of life, with educators, officials, and rich merchants. He was generous and ambitious. He had intended to give his son the best education possible in order to contribute to the glory of his family. But, as he died early, his son had to start pushing himself ahead on his own.

Chang arrived at his present position—Chief of the Administrative Section of the county government—through a long period of struggle. He was a self-made man. His success came not only from hard work in studying and home practice in the arts of calligraphy and of letter-writing but also from flattery and extensive and ingenious grafting. He was an upstart, an opportunist; as a result, many members of the gentry would place no faith in him, even though he was in power. He put on an air of great pride to cover up his difficulty in relating.

Chief Chang's wife was very pretty. She was thirty-nine years old in 1946 and had one daughter and one son. She often went to the temple to pray for the health of her children and for more children.

This case illustrates what could happen when a gentleman died early and consequently broke the regular track.

In sum, the gentry family was larger, more prosperous, and more powerful. These advantages improved its members' life chances considerably. Some gentry families had been able to maintain their social position for centuries. The continued renown of the gentry family was based on a regular track. In order to proceed along this track, every generation had to follow a specific life cycle, and the simultaneous close coordination among three successive generations was essential.

THE DISPLAY OF PRESTIGE

In order to gain and to hold esteem, it was not sufficient merely to possess wealth or power. The wealth or power had to be put in evidence, and a display of prestige was the most important way of giving evidence of status. The members of the gentry therefore competed with one another for prestige all the time. They tried to outdo their fellows in ritual and ceremonial showings during such events as births, weddings, and funerals. On ceremonial occasions the idea of thrift gave place to competitive magnificence. Wealth was expended on the fabulous funeral, the lavish wedding, and sumptuous feasts. The elaborate ceremony pointed up the social status of the family. The guests who had been invited were evaluated by the community and assigned varying degrees of social prestige. The honor of the host depended upon the characteristics of his guests. As officials had high status in the eyes of the local people, it always gave the host prestige to be esteemed by the high officials. Gentry members eagerly played up the slightest recognition shown to them by officials. This display did not aim to annihilate equals or superiors, but each member of the gentry attempted to reach a more advantageous position in the hierarchical social framework and put himself in a more favorable light. Occasions raised the popularity of the gentry member and broadened the associations of his family. It was the inherent glamour of this social game that was responsible for the gentry's struggle for more wealth and more power.

For the most part, life for the gentry was an affair of constant display. Its members had constantly to bolster up their prestige; otherwise they would lose their social status. But the most important events were those involving the *rites de passage*—birth, marriage, and death. Other occasions included building a new house, obtaining a distinguished honor, and establishing one's ancestors' glory. We shall illustrate all six one by one.

First, the birth of a male child was a great event in the gentry family. Through the period of pregnancy the mother was referred to as *yu hsi,* or "having happiness," in her body. All the members of the family looked forward primarily to the birth of a male child. The life history of Mr. Fan furnishes an illustration:

When Mr. Fan was born, his father had just been appointed secretary to the Magistrate. All the members of the family were very happy. Fan's father, Tao-yuan, felt that his becoming an official and the birth of his son were *shuang hsi lin mên,* or "double happiness descending upon his family." He thought it was the outcome not only of his ancestors' accumulated virtue but also of his own luck. When the child was *man yueh,* or "one month old," Tao-yuan therefore invited all his relatives, friends, and the officials to a series of banquets. There were about 300 guests. The banquets occurred twice a day, and the celebration lasted three days. Mr. Fan's mother also came from a noted family. His maternal grandparents sent to them many rich gifts including a pig of 100 *ching,* 1000 eggs, fifty blocks of brown sugar, and such adornments for the baby as embroidered caps (twenty), shoes (twenty pairs), clothes (twenty suits), wrappers, silver necklets, and some clothes for the mother. It took twenty-five able-bodied men to carry them. Meanwhile, each official sent silverware and piecegoods as gifts. Relatives and friends contributed sixteen catties of rice, 100 eggs, and four blocks of brown sugar. All the valuable articles were placed on exhibition in the hall. The women who came to visit all admired these showy presents. The feast was extravagant. Every guest praised the exquisite dishes, the mellow liquors. The family members had decided that they should spend some money for their *mên mien,* or literally "the front of the gate," so that they would not be criticized as stingy.

A wedding in the community was also an important occasion, bound up as it was with the prestige of the family. In the wedding ceremony, the parents on both sides tried to provide the best *trousseaux* and offer the most spectacular feasts. The following is a typical case:

When Mr. Hsieh was nineteen years old, his parents held a wedding for him. As he was an only son, his parents were especially serious and careful over his marriage. They took one year for its preparation. About five months before the wedding day, they hired four men to send the gown materials to the girl's home. The gifts consisted of 1000 silver dollars, eighty-five *ching* of glutinous rice, twenty catties of pork, ten *ching* of wine, ten *chang* of red cloth, twenty *chang* of green cloth, ten *chang* of blue cloth, a pair of jade bracelets, and a pair of jade cases. The girl's parents held a party and invited the elders of their lineage and important relatives to be present as witnesses. This procedure was called *k'ai k'ou,* or "to propose the wedding day," and *kuo li,* or "to offer the wedding presents."

A few days before the wedding, Mr. Hsieh's parents sent the clothes, hairpins, and earrings to the bride-to-be. A living pig of eighty *ching* was also sent to the girl's family. This occasion was called *sung ch'uan tai* or "offering the clothes and jewels."

On the wedding day, Mr. Hsieh's house was brightly decorated. His parents used two red sedan chairs for the bride and groom, two green sedan chairs for the best men, and two blue sedan chairs for the marriage-arrangers. They went to the girl's home to receive the bride-to-be in a long procession. Four musicians were hired for the occasion. As the girl's family was also rich, the dowries were as lavish and as fashionable as imaginable. The guests included all the relatives and friends of the Hsieh family and the officials of Kunyang. Many friends and officials of Kunming also came to congratulate them on the occasion. The blessing couplets covered every wall in the house. The people of Kunyang unanimously admired the broad associations of the family and its prestige. The amount of gifts offered by the officials was five times greater than usual. Even the banquet was differentiated into two kinds: One was for the officials and the gentry, one for the common guests. The officials and the gentry were entertained with particular hospitality, and the big feast was given for three days in succession. The food served was extraordinary, and the liquor was unusually abundant. Altogether, there were about 500 guests.

The elaborateness of a funeral was in direct proportion to the social status of the deceased during his life. It expressed social prestige in the most tangible ways. A gentry funeral always involved an ostentatious display. The family converted mourning for a near relative into an ambitious parade. The funeral of Commander Chu's mother was an exciting event in Kunyang. A member of Commander Chu's lineage said:

In 1933 his mother died. Commander Chu suggested to his two brothers that they should jointly arrange an expensive funeral for their late mother, as the reputation of their family depended on what they did at that time. They invited more than twenty Buddhist monks and Taoist practitioners to make up many idols, spirit banners, lions, elephants, and pavilions of colored papers. Besides these things, couplets and condolence banners were obtained from their relatives, friends, and officials. A big picture of the deceased was displayed, and the coffin was decorated with a silk cover and flowers. They hired an army band from

Kunming, and the Buddhist and Taoist monks also played various musical instruments. There were about 1600 guests for meals, which were served continuously for two days. The funeral procession stretched out for a mile and attracted people from the four corners of the county.

Building a new house was the most manifest expression of wealth and prestige. A fine house was the obvious indication of the social status of a family in the community, and it was always therefore an ostentatious display. Chief Chang's case is typical:

Chief Chang built a house of six rooms in both foreign and Chinese styles. The design of the house was the most modern in the community. There were water troughs to drain off rainwater—a thing not seen before. On the day the beams of the house were to be set up, the guests, about 240 of them, came in an unbroken line. Two-thirds were officials or gentry of the county. As the host had high prestige, the congratulatory presents were ten times the usual number. Unfortunately, the elder of the host's two sons died the same day. So the righteous people whispered that Chief Chang had been *pao ying*, had received retribution.

Like its worldly counterpart, a fine graveyard residence was a source of pride.[19] The prosperity of a family depended upon *feng shui*, or "wind and water." This belief was based on the idea that the ancestor living in the other world was endowed with supernatural powers that he might use to help his descendants. Although the Confucian stress on education and human effort always prevailed, it was fairly common for the Chinese to share folk beliefs attributing unusual academic-bureaucratic success to geomancy or to something supernatural and predestined.[20] There are plenty of examples that indicate that when they achieved fortune or official position, gentry members would rebuild their ancestors' tombs. The life history of Commander Chu demonstrates this point:

After residing at the border of Kwangsi and Yunnan for five years, Commander Chu returned to Yunnan with his troop and visited his home, bringing with him ten boxes of precious goods including 5,000 *tael* of silver. The boxes were loaded on five horses. He bought fifty *kung* of farmland with his money and decked all his family out in new clothes.

After being stationed at Yüchi two years, his troop was ordered to move to the border of the provinces of Szechwan and Yunnan to suppress more bandits, the notorious leader of whom was named Lee Sannew. After fighting several battles, Chu defeated them and killed Lee. He was immediately promoted to commander of a regiment.

He then returned to Yunnan with his troop and visited his home again, this time with thirty boxes of captured silver and other precious articles. These boxes were carried by fifteen horses. He bought more than

100 *kung* of farmland. He was talked about by the people everywhere in Kunyang and was praised to the skies.

When Commander Chu returned home the second time, he rebuilt the tomb of his great-grandfather with granite and set up columns and sculptured lions and horses of stone on the ground in front of the tomb. This decoration made clear not only that some of the descendants of the dead in this tomb had prospered but also the filial piety of the descendants. Commander Chu did it because he considered his promotion to high office the result of *hao feng-shui,* or "good wind and water," of the tomb of Chu Yuan.

From the life history of Commander Chu, we can see that the gentry was seldom satisfied with the fact of being fortunate. Good fortune had to be "legitimate" fortune. As the Chinese believed that the prosperity of a family depended upon *feng shui,* or "wind and water," a fine graveyard was a source of pride.

Attaining high civil-examination honors was traditionally also glorified by the people. The glory belonged to the individual and at the same time to his family. It reflected fame, power, and wealth. For example, *shuang chin-shih chia,* or the "family of *chin-shih* in pairs," was a distinguished family in Kunyang. There was a huge plaque over the outermost portal of a certain K'ung's house. The three dazzling characters—*shuang chin-shih*—commemorated the gaining of *chin-shih* during the Ch'ing Dynasty. There was a story about the plaque occasionally mentioned among the old people. A member of K'ung's lineage gave me the following account:

K'ung Tu-k'uei's father and grandfather both received *chin-shih* at twenty-five years of age during the Ch'ing Dynasty. The Emperor bestowed the plaque of *hsuang chin-shih* upon them. They had gained the highest honor in our memory. Their family was respected by everybody. When Tu-k'uei's father, Wei-han, received the degree of *chin-shih,* the people of the whole city talked of the news. Some said that it was due to the good *feng-shui* of K'ung's ancestors' tomb. Some people gave as the cause virtues of the past generations of the K'ung family. Some people argued that Wei-han had obtained a good education from his father. Others suggested that both Wei-han and his father were intelligent and nice-looking and that they had looked like officials from birth. Many people whose sons were studying in the school advised their sons to take Wei-han as a model. Their honor and glory were beyond description. When the plaque was placed over the outermost portal of their house amid the din of drums, cymbals, and firecrackers, the congratulators and onlookers swelled about the front door like a human sea. The plaque was decorated with red silk and the portal with flowery lanterns. The family gave a banquet, inviting about 300 guests. All were officials, scholars, and members of the gentry. The celebration featured a band of musicians. As a guest would approach, the musicians would play various peculiar soft tunes somehow suggestive of his person. This pomp and grandeur was without precedent.

From these case histories we can thus see how prestige was displayed, through the elaborate ceremonies of the birth of a male child, the wedding, the funeral, building a new house, rebuilding their ancestors' tombs, and attaining high civil-examination honors. All of these events were bound up with the status of the gentry's families.

These examples of prestige display provide by no means an exhaustive list, yet they show the nature and effects of such display. In order to show off gentry social status, wealth was expended on the fabulous funeral, the lavish wedding, and sumptuous feasts. With a view to enhancing their social status in the community, gentry members were obliged to make manifest their prestige. And equally the admiration gained from the expensive ceremonies was certainly a source of much satisfaction. The expenditure, however, was often ruinous to those gentry members who had high status but only moderate wealth. They did not have large sums of ready cash at their disposal. It could not be overlooked that some did get into financial trouble in trying to satisfy the social expectation. The conspicuous expenditure for funeral ceremonies was more difficult than that for weddings, as a marriage could be delayed and planned and saved for, whereas the time for a funeral was determined by death alone. The case of Vice-Chairman Loh of the Citizens' Political Council of Kunyang, a well-known physician, is a perfect example.

Vice-Chairman Loh died on the first of August in 1947 at the age of sixty-six. After his death, the family was in a miserable condition because the members of his family were either too old or too young. During his lifetime the responsibility of the family had been wholly on his shoulders. Now nobody could be depended upon. The Magistrate personally went to Loh's home to condole with the family on the third day. The gentry and people of all walks of life felt that the passing away of such a kind gentleman was a great cause for regret. During his life, he had been known for his high morality and *aura popularis* and never for his wealth and power. Though he had served the government for many years, he was still *liang hsiu ch'ing feng,* had "two sleeves full of wind." His family was therefore in agony of mind over its lack of money for the funeral. It attempted a simple elegance, but under the pressure of social expectation it was impossible to bring off. The members tried to sell their farmland to finance the funeral, but they found no buyers. They then decided to delay the funeral, but prices went up day after day. The longer they delayed the funeral, the higher would be the expenditure. At last, besides raising loans, they sold all the jewels and ornaments of the women to meet the urgent need and selected the twenty-fifth of November for the funeral. There were about 680 guests for meals, which were served for two days. The guests included the Magistrate, the heads of the various divisions of the county government, and the gentry. All were in a depressed mood. The total expenditure for the funeral was 30,000,000 national currency [about 4,300 silver dollars]. [My assistant commented: "The family had been compelled by social opinion to hold such a funeral lest it be criticized for being disrespectful."]

We cannot help asking what gave rise to this pattern of display, and what was its significance? Let us take the funeral as an example. Death was the specter haunting the people. It roamed through the community and inspired a dread that was not physical but social. As long as the patient was still breathing and the family could finance the projects, no effort was spared and no stone left unturned to find a cure. Various kinds of doctor, various types of spiritualist, and all kinds of god were resorted to. But finally, when all efforts had failed and the patient had died, then, and then only, did the family members believe that "medicine can cure diseases, but cannot cure fate."[21] The people believed in fate and, therefore, had no physical fear of death.

The fear of death was social. Death meant ruinous expenditure for the funeral. The proverb says, "The deceased does not eat any rice, but half of the family property will be gone." To fail in the provision of proper rites, feasts, coffin, and funeral would be terribly punished by the contempt and condemnation of the people. The family would be disgraced and its prestige lowered in the estimation of the community. Isolation from one's community was a great fear. Every person desired recognition from others; it made possible his social survival and growth. On the other hand, the ability to provide a decorous funeral secured to the gentry family a status in the community and assured it of commendation for filial piety pragmatically expressed. Whatever conspicuous elements for public consumption existed in burial practices attracted the attention of the community, bringing social approval and enabling each member to enjoy the display of prestige. Ordinary burial practice avoided public censure; the conspicuous funeral or abundant feast secured bursts of open praise. Then, from every point of view, the community considered the task well done.[22]

The display of prestige served as a means of validating one's position among the dignitaries of the community. Gentry members had conceptions of what one expected of another and of community attitudes and values. What was institutionally required of a member of the gentry was well known for almost any given situation, and if an individual was of gentry status he had to conform or lose face for himself and his family. The display of prestige was important because "mere economic" power, especially "naked" money power, was by no means a recognized basis of social honor. Nor was power the only basis of social honor. Indeed, social honor or prestige could be the basis of political or economic power and very frequently was.[23]

THE SOCIAL STRUCTURE OF THE GENTRY

The gentry was not merely a class of separate individuals; it also constituted a group related in various ways. Members met frequently in both formal and informal activities. They were educated in schools that usually brought together boys who lived in relatively distant places. Most had traveled a good deal and knew the importance of making friends. In many instances, old schoolmates and intimate friends became valuable connections in the struggle for positions. Friendships thus made were profound and lasting. Wealthy men always attracted relatives and friends. It was characteristic of the gentry to be appreciative of fine hospitality. Its members had time and money to devote themselves to such activities as gossip, visiting, teas, potluck parties, and dinner parties. The gentry was interested in community affairs and local administration. All these factors made its members willing to range outside their families, outside their immediate neighborhoods, and at times outside their own community, whereas the peasants tended to limit their social relations to their own families and neighbors. Gentry members were proud of their wide associations. Mr. Lee's life history is a good example:

> Mr. Lee's father, Lee Fu-kuei, was the richest and the only educated man in his village. He liked hunting, drinking wine, and making friends. He would on some days go to other villages to visit his friends to have a good time and on other days invite his friends to his home for conviviality. When they were together, they would drink wine, play the Chinese violin and guitar, and sing songs. Fu-kuei's parents were much pleased by their son's activities. They felt especially proud that their son had associated with some influential men and was respected by his friends. Fu-kuei was well known in the neighboring villages because, in the first place, his family was rich and, in the second place, he was generous and active in community affairs. If he wanted to do something, all his friends would come to help. By and by he became a "social lion" in the rural region.

Not only was the range of personal acquaintance likely to be broader for the gentry, but also its members' *potential* involvement with others was extended. Consequently, they had more opportunity to exert some influence on the social structure of their community. Chief Ting furnishes an excellent illustration:

> After being appointed head of the Department of Conscription of the county government, Ting climbed to the top of the social ladder in the community. As he was already rich and influential, he desired nothing more than good reputation to cover up his past evil deeds. He became mild, pleasant, careful, and righteous. He liked to be flattered and admired. If someone involved in a lawsuit or other trouble asked for help, he was willing to speak a word for him. He voluntarily bought many maps and contributed to the central elementary school of the urban district. He criticized the low salaries of the schoolteachers and the corruption of the officials.

Success in politics and the number of dinners a man gave to his associates seem to have had close correlation. In any case, gentry members paid much attention to the matter of entertainment. The case of Chu Lung, Commander Chu's eldest son, is typical:

> For convenience in smoking opium and taking bribes Chu Lung moved his office to his home. The servants of the *chên kung sao,* the government offices of the urban district, worked every day in Chu Lung's home. He smoked opium during the night and slept during the day. Every few weeks he would invite either the *pao-chang,* the head of the *pao,* or some of the gentry to have dinner with him, in order that he might be presented to the people in a favorable light. The expense of these dinners was paid by a tax levied on the families of the district.

The degree of "openness" in the status structure can be measured by the relative numbers of marriages between persons of different social origins. We have mentioned that marriage was a family affair rather than individual business; the principle of making a match was *mên tang hu tui,* "equality of gates and doors." The gentry members were bound together to form a natural group because they had such similar ways of thought and behavior. They had learned the same mode of life and thus understood one another. They felt more at ease with one another than with outsiders. They also became aware of their status system and other phases of their organized life. They looked upon their own ways as their most essential attributes. They took pride in their own material and spiritual possessions, property, kinship, family events, or whatever served as the symbol of contrast to others. It was therefore very natural that they selected their daughters-in-law from families of equal status with their own. Among the twenty-six gentry families there were eleven interfamilial marriages. Some gentry families had had nuptial connections for several generations. For example, Vice-Chairman Loh had married Commander Chu's sister. Vice-Chairman Loh's son married the daughter of Chu Hsin, Commander Chu's youngest brother. It was a case of *ch'in shang chia ch'in* ("two families are doubly connected by marrying a cousin"). Group endogamy was prevalent though not, so to speak, obligatory.

As the number of gentry families was limited, prospective marriage partners were few. Finding the proper mate was therefore not so easy. The following case is a good illustration:

When Mr. Fan was ten years old, his parents asked the go-between to look for a girl for their eldest son. Their family was wealthy and at the height of its prestige. They suggested that, in the first place, the girl must be pretty, bright, and virtuous. In the second place, the family of the girl must be on an equal social standing with their own. After half a year, the go-between had failed to find a girl for them. One day Mr. Fan's father, Tao-yuan, talked with a group of gentry members and mentioned that it was difficult to find an appropriate girl for his eldest son. One of them suggested that he see Mr. Yao's daughter. The Yao family was then the richest in the city. Tao-yuan told this information to his wife, who took an opportunity to see the girl and was satisfied. Then they sent an arranger to the girl's family to inquire about the possibility of a betrothal between the boy and the girl. The girl's parents were glad to make a marriage agreement with them because they found that Tao-yuan's eldest son was nice-looking and a good student. The two families exchanged the "eight characters"* of the boy and the girl. After respective consultations with fortune-tellers and an exchange of gifts, the betrothal was settled.

From Mr. Fan's case, we can see that, though there was a tendency toward endogamy, the practice was limited by the lack of prospective marriage partners among the gentry. Marriage between the members of two different social strata provided a means of social circulation. We shall illustrate this point later.

The gentry as a status group was stratified, and its strata were parallel to the bureaucratic hierarchy of the government. The gentry was stratified into four layers: *ts'un shên,* the village gentry; *hsiang shên,* the district gentry; *hsien shên,* the county gentry; and *shêng shên,* the provincial gentry. A county gentry member might simultaneously be a district gentry member and a village gentry member, but a village gentry member was not necessarily a district gentry member and a county gentry member because the prestige and power

---

* The "eight characters" were the year, the month, the day of the month, and the hour of the day of birth for each. If the horoscopes of two children were not in agreement, no marriage between them was regarded as possible.

of the gentry members varied to a great extent. Although some exercised only local influence, the more able, fortunate, and powerful gradually extended their activities and prestige over broader areas. In this way a group of the gentry common to the whole community developed. The different spheres of influence cut across the group and stratified it into various levels. The group thus functioned at different social levels in the larger community, as illustrated in Figure 2.

To the peasants all gentry members were prominent and substantial people, deserving deference and admiration. They were given seats of honor at dinner parties in anyone's home. The village gentry consisted of the respected elders of the village. They possessed farmland and had contact with the local officials. They were well-to-do but not rich enough to leave the village and become town dwellers. They were therefore in the lowest rank of the gentry. Numerically, however, they composed the great bulk of the gentry.

The district gentry, the county gentry, and the provincial gentry all belonged to the upper rank of the gentry. Within the levels of the gentry, however, they were also recognized gradations. The district gentry lived either in the villages or in the market town. They were in the lower upper rank of the gentry. They tried to separate themselves from the village gentry and to incorporate themselves with the county gentry. The county gentry members were in the middle upper rank of the group. Most members were city dwellers and had served in the government. They had family members or relatives in the provincial government; they thus had connections with high provincial officials and with other members of the provincial gentry. Sometimes they associated with the district gentry, but they and the members of the layers below them were well aware of the status differences and acted accordingly. The provincial gentry belonged to the upper upper rank of the group. They had been either high officials in the provincial government or had acquired national reputation. Almost all members were city dwellers. They felt superior and were leaders of the group.

The functioning of the gentry as a unified group can be seen in the mutual dependence of their sentiments and activities. In general, community affairs were potentially dominated and controlled by the leaders of the gentry. They selected, instructed, and supported the new members. In the process of selection, contacts were the necessary prerequisite. If the neophyte could develop friendly relationships with some members of the upper gentry, he might request a minor position in the local government. Gentry members of high prestige were ex-

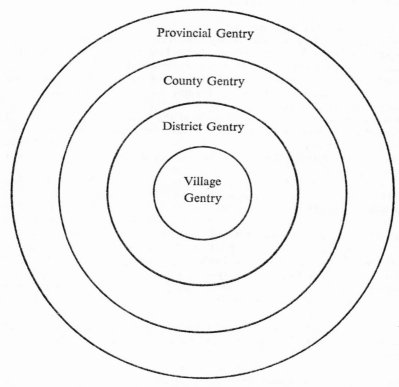

Figure 2. A Schematic Diagram of the Hierarchy of the Gentry

pected to be kind and considerate to those below them. On the other hand, members of the lower gentry were supposed to humble themselves to their superiors. Such reciprocal gestures were clearly recognizable in the success of some gentry members who rose to top positions primarily thanks to the favoritism of their patrons. The history of Chief Ting is typical:

Ever since he had become a *kung kao,* or "public opium" seller, Chief Ting had had no other occupation. Ting had been anxious to have a position in the local government for a long time. In 1939, Mr. Hsu was appointed head of the first *chu* government of the county. Ting thought it wise to approach Mr. Hsu. Consequently, Ting was appointed clerk of the district government. Because of his lack of training, this job was pretty difficult for him. His handwriting was bad. When he was assigned to write a public letter, he held the brush-pen in his hand and did not know what should be written. Then he would often sigh deeply and recite the popular couplet, "When books are being diligently used, there is self-reproach for having read little; if an affair is not passed through, you do not know the difficulty of it."

Stung by his lack of training, Ting tried to make up for it by being diligent and enthusiastic in every kind of work. If a question occurred to him, he would immediately ask Mr. Hsu to advise him. After half a year, Ting became an assistant to Mr. Hsu. During this time he learned many things, the entertainment of superior officers, general social etiquette, and the technique of grafting. At the same time he associated intimately with Chief Chang and other influential gentry members. After two years, when he was twenty-nine years old, the *chu* system was changed to the *hsiang-chên* system, and he was appointed to be *chên chang,* chief of the urban district. He was extremely delighted by his success.

After becoming *chên chang,* Ting was respectful to such superiors as Magistrate Ho, Chief Chang, and Chief Liao. He took advantage of every opportunity to send presents to them. He went to the county government offices at least once a day to report everything that had happened in the community to the Magistrate. If Chang and Liao wanted him to do something, he would do it unhesitatingly. At the same time, Ting was harsh to his subordinates. When they asked him something, he would make a show of pride and talk with them reluctantly. Because of his fawning toward his superior officials, he was labeled "Ha Pa Kou," or "Peke" [Pekinese].

When Chief Chang accused Magistrate Chao, Ting joined him in the action at Kunming. Ting was therefore discharged from his position by the Magistrate.

In January, 1945, Chief Chang resigned his position as head of the Department of Conscription of the county and recommended Ting to the Magistrate as his successor. The Magistrate agreed because he found that Ting was rich and sociable. As he was rich, when the government was in need of money, Ting could advance funds. Although Ting was not good at writing official letters, Magistrate Huang, the successor of Magistrate Chao, thought that the problem could be solved by assigning an able clerk to assist him.

The life history of Chief Ting illustrates how humble and obedient he was to his superiors. He was rapidly promoted from clerk of the district government to chief of the urban district and again to head of the Department of Conscription of the county by his patrons, in spite of his lack of training.

Sometimes the superiors were not chary in the exercise of their power and were inconsiderate of those below them. Sometimes members of the lower gentry were not humble enough. Under such circumstances, disputes between the upper and lower gentry were unavoidable. The following case provides a perfect example:

In 1937, King Pen-shuo was appointed chief of the urban district government. King was then thirty years old and considered by the people as upright and scrupulous. He was enthusiastic about this position. He was excitable, however, and not very sociable. He treated everyone as equal. Chairman Tsao of the People's Political Council was displeased with him and criticized him for being too young, too hot-tempered, and unsociable. Chairman Tsao was well known for his righteousness, but he was narrow-minded and jealous of anyone who did not flatter him. King was thus frustrated and disheartened and drastically changed his own attitude. Thereafter he grafted from public funds and entertained other gentry members. Chairman Tsao immediately held a meeting of the People's Political Council, which decided to dismiss him. King was sorely puzzled.

Furthermore, Chairman Tsao called attention to the liquidation of the account during King's term of office. As a result, King was to return to the government eighty piculs of rice and $5,000. It was said that most of the sum had been grafted by King's predecessor. But when King took over the position, he did not liquidate the account with his predecessor. King was therefore compelled to be responsible for all these funds. He refused to repay the money and was put in jail.

After one month in jail, King was full of hatred for Tsao and pledged to avenge himself. He was so anxious to be released that he secretly asked a friend to tell the Magistrate that he would give him $2,000 for his release. The Magistrate intended to accept the offer, but he was afraid of Tsao's interference. At last, the Magistrate promised to let King break jail. That night King sawed off a railing and escaped to Kunming. The next morning, the Magistrate pretended to send his men to arrest him, to avoid being blamed for the escape.

After escaping to Kunming, King dared not come home for a whole year. Through it all, he still hugged his anger and vowed vengeance against Tsao. He was waiting for an opportunity. One day he heard that some of the Kunyang natives who lived in Kunming wanted to organize an association and that some students who came from Kunyang and studied in the provincial capital also intended to organize a club. He was very happy about the news and immediately came into contact with them. He contributed part of the essential money and helped to organize the associations. After organizing the two associations, he agitated for the members to oppose Chairman Tsao. He advertised the news in the newspapers of Kunming, distributed handbills in Kunyang and the neighboring counties, and posted slogans and cartoons describing Tsao's corruption and dictatorship. As a consequence, Tsao was dismissed.

From King's case we can see the consequences of an upper gentry member's lack of consideration and control in the exercise of his power over the lower gentry. Such antagonism was often disastrous for both alike.

The gentry as a status group was not a highly organized, well-integrated social group. Relationships were mainly personal. When personal interests became contradictory, a group would split into several factions. Actions were oriented toward the acquisition of power and prestige. The opposing cliques grew out of sharp rivalries. There was considerable bitter feeling among them. All tried to use government influence to "squeeze" their opponents. As a result, resentment was fostered, and some qualities of spontaneity, intimacy, and integration seemed to disappear. Claims to prestige and power became the source of conflicts and the basis of the formation of cliques. None of the factions was really oriented to objective policies for the general good or to value systems. Members generally could not raise their political horizons beyond the boundaries of their community. There was a very prominent element of clique interest. Power, position, and remuneration always played an important part, along with other factors. Consequently, cliques were but the expressions of different interest groups. A typical case of the gentry's division into opposing factions was the accusation of Magistrate Chao described in Chapter 2.

The cliques never tried to mobilize the masses of the people of the community to support their actions. Even the *pao-chang* were only reluctantly assimilated into the two opposing cliques and did not join them voluntarily. The struggle for power was status-bound from the very beginning. Nevertheless the members of each faction were drawn together by numerous activities and common interests. We should not therefore lose sight of the gentry's over-all unity.

The individual members of the gentry were integrated with, and differentiated from, one another. This was a complex and dynamic configuration of relations in which individuals were tied together as well as separated. For example, Chief Liao was an intimate friend of Chu Lung, Commander Chu's eldest son. Yet he jointed Chief Chang to accuse Magistrate Chao, while Chu Lung was the leader of the pro-Magistrate Chao group.

The gentry thus made various networks of social relationships. Members were proud of their wide associations and paid much attention to the matter of entertainment. They were bound together by marriage. Not only was the range of personal acquaintance likely to be broader among the gentry; potential involvement with others was also extended. Consequently, members had more opportunity to exert influence on the social structure of their community. Although they were stratified and differentiated, they constituted a corporate group requiring a high degree of solidarity for joint action. Their function as a unified group can be seen in the mutual dependence of their sentiments and activities. Their struggle for prestige and power was status-bound.

NOTES

1. The term "style of life," as here used, includes the ways of earning a living so far as they contribute to the shaping of ideas of the good life. The term emphasizes judgments, implicit or expressed, of what right conduct is. And not excluded are the lesser tastes and preferences that give to a people its characteristic flavor, so to speak. When Lionel Trilling writes of *manners,* as "a culture's hum and buzz of implication . . . half-uttered or unuttered or unutterable expressions of values," he is thinking of the "style of life." See Robert Redfield, *The Primitive World and Its Transformations* (Ithaca: Cornell University Press, 1955), p. 52; Lionel Trilling, "Manners, Morals, and the Novel," *The Liberal Imagination* (New York: Viking Press, 1950), pp. 206–7.
2. Thorstein Veblen, *The Theory of the Leisure Class: An Economic Study of Institutions* (New York: The Modern Library, 1934), pp. 36–7.
3. *Ibid.,* p. 170.
4. Lin Yü-tang, *The Importance of Living* (New York: John Day Co., Inc., 1937), p. 1.
5. Y. Chu Wang, "The Intelligentsia in Changing China," *Foreign Affairs,* 36, No. 2 (January, 1958), 315–29.
6. *Ibid.*
7. Herbert A. Giles, *A History of Chinese Literature* (New York: Appleton-Century-Crofts, 1937), p. 277.
8. *Cf.* J. R. Hightower, *Topics in Chinese Literature: Outline and Bibliographies* (rev. ed.; Cambridge, Mass.: Harvard University Press, 1953), p. 104.
9. Giles, *op. cit.,* pp. 310–1.
10. Hightower, *op. cit.,* pp. 79–80.
11. *Cf.* Giles, *op. cit.,* pp. 355–6.

12. Hightower, *op. cit.*, pp. 104–5.
13. C. T. Hsia, *A History of Modern Chinese Fiction, 1917–1957,* with an appendix on Taiwan by Tsi-an Hsia (New Haven: Yale University Press, 1961), pp. 28–54.
14. A sample of his epigrams has been translated into English. See Lin Yü-tang, *The Wisdom of China and India* (New York: Random House, 1942), pp. 1083–90; Lusin, *Ah Q and Others: Selected Stories of Lusin,* translated by Chi-chen Wang (New York: Columbia University Press, 1941).
15. Hsia, *op. cit.*, pp. 237–56.
16. The "stem family" pattern, which Olga Lang named after the example of Frederick Le Play, consists of the parents, their unmarried children, and *one* married son with wife and children. Lang, *Chinese Family and Society* (New Haven: Yale University Press, 1946), p. 14.
17. *Cf.* Wolfram Eberhard, *Conquerors and Rulers* (Leiden: E. J. Brill, 1952), pp. 13–6.
18. *Cf.* Francis L. K. Hsu, *Under the Ancestors' Shadow: Chinese Culture and Personality* (New York: Columbia University Press, 1948), pp. 239–40.
19. *Ibid.*, p. 52.
20. Ping-ti Ho, *The Ladder of Success in Imperial China: Aspects of Social Mobility, 1368–1911* (New York: Columbia University Press, 1962), p. 146.
21. Hsu, *op. cit.*, p. 261.
22. *Cf.* D. H. Kulp, *Country Life in South China: The Sociology of Familism* (New York: Bureau of Publications, Teachers College, Columbia University, 1925), pp. 197, 202–3.
23. Max Weber, *Essays in Sociology,* translated and edited by H. H. Gerth and C. Wright Mills (New York: Oxford University Press, Inc., 1946), p. 180.

4

Upward Mobility
through Schooling
and
Medical Practice

In prerepublican China, as social stratification had not produced a caste system, a degree of mobility existed, both in theory and in practice. Upward mobility was widely desired and noted. Hence the oft-heard sentiments: "As generals and ministers do not originate from seeds, a man of ambition should exert himself" (*chiang hsiang yüan wu chung, nan erh tang tzŭ ch'iang*). Or, "From unpainted houses [that is, commoner houses] come lords and ministers" (*pai wu ch'u kung ch'ing*). The "social elevator" operated in traditional China, both upward and downward, though social mobility might be slow and erratic.

Schooling, scholarly activity, and medical practice were the most important channels of upward mobility. The schools were open to all people regardless of their origins and families. Theoretically at least, the "social elevator" of schooling was therefore available to everybody. It was the hope of all parents that their children would enjoy lives better than their own, and they were aware that this hope could be realized only if the children were prepared to secure better jobs in the town or city. Such preparation, however, required financial sacrifice. It was true that primary school was free in the village; but sending a child to school was an economic burden on the parents, as children could contribute useful services in the house or on the farm.[1]

Formerly, if the parents could afford to do without their son on the farm to allow him to attend a private school for ten years or so and if he were then able to pass the examinations by displaying his skill at calligraphy and his knowledge of some of the standard classical verses, he might automatically become an official. But when the traditional system was abolished and the modern school took its place, the time to complete a college course—the minimum requirement for a high official—was fixed at sixteen years. Under the traditional system he had had little need for equipment, and the old books could be used. The students could live in the village as they worked and studied. For higher education in the modern school they had to go to the urban centers and were required to wear expensive student uniforms, which cost much more than those generally worn in the villages. But the expenses of education were not only those of tuition, equipment, and clothing. The new education changed not only the outward appearance but also the whole outlook on life of the individual, so that traditional ways of life were no longer acceptable to him. Even many well-to-do families could not afford to send their children to universities, and a boy who had finished middle school alone found it almost impossible to obtain a good position in the government or with any public service.[2]

As for medical practice, the Chinese have a saying: "If a worthy man cannot become a good prime minister, he should try to be a good physician." Indeed, every society has accorded a special position to the physician. China was no exception.

THE SCHOOL AS A SOCIAL LADDER

In 1942, there were eighty-six lower primary schools with four grades each in the 259 villages of Kunyang, approximately one school for every three villages. For the higher grades, it was necessary to go to the district town. Each of the eight districts had a central elementary school. There were a junior middle school and a four-year normal school in the City of Kunyang. The income from more than ten *kung* of land was required for the support of a middle school student.[3] The census data of the Institute for Census Research show that in 1942 there were only 644 middle-school students and graduates, 605 males and thirty-nine females; there were eleven university students and graduates, ten males and one female. Besides, there were three students returned from abroad. If we examine the distribution of the tenure groups of the peasant households and their sizes of farmlands presented in Tables 7 and 8, we shall not be surprised that so few could obtain higher education. Formal education for a poor peasant's or tenant's child was patently beyond the realm of possibility.

The traditional idea that exalted the scholar class has been summarized in the epigram, "Everything is low, only the learning of books is high." It was the first thing a boy learned in starting his classical studies. The traditional idea still existed in the minds of the villagers. To be a scholar was a way to enter the government and become socially important, and it was also a way to become rich. The school was like a bridge, over which young men entered the outside world and went into occupations other than farming. Parents tried their best to send their children to school, in the hope that one day the children would reach higher social levels than their own. The "bridge of learning," however, was a long and narrow one. From the elementary school to the high school took twelve years; during those twelve years the children certainly could not help on the family farm. And parents had to pay not only for the food their children ate but also for all kinds of expense in the school, which meant that only the rich could afford to send their children to school. The young men of the poorer houses had no chance to pass over this bridge.[4]

It was a narrow pathway, indeed. Yet there was no broad highway provided by agriculture, business, or industry. Education gave respectability in itself, and the scholars were accorded very high esteem and were given prominent positions and higher incomes in the government, and the school therefore played a large part in promoting social mobility. It was the center of hope and concern.

Three life histories illustrate three aspects of modern China's educated man. The life history of Chairman Wang symbolizes the transitional period from the traditional to the modern educational system. As he was a *hsiu ts'ai* of the Ch'ing Dynasty, he was able to compose various classical literary pieces, couplets, birthday scrolls, elegiac prayers, and so on, which were still necessary for social intercourse. In order to survive the social transition, he had re-educated himself by entering the provincial normal school. He thus occupied a unique position in the community. He was not only a Confucian scholar but also a graduate from a modern normal school. Among the older generation of the gentry, nobody was better educated than he. Eventually, he even helped to promote the educational transition in Kunyang.

The life history of Director Shen is typical of that of an educated man of the younger generation. After the Nationalist Revolution of 1925–1927, China was strained by civil war between the Nationalists and the Communists. Director Shen's ideas reflected the important ideological strife among the younger generation.

The life history of Director Tai depicts the beginning of the transformation from traditional literary education to modern scientific and technical training in such areas as engineering and agriculture. During Director Tai's life, scientific and technical training in China was in its infancy.

The Life History of Chairman Wang

Chairman Wang was a typical Confucian scholar. But he was not only a Confucian scholar; he was also graduated from the provincial normal school. Among the older generation of the gentry, he was the best qualified to be a member of the gentry. Furthermore, his children had added to his prestige. His first son had studied in Japan and was working in the provincial government; his second son was in the United States; his third son was the principal of a primary school in his native district and the head of the *hsiang;* his fourth son was studying at the National Southwest Associated University in Kunming. As scholars were traditionally respected by the people, his family was regarded as most promising and was well known as *shu hsiang shih chia,* "scholar's family." Chairman Wang had been a leading member of the gentry for more than twenty years.

"Wang I-chang," or Chairman Wang—Chairman of the Citizens' Political Council of the county—was born in a village about thirty miles west of the walled City of Kunyang. One of my assistants visited there twice. He described it this way: "The village is on a mountain, and communications are very difficult. Also the climate is very bad. The main occupations of the 585 villagers are blacksmithing, acting as merchants for the selling and buying of iron, mining iron, hiring out as day laborers, and farming. Every day at dawn we could hear the sound of the hammers pounding iron. The village seemed full of activity."

Chairman Wang's great-grandfather, Wang Kai-hsin, had studied six years in a private school. He was good at writing and at figuring with the abacus. Probably because of a decline in business in Kunming, he moved to Kunyang when he was thirty years old and operated a shop there. After his arrival there, he was informed that there was an iron mine in the vicinity west of Kunyang. The area was mainly mountainous and inhabited by Lolos and filled with bandits. He risked his life several times in going to this site to make a survey.

At last, he decided to move into a nearby village named Liu Ho Ts'un in order to try to mine the iron.

He brought with him several workers, some money, and simple household goods. But because he could not understand the Lolo language, he was suspected by the inhabitants of being a spy. He was indeed in a precarious position. He knew that, if he could not improve his relations with the Lolos, he not only could do nothing but also would be in great danger. Wang invited the leaders of the Lolos to have dinner at his home and talked with them frankly and pleasantly. He tried to tell them of his ambitions and plans and offered to lend them money when they were in need. As a result, many Lolos became his good friends.

As he then felt quite safe living in Liu Ho Ts'un, he moved his family to that village. He began by engaging simply in buying and selling wood. He bought several hundred *mow* of thickly wooded mountainside and hired Lolos to work for him. If they were in need of money, he paid them their wages in advance. As the Lolos won such favors from him, they were grateful and obedient to him. He then bought more mountains, which were not only covered with forest but also rich in iron. As the Lolos were backward and always in need of money, he was able to buy their mountains and forests very cheaply.

After buying the forests, he associated himself with some merchants who bought and sold lumber in the city and began to have the trees chopped down in order to sell them to the merchants at market prices. In a year's time he had made a lot of money. He used part of the money to buy twenty *kung* of farmland, which he rented to tenants. The rice collected from the tenants was quite enough for his family's consumption.

He then decided to mine the iron and hired many workers to dig it. He failed again and again but still kept his confidence. He hired more workers and continued to look for ore. At last, he discovered a rich vein. He was very happy and organized the mining of the ore, the melting of it into blocks, and its transportation for sale to the city. But, because of the isolated location of the village, the limited demand for iron in the market, the high cost of production and transportation, and the backwardness of mining techniques, he could not expand his enterprise. Nevertheless, he laid a foundation for prosperity in iron-mining for his family. The village was becoming the center of iron-mining in the district. This enterprise prospered particularly during the years of the War of Resistance against Japan.

Chairman Wang's grandfather, Wang Chu-tung, was the elder of two brothers. He began to study when he was eight but left school at eleven. After leaving school, Chu-tung did nothing but hunt and practice weight-lifting. He was tall and strong and with his strength could beat everybody in his native place. He passed the military examination of the county when he was twenty-four and received the degree of *wu hsiu ts'ai*. He served in the army for three years and later engaged in farming and mining.

Chairman Wang's father, Wang Hai-liang, was the eldest son among the brothers. He began his education when he was seven and worked diligently in school, making a good record. When he was around fifteen years old, the economic condition of his family became much improved. Both businesses, iron-mining and selling wood, prospered. He had no need to worry about his family and devoted himself completely to his studies. When he was twenty-three years old, he became a literary graduate, receiving a grant from the government through a competitive examination. After three years, however, he was compelled to stop his studies because of his father's death. He then returned home and taught in a private school, and because of his devotion to his job he gained a very high reputation.

Chairman Wang was the oldest of three brothers and two sisters. The brother next to him in age, Chun-hui, studied in a private school for eight years. He passed the civil-service examination and received the degree of *hsiu ts'ai*. He served in his native place for thirteen years as a special representative to encourage self-government. He was honest and righteous. Chairman Wang's second brother, Chun-chi, studied in a private school for five years. Later he graduated from the provincial normal school. He assumed teaching duties in a private school when he was twenty-two years old and remained at this job through his life. He was enthusiastic and satisfied with his occupation. He said, "As teaching is the spiritual life, we should be contented with our poverty."

Chairman Wang was born in 1881. He started to study in a private school at the age of eight. Even when he was a boy, he worked very hard. Because of the reputation of his family, his teacher paid special attention to him, which enabled him to progress faster. He received a great deal of encouragement from his father. Wang's father arranged a special room for him and his brothers, so that they could continue their studies at home. He liked to recite poems and tell stories about men who had become famous scholars. These tales inspired the young man.

Chairman Wang's father sometimes brought him to the city of Kunyang and to Kunming, the provincial capital. The urban scene stirred him to work still harder and gave him some knowledge of other ways of life that his schoolmates did not have. He came to the City of Kunyang to study at the age of fifteen. As he had been brought up in the country, he felt proud of his association with city students at school.

At twenty-two he passed the civil examination and received the degree of *hsiu ts'ai*. After receiving the degree, he taught at a private school in his native place. Because of the additional income contributed by him, the economic condition of his family improved, but he felt that there was no future in a career at home. His father served as a warning to him. He had labored as a teacher all his life and had never raised himself. Furthermore, the political situation was in a transitional stage. And, as the old system of education had already been abolished, he decided to continue his own studies. He went to Kunming and enrolled in the provincial normal school. This decision eventually proved to be a crucial one in his long career. The new system of schooling was quite different from that of the private school he had attended. In the latter only Confucian classics had been taught, but in the new school there were various courses, foreign languages, national and foreign histories, geography, mathematics, chemistry, physics, and physical education. All these subjects broadened his curiosity. Furthermore, he had had to struggle and worry, and he was not going to waste his opportunity. In the four years he was there, he made great progress.

After being graduated from school, he was appointed teacher in the primary school of Kunming. The salary in Kunming was ten times higher than that in his native place. His life was certainly much improved. He was most conscientious in his work. He was praised for his modesty, his consideration for others, and his high sense of responsibility. The students liked his teaching methods. He was courted by a number of schools to take up employment with them, but he declined all invitations because he did not want to change his school.

In 1913 the gentry of Kunyang suggested to the Magistrate that he invite Wang to return and serve as the principal of the primary school of that county. Wang knew that, if he refused their request, he would be thought too proud, and for that reason he accepted. At that time everybody admired his ability. The school improved daily under his direction. In the next year, he was also appointed chairman of the Office of Compulsory Education and general inspector of education of the county.

During those years he visited the villages of the county and gave speeches to urge the peasants to send their children to school. Up to that time, all the schools had been private. Teachers had taught only the Four Books and other ancient classics. Nobody wanted to enter school under the new system, and the teachers could not use the new books as textbooks. So Chairman Wang invited them to the city to re-educate them. By degrees the new system of education became established. Wang's reputation in Kunyang rose a thousandfold.

In 1917 an educational inspector of the provincial government came to Kunyang and found that Chairman Wang's enthusiasm and constructiveness in local education had borne good results. After returning to Kunming, the inspector sent a petition to the Governor requesting a citation for Chairman Wang.

In 1924 he was appointed head of the Bureau of Education and Inspector of Education of the county government of Kunyang. While he held this position, he carried out a number of worthwhile activities: discouraging traditional private schools, increasing support for public education, selecting good teachers, and encouraging establishment of the new educational system. Because of his brilliant service, he was, at the recommendation of the Governor, honored with a decoration by the central government. He felt very happy because his services had been properly rewarded.

In 1940 when the Bureau of Education of the county government was reorganized as the Department of Education, he was appointed chief. In addition, in 1942 he was appointed principal of the normal school and junior middle school of the county. In 1943, owing to the war emergency, the Citizens' Political Council was organized. Wang was elected chairman, the most honorable position in the community. As he was old and lacked energy to do heavy work, he was not averse to inviting able and vigorous youths to help him. Anyone requested could not refuse to help him through respect for his age.

Chairman Wang was a man of high moral sense. He felt that a good reputation was difficult to secure but easy to lose; personality and reputation were the second life of man. He behaved scrupulously at all times. He often said that good character alone could make others admire one forever; authority could force no one to be obedient in his heart. If a person played tricks in order to cheat other people, he would be discovered in the long run; the most important qualities for men, given ability, were honesty and perseverance.

The Life History of Director Shen

If Chairman Wang represents a typical Confucian scholar, Director Shen typifies the model of the "new youth" shaped on a modern pattern. They were of the same status but belonged to two different generations. The basic difference lay in their quite distinct ideologies. The ideology of the former centered on his family; the latter emphasized the individual's responsibility to his society. It was a substantial change.

Shen Chü Chang, or Director Shen—the director of the Bureau of Education of Kunyang—was born in a village named Li Jen Ts'un of Ping Ting Hsiang, about twelve miles north of the walled City of Kunyang. According to the 1942 census, the village had a population of 1,148. The villagers were Moslems. Li Jen Ts'un was located on the hillside of Mount Shan Chung overlooking Kunming Lake. The farms were not fertile and did not yield enough for the villagers. My assistant visited there twice, and I went once.

Since the outbreak of the Japanese War, several factories had moved into the region. The quiet village had changed into a noisy town. Many stalls and grocery stores had been established, and many villagers who formerly had had no jobs worked in the factories.

Director Shen's great-grandfather had studied three years in a private school. He was able and hard-working. His family had then twenty-five *kung* of farmland. He engaged in agriculture and dealt in oxen and sheep.

Shen Wei-ya, Director Shen's grandfather, was the younger of two brothers. He entered school at the age of seven. He studied very hard and became one of the best students. He received the degree of *Hsiu Ts'ai* when he was twenty-two years old. He was engaged in teaching.

After dividing the family property with his brother, he received eighteen *kung* of farmland and a house of two rooms. As a teacher in the village, he was respected by the people, though he was not rich. He was enthusiastic about the public affairs of the village. The building of the mosque and the primary school were both carried out under his sponsorship. He often said, "The progress of the village rests upon the advancement of education." He was elected chairman of the Association for the Advancement of Islam in Kunyang. He was still healthy and in good spirits at eighty-five years of age. The Chairman of the United Association for Saving the Country of the Moslems of Yunnan bestowed upon him a plaque with four characters, *teh shou ping chên* ("attaining to both virtue and longevity"). Magistrate Wei presented him with a plaque with the characters *jê hsin hsing hsüeh* ("enthusiastic in promoting education"). Magistrate Ho also conferred a plaque on him with the characters *wang ch'ung hsiang li* ("becoming prominent in his native place").

Director Shen's father, Shen Hsiao-ming, was the second born; he had three brothers and three sisters. His elder brother was engaged in studying, and his two younger brothers had joined the army. Hsiao-ming studied seven years in his father's school and could keep accounts and handle correspondence and official documents. He took as his career both business and agriculture. He was eloquent, humorous, and sociable.

Director Shen was precocious and ever encouraged, as his grandfather and father loved him very much. He started to study in his grandfather's school at the age of six. He had a very good memory. He entered a primary school at twelve. After graduation from the primary school with an excellent record, he was enrolled in a junior middle school in Kunming. Because of the financial condition of his family, it was barely possible for him to study in Kunming. He felt very lucky and worked extremely hard in the school.

After graduation from the junior middle school, he returned home. He discovered that his family had gone into debt for his schooling. It was impossible for him to continue his study. Still he was inadequately trained and not at all well prepared for a good job. He worried over his future and went many nights without sleep. His grandfather also worried for him and thought that if he discontinued his study it would be as if "they had raised a mound nine fathoms high only to fall short by a single basket of earth." After careful consideration, his grandfather decided to deprive the family still more to let him continue his study. This decision was crucial. Otherwise, Shen would have been "half-baked," so to speak.

Shen went to Kunming with mingled feelings of happiness and sorrow. He was delighted because his future looked bright but sorry because of his family's suffering for him. He decided he could enter only the normal school because it provided an aid of $10 a month for every student. If he were thrifty, his family might not have to send him any money.

Fortunately, after he had entered the provincial normal school, his lineage also gave him an aid of $10 a month. He not only could cover all his expenses but could also save a little money.

After his graduation from the normal school, he was considered one of the most intelligent scholars in his native district and was immediately invited to be a teacher at the central elementary school. He was highly praised by his students and colleagues for his new methods of teaching, his clear explanations, and his spirit. Admiration for him spread to every quarter of Kunyang.

In the next year, he was invited to be a teacher in the normal school and junior middle school of the county. All his students liked him there too, for he introduced new ideas and modern knowledge. He was enthusiastic about his job and very responsible. After one year, he was appointed principal of the school by the Magistrate. Under his leadership, the normal school and junior middle school improved steadily. But, after two years, he resigned his position because he could not carry out his projected plans without essential funds.

After resigning his office, Shen returned home and went into the business of buying and selling rice. Meanwhile, he kept studying and began a diary. After two years, he was invited to be principal of the central elementary school at Ping Ting Hsiang. At first, he was enthusiastic in his new position. But later he began to realize that he was *ta ts'ai hsiao yung,* "a great talent employed in a small capacity." In addition, he wanted to engage some good teachers, but the school was short of funds. If he let matters stand, he felt no good would ever come of it. He submitted a plan for reforming the school to the government, but it was turned down. He resigned the position.

When Director Shen was thirty-three years old, he became interested in educational administration. Meanwhile, Magistrate Chao had come to Kunyang and wanted to give him the position of chief of the Department of Education of the county government. But after Shen talked with Chao, he refused to accept any position in the county government. Later, he told his friends: "Magistrate Chao is a greedy official. Black and white are not the same color. I would prefer to suffer poverty rather than humiliation." He also said: "As we are the new youths, we should not stand together with the evil gentry and corrupt officials. If everybody keeps grafting money and swerving from his principles, however mean and poor his condition, how can the country avoid becoming weak and eventually invaded by foreign powers? Our sacred responsibility is to save our country and to reform our society." After two years, when the people complained about

Magistrate Chao's corruption and inefficiency and the gentry accused Chao before the provincial government, the people had reason to admire Shen's quick insight and sound judgment.

After Magistrate Chao was dismissed, the provincial government appointed Magistrate Huang. Magistrate Huang considered Director Shen one of the most able men in Kunyang and insisted upon his accepting a position in the county government. For his part, Shen felt that Magistrate Huang was a good man. So he accepted the post of head of the Department of Education of the county government. His first suggestion was that the financial budget of the schools of the county should be doubled, and it was accepted by the county government. It greatly heightened the morale of the teachers. Then he organized the Association of Schoolteachers of Kunyang, the first professional association in the community. This organization backed up his many further demands for the improvement of education in Kunyang. His enthusiasm was highly appreciated. As Magistrate Huang trusted him, most of his suggestions were adopted.

In January 1946, the Department of Education of the county government was changed back to the Bureau of Education, which was directly related to the Department of Education of the provincial government. The financing of the Bureau became independent from the county government. The Bureau thus had much more power than the Department. Shen assumed the directorship of the Bureau of Education. He was also elected to the Citizens' Political Council in Kunyang. He thus climbed to the top of the social ladder in the community.

In August, 1946, he instituted a summer school and gathered all the schoolteachers of the county in the City of Kunyang. He invited a dozen professors from National Southwest Associated University in Kunming to come to Kunyang as visiting lecturers. This program of challenging ideas was an unprecedented event in Kunyang.

Shen was bright, energetic, and sociable. He spoke with moving eloquence. He was industrious and persistent and good at writing official letters. He was sometimes criticized, however, for being inconsistent in his speech and deeds and thus for being insincere. He liked to read books about social history and also about revolutions. He had said: "Both the 'Three Principles of People'* and Communism are good for China. But when they are carried out, the former

---

* "The Three Principles of People" were Dr. Sun Yat-sen's doctrines. They were nationalism, democracy, and livelihood. Dr. Sun's book, *The Three Principles of People,* became the bible of the Nationalist Party.

easily changes course, while Communism has a definite program and, hence, is the more efficient."

The Life History of Director Tai

The tradition was for boys to enter the middle school or normal school and then go on to take jobs in the government or become teachers. These two professions were thus overcrowded. There was no movement toward a more technical kind of education in agriculture, engineering, or business. Director Tai was perhaps an exception. He entered a school of agriculture.

Tai Chü Chang, or Director Tai—the director of the Bureau of Reconstruction of the county—was born in a village named Ning Mo Ts'un, which was seven miles south of the city and located by the side of the highway from Kunyang to Yüchi. There was a river between the highway and the village. Behind the village were high hills with thick forests. According to our 1942 census, the village had a population of 333 people.

Director Tai's great-grandfather had studied five years in a private school in the city. As he came from the country, he was often ridiculed by his schoolmates. But he worked very hard and was praised by his teacher for his good marks. After half a year, all his schoolmates changed their attitudes toward him. He often said, "if one wants to be respected, he must become superior to others." When he was thirty years old, he was elected by his villagers to be manager of the public affairs of the village. Almost all the documents in the village were written by him. His family had then ninety *kung* of farmland and was the richest in the village. His wife bore him three sons and one daughter; all died except a son.

Director Tai's grandfather started to study at nine and received the degree of *hsiu ts'ai* at the age of twenty. He employed two regular laborers to take care of his farms. He himself simply gave them daily orders. He visited either the market town of his native district or the city almost every day. He had no ambition about money but was anxious to have prestige. He liked to associate with the gentry of his county. When he was forty-five years old, he began teaching in a private school. He kept this job for the rest of his life.

Director Tai's father was the youngest of three brothers. When he was only two years old, his parents died successively, and thus he was brought up by his eldest brother and sister-in-law. He studied three years and then engaged in agriculture. When he was twenty-five years old, the family property was divided. He received twenty-eight *kung* of farmland and a house of two rooms. He was thrifty and industrious. Later, when he was sixty years old, he bought thirty-five *kung* of farmland and became one of the richest farmers in his village. His first wife gave birth to three sons and two daughters and died. His second wife bore him two more sons.

Director Tai was the third of the five brothers. When he was only fourteen months old, his mother passed away, and he was brought up by his elder sister. He entered school at the age of nine. He had a good memory and studied very hard.

When he had finished the Four Books and the Five Classics, he was seventeen years old. He felt that he had accomplished nothing and could find no job in the village. Fortunately, his father agreed to let him continue his schooling in Kunming. He entered the Provincial Agricultural Middle School. He thought: "China is an agricultural country. After graduating from the school, I may be able to do something in reforming agriculture."

After graduation from the agricultural school, he returned to his native place and was invited to be a teacher at the elementary school of the county located in the City of Kunyang. He was renowned as a good teacher. One day the Magistrate visited the school and was informed of his high qualifications. Educated men were rare in the community, and the Magistrate appointed him head of an office for advancing agriculture and industry. Director Tai was, of course, delighted.

After taking up the position, he founded an experimental and demonstrational agricultural station. He distributed the young shoots of trees to every village and urged the people to plant them. He divided all the hills in the county into ninety-seven areas and appointed a supervisor for each area to protect the forest. He inspected the areas twice a year. He also invited the supervisors to the city for a short period of training in the methods of forestry and irrigation. After ten years, the trees grew up, and there was thick forest in every area. The people admired him for his wise guidance and great service. Once the provincial government sent an official to Kunyang to investigate local administrative conditions, and, after he had gone to Kunming and reported Tai's accomplishment to the Governor, the Governor awarded Tai a plaque with four characters—*shu mu kê feng* ("the trees beautify the landscape").

In 1927, when he was forty years old, Director Tai was appointed director of the Bureau of Reconstruction, where he had much more power than in his former office. He became one of the distinguished gentry in Kunyang. During his time in office he rebuilt the tomb of Cheng Ho's father,[5] built two dams, repaired roads and bridges, and dredged and diked the canal that connected the city and Kunming Lake. He personally supervised every reconstruction and almost always worked through the night.

In 1933, he was ordered to build two highways, from Kunyang to Yüchi and from Kunyang to Chinning. The respective distances were twenty miles and ten miles. There were to be a total of seven stone bridges and 120 sluices. He had never undertaken such a large-scale project. But the provincial government urged the county government to start the construction work immediately. Tai requested the Magistrate to notify the officials of the district governments to hold a meeting for sharing such tasks as the recruitment of laborers and the appointment of supervisors. He made plans at night and purchased materials and directed the construction work in the daytime. There were several thousand laborers working daily along the thirty miles of highway. As they were drafted and worked without payment at all, they were reluctant to work. When the supervisors came, the laborers pretended to work very hard. When the supervisors left, they sat down again. Finally, the supervisors became lazy too. The construction work thus went far behind the time schedule.

Although it was easy for Tai to take graft, he remained honest, prudent, and impartial. His subordinates, Mr. Tung and others, however, took advantage of every means to extort from the people. The highway, for example, was to cross the farms of the peasants. The supervisors thus would purposely set up the roadmarks at the centers of farms to indicate that the route would cut across them. The peasants whose farms were to be crossed would offer bribes. The officials would then move the roadmarks to other farms. The peasants were outraged and began to stir.

After the highway was half done, Tai felt better. His next plan was to plant trees along the two sides of the highway. He thought that, after this long period of anxiety and hard work, he would surely be rewarded. He did not know that his subordinates had greatly angered the people by their grafting and that complaints could be heard everywhere. Some people even wanted to assassinate Tai. The trouble was reported to the Magistrate. After learning what his assistants had done to him, Tai was greatly dejected. Although the trouble was smoothed over, he was so discouraged that he resigned his position. He then returned home and began to farm. He felt unhappy, though he was still respected by the people.

In 1944, two agents of a commercial lumber company financed by the American army and operated by a university in Kunming came to Kunyang and wanted to buy the trees on the hills behind Director Tai's village. The villagers refused to sell. The agents bribed the magistrate with $160,000 (equivalent to 210 silver dollars in 1944) and hired 100 workers to chop down the trees first and talk about the price later. Director Tai led more than 200 villagers to prevent the workers from chopping down the trees. When he argued with the agents and the secretary of the Magistrate, he was humble and polite but brave and determined. He forced the agents to abandon their scheme.

Director Tai was often criticized for being backward, incompetent, and even unsociable. The consequences of his utter concentration on his job and career were inevitable isolation from the people and the limited numbers of friends and acquaintances he had. To be truly a member of the gentry and to achieve solid status at the top level of the community, one had to be able to interact with people easily and to become part of his community. It seemed that Director Tai's approach to his life carried the seeds of his failure. Nevertheless, many people knew that he was modest, honest, and conscientious and that among the gentry few others had done so many constructive things for the community as a whole.

MEDICAL PRACTICE AS A SOCIAL LADDER

The medical profession was not only respectable; it was also an avenue to fame and fortune. Yet even the specialist might not have received any formal training. At best, he might have been the disciple of some eminent practitioner. In the more primitive societies, the medicine man learns from experience that some leaf or plant is a specific medicine for a particular disease, and this knowledge gives him a definite superiority over the ignorant populace. The success of the medicine man greatly depends upon his skill in, and his knowledge of, roots and herbs, no less than upon his acquaintance with the psychology of his patients. Furthermore, the medicine store stocks herbal medicines. These medicines are often needed at a moment's notice. The store therefore finds a place in the rural community. The life history of Vice-Chairman Loh illustrates how medical practice served as a channel for upward social mobility in China.

The Life History of Vice-Chairman Loh

Loh Fu I-chang, or Vice-Chairman Loh of the Citizens' Political

Council of the county, was born in the City of Kunyang. His great-grandfather, Yeh Nang-sheng, lived in a village named Yeh Chia Ts'un. Vice-Chairman Loh's grandfather, Loh Ping-shu, adopted his wife's family name.[6] Vice-Chairman Loh's father was an only son. After studying nine years in a private school, he went into agriculture and later operated a grocery store.

Vice-Chairman Loh was the second of three brothers. His elder brother studied ten years and received the degree of *hsiu ts'ai*. His younger brother also received the degree of *hsiu ts'ai* and engaged in medical practice.

Vice-Chairman Loh entered a private school at the age of six. He was noted for his very good memory and admired for his handsomeness. He married at seventeen and received the degree of *hsiu ts'ai* at the age of twenty-one. After receiving the degree, he became a teacher.

After teaching three years, he decided that for one who stayed in his native place there was no future and that he must go away to seek his fortune while he was still young. He needed to broaden his experience. Fortunately, his brother-in-law, Commander Chu, was then promoted to the rank of battalion commander and asked Loh to be his secretary. Loh eagerly accepted the position.

In the army he liked to visit scenic places, and he read books and practiced calligraphy as pastimes. Once he made the acquaintance of a well-known scholar-physician. He felt that a man who did much traveling should have some knowledge of medicine for emergencies and that, in the meantime, he might accumulate virtue for the next world by curing the diseases of others. He thus requested the scholar-physician to teach him the medical practice. He bought some medical books and started to study. After one year, he could cure common ailments and became an amateur doctor.

After several years in the army, Loh returned home. He was respected by the local people and often asked for advice when there was any public affair to be arranged. He was especially zealous about such religious matters as building temples and the festivals of the Birthday of the Goddess of Flowers, the worship of the Dipper (for longevity), and the Birthday of the Goddess of Mercy. He contributed money generously and was often asked to supervise the festivals. He believed that his participating in these religious affairs would help him to obtain male children. He had then only a daughter and was anxious to have a son.

When he was thirty-seven years old, he felt that he needed a proper occupation. Medical practice seemed to suit his needs: He liked it, and it was respected. Furthermore, as he already had some knowledge and actual experience in curing people, it would be easy to continue advanced study. He bought many such medical books as *The Medical Dictionary* and *The Medical Herbs of Southern Yunnan* and asked the esteemed physicians of Kunyang for guidance and direction. In addition to medicine, he also studied chronomancy and geomancy. He emphasized a close relationship between theory and practice. He became well known as a very skillful physician, geomancer, and chronomancer in Kunyang. He also kept a medicine store.

He was noted for his careful diagnosis of pathological states. He took a long time in feeling the patient's pulse. He systematically asked the patient about the symptoms of his disease. When he wrote a prescription for his patient, he usually requested weak medicine in small quantities for testing. It did not bring the patient immediate recovery from his illness, but, on the other hand, he avoided all drastic reaction. After the patient had taken his medicine once or twice and Loh could make sure that the prescription was suitable, he would give stronger doses so that the patient would recover as soon as possible. He sold his medicines at low prices. If his patient was poor, he would even give him the medicine free of charge. Should the patient ask him about his disease, he would tell him in detail. When the patient left his store, he invariably felt kindly toward Doctor Loh.

Loh fixed the price of his medicine according to the principle that stated "30% higher than the cost is reasonable, but 70% higher than the cost should be condemned." The patients came continually, and his store did very good business. During the years between 1940 and 1945, he accumulated about $2,000,000 (equivalent to 487 silver dollars in 1945). He had twenty-five *kung* of farmland, which were rented to tenants, and a house of four rooms.

Successful at forty-five years of age, he wanted to have still higher prestige. When the Kunyang representative of the People's Political Council of the Province of Yunnan was to be elected, he enthusiastically joined the campaign. He reported his name and background to the provincial government. Loh was approved as one of the two candidates for Kunyang. Before election day, his rival tried to bribe some gentry members to use their influence in favor of himself. Vice-Chairman Loh knew that, even though he had a fine reputation in Kunyang, his rival's money could still buy many minds.

He therefore campaigned vigorously. His younger brother-in-law, the younger brother of Commander Chu, also helped him to propagandize everywhere. As a result, he was elected. He was very happy and seldom missed the meetings at Kunming.

In the next year, Magistrate Tsou came to Kunyang. The Magistrate had great respect for Loh and selected him to run the Department of Civil Affairs of the county government and gave him the command of the county guard. He thus became one of the most powerful gentry members in Kunyang. He remained noted for his honesty and sense of justice.

After three years, he resigned his posts and settled down to medical practice. He felt that a perfect gentleman could not make friends with the mean "clowns" of officialdom. He often said: "The current society is turned upside down. The able and honest man is expelled by mean and contemptible rascals. Just recently our Mr. Hsiao was seriously beaten by a group of soldiers led by Captain K'ung because Mr. Hsiao suggested that the government should dissolve public funds and public farmland managed by K'ung Chin-shih, Captain K'ung's father, for more than thirty years. Even the magistrate who came to settle the dispute was insulted. As I am engaged in medical practice and have nothing to do with them, I can avoid these distresses and vexations. I am one who seeks an ivory tower, an escapist from that society at least."

In 1945, Loh was elected Vice-Chairman of the Citizens' Political Council of Kunyang and a member of the editing committee of the county gazetteer. He bitterly hated the corruption of the officials and suggested in the Council meetings that they deserved severe punishment. Though he knew that the Council had no power, he aimed for rhetorical effect. He wrote essays and poems for the gazetteer to express his views and feelings.

Although Vice-Chairman Loh's degree, relatives, and official positions all made him prominent, he eventually established himself as a medical practitioner. He was well known as a very skillful "scholar-physician" (ju-i). He operated a medicine store and sold his medicine at low prices. If his patient was poor, he would even charge him nothing. He bitterly hated the corruption of the officials and deplored the society he called "turned upside down." He conveyed the message that those were times when strong men won regardless of class background or moral conduct. He had a high sense of social justice, and thus his mobility function was coordinated with his own deep moral convictions.

NOTES

1. Hsiao-tung Fei and Chih-i Chang, *Earthbound China: A Study of Rural Economy in Yunnan* (Chicago: The University of Chicago Press, 1945), pp. 129–30.
2. *Ibid.,* pp. 278–9.
3. *Ibid.,* p. 130.
4. *Ibid.,* pp. 273–4.
5. Cheng Ho, a eunuch and famous navigator under the Ming Dynasty, was born in the village named Ho Tai Ts'un, Kunyang. During the period of 1405–1433, he led 27,800 officers and soldiers with sixty-two large boats, each of which was about 440 feet long and 180 feet wide, to visit forty countries, including Indochina, Siam, Singapore, Malacca, Sumatra, Java, India (East and West), Ceylon, Aden, Mecca, Madagascar, seven times. For details, see Liang Chi-ch'ao, "The Biography of Cheng Ho," in *In Ping Shih Ho Chi (The Collected Essays of In Ping Shih)* (Shanghai: Chung Hua Book Co., 1936); Lee Shih-hou, *Cheng Ho Chia P'u Kao Shih (A Study in the Family History of Cheng Ho)* (2nd ed.; Kunming: Chung Wen Press, 1937). The huge stone tablet in front of the tomb was valuable for studying Cheng Ho's family history.
6. A person who had only a daughter sometimes did not take a nephew as adopted son but preferred to "adopt" an unrelated boy as a "live-in son-in-law" (*chui hsü*). The boy later on had to marry the daughter and was supposed to carry her family name and to give up his own family name. The boy moved up economically by this marriage arrangement, but he lost social status. This regulation went against established tradition and was regarded as dishonorable for men. Wolfram Eberhard, *Social Mobility in Traditional China* (Leiden: E. J. Brill, 1962), pp. 233–4.

5

Upward Mobility through the Army, Government, and Commerce

The army, government, and commerce played important roles in upward social mobility. In a period of militarism or of international or civil war, the army played an especially significant role as "social stairway." The frequency of international and civil wars in modern China afforded comparatively so wide a scope of opportunity that soldiers were able to gain easy ascendancy.

Political organizations, beginning with the government and ending with the political party, also played the role of social elevator. What was true of large political organizations was also true of the small local political organizations, whatever their names may have been. Every village and town had its political bosses and leaders. One channel for local promotion was the local political organization.

Commerce was one of the most important roads to wealth, like the roads of landowning, mining, and manufacturing, which had always served as social ladders. There was some correlation between wealth and social position. Indeed, it was difficult to maintain prestige while being poor. In China, the old tradition of class division gave the scholar the highest rank, the farmer next, then the artisan, with the merchant at the bottom. The merchant who had money power could never really be at the bottom of the social scale, however. Being a businessman—or, at least, a successful one—meant status.

During the last Sino-Japanese war, the successful money-makers rapidly promoted themselves and superseded, in considerable part, the petty officials and schoolteachers in top social positions. Because of inflation many *bona fide* gentry members were silent partners in commercial ventures or became occasional traders.

THE ARMY AS A SOCIAL LADDER

The main income of the villagers was from the farmland. Unless a peasant had gained title to some land, he was afloat in the community and likely eventually to drift anywhere. The extreme importance of land ownership to the peasants was mirrored in the saying that "the boat has to be anchored against the wind." Still, the very small portions of land owned by most peasants revealed their almost helpless condition, for a small farm not only provided no leeway to meet such emergencies as flood, drought, and locusts but it also reflected the trend toward rapid reduction in economic status of the well-to-do peasant family. This latter point explains why the peasant exodus was more or less continuous, regardless of whether there was a good harvest or natural calamity.[1] When the agricultural laborers, forced by circumstances, left their native areas and set themselves to wandering in strange places, they usually hired themselves out as farmhands, peddlers, coolies, handicraftsmen, factory workers, or mercenary soldiers. The last-mentioned vocation laid the real foundation of China's warlordism.

According to the statistics registered by the Institute for Census Research, during the period between August, 1943, and January, 1946, 1,488 men left their native villages. The causes of their emigration are listed in Table 14. Of the 1,488 men who left their native villages, 1,090, or 73.25%, entered the army.

Under the mercenary system, the officers and soldiers had quite different family backgrounds. Most of the officers had been recruited from the middle or upper classes. The officer's usual motive was economic gain; he sought to secure an official position and to rise, for "to be promoted in official rank is to become richer and richer." Nevertheless, to become an official required education, and schooling was not easy for the villagers. There followed a tendency for young men to enter military academies, not only because they were free, but also because quick success could be achieved. After a short period of training, a man could be commissioned an officer in the army and, with luck, might be promoted to the higher ranks.[2] The military cadet schools trained young men to be "officers and gentlemen." And

Table 14. The Causes of Emigration for the Males in the Four
Districts of Kunyang, August, 1943–January, 1946

| | Emigrants | |
Causes of Emigration	Number	Percentage
Joining the army	1,090	73.25
Seeking livelihood	211	14.18
Family discord	96	6.45
Marriage	51	3.43
Public service	19	1.28
Evacuation due to air raids	1	0.07
Unknown	20	1.34
Total	1,488	100.00

Source: The Institute for Census Research, National Tsing Hua University, "A Report on the Registration of Vital Statistics in Chengkung and Kunyang, Yunnan" (unpublished).

as gentlemen, they did not share in the hardships and dangers of their soldiers.

The following three life histories are typical representations of three kinds of Chinese military man. First, the life history of Commander Chu is that of an officer from a well-to-do family who went through the military schools in the earlier days. We find him proud of his descent from outstanding military people and of his ability to lead and promote the welfare of his troops. Major Chang's life history illustrates how the army elite, although largely middle-class in origin, provided a channel by which sons of poor and little-educated peasants could reach the top, in Chang's case, through extreme self-sacrifice. A man who entered the lower ranks of the army or the personal service of an influential ruler might be carried up by the promotion of his superior officer. A poor boy from any family might fight his way to success and official position and thereby raise his family from the depths of penury to prosperity and high social status in the community. Finally, the life history of Colonel Fang illustrates the popular saying that "good iron will not be made into a nail; a good man will not become a soldier."

The Life History of Commander Chu

Chu Ssŭ-ling-kuan, or Commander Chu, was born in the walled City of Kunyang. His great-grandfather, Chu Yuan, had resided originally at a village named Wang Sien, which is situated at the edge of Kunming Lake three miles east of the city. He was a well-to-do farmer. As the location of the village was close to the lake, a flood occurred every two or three years. When there was no flood, there might well be drought instead. He felt that there was no future for him in the village.

Because of the difficulty of living in the village, Chu Yuan decided to move his family to the city. In the city he rented a room facing the street and opened a grocery store to sell such items as salt, wine, tobacco, bean oil, sugar, and soap. The first two years in his venture were dull and unsuccessful, for he lacked experience in business. Little by little, Chu Yuan changed his stern and zealous mien for a pleasant one and took for his motto "the customer is always right." Soon after, his business began to prosper by leaps and bounds.

Commander Chu's grandfather, Chu Hun, was an only son. He entered a private school at the age of nine but left after five years to assist his parents as a salesman at their shop. He kept accounts during the day and in the evening turned them over to his father.

Commander Chu's grandmother was a well-bred woman. She encouraged her husband to pursue his studies and to take the civil-service examination. He came to feel, too, that, although his family was wealthy, he himself had no real prestige. A wealthy man without other attainments was not respected by the people. At twenty-one he began to study military science and art. He also arose very early to practice weight-lifting. Everyone soon came to admire his great strength and ability in feats of this sort. After three years he passed the county civil-service examination and received the degree of *wu hsiu ts'ai*. In another three years he passed the provincial civil-service examination and received the degree of *wu chü jen*.

After receiving his degree of *wu chü jen,* he was highly respected by all the local people. Those who met him would bow to him. If there was an important military affair, he would be consulted by the Magistrate of the county before any action was taken.

Commander Chu's father, Chu Kan, studied in a private school for three years. Though he was intelligent, he had no interest in the academic field. During his years in school he often played truant. One day he told his father that he was going to school, but in reality he gathered a group of children and led them to a hill to play war games. He instructed each one to bring his own weapons, such as clubs and stones, and he divided them into two groups of equal strength and then ordered them to fight each other. As a consequence, many of them were injured. This incident was told to his parents. His father punished him by having him kneel on the ground and beating him until he promised not to play truant any more and to study harder in school. Thereafter, he applied himself to his school work but made no real progress.

Chu Hun decided that, as his son was tall and strong and had no wish to become a man of learning, he would probably do better to study the military art. So Chu Hun allowed his son to stay at home and look after the business at the shop, where he would tell him of his own enthusiasm for and experience in the field of military art. Chu Hun's wife also told her son about her experience in handling the business, but Chu Kan showed no interest in anything except military art, which he began to practice at twenty.

Chu Kan had a great deal of strength and could beat everyone in boxing and fencing. He could raise a square stone of sixty *ching* with one hand. He passed the civil-service examination of the county at twenty-six and later passed the examination of the province to receive the degree of *wu chü jen* at twenty-nine. His family became known as *i mên wu jen,* an "outstanding military family." He was then chosen by the gentry and appointed by the Magistrate to be captain of the county guard. He collected a group of volunteers and trained them daily in the use of the sword and spear. He was adventurous and brave.

Chu Ssŭ-ling-kuan had two older brothers and one younger brother. When he was a young boy, he was quite handsome and imposing. He was quiet and reserved but stubborn. If there was something that did not suit his fancy, he would cry unceasingly. He often bullied other boys, and they could not retaliate because Commander Chu was too strong for them. Because of this strong individuality and unrivaled courage, his father later let him serve in the army.

Commander Chu entered a private school when he was eight. He was very interested in school work and made rapid progress in it. His teacher praised him highly, and his schoolmates respected him very much. This praise made him study still harder.

After four years in the private school, a friend of his father recommended that he enter a military primary school in Kunming. He felt most fortunate in being able to study there, as few persons in his position received such opportunities. Because of his good record there, he was sent to the military middle school in Nanking on the recommendation of the military primary school. He was very happy at this opportunity. He felt that his native place was comparatively backward and that Nanking would give him a fine chance to widen his knowledge.

After three years he was graduated from the military middle school and entered the military academy at Pao-ting, then capital of Hopei Province, through competitive examination. This step was the real start of his future career because the academy was then the center for Chinese military training. He studied there for another three years. After graduation, he returned to Yunnan Province and served in the army as a low-ranking officer.

Commander Chu began his career as a first lieutenant in the army. After serving one year, he was promoted to the rank of captain and became commander of a company. He shared the money given him with his company.* He cared for his soldiers and respected the people. His troop was then stationed at the border of Kwangsi and Yunnan. His mission was to suppress the bandits—which he carried out with complete success. From the bandits he captured a good deal of money and goods. He used the regained loot to improve the living conditions of his soldiers and to supplement the expenses of the junior officers, thus encouraging them to serve loyally. This attitude satisfied his troops, and he accomplished his mission very easily. After three years he was promoted to the rank of major and became commander of a battalion.

Commander Chu did not want money; he wanted power and honor. But this ambition was only one factor in his success. Another important factor was his quality of leadership. He knew how to lead men. Once he said: "The most important thing in soldiering is morale. Leadership, good living conditions, training, and the relations between the officers and soldiers, between the commander and the junior officers, are the fundamental basis of good morale. We should not let the junior officers feel that they are only fighting for the commander. The whole group is a team, and every member should be working toward the same goal. During peacetime we should pay special attention to discipline, but it should be self-respecting and self-governing. Moreover, the troops should co-operate with the local people. The seizure of private property should not be brooked."

Following his promotion to battalion commander, Chu became most ambitious. His chances were good: He had a very strong sense of duty, and he had been most successful in suppressing the bandits. The rich people, the merchants, and especially the local civil officials

---

* Commanders of sizable companies usually were given sums of money to be passed on to the soldiers. Commanders, as a rule, however, kept most of the money and distributed only small portions to the soldiers. Commander Chu, therefore, was doing something unusual.

were most grateful to him and they presented him with various gifts.

After residing at the border of Kwangsi and Yunnan for five years, Commander Chu returned to Yunnan with his company to visit his home, bringing with him ten boxes of precious goods including 5,000 *tael* of silver. The boxes were carried by five horses. He bought fifty *kung* of farmland with his money, and all his family bought new clothes.

After being stationed at Yüchi for two years (Commander Chu had taken a concubine there* because his wife had borne him no child), his troop was ordered to move to the border of the Provinces of Szechwan and Yunnan to suppress more bandits, the notorious leader of whom was named Lee San-new. After fighting several times, Chu defeated them and killed Lee. He was immediately given command of a regiment.

After being promoted, he returned to Yunnan with his troops and visited his home again, this time with thirty boxes of captured silver and other precious goods. These boxes were carried by fifteen horses. He bought more than 100 *kung* of farmland. He was talked about by the people everywhere in Kunyang and was praised highly.

When Commander Chu was promoted to regimental command, his brothers and nephews began to outrage the local people with their unreasonableness. Commander Chu's younger brother, Chu Hsin, twenty-nine years old, who had been previously despised by the people, saw his chance for revenge. Even members of the active local gentry felt oppressed by the power of the Chu family. They feared that they would be foremost among the hated and the attacked. They deemed it better to give Chu Hsin a position. They appointed him head of the Bureau of Finance of the county government. The Magistrate, for his part, praised him openly for his ability. At that time county government financial matters were controlled by a committee, made up of the Magistrate and twelve members of the gentry, which was independent of the provincial government. After Chu Hsin assumed this position, he became the most powerful individual among the gentry of the county. He controlled not only finance but also education, construction, and other public affairs. If he vetoed a plan, it was not carried out. People filing lawsuits against others had necessarily to ask him for help. As to his income, nobody knows how much he profited, but after four years he resigned his position and later built a big house and bought thirty *kung* of farmland.

* The girls of this region have long been known for their light skin and physical beauty.

During the revolution of 1911, Commander Chu saw action in both Shanghai and Canton. In Canton, he served as commander of a guard battalion for Dr. Sun Yat-sen for almost two months. After returning to Yunnan, he continued to serve in the army and fought the Manchurian army in the provinces of Szechwan and Kweichow. During his stay in Kweichow, Commander Chu recommended his eldest brother, Chu Fu, to the Governor of Kweichow Province for the position of magistrate of a county. Later Commander Chu was appointed vice-commander of a division in Kwangsi Province.

When he took the junior command, he saw that the soldiers of the division were not well trained and that his superior was incompetent. The enemy facing them was very strong. Nevertheless, he had to stay there and do his best. At last, they were attacked by the enemy. After fighting one day and one night, his division collapsed. The commander was dismissed, and Chu was promoted to succeed him.

Commander Chu tried to withdraw his troops to the bank of a river in order to improve his position. He hoped to hold the enemy there until the arrival of reinforcements. But the enemy kept at his heels. He retreated, taking with him his personal property, but when he was barely at the middle of the bridge, the enemy rushed up and gained the bank of the river over which Commander Chu was escaping. The soldiers became disorganized, each struggling to get across the river first. As a result, the pontoon bridge collapsed. Many soldiers and Commander Chu fell into the river. Fortunately, he was not far from the bank and was able to swim this short distance. He very narrowly escaped being captured and killed. All his money, silver, and precious articles accumulated through the years were lost. He went to Kweichow to meet his eldest brother and requested him to return home with him. Chu Fu refused because he had amassed more money than could be transported on such short notice. Chu Fu was afterward killed by the enemy coming from Kwangsi.

Commander Chu regretted deeply his defeat and the death of his eldest brother. The local people censured him behind his back and said that the cause for his failure lay in the evil-doings of his family. After he had become an officer, his brothers and nephews had done many wicked deeds, beating the common people and extorting from them. Commander Chu felt that the criticisms of the people were reasonable and blamed most of his failure on his family. He was too discouraged to serve as an officer again.

Commander Chu was fifty-nine years old in 1946 and still very strong. He was of volatile temperament; his speech was quick, frank, and direct. He often criticized the hostility and lack of cooperation among people. He said in his speech delivered at the inaugural meeting of the Association of Veteran Officers in Kunyang: "One person always takes advantage of another person; there is no attempt at equal exchange. Everyone does everything in his own interest. The people have no idea of ethics."

The social structure he found unjust: "Everyone who has money and power can remain independent, even though he gained his wealth by illegal means. On the other hand, one who has no money and power, though he earns his living by his own blood and sweat, still must bear the pain of being oppressed and insulted. This is a society of devils."

He criticized politicians as corrupt and incompetent: "The officials speak in high sounding terms but do nothing worthwhile for the public. Their administration is inefficient. From the most important officials to the lowliest clerks we find corruption. There is no bright future in politics."

He gave few public speeches and did not like to interfere in public affairs. He seemed very depressed and stayed passive. Yet he still hoped that each of his sons would become a man of some distinction.

The Life History of Major Chang

Chang Fu-kuan, or Major Chang, an *aide-de-camp* to the division commander, was born in 1904 in the village named Pei Chuang, which was located fifteen miles northwest of the walled City of Kunyang. According to our 1942 census, the village had a population of 208 people. Almost all the villagers were engaged in agriculture. Only a few could read and write.

Major Chang's great-grandfather had been an illiterate farmer. His family had had fifteen *kung* of farmland. As the products of the farmland were not enough for his family's consumption, he had to increase his income by gathering and selling firewood and hiring himself out as an agricultural laborer. When he was sixteen years old, there was a drought. His farm produce was greatly diminished. He then worked as a long-term farm laborer for a landowner. His yearly compensation was 240 *ching* of rice and two suits of clothes in addition to his board and room. His compensation in kind was raised to 300 *ching* of rice for the second year and 400 *ching* for the third year because he was honest, diligent, and dependable in many ways. When he was twenty-five years old, he came home and rented ten *kung* of farmland. The economic condition of his family improved gradually. After ten years he was able to buy fifteen *kung* of farmland. He built a new house of two rooms when he was forty-seven years old. After that, his family was considered well-to-do in the village.

Major Chang's grandfather was the older of two brothers. He had never entered school. When he was thirty-two years old, the family was divided. He received fifteen *kung* of farmland. He was industrious and thrifty throughout his life. He bought seven *kung* of farmland when he was sixty years old.

Major Chang's father was also illiterate. Since boyhood, he had never had an easy day, eaten a good meal, or worn a good suit of clothes. When he was fifteen, there was a calamity of locusts and a murrain among the domestic animals. As the family could not make ends meet after that, he was ordered by his father to seek work as a farmhand. When the family was split, he received eleven *kung* of farmland and one horse. Though he was industrious and painstaking, his economic condition did not change very much. He had two sons and two daughters.

Major Chang was the elder of the brothers. As his father knew that there was no one in the family who had been able to read and write for three generations and as his son seemed very clever, the son was sent to the village school when he was eight years old. He had a good memory and was interested in learning. After two years, however, he had to discontinue his schooling because of the family's stringent economic condition. It deeply hurt his hopes.

Major Chang married at the age of twenty-two. His wife also came from a poor family. Though not pretty she was very strong. His family went into debt for his wedding. He felt humiliated by his poverty, and there was no prospect in the village. When he was twenty-three years old, he therefore entered the army as a volunteer. After his six months' training, he became interested in army life. He was naturally adventurous and brave. Because he was tall and strong, he was chosen for the cavalry and trained for two more years. Because of his good record, he was selected as a bodyguard for the army commander, who later became the Governor of Yunnan Province.

The Governor's eldest son, who was then a battalion commander, liked Chang and accordingly chose him as his *aide-de-camp*. Chang was given the rank of second lieutenant. The Governor's eldest son was hot-tempered. Once Major Chang was ordered to wash the

Commander's horse. The Commander grew angry because Chang had not washed the horse well enough. He kicked Chang and struck him with a whip more than ten times. Major Chang's body was black and blue. But throughout the ordeal he did not alter his stance of attention a whit. He was absolutely obedient to his superior officers. After five years he was promoted to first lieutenant.

After he became an officer, his family's position changed greatly economically and socially. He could send money to his family, and because he was an officer his family was respected by the villagers. Some people who formerly had bullied his relatives came to flatter them lest they seek revenge. If there was any public affair to be discussed in the village, his father was the first invited to be present.

In 1939, Chang was promoted to a captaincy. The army had moved into Kunming. He had accumulated about $10,000 (equivalent to 4,000 silver dollars) cash on hand. He sent two soldiers to Yüchi to import opium into Kunming for him. As opium trading or transporting was illegal, the opium dealers were covetous of his privilege and willing to provide him with capital to do opium trading. The profit was to be equally shared between him and the merchants. Chang sent armed soldiers to Yüchi to import large quantities of opium into Kunming. In one year, he earned about $1,000,000 (equivalent to 111,000 silver dollars).

In 1942, he became a major. (The Governor's eldest son had been promoted to division commander and, at the same time, vice-commander of the garrison troops in Kunming, the capital of the Province of Yunnan.) He was then not only rich but also powerful. As the Commander had faith in him, he was respected by all the officers of the division and of the provincial government. He was running the opium trade, on the one hand, and searching out opium smugglers, on the other. He operated gambling houses and, at the same time, was sending his men out to arrest the gamblers. All the opium smugglers therefore came to request him to be their honorary partner without any endowment but with the privilege of sharing in their profits. The owners of opium dens and gambling houses in Kunming turned to him for protection and sought his favor. His income rose immeasurably. It was estimated that he accumulated more than $3,000,000 in a single year. He sent part of his money to his family. His father bought sixty *kung* of farmland and built a fashionable new house of seven rooms with this money. As his wife was no longer adequate, Major Chang remarried in Kunming. He was eulogized to the skies and regarded as a paragon by the gentry and the people of Kunyang for his extreme perseverence and long struggle to achieve a successful career.

One day Major Chang was informed that there was a large opium house operating in his area. He reported to his commander. The Commander instructed him to lead a group of soldiers to encircle the opium den and thoroughly search the house. Consequently, they arrested one opium smoker with the manager and seized more than 100 loads of opium and 200 catties of gold bars. The manager was sentenced to death, and the smuggled goods and gold bars were confiscated by the garrison troop headquarters. The shareholders in this den happened to be certain influential officials. After quick consultation behind the scenes, the owners were allowed to substitute a beggar to be shot instead of the manager. Major Chang was highly rewarded for this action.

Another time Major Chang took over two automobiles that were being used for smuggling opium. He also reported the case to the Commander. As a result, the automobiles and smuggled goods were confiscated. He was rewarded with one of the two automobiles.

Chang rented a house in Kunming for his residence until a fellow Kunyang native named Dao Fa-chuan asked him for help. Dao owned a house that was rented to several influential men. They had neither paid rent for five or six years nor would they move out. Major Chang drove them out of the house, and he himself moved into it. He paid no rent to Dao either.

In 1943, the gentry of Kunyang accused Magistrate Chao of malfeasance. It was mainly due to Chang's influence that Magistrate Chao was dismissed. Chu Lung, the eldest son of Commander Chu and the leader of the group for Magistrate Chao, was then beaten up by Major Chang in Kunming. Major Chang had hated the corrupt men of Kunyang and had hoped that the local administration would be honest and efficient. Though the people of Kunyang had generally a very good impression of him, Chang won out.

In 1945, the central government reorganized the provincial government of Yunnan by force. When the soldiers of the Fifth Army of the central government were sent after the Governor's officers and soldiers, Chang hid at home and dared not go out for a whole month. After that his prestige in Kunyang vanished. His glory was gone. He entered business in Kunming.

Major Chang was generous and sociable. Although he did not talk very much, when he did talk, his speech was straightforward and forcible. Usually he was kind and gentle, but when he became angry he was temperamental and even violent. He was always in high spirits and arose very early in the morning, yet his life was very irregular. As he saw no more bright future in his own career, he hoped that his two sons and one daughter would be graduated from the university and would become worthy persons.

The Life History of Colonel Fang

Fang Ssŭ-ling, or Colonel Fang, the commander of the guerilla troops, was born in 1890 in the village named Ta San Ts'un, which was situated about ten miles north of the City of Kunyang. According to the 1942 census, the village had a population of 369 people. It was located on the side of a mountain. Irrigation was a big problem for the village. Most of the farms there were so-called *lei hsiang tien,* "thunder-sounding fields," which means that the irrigation depended on rain water. During 1943, 1944, and 1945, there were three successive droughts. As a result, most of the villagers were half starved and dressed in rags.

Colonel Fang's great-grandfather had engaged in agriculture. His family had sixty-five *kung* of farmland. All his farms were used for planting opium. He could harvest 1,600 *liang* or *tael* of opium each year. His family became one of the richest in the village, which was prosperous at that time.

Colonel Fang's grandfather was the elder of two brothers. After dividing the family property with his younger brother, he received thirty-three *kung* of farmland. He never worked very hard but simply kept up his estate.

Colonel Fang's father was also a farmer. He had studied three years and could write and keep accounts. He was intelligent and had a good memory. Though he quit school, he read books like *The Romance of Three Kingdoms* at his leisure. When he was thirty years old, he was elected to manage the public affairs of the village. He was a careful, enthusiastic, and responsible man.

Colonel Fang was the younger of two brothers. His parents loved him very much because of his "cuteness." When he turned seven, he suddenly became a wretched boy. He was bold and liked to bully others. He would knock down any boy who did not obey him. He was tall and strong for his age, and no other boy could rival him in pugilistics. He entered a private school when he was eight years old but had no interest in studying. After five years, he had learned nothing but gambling. When he lost money, he would steal things from his home to sell. When he was sixteen years old, his father died. His mother could no longer control him. He was married at the age of twenty-one, but the young couple was ill matched. All these factors encouraged his dissipation.

He gambled every day. Sometimes he did not return for several days. In fact, he came home only when he needed money. His mother and wife often cursed him. He wandered around the gambling houses, opium dens, and bordellos in the market town a mile or so from his village. The villagers despised him for his base character. He was treated coldly everywhere. After losing a great deal of money in gambling on credit, he was dunned by his creditors and had to flee by night.

He went to Kunming. After a few days, he squandered all his get-away money. He asked some acquaintances for help, but all considered him a man of bad conduct, and nobody was willing to help him. As he could find no other job, in desperation he volunteered for the army. He knew that the soldier was held in low esteem.

He started as a private. He rationalized his embarrassment by saying, "Everything has a beginning." When he was treated harshly by his officer, he would muse, "The bitter experience of a private is essential for the officer." He overcame his discouragement even though he suffered great hardships. During the period of training, he fought against his bad habits. He studied very hard. He became pleasant and learned to speak distinctly. After completing his training, he was appointed to a second lieutenancy. He felt happy and resolved to quell all extravagance.

When he was twenty-seven, his group was ordered to suppress bandits. Though he had been in the army for almost three years, it was his first time to fight at the front. He conducted himself bravely and shrewdly. When the whole battalion was surrounded by the bandits, he led the small group of soldiers under his command in a break through the enemy's lines and rushed to headquarters to report the situation to his colonel. The colonel immediately sent out reinforcements. As a consequence, the bandits were defeated, and the life of the battalion was saved. The colonel promoted him to captain. He was greatly encouraged.

After three more years, the army was ordered to move to Kwangsi Province, and he became a major and a battalion commander. He had become so ambitious that he thought, if he could defeat the enemy, he might be promoted to be a colonel. He was ready to display his heroic boldness on any front. Unexpectedly, when the army reached Pai Sê, he was confined to bed by sickness and could not go on with his troops. After recovering from his illness, he decided to return to Yunnan. There were scattered soldiers everywhere. He gathered about 300 men. When he arrived at Hsi Ch'ou, he by chance met Director-General Pai Chiao-jen, who had been driven out of Ho K'ou by the bandits. He led his 300 men and Director-General Pai's remaining soldiers in a counterattack on Ho K'ou and soundly defeated the enemy. After resuming his office, Director-General Pai advanced Fang to lieutenant-colonel. There were now six districts under his regime. He secretly set up a customs office to collect taxes on imported goods. The taxes collected were used for military supplies for his troops. After two years, with his troops thriving, he secured a colonelcy.

During his five years in this position, besides his military activities, he was engaged in opium trading. He accumulated $15,000,000* from this business. He sent part of his money to his home. His mother bought eighty-five *kung* of farmland and built a large house styled on Western architecture. His family almost overnight became one of the richest in his native district. He bought another house in Kunming, and he took a concubine in Ho K'ou, all for gentility.

Occasionally, he visited home for a few days. When he was at home, he did not associate with the multitude but with a few intimate friends. He did not interfere with local administration. The people who formerly had taunted him became his sycophants.

He still liked to gamble in Ho K'ou and often promoted games among the local prominent gentry. On one occasion he lost $400,000 at the beginning but was able to offset the loss and ended up $150,000 to the good. He remarked that this coup symbolized his entire career.

In 1936, Colonel Fang was reappointed commanding officer of a regiment for suppressing contraband in the area of Yeh Ching. Before leaving Ho K'ou, he bought ten loads of opium to be transported by his troops to the appointed place. Unfortunately, his troops were intercepted by Brigadier-General Ma Ch'ung. Fang lost all his valuables, fourteen pistols, 300 rifles, and ten loads of opium. His loss was estimated at about $5,000,000. Furthermore, Ma Ch'ung reported Fang's opium dealings to the provincial government. In order to escape court-martial, Fang had to ask some influential offi-

* This sum was in the provincial notes of Yunnan, the official rate of which to a silver dollar was ten to one. The silver dollar was worth about half a United States dollar at the normal rate of exchange.

cials of the provincial government for help. To pave the way, he had to use a great deal of his savings. After the trouble was over, he immediately resigned his position. A company commander under Fang said that Ma hated him because Colonel Fang had an opium pipe inlaid with three *liang* of gold, which Ma Ch'ung liked very much but which Colonel Fang had refused to present to him.

After a few months, he was appointed *aide-de-camp* to the provincial government. In 1938, he was reappointed by the Governor to command the guerrilla troops in Ho K'ou. They were to defend the border of Yunnan and Indochina. He was extremely happy, because once again he had a golden opportunity.

After four years, he accumulated $12,000,000 (equivalent to 444,000 silver dollars). He believed that he was wealthy enough and that it was time to retire. He was fifty-two years old. He resigned his position and came back to Kunyang with his family. He bought 150 *kung* of farmland, landscaped a magnificent garden, and rebuilt his ancestors' tomb. When he was at home, he watered flowers and fed fish or birds in his garden. He simply enjoyed himself. He seldom went to the walled City of Kunyang but went to Kunming very often. Although he was admired by the gentry and the people, he was criticized because he had made no contribution to the welfare of Kunyang.

THE GOVERNMENT AS A SOCIAL LADDER

In the community of Kunyang, the public service provided a recognized channel of upward mobility. The careers of a number of prominent gentry members began through officialdom at low ranks. By grasping every opportunity, they succeeded in promoting themselves from the less important and lower-paid ranks to the higher positions. In the village, however, opportunities were limited. Most of the young educated men therefore tried to find positions in the government.

Many bureaucrats were men with slight education but considerable experience. They not only were ambitious but also had learned traditional Chinese official practice and those social techniques that were essential for the successful bureaucrat. For example, according to special official practice, it was customary to address a superior in one way and an inferior in another. The former was addressed "my exalted sir" and the latter "I order you." Although scholarly writing was almost entirely in the vernacular style, the government documents were still couched in a semiclassical style. A bureaucrat was therefore usually the man who was clever enough to master this style and, of course, to outwit his fellow natives. Two life histories are illustrative.

The Life History of Chief Chang

Chang Ko-Chang, the chief of the Department of Civil Affairs of the county government, was born in the city. Chief Chang's ancestors were the residents of a village named Miao Lin Ts'un, which was situated fifteen miles north of the city. They were agricultural people and had about sixty *kung* of farmland. His great-great-grandfather, Chang Fu-tung, had rented out his farmland to tenants and had moved into the city to escape disturbances from bandit raids. After he had settled down in the city, he bought a small house and fifteen *kung* of farmland near the city. He left off farming entirely and turned to business and returned to the village only once a year to collect his rents.

Chief Chang's great-grandfather, Chang Su-sen, was born in the city. Because he was an only son, he inherited all the property of the family and from boyhood had an easy life. When he was twenty-four years old, he began to make friends with gamblers. Every year he spent the rents he had collected from the village, always within a few days. When he was penniless, he would sell land that he owned in the village.

Chief Chang's grandfather, Chang Chia-lin, was also an only son. Since boyhood, he had seen how his father had wasted most of the family property. It served as a warning to him, and he tried very hard to recover the lost property for his family. Although he was illiterate, he was very clever and expressed himself with great force and fluency. But as he was also miserly, he made very few friends.

Chief Chang's father, Chang Wei-lung, was the elder of two brothers, but his younger brother died at eighteen. Since the time of Chang Fu-tung every generation had had only one surviving son. Because of the scarcity of children in the family, Wei-lung was especially loved by his parents from the moment he was born. He began to study in a private school at five. After nine years, he finished the study of the Four Books. He then entered a four-year provincial normal school in Kunming. He studied hard in school but showed special talent only in arithmetic.

After graduation from the normal school he came back to Kunyang and taught arithmetic in the primary school of the county. After two years all his colleagues and students came to respect him as a teacher. He felt very happy, but he had to resign his job in the third year because of an awkward situation. One day, while solving an arithmetic problem on the blackboard, he made a mistake. The students clapped their hands and shouted gleefully, "It is wrong! It is wrong!" He blushed with shame and became quite rigid. One of his colleagues quickly came over and helped him out of his difficulty. But, though the students kept silent about it, he felt so mortified that he resigned his job at once and swore off teaching forever. After resigning his job, he could not find another for almost a year. He was disappointed and depressed.

Later, Wei-lung felt that being a doctor would be a noble occupation and would benefit his family as well as would any other; it not only would bring money but also would win him a reputation. Furthermore, it was an occupation free from the interference of others. He bought some Chinese medical books, *The Medical Herbs of Southern Yunnan* and *The Medical Dictionary,* for example, and studied very hard. When he encountered problems, he would ask the advice of noted doctors in the city. He often invited these men to dinner, asked them to tell him about their experiences, and borrowed medical books from them. He paid special attention to typhus. After studying five years, he began his practice. Owing to his lack of experience, he still felt unsure, and he often consulted with other doctors about the prescriptions he gave his patients. He studied the causes of his patients' illness, and after another four years he became a well-known physician in Kunyang. He passed away at the age of forty-four.

When Wei-lung died, Chief Chang was only twelve. He was too young to assume responsibility for the welfare of his family. Wei-lung's wife was by nature very happy and willing to do any kind of work. After the death of her children and her husband, however, she became so moody that she was forced to look for distraction in order to forget her troubles. In her depression she took no more interest in farm, business, or household. After several years her grief lessened, but by that time the economic condition of her family was very bad.

Chief Chang was Wei-lung's last son. By the time Chief Chang came along, his two brothers and two sisters had died. Chief Chang was thus especially loved by his parents. In the community, one who had no heir was pitied. According to the custom, he could not be buried at the cemetery of his ancestors' tomb. He would be despised as well as pitied by the people because to have no son was considered most shameful. It was the *er sun man tang,* or "the one who has his hall full of children and grand-children," who was rated most highly by the people.

Chief Chang began to study at the age of six. Before then, he had had no opportunity to play with other children, as his parents overprotected him and would not let him out of their sight. When he wanted something, his parents would always give it to him. Perhaps this indulgence was the main cause of Chang's headstrong character. When he began to go to school, he liked it not only because of his parents' encouragement but also because of the companionship of the other children. He was clever and had a very good memory from boyhood on.

Wei-lung's early death made more difficult his family's ascent into the gentry. The last few generations of Chang Wei-lung's family had all been illiterate. But Wei-lung was a graduate of a normal school and, as a schoolteacher, was qualified to be a member of the gentry. His methods in the treatment of disease, which he had learned on the side, made him well known in Kunyang, and gradually this reputation had raised his position to gentry status. He had also made friends in every higher walk of life, educators, officials, officers, and rich merchants. He was generous and ambitious. He intended to let his son have the best education possible in order to contribute to the glory of his family. And, as he died early, his son had to start pushing himself ahead while still young.

After Chang's father's death, his mother wept every day, and he stayed home to look after things. The situation made him fear that he might be taken out of school entirely. He worried: "If I could not continue my study, what could I do then? On whom could my mother and I depend?" Happily enough, three months after his father's death, his mother told him he might go back to school again, impressing on him the hardship it would incur. When he went to school with mingled feelings of sorrow and joy, his teacher and fellow schoolmates came to console him, but their sympathy made him cry the more. Many other schoolmates, who were jealous of his good record, could only talk about his dark future. The alternate coldness and warmth of men's feelings impressed him so deeply that he never trusted them again. His mother was still in deep sorrow, but, when he came home from school, she would dry her tears at once and smile at him. He was deeply inspired by her. He studied hard to prove himself to her, and he drew consolation from reading.

He left the private school when he was thirteen and entered a primary school that had been formed under the new system of education. After three years, he was graduated. At that time the question of his future arose again. He was anxious to continue his studies, but the financial condition of his family did not permit him to do so. He could only study on his own at home during his free time from farm and household.

He married at the age of seventeen. His wife was the daughter of his mother's brother. Though making ends meet was difficult, they had very deep affection for each other. She became his able helper and encouraged him to improve himself.

During those years, he tried his best to find a job but failed again and again. Fortunately, when he was twenty-one years old, he was sent by the county government to the Short-Term Training School of the Bureau of Industry of the Provincial Government on the recommendation of his father-in-law, who was one of the leading gentry members of Kunyang. After three months he was graduated from the school and expected an appointment to an official post, but he did not receive one. He then taught in a primary school. After half a year, he was chosen as technician in the County Bureau of Reconstruction, again on the recommendation of his father-in-law.

At that time his mother's brother encouraged him to practice calligraphy. He used a board painted with red lacquer instead of the usual paper. After filling the face of the board with written characters, he would wash them out, so that he could use it again. Even when he was very busy, he continued to write fifty large characters and 100 small characters daily. After two years he began to be asked by many people to write couplets and scrolls. A year later he had to leave the Bureau. Originally when Chang went with the Bureau, he was enthusiastic about everything and was polite to his colleagues because he knew that both knowledge and experience were lacking to him. After a year, however, he became conceited and self-satisfied. He showed that he despised his colleagues, including the director of the Bureau. As a consequence, he was dismissed by the director.

After leaving, he was appointed clerk under Commander Chu, again through the recommendation of his father-in-law. He was then twenty-four years old. After two years he returned to Kunyang because he could not bear the hardships of a soldier's life.

As he had nothing to do at home, he devoted himself to the study of writing public letters and characters and to the reading of many practical books like *A Manual of Social Intercourse, Daily Practical Literature,* and *Essentials for Writing Good Letters.* After one year, he was appointed clerk in the county guard. Because of the low salary, he resigned after serving one year.

He then went into the rice business. Because he had no capital, he had to borrow money at high interest from others. He profited little.

As he had suffered a great deal and taken many beatings, he had learned a great deal about how to act toward others in order to get on in the world. He saw clearly that, if a man wanted to ascend in the social scale, he had to be an opportunist and do everything possible to gain the approval of society. His words and actions had to conform to the psychology of the gentry and the educated younger generation of the community. He had also to be generally sociable and to secure friends in powerful positions. He himself followed these principles and gradually won the confidence of the public.

The people—especially the young educated people—thought that Chang was an able youth. When the system of voting for the people's political representative of the county was first established and the election for representative was held, Chang was elected. At that time there was only one representative for each county. His name was posted on the gate wall of the county government, and he suddenly became well known in Kunyang. He was only twenty-nine years old.

After he was elected people's political representative, one could hear people talking about the reasons for his success in teashops and restaurants. Some said that he had struggled hard, some that he owed his success to his fine handwriting, others that he was supported by his father-in-law. Many peasants, who had had no chance to see him, even fancied that he was a man of extraordinary talent. During that period he was in high spirits, elated with his success. He played tricks to cheat others. If he had to ask a favor of someone, Chang would flatter and show great respect to that person. Otherwise, he would show him no more consideration than if he were an ant. He became very conceited and cared solely for profit.

When Chang was thirty-four, Magistrate Chen came to Kunyang. Chang visited him very often as people's political representative. He described the general situation at Kunyang to the Magistrate and told him how greatly drought had harmed the crops of the county. He suggested to the Magistrate that a dam be built at the foot of Sung Shan, Mount Sung, to collect the water for irrigating the farms west of the city and that the owners of the farms south and east of the city be taxed so that a twenty-horsepower water pump could be bought. The problem of drought in the area near the city would then be solved completely. With this proposal he won the admiration of the Magistrate and was appointed director of the Bureau of Reconstruction for the county government as successor to Director Tai.

At that time he was happy in his success and promotion. Promotion meant prosperity. He felt that, if his plans were to be carried out, it would be possible both to add to his reputation and to "squeeze" money. Though his suggestions had not been put into action, he was ordered to complete highways from Kunyang to Yüchi and from Kunyang to Chinning, which had been half-done by his predecessor. (The distances were twenty miles for the former and ten miles for the latter.) He selected the workers and supervisors himself and sent a petition to the provincial government to ask for an appropriation of money. The provincial government promised to give ten cents a day for each worker. He, however, withheld the appropriation money from the workers and kept 4,000 silver dollars for himself.

The highways were to be paved with basalt. This stone should have been mined by stonecutters from a region fifteen kilometers away. Expenses were to be paid by the Department of Reconstruction of the provincial government. But he told the workers to pave the highways with stones that could be gathered from the mountains nearby and to mix in only a little basalt. He received a sum of 6,000 silver dollars from the provincial government for further expenses. He "squeezed" all this money too, and with it he built his magnificent house.

The Chinese proverb says, "Everyone respects the rich; but the dog bites those who wear shabby clothes." As he had become the director of the Bureau of Reconstruction and had grafted a great deal of money, the rich and great came running to pay respect to him like so many flies hurrying to sticky flypaper. People who flattered him or sent him gifts came to his home incessantly. The economic condition of his family changed suddenly. He dressed well every day and demanded wine and meat at every meal.

The next year he asked a stonecutter to cut five tombstones and twenty feet of big stone to be placed at his ancestors' tombs. While the work was going on he invited twenty monks and Taoists to chant the canon of Buddhism and to recite dirges. At the same time he built a house of six rooms in both foreign and Chinese styles. The design of the house was the most modern in the community. There were water troughs to drain off rainwater—an innovation unseen before. On the day the beams of the house were to be set up, the guests, about 240 of them, came in an unbroken line. Two-thirds were officials or gentry members of the county. As the host had high prestige, the congratulatory presents were ten times the usual number. Unfortunately, the elder of the two sons of the house died the same day. The righteous people, who saw the hand of heaven in it, whispered that Chang had been *pao ying,* punished in vengeance.

In 1939, Chang was thirty-seven years old. The Magistrate was then Mr. Ho. The Bureau of Reconstruction had been changed to the Department of Reconstruction, and Chang was appointed its head. After half a year, the county government was ordered to construct a highway from Kunyang to Anning. The route of the highway cut across many farms. Many of the farmers who wished to save their farms bribed Chang to change the route. He made a great deal of money. He also sold the government basalt to the stonecutters who built the stone bridges. It was estimated that he filched about $200,000 (equivalent to 8,000 silver dollars).

In 1940, he was reappointed head of the Department of Civil Affairs. Though he had no chance for graft in this job, he took advantage of his position to run a business. He borrowed a large sum of money from the Society of Farm Loans of the Farmers Bank of China. He borrowed it at a very low rate of interest, but the interest accumulated rapidly due to inflation. He used the money to buy iron and hoarded it until prices went up. He bought iron at $5 a *ching* and after three months was able to sell it for $25 a catty. Then he bought salt at $8 a *ching* and sold it after four months at $16. He again bought iron and sold it when the price went up. It was estimated he made about $1,500,000 (equivalent to 166,000 silver dollars) on this type of speculation. The profit was equally divided between the head of the society and himself.

He cultivated a close friendship with Magistrate Ho. For the Magistrate's birthday he suggested to the members of the gentry that they present him with a eulogistic scroll along with gifts in honor of his virtuous administration. As a result, Magistrate Ho liked Chang very much and often invited him to his bedroom to teach him the music to various verses. As Chang was a good friend to the Magistrate and the Magistrate agreed with his opinions and honored his requests, he took advantage of his position to obtain bribes of various sorts. When Magistrate Ho was dismissed by the provincial government, Chief Chang suggested that the gentry build a pavilion in his honor.

In 1943 the people complained about Magistrate Chao's corruption and inefficiency. Chief Chang felt that backing the people's complaints to the government was a golden opportunity. He solicited the aid of Wu Li-shih, Chairman Wu (of the Chamber of Commerce of Kunyang), Liao Ko-chang (head of the Department of Conscription), Ting Chên-chang (chief of a district government), and others to suggest that the Citizens' Political Council hold a meeting. In the meeting a special committee to accuse the Magistrate was organized. Chairman Wu, Chief Liao, Chief Ting, and Chang himself were elected by the committee as representatives. They went to Kunming for this purpose.

This task was not easy because the wife of the Magistrate, Mrs. Chao, and the Governor's wife were sworn sisters. Mrs. Chao went to Kunming for help. At that time the gentry of Kunyang was divided into three groups: one anti-Magistrate Chao, the leader of which was Chief Chang; the second pro-Magistrate Chao, the leader of which was the eldest son of Commander Chu; the third group neutral, the leader of which was the third son of Chairman Wang. It was difficult to judge who would win in the struggle to overthrow Magistrate Chao.

In this crisis, Chief Chang used desperate measures. He was advised by his nephew, who was *aide-de-camp* of the commander, to offer a bribe of half a million dollars to the eldest son of the Governor, who was then the commander of a division. As he was a very good friend of ex-Magistrate Ho, who was then the general secretary of the Provincial Administrators Training School, he asked Mr. Ho to help him write the petitions. He also published the facts of Magistrate Chao's corruption in the newspapers in Kunming and distributed handbills in Kunming and Kunyang to enlist favorable public opinion. After four months of heavy propaganda he attained his goal, and Magistrate Chao was dismissed.

During Chief Chang's stay in Kunming to accuse Magistrate Chao, his position in the county became insecure. He did not dare go home for fear of reprisals from Magistrate Chao until the latter was actually dismissed and a new magistrate appointed. When the newly appointed Magistrate came to the county to take over his office, Chief Chang and the other representatives of the Committee to Accuse Magistrate Chao followed him back to Kunyang.

After their return to Kunyang, reaction was rife. There was street fighting between the pro- and con-Magistrate Chao groups;

and the Committee to Accuse Magistrate Chao was renamed the Committee for Settling Magistrate Chao's Accounts and Debts. Magistrate Chao was detained in Kunyang by the new Magistrate and the committee.

The total expense of bringing charges against Magistrate Chao was $1,002,000 (equivalent to 3,800 silver dollars). The money was advanced by Chairman Wu, Chief Liao, and Chief Chang himself.

After several meetings of the Committee for Settling Magistrate Chao's Accounts and Debts and the Citizens' Political Council, a preliminary report was published. It said that Magistrate Chao had taken more than 400 *shih* of government rice for himself. Other items of Magistrate Chao's corruption were still under discussion.

When the new Magistrate arrived at Kunyang, a big dinner party was given by the county government in his honor. I was sitting at the same table with the two magistrates, Commander Chu, and others.

During the dinner, Commander Chu said: "After having served the government for a long period, I could only build a small house like this. But he [Chang] served the government only a few years, and has built a house far bigger and better than mine." Chu shook his head with a deep sigh.

At the beginning, the new Magistrate did not appoint Chang to any position because he had been the main instigator in the action against Magistrate Chao. After three months, however, the new Magistrate made Chang head of the Department of Civil Affairs of the county government. At that time Chang considered himself a bringer of progress to his native place. He made a great show of his conceit. When common people bowed to him in the street, he raised his head and did not pay any attention to them. When he met a superior, however, Chief Chang would beam on him politely and earnestly.

The following year he was reappointed head of the Department of Conscription of the county government. He knew that martial law was much stricter than ordinary civil law and thus acted very carefully. If corruption were reported to him and the investigation proved to be true, he would petition the magistrate to file charges. He seemed very just.

In 1944 Colonel Liang, once an army officer, came to Kunyang to enforce conscription. Chief Chang sent $50,000 (equivalent to 64 silver dollars in 1944) to him. The officer was honest and refused to accept the money. With urging, however, he finally accepted $20,-

000 for his daily expenses. Because of the officer's purchased leniency, conscription was not carried out satisfactorily. The officer was recalled. Another officer, Colonel Su, came to Kunyang in his place. Colonel Liang told the story of the bribe to Colonel Su. The latter pretended to be incorruptible and sent his helpers to the county government to investigate the report. The Magistrate was asked to send Chang to Colonel Su. Chief Chang knew that the officer simply wanted to extort money and presented $100,000 to him immediately. Later Chief Chang told others that "with money you can make the devil turn your mill."

In January, 1945, Chief Chang was invited by Magistrate Ho, who was then Magistrate of Yi-mên, to be his general secretary. After half a year Chang returned to Kunyang and was appointed head of the Department of Civil Affairs of the county government.

The main reason for Chang's success was his shrewdness. He saw how local affairs stood and guided himself accordingly. He did not get into trouble with his grafting. A "self-made" man without much schooling, he was proud, cold, and snobbish as well as able and realistic. Even in 1946 at forty-three he was prominent among the gentry of middle age. Many people were afraid of him because of his malicious ways. If one were not on good terms with him, he might make trouble. On the other hand, one could never count on his remaining friendly.

The Life History of Chairman Tsao

Both Chief Chang and Chairman Tsao were capable men. Their successes depended not on their family backgrounds but on their abilities. They had quite different personalities, however. Chang was an opportunist and an unscrupulous bureaucrat, while Tsao represented an energetic fighter for justice and honesty.

Chairman Tsao was born in a village named Hui Ch'ang. The village was located four miles north of the walled City of Kunyang, and, according to the 1942 census, had a population of 815 people. Chairman Tsao's grandfather had been a farmer and had had fifteen *kung* of farmland. Because of his industry and thrift, the family managed well enough.

Chairman Tsao's father was the elder of two brothers. When he was thirty years old, he and his younger brother divided their property. After five years, the economic condition of his family began gradually to improve. It kept improving until he died at the age of forty-six.

When his father died, Chairman Tsao was only nine years old. Under the economic pressure of his family, he was made to seek his own fortune at an early age. He went to the walled city and served as an assistant in an opium den. He worked without wage except board and room. As he was very witty, everyone liked him very much. The customers often gave him tips for service. He saved the money and gave it all to his mother. Meanwhile, he learned to read and write from his master's son, who was two or three years older than he. After two years, he went to serve as an apprentice at a grocery store. His annual wage was 40 catties of rice in addition to his board, room, and clothes. He learned to keep accounts and to figure with the abacus there. After three years, his annual wage was increased to 160 catties of rice. In this way, the economic condition of his family gradually improved.

When he was sixteen years old, he requested his mother to allow him to enter a private school. Because he was very intelligent and had an excellent memory, he easily proved himself the best student in the school. When he was twenty years old, he entered the Provincial Policemen Training School in Kunming through competitive examination. After six months, he was graduated from the school and was made a sergeant. During these years he found that the officials were corrupt, that the local hoodlums were savage and unreasonable, and that the people had little moral sense. He saw that the feelings of the people changed with the winds of fortune, that social justice was all but nonexistent. He was discontented and grumbled every day. He lessened his wrath somewhat by unburdening himself in a diary he regularly kept.

But he could not keep silent about what he knew any longer and started to contribute some reports to the newspapers. But the newspapers did not publish his reports because his literary style was not good enough. He tried many times and failed again and again. Only once was a report of his published. He was very happy at his success.

He was not interested in the work of the police force. After serving for two years, he resigned his post and became a reporter for a newspaper in Kunming. He paid special attention to injustice. On one occasion, he investigated the Provincial Bureau of Taxation. He reported the corruption of the Bureau and the dark dealings of the tax-collecting administration. He described in detail how the powerful and wealthy evaded their taxes with personal letters or simply visiting cards, while the small businessman's goods were confiscated on the basis of false reports. As a consequence, he was arrested on charges pressed by the director of the Bureau of Taxation, found guilty, and sentenced to work as a laborer on the highway for three days. Meanwhile, he was dismissed by the newspaper under the influence of the director of the Bureau. As he could not find another job, he went back to Kunyang.

When he was twenty-six years old, he entered the Provincial Administrators Training School through competitive examination. He studied diligently in the school. He was graduated number one in his class. He was then appointed to the directorship of the Bureau of Reconstruction of Kunyang. He suddenly became one of the leading gentry members in Kunyang. He was especially admired for his great courage and sense of rightness. He was good at writing official letters. He was sociable and eloquent. He was sagacious and full of stratagems.

In 1920, a battalion of the irregular army arrived at Kunyang. The soldiers looted the people and raped the women of the region. The residents escaped to the mountains and dared not come back home. Chairman Tsao fabricated an official letter from the provincial government, which exhorted the county government of Kunyang to hold up under the devastation of the bandit raids until the arrival of a vast army slated for arrival in a few days. The fabricated official letter stated that the whole group of bandits would soon be annihilated. Tsao counterfeited the seals of the provincial government with soap. He then visited the colonel of the army with the forged letter and pretended to be sympathetic with him. He said: "As your officers and soldiers have been on good terms with the people of Kunyang, I come to inform you of this secret order out of my own personal feelings for you. It has some bearing on the life of your army." He showed him the spurious official letter. The colonel apparently regarded it as true because the troops moved out of Kunyang that very night. After Tsao had brought off this coup, the gentry and the people of Kunyang held him in high esteem. He was selected commander of the county guard of Kunyang and a member of the Committee of Public Finance of the county. He became one of the most powerful members of the gentry. He not only had high prestige but also enjoyed a high standard of living. His mother moved into the city to live with him.

In 1931, he proposed to repair the Confucian temple and the Palace of the God of Literature. He urged that the County of Kunyang increase its educational funds and reform such backward customs as keeping queue for the men and binding the feet of the women. In order to expand the sources of public finance, he suggested that the people investigate the public funds and public farmland of the county. As a result, a total amount of 110 *kung* of farmland that had formerly been kept hidden by juggling with the surveyor's figures was restored. Tsao also charged the chief of the district government with corruption and had him put in jail. After that, all the local officials and members of the gentry who were suspected of being corrupt hated him.

In 1932, when the People's Political Council was organized, he was elected the first chairman. The next year, when he was fifty-two years of age, Chairman Tsao suggested that the Tower of Jade Emperor, the Most Exalted Highest Emperor God, be built on the peak of Mount Moon in the walled city. This temple had three stories, and the buildings and grounds were to be magnificently adorned with paintings and sculptured pieces.

In 1943, the village named Pa Li Ts'un of Kunyang had a dispute with two villages named Jou San and Liu Mu of the County of Chinning over a reservoir that was important for the irrigation of the villagers' farms. Jou San and Liu Mu sent more than a hundred able-bodied men to Pa Li Ts'un and threatened to fight. Pa Li Ts'un could not rival them in manpower and thus invited Chairman Tsao to mediate. The people of Jou San and Liu Mu were headstrong and did not heed his mediation efforts. He therefore wrote a petition to the provincial government for Pa Li Ts'un. The provincial government sent an official to the villages to investigate the case, and he gave his verdict in favor of Pa Li Ts'un. The people of Pa Li Ts'un were grateful to Tsao. They accordingly presented him with 1,000 silver dollars and five *kung* of farmland and established a memorial tablet in the village in his honor as a reward for his service. In the meantime, he bought a piece of land in the city and built a store of two rooms with painted pillars and carved beams. His son sold books and imported medicine for the store. Consequently, the gentry and the people suspected him of corruption and grafting with the fund for building the Tower of Jade Emperor. His house was thus nicknamed Hsiao Yü Huang Ko, "Little Tower of Jade Emperor." He was immediately put in an unfavorable light.

As he was then Chairman of the People's Political Council, a member of the Committee of Public Finance of the county, commander of the county guard, and a secretary and part-time teacher at the normal and junior middle school, he was accused of being a dictator in local affairs and of being corrupt. King Pen-shou, his enemy, agitated the members of the Association of Kunyang Fellow Natives Who Lived in Kunming, and the members of the Association of the Students from Kunyang who studied in the provincial capital to oppose Chairman Tsao. They accused him in the local court in Kunming of stealing from the public fund. During the hearing, his speech was clear and forcible, and his appearance was serious but undisturbed. King, the plaintiff, became afraid of losing the case and bribed the judge with $10,000. Chairman Tsao was put in jail. Later he found out about the bribery and appealed to the high court. Eventually, his character was publicly cleared.

After release from jail, he rid himself of all community involvement. He simply taught civics at the normal school and junior middle school and now and then wrote petitions for litigants. If the suit was serious, the fee was 240 *ching* of rice for each petition.

During his twenty-five years in power, he had never blackmailed a soul. He might have grafted a little money, but he bought no farmland at all except enough to build a store of two rooms upon. After his death in 1940, his family rapidly declined. This decline was the most convincing proof of his honesty. During the years of the Japanese War, although a certain amount of corruption was expected, the people considered the officials and the gentry who controlled the local government excessively greedy. By contrast, the people remembered Tsao, in the long run, as a talented, upright, and honest gentleman.

COMMERCE AS A SOCIAL LADDER

There were seven market towns in Kunyang. The total residential population of the seven towns, according to our census taken on March 1, 1942, was 5,927 persons, most of whom were engaged in business of some sort. Almost every day of every lunar month (twenty-nine or thirty days) was a market day. Though the residential population of the seven towns was only 8.6% of the total residential population (69,234) of the county, it is evident that the importance of commercial activities was much greater than the actual number of established shops would indicate.

The *hsien cheng,* the City of Kunyang, was a political, educational, cultural, handicraft, and commercial center with market days on the fifth, ninth, fifteenth, nineteenth, twenty-fifth, and twenty-ninth days of every lunar month. It was the largest among the seven market towns. The residential population of the city in 1942 was

3,547 persons. The richest merchants of the county lived there, and the Chamber of Commerce was the most powerful organization. In the city, of course, commercial activity was a part of the routine of living. Much of what was consumed had to be bought. Commercial activities might be carried on entirely in a shop, directly between homes and periodic markets, or between Kunyang and outside districts like Yüchi and Kunming on particular commercial trips. It was on market days, however, that business life was in full swing. The people coming from the villages and the neighboring counties might swell the figures to a hundred times more than the residential population of the city. The main street and avenues were crowded with trading people. Varieties of commodities were assembled in different sections—grain, livestock, farm implements, vegetables and meat, charcoal and firewood, and so on. Every available space was used. Two life histories are cited for illustration.

The Life History of K'ung Tu-k'uei

K'ung Tu-k'uei was born in the City of Kunyang. His great-grandfather, K'ung Lian-sung, had studied in a private school for ten years and had then become a teacher. His wife had operated a grocery store.

Tu-k'uei's grandfather, K'ung Tan-ching, entered his father's private school at the age of six and was especially trained by his father. He received the degree of *hsiu ts'ai* at the age of seventeen, *chü jen* at twenty-one, and *chin shih* at twenty-five. He was admired by the gentry and the people as *shao nien te chih*, "a youth who has realized his wishes."

Tu-k'uei's father, K'ung Wei-han, was an only son. He had an easy life from childhood. He entered a private school at eight and had for his teacher a friend of his father. He was given special care by his teacher in the daytime and again taught by his father at night. He became the best student in the school. He received the degree of *hsiu ts'ai* at nineteen years old and *chü jen* at twenty-one. After receiving the degree of *chü jen,* he took up teaching, but he still studied very hard. He received the degree of *chin shih* at twenty-five. As both he and his father had received the degree of *chin shih* at the same age, the Emperor bestowed upon his family the plaque of *hsuang chin shih, "chin shih* in pairs."

Tu-k'uei's mother was very capable. All the affairs of the household were managed by her. The family had ninety-seven *kung* of farmland and operated a large grocery store of three rooms. Because of her mild and pleasant disposition, the business of her store was quite prosperous. She gave birth to four sons and two daughters, all of whom were more influenced by their mother than by their father.

Tu-k'uei was the eldest of the four brothers. His first younger brother, Yao-kuang, studied six years in a private school. He was very clever and precocious but mischievous. He started chasing girls when he was only eleven or twelve years old. When he was fifteen or sixteen years of age, he devoted himself to learning such musical instruments as the guitar, flute, and Chinese violin. All these musical instruments he could play very well. After his marriage at eighteen, he still did nothing significant. His friends among the fair sex were numberless, and he never changed his direction throughout his life. He was therefore despised by his family and lineage members. Fortunately, his wife was able and virtuous. She kept the grocery store going. Tu-k'uei's second younger brother, Mao-sen, studied five years in a private school. He had a very strong character and a hot temper. He was both bold and shrewd. He served in the army from his twenty-first birthday to the age of thirty and when he resigned was a captain and a company commander. Later he also operated a grocery store. Tu-k'uei's youngest brother, Chi-nan, studied three years in a private school. He also operated a grocery. But among the four brothers, Tu-k'uei was the only one who became a really successful merchant.

Tu-k'uei entered a private school at the age of seven. Though he was encouraged by both his father and grandfather, he had no interest in academic work. He studied five years but made little progress. He was married at seventeen years of age to a girl from a wealthy family.

Because his father did not care about the affairs of the large family, Tu-k'uei had to help his mother manage the farm and business of the household from his sixteenth year. He carried out his mother's daily orders for the business and farm and had all her trust because he was careful and responsible. After several years, he was quite well versed in both agriculture and commerce. And, as his father was a member of the gentry, he usually had his way with the people. If he wanted to do any business, the people would be glad to help him. Between the ages of seventeen and twenty-seven, he engaged in various kinds of trade, such as the buying and selling of rice and pigs and the smuggling of opium.

When he was thirty-seven years old, the family wealth was divided because the sisters-in-law often quarreled with one another. Though the family had ninety-eight *kung* of farmland and a house of seven rooms, it was quite large, and after the division no single portion was worth mentioning. While managing the household, however, Tu-k'uei had taken various means to amass a sum of 500 silver dollars for himself. He asked his wife to send the money to his father-in-law to lend it out at usury for him. After thirteen years, the money grew to a large sum, and Tu-k'uei at last had the capital for real business. He bought rice in Kunyang and transported it for sale in Kunming. His grocery store and twenty-five *kung* of farmland were mainly managed by his wife. After ten years, he bought ten more *kung* of farmland.

In 1939, he established a liquor factory to produce alcohol. It required a large sum of capital. He organized four credit unions for $10,000, $20,000, $30,000, and $40,000 respectively, amassing a total sum of $100,000 (equivalent to 40,000 silver dollars at the end of 1939). As prices kept going up, so did his stockpile of hoarded goods.

Tu-k'uei used the $100,000 to purchase 240 piculs of barley and millet and thirty pigs. All his farms were used for growing barley and millet instead of rice. In this way he could harvest eighty piculs of barley and millet each year. The distillery's grains were used for feeding pigs, while the pig-raising itself made fertilizer for his farms. The pigs were sold after being raised for half a year. He thus sold pigs twice a year, and each time he earned a profit of $1,500,000. His alcohol business was equally prosperous. After two years, he accumulated $5,000,000 (equivalent to 178,600 silver dollars). He bought thirty *kung* of farmland.

Each year he bought his extra barley and millet at harvest time because at that time prices were lower than at any other time of the year. The quantity of barley and millet he bought would be enough for brewing liquor for a whole year. In the meantime, he lent money to the farmers when he could between crops, under the guise of buying their goods in advance. The farmer thus sold his goods before the harvest at still lower prices. For example, in May, 1944, Tu-k'uei lent money to farmers at the price of $400 for each local *sheng* (eight catties) of barley. When the farmer repaid with barley in October, 1944, the price of barley was $1,800 for each *sheng*.

In 1944, when the price of gold went up rapidly, Tu-k'uei bought 40 *liang* of gold in Kunming at $130,000 each. After half a year, he sold the gold at $250,000 for each *liang*. He easily netted $4,800,000. He bought twenty-five *kung* more farmland.

After one month, he bought thirty *liang* of gold at $280,000 each. With the surrender of Japan, the price of gold suddenly dropped. He had to sell out for $180,000 a *liang*. This time he lost $3,000,000. After the start of civil strife between the Nationalists and the Communists, prices went up again. In November, 1945, he bought twenty *liang* of gold at $65,000 each and hoarded it until the price went up to $360,000 a *liang*. He made a net profit of $5,900,-000. He profiteered during the Japanese War and the civil war and became one of the richest merchants in Kunyang in a few years. In May, 1946, he usually kept $20,000,000 (equivalent to 5,500 silver dollars) cash on hand for conducting business.

In 1946, some members of the gentry accused Magistrate Huang of corruption and the Magistrate was dismissed by the provincial government. The move was backed up mainly by the wealthier merchants. The Magistrate had offended them by his severe suppression of opium dealing and by prohibiting the use of grain for brewing liquor. Tu-k'uei was one of the figures behind the action. When Magistrate Chao had been accused and dismissed, seven-tenths of the gentry had joined in the action. But when Magistrate Huang was accused and was dismissed, only three-tenths of the gentry participated. Even the Citizens' Political Council was pro-Magistrate Huang. These actions illustrated the rise of the merchant class during the wartime.

Tu-k'uei was humble and modest. He was amiable to all kinds of people but carefully selected his friends. He was diligent, thrifty, and cautious all his life. He never smoked but occasionally drank a little wine. He was sixty-four years old in 1946 and still very strong.

The Life History of Hsia Shou-kai

Hsia Shou-kai was born in 1894 in the City of Kunyang. His great-grandfather, Hsia Fa-ken, had originally lived in a village named Nan Tou Ts'un, which was about fourteen miles northwest of the walled city. Fa-ken was a poor farmer.

Hsia Shou-kai's grandfather, Hsia Chung-tai, was an only son. When he was fifteen years old, he started in business by buying and selling charcoal. He usually transported charcoal from Erh Chieh to the City of Kunyang with his two horses. He could save money equivalent to sixteen *ching* of rice each trip. After two years, he bought two more horses. He worked from daybreak to evening every day. After thirty years, he had accumulated quite a bit of money. But one day he went to a village twenty miles away, taking all his money and four horses to buy lumber. To his ill fortune several robbers took all his money and the four horses and bound him in a cave. He was able to free himself and came back home. But the earnings of more than thirty years toil were completely gone. Hsia Chung-tai went out of his mind. He sat and cried every day until his death.

Hsia Shou-kai's father, Hsia Fo-sen, had to be hired out as a cattle tender for a landowner without any compensation except food and shelter. After four years, he was raised to eighty *ching* of rice a year. When he was nineteen years old, Fo-sen's wage was raised to 400 *ching* of rice a year. It was the highest wage for a farm laborer in the area. The economic condition of his family improved gradually.

The family's calamity served as a sharp warning that there was no safety in the country. Fo-sen determined to go to the city even if he had to become a beggar there. After his father passed away, Fo-sen took the opportunity to realize his wishes. He leased his house and farmland and went to the City of Kunyang, with his mother and his wife, to seek his livelihood.

Once in the City of Kunyang, Fo-sen rented a room, and he, his wife, and his mother hired themselves out as casual laborers. After two years, he rented twenty *kung* of farmland. By the age of forty-two, Fo-sen was able to buy ten *kung* of his farmland and still rent the other ten *kung*. His economic condition was improving steadily.

Hsia Shou-kai was an only son. His parents loved him very much. After he was born, his mother consulted one fortune-teller after another, and all informed her that, according to his "eight characters," he was a child of good fortune and would have no need to worry about his livelihood. She was overjoyed to hear it and became confident. When he was seven years old, Shou-kai was sent to a private school at his mother's insistence. He was especially encouraged by his mother and studied very hard in the school. After three years, however, he had to discontinue his schooling because of the drought and a setback to his family.

Two years previously, when he had been eight years old, his family had been fairly comfortable, and all the neighbors considered it a "newly rising family."* He was engaged to the only daughter of a wealthy merchant. Though the social standing of the two families was not equal, the "eight characters" of the boy made up in fate what he

* The proverb says, "Chia hsin chi, t'ao lao chia," which means "choose your son-in-law from a newly rising family; choose your daughter-in-law from an old family." A newly rising family was one with good prospects.

lacked in fortune. His fiancee was clever and pretty, but after the engagement his family declined because of the droughts. Still, though many people said that the engagement was a big mistake, the parents of the girl believed it to be predestined and did not complain.

Hsia Shou-kai married at the age of twenty. After marriage, he and his wife came to love each other. When he was in distress at his poverty, she would console and strengthen him. She had accumulated a large sum of money when she was still with her family. She used part of it as capital to set her husband up in business. He engaged in buying and selling rice. And because his father-in-law was a wealthy merchant, he was held to be a good credit risk.

After five years, he bought twenty *kung* of farmland. When he was thirty-two years old, he added another twenty-five *kung* of farmland. His investment in the rice business was also enlarged. He often bought thirty piculs of rice at a time.

When he was thirty-three years old, Shou-kai's eldest brother-in-law was also in the rice business, his second brother-in-law was an agent of salt transportation in Hai Kou (twelve miles north of the city), and his third brother-in-law was running a grocery store. All their businesses were large and prosperous. Hsia Shou-kai channeled all his money into the business of buying and selling rice. He bought rice in Kunyang and transported it to Kunming. He would go to Kunming with his eldest brother-in-law, who had more extensive connections there than he had himself. His wife operated a store selling salt, which she put on the market for her second brother. She simply paid the money after the salt had been sold, and she therefore needed no capital. Shou-kai's mother had also set up a stall to market salt.

By the time Hsia Shou-kai had turned thirty-six, his second brother-in-law was the agent of salt transportation for three counties —Kunyang, Yüchi, and Tung Hai. Shou-kai invested all his own money in 20,000 *liang* of opium and hoarded it. He then devoted himself to marketing salt, which he transported from his second brother-in-law in Hai Kou, and he therefore needed no capital. He monopolized the supply of salt in Kunyang. When the price of salt was going down, if a merchant wanted to buy salt from him, he would demand that he pay all the money in advance. Then he would go off to Hai Kou to transport salt for his contract. When the price of salt was going up, he would not accept any money in advance but would require that he be paid at the time of delivery. He was well informed by his brother-in-law about the current market and the conditions of the salt supply. He accumulated $20,000 in a single year. He also made loans to others at a monthly compounded interest of 8%. If someone wanted to borrow money from him, he had to pledge his farmland for security. Shou-kai was thus able to obtain fifty *kung* of farmland in 1924 and eighty-five *kung* in 1926. All his farmland came from his debtors. He became a prominent landlord with 186 *kung* of farmland. He also bought a store of three rooms for $30,000. He rented his farmland to tenants and collected 336 piculs of rice each year.

In 1928, the price of opium went up because of the government's policy of suppression. Hsia Shou-kai traveled the country buying opium every day. He worked for two months and then stopped because he felt it did not pay. He bought opium on the market in Kunyang and smuggled it to Kunming. He operated a grocery store in the City of Kunyang as a front.

In 1933, he sold half the 20,000 *liang* of opium that he had hoarded and bought a house outside the West Gate of Kunming to establish a factory for husking rice. Later, he moved his family to Kunming. After three years, he had accumulated $50,000. He felt that it was inconvenient for him to go back and forth to collect the rice rents from his tenants. He therefore rented his rice store and moved his family back to Kunyang. He operated the original grocery and started a wholesale business selling salt. In one year, 1937, he bought 130 loads of salt and netted a profit of $150,000. He bought another fifty *kung* of farmland and a house of three large rooms. He became one of the wealthiest merchants and landlords of Kunyang.

Although he was rich, he was frugal, industrious, prudent, and in fact stingy. Usually he did not associate with people except for business. In order to evade conscription and various provincial taxes, he and his family moved to Kunming again. At the same time, he transported 12,000 *ching* of tobacco with him. In Kunming he resumed control of his rice store. He came back to Kunyang for his rents once a year. After collecting the rents, he would take rice with him back to Kunming. When he was at Kunyang, he stayed either with his relatives or tenants and paid them nothing. Shou-kai was often criticized for his cunning and his sharp dealings. Though his wife and children liked good meals and handsome clothes, he himself usually dressed in rags and ate worse than his tenants. He was nick-named *yu ch'ien ti hua-tzŭ,* "rich beggar." Though he himself had had little schooling, his two sons were graduated from middle school and the military academy, and his two daughters studied in a middle school in Kunming. His family was considered promising.

NOTES

1. *Cf*. The Institute of Pacific Relations, *Agrarian China: Selected Source Materials from Chinese Authors,* translated and edited by Research Staff of the Chinese Secretariat (London: George Allen & Unwin, 1939), p. 251.
2. *Cf*. Hsiao-tung Fei and Chih-i Chang, *Earthbound China: A Study of Rural Economy in Yunnan* (Chicago: The University of Chicago Press, 1945), p. 279.

6

Upward Mobility
by the
Avenue of Marriage

Marriage had been regarded as a family affair and had been customarily defined as an alliance of two families. Choice of mate was made on grounds of family status. Through marriage big families were often confederated into powerful groups. Sometimes there was a mutual "gravitation" between the wealthy but politically powerless family and the powerful but comparatively poorer family. In that way, one obtained political protection, the other financial support. For example, when Captain Yang was at the height of his power, his daughter was betrothed to the eldest son of Wu Chi-min, who was one of the wealthiest merchants in the City of Kunyang. After Captain Yang was assassinated, however, the engagement was dissolved.

The "equality of gates and doors" principle applied to the influence of intermarriage on the individual's social mobility. Marriage between two families of different strata provided an important means of social circulation. In that way many lower-status people made successful careers. We have given Mr. Hsia's life history, emphasizing commerce as a social ladder. But it should be noted that, following his marriage, his father-in-law's influence and money started him up the ladder of success in trade.

The life history of Chief Ting furnishes a typical example of upward mobility through the avenue of marriage. Chief Ting came

195

from a leading gentry family. But when Ting's grandfather died, Ting's father was only fifteen years old. Because Ting's uncle squandered the family property, Ting received only a small amount of education and little training for a career. Following his marriage into another leading gentry family (through his distinguished family line instead of his own efforts), the influence and wealth of his father-in-law helped him to achieve a brilliant career in business and the bureaucracy.

The Life History of Chief Ting

Chief Ting's remote ancestors came from Lan Chi (the famous commercial center of eastern Chekiang), Chekiang Province, during the Yuan Dynasty. His family was descended from Ting Huai-yin.* His ancestors had been either high officers or scholars. The first to come to Kunyang came as commander of the army and brought with him prosperity for succeeding generations. Chief Ting's great-grandfather, Ting Nai-huan, had been the richest man in Kunyang. His business was the transportation of salt from where it was produced to Kunyang.

Chief Ting's grandfather, Ting Mu-tseng, inherited a great fortune from his father. After Nai-huan's death, Mu-tseng devoted himself to trading in rice. He also managed thirty *kung* of farmland with the help of two long-term laborers. Although he had had only four years' schooling, he could keep accounts and was good at calculating on the abacus.

When Chief Ting's grandfather died, Chief Ting's father was fifteen. On his deathbed, Ting Mu-tseng called his two sons to his side and gave them his final message: "Our family is a family that has cultivated the polite arts, loyalty, filial piety, and etiquette. The fortunes of our family have never declined. This may be attributed to our care for our ancestors. You should preserve this prosperity for those to come. All of the Tings have kept on the proper road. I hope that both of you may follow along it when I am gone." This statement Chief Ting's father tried to remember well. But Chief Ting's uncle put it out of his mind.

After the death of Chief Ting's grandfather, their home was wholly under the management of Chief Ting's uncle. Although this

* It was said that Ting Huai-yin had been a magistrate of Ch'ü Fu in Shantung Province during the Ming Dynasty and had been nationally famous for his honesty and justice. He was called Ting Ta Sheng Jen or "Great Saint Ting."

uncle was also an educated man (he had studied in a private school for five years), he was not following the right road. Through drinking and gambling he squandered most of the family property. Ting's father had no right to interfere in what his elder brother did, and therefore, a few years later, when the property was divided, Chief Ting's father received only ten *kung* of farmland and six rooms of what had been an immense household.

Chief Ting's mother was very bright and capable. After her marriage, she foresaw that the property of their household would be quickly squandered by her brother-in-law and insisted that her husband make the division then and there. But before reaching her thirty-fifth birthday, despite her thrift, she was so poor that she had to support her family by selling doughnuts. Though all her neighbors laughed at her in secret, she was confident that she would rise above them again in the future. She often said that she was "Pin kuo ming, lao lai hung" (Her fate will be like that of an apple, which becomes red when it ripens, that is, she would be prosperous when she became old; the color red symbolized prosperity). She also said, "Suffering while young is unimportant; it is suffering while old that should be avoided." She was fifty-eight in 1946 but was still going strong.

Chief Ting's father, Ting Hsiao-chih, was a mild and honest fellow. Though he did go at times to a teashop or to a restaurant for a little wine, he sat in a corner and did not gossip with others. When he was young, he was rather handsome. He studied in a private school for more than ten years, finished the Four Books and the Five Classics when he was fifteen, and received the degree of *hsiu ts'ai* at seventeen. He then devoted himself to teaching. But he cared nothing about his family, even when there was no more rice or salt at home, and let his wife take the whole responsibility for the family. Only once, when his wife was about to have a child and could not support the family, did he lease five of his six rooms to obtain money for support. As he was always in debt, he was always discouraged.

Because of the poverty of his family, when he was still a child Chief Ting had to work to help his mother. When he was six years old, his father sent him to school to study, but he often played truant. He studied in a private school for four years. After leaving school, he could find nothing to do. He simply wandered.

When he was eighteen, Chief Ting's mother tried to find a girl for him. Though the go-between asked many girls, no one was interested. When the go-between mentioned that the young man was Ting, the girls' parents immediately refused. After half a year, however, one of the leading gentry members promised to marry his daughter to Ting. This gentleman, named Su Po-lan, was the commander of the Corps of People's Self-Defense of Kunyang. He had a high regard for morality and thought that the success or failure of a person depended wholly on his virtue. If the ancestors of a family were able and virtuous, even though the descendants were in adversity, the family would still be a *fa chia,* or "rising family." When he traced the genealogy of Chief Ting and found that he was the descendant of Ting Huai-yin, he decided to give him his daughter. As Ting's family was poor, the engagement gifts his parents sent to Su Po-lan's family were insignificant. Su Po-lan knew in advance that he would have to help his son-in-law.

Chief Ting married at twenty. The wedding ceremony was arranged as simply as possible. On the other hand, because the girl was Su Po-lan's only daughter and because Su was wealthy and had high status, he invited more than 400 guests. According to custom, half the dowry was to be paid by the bridegroom's family and the other half by the bride's family. But Ting's family paid nothing at all.

After the marriage the young couple came to love each other very much. Ting's wife was virtuous and capable. She would console him when he worried about his economic condition and encourage him when he was disappointed. She told him that she would persuade her father to advance some capital for some sort of enterprise. Ting admired his wife and complied with whatever she said. At the same time, Su Po-lan was thinking that it was not good for his son-in-law not to have a permanent occupation. He requested his friend, Chien Tsai-wan, who was one of the area's richest merchants and opium dealers, to accept Ting as an apprentice in his shop. Chien Tsai-wan thought, however, that it was improper to accept Commander Su's son-in-law as an apprentice and declined his request. At last, Commander Su invested 300 silver dollars in Chien Tsai-wan's shop on the condition that Chien would accept his son-in-law as an apprentice. Chien Tsai-wan then felt that, as Commander Su was nominally a partner, the youth could be employed.

Thenceforth, not only had Ting a place to earn his living, but he also had the beginnings of a career. Though his reputation with the local people was bad, he became careful and industrious. He decided to get ahead in earnest. He was the last one to go to bed and the first one to get up in Chien's shop. He would do every kind of work—sweep the floor, move the goods, clear up the counter, and serve the customers. He was honest and faithful.

As he believed that Ting was trustworthy, Chien Tsai-wan taught him all his secrets and passed on his experiences in business, all the sharp practices in buying and selling and the proper speech and manner to be used with various types. As he was successful in carrying out whatever Chien Tsai-wan suggested, Ting felt very much heartened over his future.

After four years of working in Chien Tsai-wan's shop, Ting decided to try to trade independently in opium and told his plan to his father-in-law. They agreed immediately, and Su Po-lan advanced the money for the enterprise on the condition that, if there was any profit, it should be shared equally. Su Po-lan was then the greatest opium dealer in Kunyang. Ting collected the opium from producers in the country and transported it to Kunming to be sold. On each trip he transported more than a million *liang* or ounces. At that time Ting bought as much opium as possible under the name of his father-in-law. If he did not have enough money, he bought on credit. Because of the ignorance in the country of the city market, he could often buy the opium at a much lower price and make a high profit, but, when he reported the transactions to his father-in-law, he quoted the sale prices current in the city.

After two years, Ting redeemed the five rooms that his father had leased out and had saved a lot of money. But, unexpectedly, all his creditors came at once for the payment of old debts. This event was a real setback, and he was greatly discouraged. He had no more money left for his business. Then Ting's wife went to her father for help. Commander Su was compelled to lend him 300 silver dollars and to organize a credit society* of 400 silver dollars for him.

* This kind of society was a savings-and-loans association, into which each member paid a certain amount at certain intervals and from which he was paid a certain sum on a specified date. The size of the payment to be made by each participant and the time at which he was to be paid were prearranged. Anyone in need of money might organize a society by enlisting ten other members. Each would pay a predetermined proportion of the $400 that the organizer received. Thereafter, the society would meet every six months, usually in March and September, at which time one member would receive $400 and the rest would make their payments. Members other than the organizer paid sums directly proportionate to the order in which they were paid, so that, in effect, the first five were paying interest on loans they had received, while the last five were receiving interest for money they had deposited. The organizer, on the other hand, repaid only $400 during the five-year life of the society and had thus secured a loan without interest. But he was obliged to offer a feast at each meeting and had the responsibility of collecting the money. Furthermore, in case of default by any of the subscribers, he was

Ting continued in the opium trade and, after one year, was able to repay the 300 silver dollars he owed his father-in-law; the economic condition of his family was greatly improved. Unfortunately, at that time he caught such a severe case of typhoid fever that he was subject to frequent vertigo. His father-in-law came to his home and personally took care of him for more than a month.

Under constant medical care his health was gradually recovered, but his debts steadily increased. His father-in-law made a deal for him with the county officials that he was to take over the collection of taxes. The sum paid by his father-in-law was 800 silver dollars. As a result Ting received the job of collecting the opium tax and, in a single year, accumulated for himself more than $2,000. Later the government began to control opium smokers under the Bureau for the Prevention of Opium Smoking. The Bureau sold a kind of opium named *kung kao*, "public opium," which was mixed with morphia. According to the regulations, every opium smoker had to go to the Bureau to register his name and to report the quantity of opium smoked in a definite period. After registering, the opium smoker had periodically to buy *kung kao* from the Bureau or its agent and could not smoke his own opium any more. If an opium smoker still had some opium upon registration, he was to sell his opium to the Bureau. After a certain graduated period, the opium smokers would refrain from smoking entirely. Ting bought the right of selling *kung kao* from the Bureau for a nominal sum of money. From this business he accumulated for himself about $3,000.

While he was selling *kung kao*, Ting ordered every opium smoker to buy a definite quantity of *kung kao*. If an opium smoker did not buy it and secretly smoked his own opium, he would be arrested and punished severely by Ting. If Ting had a chance for extortion, he showed no mercy. As he knew that his father-in-law was an opium smoker and would certainly not smoke *kung kao* instead of his own opium, the quality of which was much better than that of *kung kao*, he sometimes brought his men to the home of his father-in-law to investigate him in the daytime; sometimes he went alone at night to the outside of the home to listen for the sound of smoking. At last he heard the sound of smoking and discovered that

---

held accountable. The functioning of this system depended on the unvarying discharge of their obligations by the subscribers, and this dependability was secured only by existing ties of friendship and kinship. Perhaps such a society was somewhat comparable to a credit union in the United States.

the opium his father-in-law was using was not *kung kao*. Ting arrested him immediately. He did not remember his father-in-law's help in the past. Although many of his relatives and friends appealed to him with regard to Su Po-lan, he remained adamant. As a consequence, his father-in-law was fined 50 silver dollars for breaking the law.

Once when he went to Nei Tien Hsiang and Chiu Tu Hsiang to sell *kung kao,* Ting, under the guise of suppressing opium, threatened the people with arrest and punishment. Many opium smokers and opium dealers came to bribe him. One day he led his men to a crossroad, set up a block, and searched the passers-by. From this venture, he obtained more than 1,000 *liang* of opium. But as such action exceeded his authority, he was afraid of being reported to the Magistrate. To quash a possible accusation, he offered 400 *liang* of opium to the Magistrate. This event gave him a hint that one who had no connection with officialdom would have no security even if he had money.

After he became a *kung kao* seller, Ting had no other occupation. He had been preparing himself for a position in the local government for a long time. In 1939 Mr. Hsu, a relative of Su Po-lan, was appointed head of the first *chu* government of the county. Ting, again through his father-in-law's influence, approached Mr. Hsu. Shortly thereafter, Ting was appointed to a clerkship in the district government. Because of his lack of training, this job was quite difficult for him. His handwriting was bad. In order to make up his deficiency, he was diligent and enthusiastic in doing every kind of work. If any question occurred to him, he would immediately run to ask Mr. Hsu to advise him. After half a year, Ting became Mr. Hsu's assistant.

In 1941, when Ting was twenty-nine years old, the *chu* system was changed to the *hsiang-chên* system. Mr. Hsu resigned his position, and Ting was appointed *chên chang,* head of the urban district. After becoming *chên chang,* Ting was respectful to his superiors, Magistrate Ho, Chief Chang, and Chief Liao. He took advantage of every opportunity to send presents to them. He went to the county government offices at least once a day to report everything that had happened in the community to the Magistrate. If Chief Chang and Chief Liao wanted him to do something, he would do it unhesitatingly. In direct proportion, Ting was harsh to his subordinates. When they asked him something, he would make a show of pride and talk with them reluctantly. Because of his fawning on his superior officials, he was labeled "Ha Pa Kou," or "Peke" (Pekinese).

As he found that Magistrate Ho, Chief Chang, and Chief Liao trusted him, Ting felt that he need fear no more. He often used the public funds of the district to buy planking and salt, which he hoarded until prices went up. As in wartime prices kept going up because of inflation, he made great profits very easily. It was said that he had saved more than $500,000 (equivalent to 10,600 silver dollars in 1942) from this business. Then he was ordered to build several barns to store the tax rice of the government. As he did not make public the account, nobody knew how much he had grafted. According to the government regulations, the tax rice was lent to the people at a yearly interest rate of 20%. But he secretly raised the rate to 40%. Then, when he was ordered to collect telegraph poles from the people's forest for military use, he collected more than were needed and "squeezed" more than fifty of the best poles for himself. Again, when the army passed through Kunyang, the local government was ordered to supply rice, firewood, and corn or beans. (The rice was used to feed the soldiers, the corn and beans to feed the horses.) Ting collected more than was needed and transported the remainer to his home in the dark of night. After three years his family became one of the richest in Kunyang.

From graft money, Ting became very rich. He associated with wealthy and influential men and despised the common people. To top it all, although his father-in-law had helped him many times, he not only made no repayment for his kindness but even talked about him behind his back. Some people therefore said of Ting, "One who makes a great fortune will surely be a cruel man." Some other people quoted the ancient saying, "The benevolent will not be rich; and neither will the rich be benevolent."

When Chief Chang accused Magistrate Chao, Ting joined him in his action in Kunming. Ting was therefore discharged from his position by the Magistrate. Later Chao was also removed by the provincial government. Ting then returned to Kunyang and again dealt in salt.

In 1944 Ting's father-in-law decided to become a wholesaler in salt, buying salt from the government and transporting it to Kunyang, whence it would be distributed to different stores for retail trade, a profitable business. After receiving inside information, Ting immediately hot-footed it to Kunming to secure the franchises for himself. He presented some *tung-tiao* rice* and four salted ducks to the authority of the District Directorate of Salt Administration. As a result, he became a wholesale dealer in salt in Kunyang.

In January, 1945, Chief Chang resigned his position as head of the Department of Conscription of the county and recommended Ting as his successor to the Magistrate. The Magistrate agreed because he found Ting sociable as well as rich. And, as he was really rich, when the government was in need of money, Ting could advance funds. Although Ting was not good at writing official letters, Magistrate Huang, Chao's successor, thought that this work could be handled by an able assistant.

In November, 1945, Ting's third brother-in-law was being sought by the military police (he was a private in the provincial army of Yunnan) because he was absent without leave. His commanding officer sent two soldiers to Kunyang to arrest him. When Ting's brother-in-law was arrested, Su Po-lan came to ask Ting to make an appeal to the soldiers. As he was then head of the Department of Conscription of the county, it would have been possible for him to secure the release of his brother-in-law. But Ting refused. Consequently, his brother-in-law was sent to Kunming and shot.

After being appointed head of the Department of Conscription of the county government, Ting climbed to the top of the social ladder in the community. As he was already rich and influential, he desired nothing more than a good reputation to cover up his past evil deeds. He became mild, pleasant, careful, and righteous. He liked to be flattered and admired. If someone involved in a lawsuit or other trouble asked for help, he was willing to speak a word for him. He voluntarily bought many maps and contributed them to the central elementary school of the urban district. He criticized the low salaries of the schoolteachers and the corruption of the officials.

---

* This kind of large-grained rice is of very good quality, especially white and with a peculiar flavor. It is a special product of Kunyang and well known in Yunnan.

7

The Types of Upward Mobility

In the previous chapters we have described the various routes of upward social mobility and the many varieties of men, in terms of careers, skills, and personalities, who found many ways to work up to high social positions. We found that the underlying reality of Chinese society was flexibility, not rigidity. The status barriers were surmountable. Now we want to change our focus of attention a little and to see the life drama of the mobile men and families from a different angle. We can do so by reconstructing the picture of upward mobility with special attention to the different types and their rates of mobility. This analysis will reveal the working of the total mobility forces more pointedly. What were the processes and rates of upward mobility? Did upward mobility have a gradual or a sudden character? What were the social and economic backgrounds of the gentry? What were the routes toward wealth-accumulation? These problems will be examined in this chapter.

THE TYPES AND RATES OF UPWARD MOBILITY

From the point of view of their family backgrounds the members of the gentry can be classified into two different groups. The first was the birth elite, the men whose fathers or grandfathers were already members of the gentry. Although the gentry had no legal foundation and birth was not a factor in selection for either higher education or

204

administrative posts, opportunities were socially unequal. The second group was that of the mobile men, whose fathers had been farmer-peasants. They had to pass through the maximum social distance to reach the top. These two groups differed most from each other in the social and occupational positions from which their members began their careers. When we look at upward mobility, we must keep in mind two different types of mobility.

The birth elite were the inheritors who retained the social positions their fathers had held before them. The backgrounds of these men made their careers seem less trying, less difficult, than the career tasks of the mobile men. They usually had various kinds of advantage. The influence of a father's status could be felt as economic or political power or, less directly, through the aid of the family's relatives or friends. The life history of Chu Lung, the eldest son of Commander Chu, is a case in point.

Chu Lung, twenty-four, was graduated from a middle school especially built by the Governor for educating the children of the officials in Kunming. After his graduation, however, as he could not pass the entrance examinations into any college, his father sent him to a military academy. But after one month in the academy he ran away because he could not bear the regimentation. Chu Lung lived in Kunming and Kunyang according to his fancy. When he was in Kunming, he did nothing but go to see movies and Chinese operas, gamble, and smoke opium.

One year after graduation, Chu Lung received, through the recommendation of a friend of his father, the position of secretary of a county government, but he was quite incompetent. After half a year the Magistrate gave him $50,000 [equivalent to 4,100 silver dollars] and sent him home.

In 1943, a complaint was made by the local gentry to the provincial government of the corruption of the Magistrate of Kunyang. Chu Lung felt that it was his opportunity to exercise his family's influence. He had printed the testimony of a number of people as to the honesty of the Magistrate in the Kunming newspaper and presented a petition to the provincial government to hold off judgment on him. Chu Lung was appointed head of the Department of Military Affairs by the Magistrate of the county government.

At the end of 1943 a new magistrate came into office in Kunyang. The new Magistrate wished to dismiss Chu Lung but feared that it would hurt the feelings of Commander Chu, and no action was taken.

Chu Lung's case history shows that the birth elite were expected to attend school and in most cases to take advanced training. They were educated as desirable members of society. Their families met and knew the officials. They obtained jobs through the influence of important family members, even though sometimes they were actually incompetent.

The birth elite opened up further opportunities to the family, often to an even greater degree than to the successful individual himself. It centered on the process of entrenchment: The kind of success that was the basis for an individual's rise normally tended to repeat itself simply because, as a rule, the individual managed to carry out the same kind of task again and again and because success generally paved the way for further success. In the vast majority of cases success brought in its wake important functional positions and other powers over material resources. The individual became entrenched and with him his family.[1] Entrenchment then became traditional and conferred prestige. The case history of Chairman Wang's family provides an illustration:

Chairman Wang was a leading man among the gentry in Kunyang. At that time he was the principal of the junior middle school and the normal school of the county. His family was well known as *shu hsiang shih chia,* a "scholar's family." Chairman Wang's father had been a literary graduate and a schoolteacher. Chairman Wang himself received the degree of *hsiu ts'ai* and was graduated from the provincial normal school in Kunming.

Chairman Wang's oldest son, Wen-hung, studied in a primary school in the city of Kunyang. After graduation from primary school, he went to Kunming and entered a middle school, and from there he entered the Central Political Academy of the Kuomintang in Nanking. Being graduated from the Academy at the age of twenty-eight, he returned to Yunnan and served as the head of a division in the Department of Finance of the provincial government of Yunnan. After one year he went to Japan and entered Waseda University in Tokyo, where he received the degree of Master of Arts. He was the first to go abroad from Kunyang. After returning to China, he served as a secretary in the provincial government of Shansi. After six years he returned to Yunnan and served as a head of a division in the Department of Education of the provincial government. After two years he was recommended by the director of the Department of Education to the Governor as a candidate for magistrate.

Chairman Wang's second son, Wang Wen-ta, studied very hard in school. In the middle school he obtained a scholarship twice. When he was twenty-three years old, he entered the National Tsing Hua University in Peiping through competitive examination. After study there for two years, he left the University to serve as a member of the Provincial Headquarters Committee of the Nationalist Party of Yunnan. In a year he won a scholarship to study abroad from the Central Headquarters of the Nationalist Party through a competitive examination among the members of the Party. He went to the United States in 1931. Wen-ta received the degrees of Master of Arts and Doctor of Philosophy from universities in the Midwest. He married an American girl and remained in the United States.

The brilliant academic careers of Wen-hung and Wen-ta brought Wang's family to new heights of prestige. In the community no other family could challenge its status as a "scholar's family."

To succeed easily to the father's position, a man had to be able, ambitious, and energetic. He had to be on the whole an independent person who could function in a position of major responsibility.[2] Even though a member of the birth elite was usually equipped with elaborate education, helping to fill out his background as a proper successor to positions of power, he had also successfully to prove himself as good a man as his father had been. He had to be able to establish himself with persons of his own social level. The advantages of the birth elite were, however, to some extent offset by the deadening effect of exalted position and security on the original impetus, by the diversion and complication of interests, and perhaps also by the sheer exhaustion of energies.[3] Chairman Wang's third and youngest sons furnish typical examples of exhaustion in the birth elite:

Chairman Wang's third son, Wang Wen-chang, studied in Kunming when he was a boy. He seemed to be spoiled by his father. He liked to play and eat and did not like to study in school. His father let him come back to Kunyang, where he entered the county normal school. After graduation from the normal school, he taught in the primary school of his native place and, at the same time, managed his home and farm. During those years he became an opium smoker. He would smoke opium the whole night. He went to bed in the early morning and got up around two o'clock in the afternoon. He was lazy and low-spirited. Nevertheless, because of the prestige of his father and brothers, he was respected by the local people and elected *hsiang chang,* chief of a district government, and principal of the central primary school of his native district.

The youngest son of Chairman Wang, Wang Wen-hua, commenced his studies in the City of Kunyang. After graduation from the normal school of the county, he went to Kunming and entered the provincial normal school. He then entered the teachers college of Southwest Associated University in Kunming. After graduation from the University, he went back to Kunyang. In 1946 Wen-hua took over the long-coveted position of the principal of the normal school and junior middle school but found that the salary was not enough to live on and that it was not paid regularly. The teachers could not support themselves by their salaries and therefore did not take their jobs seriously. Many of the students were encouraged to create disturbances by some gentry members who were against him. He was indecisive in everything and could not control his junior staff members. In a word, he lacked experience. After he became the principal of the school, he felt that it was necessary to be sociable. He would smoke cigarettes, drink wine, and play mah-jongg. He would go to bed late and get up late, like an old man.

The life histories of Wen-chang and Wen-hua do not fit into the ever fascinating family drama of hard-won success. Indeed, their careers, by virtue of the seeming ease of achieving high social position, had been made more difficult by the looming figures of their highly esteemed father and elder brothers. Under the shadow of their father and brothers, they seem to have been frustrated by a losing battle.

Success, once achieved, exerts a continuing effect, without accomplishment, for the reason that the prestige it engenders assumes a life of its own. It does not necessarily disappear when its basis disappears; for that matter, its basis does not readily disappear. This observation is the very heart and soul of the independent organic existence of social status.[4] The case history of Chief Ting's family, which we cited to illustrate marriage as a social ladder, corroborates this statement. Even though Ting's family had declined, it was still considered promising. Interestingly, Ting's family did rise again with the assistance of Su Po-lan, Ting's father-in-law.

The mobile men were those who had risen from farm labor. They had done *something novel,* something odd that meant their getting out of the conventional rut. Because of the limited opportunities open to poor peasants, novelty was virtually the only method by which they could make the great leap out of their original status. They were men with little formal education who learned as they advanced. They were the *nouveaux arrivés* and were identified by the fact that their high positions, in terms of income, prestige, and power, were far removed from the statuses of their fathers—the statuses into which they had been born. The life histories of Major Chang, Colonel Fang, Chief Chang, and Chairman Tsao are signal examples. Each struck out along unconventional paths, becoming a mercenary soldier, a policeman, or a clerk and moved up into the gentry in his own lifetime. These routes were quite hazardous, however, and the positions were not firmly established. These men rose suddenly, but their prestige waned as quickly. Chairman Tsao did not buy any farmland, and after his death his family declined rapidly. The permanence of Chief Chang's and Major Chang's statuses was still uncertain because their children were still young. Only Colonel Fang's family seemed promising because his two sons were studying in the middle school.

These two types, the birth elite and the mobile men, had different patterns of upward mobility, which are suggested in Figure 3.

In the diagram the capital letter P represents landless peasants, G gentry, L landowners, S shopkeepers, E educated, M mercenary soldiers, N policemen, and C clerks. The arrows show the direction of mobility. Each short solid arrow denotes one generation. The combined solid and dotted arrow symbolizes tremendous upward mobility in one generation. The entire distance covers six generations.

On the route of the birth elite, a poor peasant who wanted to climb into the gentry had to pass through two big stages: landowning or shopkeeping and the acquisition of education. The purpose of both landowning and shopkeeping was to accumulate wealth. After the family had become wealthy enough, the children would be able to acquire higher education. Each step took one or two generations, and the entire social ladder might take five, six, or even seven generations to climb. The families of Chairman Wang and Commander Chu are good examples.

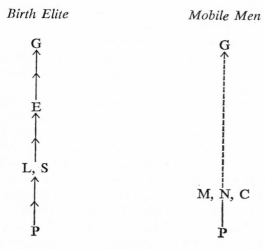

Figure 3. A Schematic Diagram of the Upward Mobility of the Birth Elite and Mobile Men

On the route for mobile men, a poor peasant might climb to the top rung of the social ladder in a single generation. Indeed, there were shortcuts for the poor but ambitious peasant. A mobile man, however, had to show extraordinary ability and energy. Many years of training or work were essential to achieve this goal in a single generation. When Major Chang was promoted to major, he was thirty-eight years old. When Colonel Fang was appointed colonel, he was thirty-two years of age. Chairman Tsao became self-supporting at the age of nine and the director of the Bureau of Reconstruction of the county at twenty-seven years of age. When Chairman Tsao was elected chairman of the People's Political Council, he was fifty-one years old. The social rise of the climbers was in any case by no means a "sudden jump."

The length of time to reach the top official position was shortest for the sons of the most prominent gentry members. When Commander Chu's eldest son, Chu Lung, became head of the Department of Military Affairs of the county government, he was only twenty-four years old.

The birth elite had great advantages in their careers over the mobile men. Their promotions were faster, and the time to achieve really top positions was far shorter. The mobile men had to follow hazardous routes, and their positions were not firmly established. They rose suddenly and as suddenly fell.

When people talk of success, we sociologists are perpetually amazed to hear the stress placed upon individual capacities. Although individual capacity or talent is one criterion, there are certainly other factors that go into shaping a successful career. An important factor is the "tradition of success." It is almost impossible to think about preparing for a career when no precedent has been established for participation in that career by any of a man's own group. To be able to say, "My father did it" or "My grandfather did it," is an important and powerful factor in the shaping of a career. On the other hand, if one is a pioneer, he will take faltering steps and possibly stumble along the way; people will look askance at his activity and make it much harder for him. If he can establish this tradition of success, he has a powerful force on his side.[5] It is remarkable that, deprived of any such tradition as were Major Chang, Colonel Fang, Chief Chang, and Chairman Tsao, so many people attained to social heights. But the "tradition of success"—the tradition of upward social mobility— was an all-important factor, as shown in Table 15.

An analysis of Table 15 reveals that among twenty-six upper gentry members of Kunyang, twenty-four had had fathers who were in the gentry, nineteen had had gentry grandfathers, fourteen had had gentry great-grandfathers, and eight had even had gentry great-great-grandfathers. On the average, between two and three preceding generations of the gentry were already gentry.

The birth elite and mobile men shared a common sense of belonging to the higher social status. Most of them felt, even though they may not have explicitly recognized it, that they were socially above the ordinary people. They knew they were in the spotlight. The case history of Chief Chang, a mobile man, is typical.

At the beginning the new Magistrate did not appoint Chief Chang to any position because he was the main instigator in the action against Magistrate Chao. After three months, however, the new Magistrate appointed him Chief of the Department of Civil Affairs of the county government. At that time he considered himself a bringer of progress to his native place. He made a show of his conceit. When common people bowed to him in the street, he raised his head and did not pay any attention to them. When he met a superior, however, Chief Chang would beam on him politely and earnestly.

This sense of status was stronger in gentry families. The case history of Commander Chu, a member of the birth elite, confirms this statement.

During those years Commander Chu's family was in difficult economic straits on account of a bad drought. The family was large, including seventeen members, which meant that everyday expenditures were high. Although the family members ate very poorly, had few new clothes, and reduced unnecessary expenditures to a minimum, they could not make ends meet. At that time all the brothers were struggling very hard for livings. The eldest brother, Chu Fu, had borrowed a large sum of money and gone into the rice export-import business between Kunyang and Kunming. Chu Fu was intelligent and careful, for he had studied nine years in a private school. He made a great deal of money, and the family depended on him for support. Commander Chu's second eldest brother, Chu Lo, also borrowed a sum of money to go into the rice-noodle business in a nearby village. Because of his lack of experience, he lost money. Later he rationalized, "Failure is the beginning of success." He borrowed another sum of 100 *tael* of silver to start a wine factory. Because of the small amount of capital, he lost money again. Owing to these failures, he felt too discouraged to try again. But the debts had to be repaid. He liquidated all his assets in the wine factory but still owed 175 *tael*. When he returned home in disappointment, his creditors were still pursuing him.

But when the news of Commander Chu's position became known in his native place, the condition of his family changed completely. His parents and brothers showed a sense of their new high position. At once the local people one and all began to speak of his father as Lao Tai Yeh, "Great Excellency." When Chu Kan stepped into a teashop or a restaurant, he would immediately be greeted with enthusiasm. Commander

Table 15. *The Social Status of the Forebears of the Twenty-six Upper Gentry Members in Kunyang, 1946*

Status of Gentry Forebears

Stratum of Gentry	Father					Grandfather			
	provincial gentry	county gentry	district gentry	village gentry	sub-total	county gentry	district gentry	village gentry	sub-total
Provincial gentry (three members)		3		3	3	1	2		3
County gentry (thirteen members)	1	4	3		11	1	4	4	9
District gentry (ten members)			3	7	10		1	6	7
Total	1	7	6	10	24	2	7	10	19

Chu's mother was especially proud. When she went to the market to buy something, she purposely asked the price of this or that. If the salesman knew her and lowered the price, she might buy it; otherwise she would ask: "Are your stupid eyes blind? Don't you know who I am?" Commander Chu's second older brother was no longer in great debt because the creditors dared not ask him to repay the money any more. Commander Chu's younger brother, Chu Hsin, had become an opium smoker and gambler and had long been despised by the local people, but now he was called Sze Lao Yeh, "The Fourth Excellency," and flattered with flowery remarks.

Both the birth elite and the mobile men had a sense of their higher social status in the community. This sense separated man from man and group from group.

The security of elite position allowed a gentleman to be an individualist; by accepting certain traditions without question, he became free to deviate a little and not to be criticized so long as he did not overdo it. Mr. Ku's case is typical. My informant said:

After Mr. Ku was appointed chief of Pao Shan Hsiang, a rural district, and principal of the central elementary school of the district, he held the power of both administration and education. He was praised for his enthusiasm and effort. The old people shouted approval of him, and the young men looked up to him as a superior being and longed for the time when they might emulate his deeds.

Indeed, he devoted himself to his responsibility. Meanwhile, he also showed off his conceit and vainglory. He was elated with his success and conscious of distinction in personal appearance and manners. Strutting

Table 15. *(continued)*

Status of Gentry Forebears

Stratum of Gentry	Great-grandfather				Great-great-grandfather		Grand total
	county gentry	district gentry	village gentry	sub-total	village gentry	sub-total	
Provincial gentry (three members)			3	3	2	2	11
County gentry (thirteen members)	2		6	8	6	6	34
District gentry (ten members)			3	3			20
Total	2		12	14	8	8	65

proudly through the town, he became an object of envy to his peers and of tender interest to the girls of the region. He was most "greedy" of pretty girls. When a beautiful woman passed by, he would surely gaze on her twice.

The case history of Mr. Ku has illustrated that the gentry members held themselves aloof from the common people. Although they frowned upon deviations, a gentleman could be a little odd and not be punished. Indeed, his actual community power guaranteed enough security to permit individualistic expression and variation.

Although the unusual cases in which men rose from nothing practically overnight are dramatically interesting, they are after all sociological exceptions, especially in a relatively stable state of society. Whatever historical period, whatever set of social circumstances we may select, we shall always be able to make two assertions that are not likely to be successfully contradicted: In the first place, only in very exceptional cases—so exceptional that they are of no particular significance to the explanation of social processes—is it possible for an individual to enter a "higher" status at a single bound. In the second place, it is *as a rule* practically impossible for the individual to effectuate the transition to a higher status *for himself;* it is impossible for him during his own lifetime to modify decisively the status situation of the true status holder, the family.[6] When we study social mobility, both individual and family should therefore be equally emphasized.

THE SOCIOECONOMIC BACKGROUNDS OF THE GENTRY

The distinction between the gentry and the farmer-peasants was a real one. Both education and wealth played a considerable role in determining the status of the gentry. The cleavage between the educated and the uneducated people was sharp. The uneducated people were called *wu chih yü min,* "stupid people without learning," which carried with it a sense of contempt. The difference in education became a distinction in status and prestige. The villagers therefore regarded education as a means by which a family could raise its social position.

Education became a stepping stone to social ascendance for many reasons. First, it was in school that children were taught to recognize characters, practice calligraphy, keep accounts, and use the abacus. The children also learned good manners, wore long gowns or student uniforms, and absorbed the teachings of ancient worthies. The country boy gradually changed his way of life. Second, as educated people were so few in the village, they acquired a scarcity value. There were still fewer who had leisure and were at the same time willing to take the responsibility for community affairs without reward. Their ability and service thus gave them authority and status. Third, up to very recent times the most important goal of life for the majority of those who were gifted and motivated toward success was to attain high positions in the bureaucracy, and education furnished one of the most favored and surest ways of realizing this dream. It was the personal ambition of everyone to have education. Consequently, education commanded considerable social prestige. Fourth and finally, the intellectual distinction soon developed into a psychological discrimination, which in turn created a sense of superiority among the educated people and a sense of inferiority among the peasants.

More than half the gentry members had received at least a senior middle school education. From Table 16 we can also see that the education of the gentry was higher than that of its ancestors. The average years of schooling for the gentry were 12.9; for fathers 10.3; for grandfathers 6; and for great-grandfathers 2.6. By sacrificing themselves to enhance the prestige of their families, all the parents sought to give their children better education and to start them higher up the social ladder. Sometimes they may have projected upon their children their own frustrated educational ambitions.

The gentry generally consisted of educated people, as shown in Table 16.

Table 16. Educational Levels of the Twenty-six Upper Gentry Members and Their Forebears, Kunyang, 1946

Years of Schooling	Gentry Members	Fathers	Grand-fathers	Great-grandfathers
0			5	13
1				
2				
3		2	3	1
4		3	6	4
5			4	4
6		2		2
7	1	3	1	1
8	1	1		
9	3	2		1
10	2	1		
11	2	2	1	
12	6	2	4	
13	1	1		
14	3		1	
15	1			
16	1	1		
17	2	4		
18	1			
19		1	1	
20	1	1		
21	1			
Total	26	26	26	26

The difficulties in acquiring formal education for a country boy were numerous. They were not only economical and ecological but also psychological. Nevertheless, as education was a source of prestige and a stepping stone to social advancement, the zeal for education was remarkable. Enthusiasm was shown not only by the father of the boy but also by relatives and friends of the family. The life history of Liu Tsung-tao is typical:

Liu Tsung-tao started to study at nine. In his native district, education was backward. Usually there was a single school for more than ten villages. He entered a private school located five miles from his home where he had to reside and board at the school. Only a few families could afford to send their children to such schools.

Although Liu Tsung-tao's father, Yen-tau, was illiterate, he was well disposed and farsighted. He felt that there would be no future for his family unless he allowed his children to study. But if one of his children were to become an official, there would be fame for his family and ancestors. A farmer was not in a position to develop greatly. He was very glad when his son's teacher told him that Tsung-tao was clever and had a good memory. The teacher also said that, although Tsung-tao liked to play, his record was one of the best.

After eight years in the private school, Tsung-tao went to the city of Kunyang to compete in the entrance examination for the junior normal school of the county. When Yen-tau was informed that his son had gained entrance, he gave a big feast for his relatives, friends, and the local gentry. Each person who came to congratulate him on the success of his son contributed one or two silver dollars toward the school expenses.

While he was studying in the normal school, Liu Tsung-tao felt very proud of himself because he reveled in the thought that, although he had been born in a mountainous region, he had come to the city to study with city boys. As he knew that the other boys of his village could not enter a city school, he tried to study very hard and not to disappoint the expectations of his father. At the same time, he really had a sense of inferiority because the clothes of the other boys were better than his. He had not eaten what the others had eaten, and he had not seen what the others had seen. During his study at this school, Tsung-tao often fought with the others. After four years he graduated from the normal school.

It is apparent that education, although not entirely limited to wealthy classes, required some leisure time. Manual labor and leisure were mutually exclusive. A farmer who engaged in long hours of work in the fields exhausted his energies in grinding physical labor. As the income of a farmer was small, he could not hope for long periods of leisure. Those who had leisure had to be supported by others. They were big landowners or wealthy merchants. They could secure enough income either from their farmlands in the form of rents or from their businesses in the form of profits. A man who had to work for bare existence had absolutely no opportunity to enter school. The members of the gentry of Kunyang were, as a rule, either landlords or wealthy merchants.

As Table 17 reveals, half the twenty-six gentry families had more than 100 *kung* of farmland. The average-sized holding was 138.5 *kung*. It is obvious that the gentry families could live entirely on their rents, except for a few merchants who had other sources of income. The gentry class was based in the Chinese economic system.

Wealth did not automatically lead to education. It is well known that the Chinese writing system was not a convenient device lying ready at hand for everybody to pick up and use as he prepared to meet life's problems. One might well have greater "natural" disposition for doing what another could do only by exertion. A wealthy man who could find the time for long study might still be debarred from social advancement through lack of education. For example, the biggest landlord in Kunyang, Chiang En-tsê, had six sons, all of whom turned out worthless and lived parasitically at home. They became a regret to all the community.

Table 17. The Farm Sizes of the Twenty-six Upper Gentry Families

Farm Size (in *Kung*)	Gentry Family	Farm Size (in *Kung*)	Gentry Family
50	3[a]	150	1
60	2[a]	160	1
65	3	170	1
70	2[b]	200	1
80	2	245	1[a]
97	1	260	1
100	3	500	1
115	1	520	1
120	1		—
		Total	26

[a] These families are also wealthy business owners.
[b] One of these families also owns an iron mine.

It is, of course, not to be overlooked that wealth itself was a primary route to ascending the social scale in a society of money economy. It was a mark of prestige to say that a family possessed inherited wealth. Without inherited wealth, one could not afford the style of life of the true gentry. In addition, generosity and hospitality were generally valued and brought repute and esteem for those who were ready to entertain their relatives and friends or to bestow gifts upon them. Wealth was, however, a prerequisite for the development of these virtues on a large scale. Above all, to the common people, leaving property was the most important way of being remembered after death. Parents who left nothing to their children would either be blamed for a long time after death or be forgotten immediately. The names of parents who added something to the property or who restored the original fortunes of a family were inscribed on the family record. They were celebrated by their descendants and talked about with pride as long as the family existed.[7]

THE ROUTES TO WEALTH ACCUMULATION

The agricultural laborer could earn a yearly wage at maximum of 400 *ching* of rice plus board and housing. With this meager income, the worker could maintain only a hand-to-mouth existence for himself and his family. There was hardly anything left when a whole year of drudgery was over. Under such circumstances the farm laborer could not hope to save enough money from his wages to buy farmland and climb higher on the agricultural ladder. At the same time, in a society of dense population and scarce land, a tenant had to pay rent of more than 50% of the main product for the use of land. The chance of ascending to ownership was very small. One might borrow money to purchase land. But as the monthly rate of interest was as high as 8%, the climber would likely slip down to the lower rungs because of the heavy burden of interest. A farmer-peasant who worked on the land seemed bound to it. We cannot help but ask how wealth was accumulated and how the gentry eventually emerged.

Of course, we must admit that, as there was no social barrier to prevent a poor peasant from entering the gentry if he could afford to lead a leisurely life, there would be those hardworking peasants who would strive to rise from the bottom. But it would take them several generations to climb the social ladder, each generation a little higher. Despite thrift and endurance, it was not only a long but also a haphazard way, because in the rural community misfortunes of all kinds were not uncommon. Drought and flood might cause famine. Epidemics might ruin a family. In periods of political disturbance, bandits were as bad as locusts in dry years. It would have been most rare for a family to keep up its morale for several generations and to have no misfortune strike it in the meantime.[8] Even under ordinary circumstances, resources would constantly be drained by the expenses of ceremonies like weddings and funerals. It is pertinent to ask what were the routes to prosperity for the village families.

The way to great wealth lay outside the occupation of farming, and ambitious villagers had to seek their fortunes beyond agriculture. If they were fortunate enough to achieve their goals, they bought land and became large landowners. The village was filled with landless farm laborers. Such men might in the end die in disgrace or disappear from the village. These outcasts were desperate. They had nothing to lose but their lives of drudgery. They left the village and plunged themselves into banditry or smuggling, joined the army, or sought employment as servants in big gentry houses. These jobs were economically unproductive, but only by taking them, in addition to enjoying good luck, could the outcasts from rural society hope to obtain wealth quickly. Of course, hundreds and thousands of such fortune seekers died in despair and were forgotten by the world.[9] The most important routes to great wealth were the governmental office, the army, commerce, and illegal trade.

Governmental Office

In an agrarian society like that of pre-Communist China, where industrial and commercial activities were maintained on tiny profits and a very low standard of living, the chief way to acquire wealth was by becoming a high official. A man would then be in a position to turn matters to his own advantage at the expense of the people and the nation. Power was clearly the origin of wealth.[10] The life history of Tang Sheng-kuang's great-grandfather is typical:

Tang Sheng-kuang's great-grandfather, Tang Kao-hsün, was intelligent and handsome. He received the degree of *chin shih* at twenty-eight years old. Because of his excellent record, he was appointed magistrate of the County of Meng Hua of Yunnan Province. After taking over the position, he was enthusiastic and honest. All the people praised him as a good magistrate. All the gentry was on good terms with him. After one year, however, he not only came to perform his duties negligently but he also exploited the people by every means possible. After three years, all the people complained of his inefficiency and corruption. There was a case of homicide, which was considered a test of his sense of justice and honesty because both parties involved were from wealthy and powerful families. The gentry and the people of the county excitedly watched for his verdict on the case. If he should have the criminal shot, there would be the threat of the defendant's family wealth. If he should acquit the criminal of the charge, there was a threat from the family of the plaintiff, which was very powerful. Both parties bribed him with a great deal of money. After several months, he completely sidestepped the issue and decided to allow the criminal to break out of prison and at the same time to send the jailer, a nephew of his, away, thus casting suspicion on him. This turn of events caused an uproar. The plaintiff threatened to accuse him to the Governor for receiving bribes and freeing the criminal. Tang knew that the outcome of the case would be unfavorable to him. He therefore sent two men after his nephew, and they killed him. In order to prove Tang's good will, his nephew's head was brought back to the City of Meng Hua. At the same time, he put up a great reward for the criminal's capture. The people applauded him for his honesty and righteousness. The family of the criminal offered him another sum of money because he had freed the felon. He gave one-third of the money to his nephew's parents for compensation. After five years, he resigned his position. When he left the county, all the people commended him as an honest and upright official. The gentry also presented him a eulogy for his virtuous administration. He came home with fortune and honor. He bought 300 *kung* of farmland and a store with six rooms in the City of Kunyang.

This case clearly shows how government office became the origin of wealth. Being in power, Tang Kao-hsün was in a position to swing matters to his own advantage at the expense of the people.

The Army

Chaos during wartime provided opportunities for robbing and plundering. Even in peacetime, the rich people and the civil officials had to make the largest possible "gifts" in order to secure the good will of the commander of the army, so decisive for their own fates. Commander Chu's case history, cited in Chapter 5, furnishes a suitable example. From it, we can see that the army was a way to great wealth.

Commerce

If we compare agriculture with commerce, we can see how in the latter wealth could more easily be accumulated.[11] In the City of Kunyang there were eight or nine merchants who had become wealthy in one generation. Capital accumulated in commerce was not considered a stable basis for establishing a family estate, and eventually it was redirected into farmland. Consequently, the rich merchants became, at the same time, the holders of large amounts of farmland. The life history of Shu En-chuan's father illustrates this point:

> Shu En-chuan was born in the City of Kunyang in 1890. En-chuan's great-grandfather was a native of the city of Yüchi. His family had had only five *kung* of farmland and a store. He engaged in operating a teashop. His wife set up a stall to sell cold rice-noodles in front of the teashop. Both businesses were prosperous. After ten years, Shu accumulated 600 *liang* of silver. He lent the money to two men at high interest. Unfortunately, one of his debtors contracted an epidemic disease and died. The other debtor fled. Shu not only received no interest, but he also lost all his money. After three years, the debtor who had fled came back and repaid him 200 *liang* of silver. The other debtor's son paid him 150 *liang* of silver. He felt that it was a streak of luck in misfortune. He learned his bitter lesson and repented that he had not taken the warnings of his friends and relatives, who had advised him to buy fifteen *kung* of farmland with the money.
>
> Shu En-chuan's grandfather had studied three years in a private school. He could read simple letters and keep accounts. When he inherited his father's shop, he painted the room and invited in a story-teller to entertain his customers. In the beginning, his business was prosperous. But because of his conceit and rigid attitude, his business declined

gradually. He changed his business and opened a restaurant. But he could not improve his fortune. As a result, he was in debt and had to rent his restaurant to another. He obtained a sum of money equivalent to sixteen *piculs* of rice for the pledge of renting his shop. After repaying his debts with this money, he and his family moved to a village and began truck gardening. After four years, his economic condition was improving gradually.

Shu En-chuan's father was the second of three brothers. From childhood, he had experienced only poverty and hardship. His father was very severe with him. When he was only seven or eight years old, he had to help his father do various sorts of work like carrying fertilizer and irrigating gardens. His father often scolded and beat him. One day after he was scolded by his father, he ran away from home and went to Kunyang. He earned his own living by selling candies, cigarettes, and matches. He was then only sixteen years old.

After two years, he accumulated a sum of money equivalent to 160 *ching* of rice. He used this money as capital and traversed the villages to buy rice and sold it in the market town. After one year, he bought 280 *ching* of vegetable seeds for pressing vegetable oil in a factory. He went through village after village and bartered by offering two *ching* of vegetable oil for one *ching* of vegetable seeds.

After two and one-half years, he rented a factory for pressing vegetable oil. He hired two laborers to help him. When he was twenty-two years old, he was able to buy ten *kung* of farmland and take a wife in Kunyang.

After five years, he bought another twenty *kung* of farmland. He rented his land to a tenant and engaged himself in manufacturing soybean sauce. His business was prosperous.

One day in 1922 an opium dealer from Hao Ching came to Kunyang with 5,000 silver dollars to buy opium. Shu and his second elder brother intercepted the opium dealer midway between Kunyang and Anning. They killed him and robbed him of his money. This burglary was reported to the Magistrate of Kunyang. Shu and his brother fled to avoid arrest. Fortunately, the Magistrate was soon changed, and the case was forgotten accordingly. His second older brother went to Erh Chieh, a market town of Jen Teh Hsiang, to open a business, while he himself went to Pa Chieh, a market town of Anning, to do the same. He bought forty horses for transporting various kinds of goods to and from Pa Chieh and Kunyang. His family hired thirteen long-term laborers and greatly enlarged his enterprise of manufacturing soybean sauce.

When he was thirty-five years old, the large family was divided. After the division of the family, he moved his own family from the City of Kunyang to Erh Chieh, where he built a large and fashionable house. He operated a grocery store and manufactured soybean sauce. After ten years, he bought 280 *kung* of farmland and became one of the wealthiest merchants and landlords in the district of Jen Teh Hsiang.

The life history of Shu En-chuan's father illustrates that through commerce wealth could be accumulated; eventually it was redirected into farmland because, in a community without banks or joint stock companies, land was the safest investment. Indeed, insurance was unknown. Fire might destroy merchandise or a hoard of treasure, and war or banditry might ruin a merchant. Land would survive most calamities, however, and gave great stability to the agricultural society.

Illegal Trade

The traditional rural economy even forced people into criminal activity. It was quite natural for a young man to be dissatisfied with the closed economic system. A man who started from the bottom of society had to work on the farm for a meager income while he was young. Opportunities for him were very limited. But the dream of rising in the world existed in every mind. Although Chinese culture had done its best to support this limited economy by emphasizing the attitude of contentment, even in the past this doctrine had probably failed to satisfy everyone fully. In the 1940s, in the rapidly changing world that surrounded the peasants, we may say that it had become less and less effective. Desperately poor peasants were led into illegal adventures, which might take the form of political revolution or widespread banditry.[12] In Kunyang the smuggling of opium became a lamentably common means of getting wealth.

In the first days of the Republic the government adopted strict measures toward the vicious habit of opium smoking. But since the first importation of this drug, a large body of the population had developed the habit, for which unfortunately there was no easy cure. The results of the prohibition of opium were the rise of a black market in opium and the encouragement of smuggling.[13] As Kunyang was between the two large centers of the black market in opium— Kunming and Yüchi—it both profited and suffered from this trade.

To smuggle opium, one had to keep out of the hands of policemen, gangsters, and other governmental agents. The smuggler had to be daring, shrewd, and experienced. He had to be kept informed about the conditions of the market. The life history of Tseng Hsia-mo serves to illustrate:

Tseng Hsia-mo was born in the City of Kunyang. His great-grandfather had studied three years in a private school and had then taken up farming. His family had twenty-three *kung* of farmland and a house of three rooms.

Hsia-mo's grandfather had studied four years in a private school. When he was thirty-six years of age, he felt that the income from his farms was not enough, and he bought three horses to transport goods for others to and from Erh Chieh and Kunyang. He could save eight *ching* of rice from each trip. When he was fifty-five years old, he bought ten *kung* of farmland and opened a grocery store.

Hsia-mo's father was the elder of two brothers. He studied six years in a private school. When he was thirty-two years old, he sold five *kung* of his farmland and obtained 200 silver dollars. His wife used the money to open a business for buying and selling rice, while he himself operated a gambling house on the second floor of his house.

Hsia-mo studied four years in a private school. When he was fourteen years old, he was hired by a grocer as an apprentice. His monthly wage was twenty-four *ching* of rice. Every two years his monthly wage was increased by eight *ching* of rice. After six years, his master, who trusted him as a good helper, brought him to Yüchi to purchase opium. After several trips together, his master entrusted him to go alone. Each time when he went for opium he disguised himself as a horse driver or as a peasant vegetable salesman. He smuggled from 500 to 1,000 *liang* of opium on each trip. He worked for four years safely. He was faithful and careful. He thus established his reputation as a reliable man among the opium dealers of Yüchi and was able to buy 200 or 300 *liang* of opium on credit any time he wanted. He earned 300 silver dollars for each trip. Every year his master also gave him a bonus.

By that time Hsia-mo's parents concluded that, though the money was earned for his employer, Hsia-mo himself was known as an opium dealer and that gangsters would soon try to rob him of his opium. As he was in this danger, his parents let him come home and gave him 1,200 silver dollars to set up a rice business. After one year he had not made much money. He asked his parents to organize three credit societies to garner about 3,000 silver dollars. He returned to his old career of opium smuggling then with a capital stock of 4,200 silver dollars. His first trip was very successful. The price of opium in Yüchi was $2.25 for each *liang*. He could buy 1,500 *liang* with his money. When he transported the opium back to Kunyang, he could sell it at $2.75 a *liang*. He made 750 silver dollars out of this trip. His second trip brought a net profit of 1,000 silver dollars.

He set up an opium den alongside his father's gambling house. His neighbor ran a restaurant. His house was therefore considered an ideal place for opium smoking and gambling. After eight years, he built a house with three successive courts and became a wealthy merchant in the City of Kunyang.

During the Japanese War, the government suppressed the opium trade more severely, and the price of opium went up quickly. Hsia-mo's eldest son, Tseng Kan-shen, was then the commanding officer of the Kunyang Air Raid-Warning Station. Kan-shen took advantage of the long-distance telephone in the station to keep apprised of the market price of opium in Yüchi. The commanding officer of the Yüchi Station had been a schoolmate of Kan-shen and was persuaded to do this service for him. Kan-shen paid nothing for the communication but was kept informed of the conditions of the opium market in Yüchi. When the price of opium was rising there but had not changed in Kunyang, Hsia-mo would purchase large quantities of opium in Kunyang and hoard it until the price went up. At the same time, Kan-shen took advantage of his position as an officer and often went to Yüchi by bus to buy opium. Whenever he was informed that the price of opium in Yüchi was much lower than that of Kunyang, he would go to Yüchi with money immediately. Each time he would purchase at least 200 *liang* of opium. He bribed the official of the customs house at the border of Yüchi and Kunyang. Every month he presented $25,000 [equivalent to 100 silver dollars in July, 1943] to the official. He also offered bribery to the Bureau of Police Force of Kunyang and the commanding officer of the Company on Investigating of the county government. He therefore smuggled opium from Yüchi without difficulty. Some of the gangsters, however, intended to rob him of his opium at the bus station of Kunyang. One day in order to avoid robbery, when he was coming back to Kunyang from Yüchi he jumped down from the speedily moving bus about two miles from the City of Kunyang. Hsia-mo's son was immediately killed.

In 1944, Magistrate Huang had just come to Kunyang and was strict about suppressing the opium trade. As Tseng Hsia-mo was a well-known opium merchant and very wealthy, he became first prey. One day when he was selling opium, the commanding officer of the police force rushed in and caught him. The officer searched his house but found no more opium. There was a bag that contained twenty *liang* of opium hanging on the wall, but the officer did not notice it. Tseng was jailed for three days and released on a bail of $100,000 [equivalent to 180 silver dollars in March, 1944]. Another time he was caught again by the officer. This time the officer searched his house even more thoroughly. Every box and chest was opened. But the officer missed the coffin, in which Hsia-mo had hidden 200 *liang* of opium. He was again put in jail. After five days, he was released on a bail of $150,000. After that every month he contributed thirty *liang* of opium to the county government, and he conducted his business without any more trouble.

Hsia-mo had been in the opium trade for more than twenty-five years. Although he handled opium every day, he himself had never smoked it. His property was estimated at more than 100,000 silver dollars.

From Tseng Hsia-mo's case history, we can see how the smuggling of opium became a route to great wealth. The closed economic system forced dissatisfied men into criminal action.

The routes to accumulation of wealth obviously lay outside the occupation of farming, and ambitious villagers had to seek their fortunes beyond agriculture. If they were fortunate enough to achieve their goals, they became large landowners or wealthy merchants. Several conclusions may be drawn.

First, it is questionable that "frugality" and "hard work" alone could make a family prosperous. The case histories fully confirm the proverbial saying that "little wealth can be attained by diligence, whereas great wealth comes from heaven." For "from heaven" we could read "governmental office," "army," "commerce," "illegal trade," and even "banditry." Our cases supply us with the materials to formulate the concept of "unearned increment." It goes without saying that the struggle for wealth kept the community in a furor. Many people even sacrificed their own and others' lives.

Second, when we review the routes to accumulation of wealth, we cannot help but view the wealthy people as "robber barons." To gain entrance to the wealthy class, candidates had to be gifted with clannishness, audacity, unscrupulousness, and tenacity of purpose. We find under the mask of the "long gown" the grim economic reality of the gentry families.

Third, the real incentive to strive for wealth was material gain and its connotations rather than bare necessities. The way by which the money was earned seemed unimportant. It was quantity that mattered. Land was a form of wealth and a source of prestige.

Fourth, there was no guarantee that material gain would bear any relation to service or power to responsibility. The motive for private gain was scarcely an encouragement to efficient public service. But as long as the traditional conception that an official should be prosperous lingered on, lack of success in attaining wealth through public service led to a sense of frustration among those brought up with this idea.

Fifth and finally, the deprived but demanding Chinese peasants were forced to choose unhappy ways of accumulating wealth. The simple truth is that exploitation of the land, using crude and primitive technology, was not an effective method of attaining money quickly.

NOTES

1. *Cf.* Joseph A. Schumpeter, *Imperialism and Social Classes,* translated by Heinz Norden and edited by Paul M. Sweezy (New York: John Wiley & Sons, Inc., 1963), pp. 218–9.
2. W. Lloyd Warner and James C. Abegglen, *Big Business Leaders in America* (New York: Harper & Row, Publishers, 1955), p. 157.
3. Schumpeter, *op. cit.,* p. 219.
4. *Cf. ibid.,* p. 218.
5. The author is indebted to the late Professor Louis Wirth for his lectures on "Social Organization" during 1950–1951 at the University of Chicago.
6. *Cf.* Schumpeter, *op. cit.,* p. 164.
7. Martin C. Yang, *A Chinese Village: Taitou, Shantung Province* (New York: Columbia University Press, 1945), p. 82.

8. Hsiao-tung Fei, "Peasantry and Gentry: An Interpretation of Chinese Social Structure and Its Changes," *American Journal of Sociology,* 52 (July, 1946), 1–17.
9. *Ibid.*
10. Francis L. K. Hsu, *Under the Ancestors' Shadow: Chinese Culture and Personality* (New York: Columbia University Press, 1948), p. 281, note 4.
11. Fei and Chih-i Chang, *Earthbound China: A Study of Rural Economy in Yunnan* (Chicago: The University of Chicago Press, 1945), pp. 283–4.
12. *Cf. ibid.,* pp. 279–80.
13. *Ibid.,* p. 280.

8

The Forms of
Social Mobility

So far the term "social mobility" has been used to indicate the over-all changes of status of individuals and families, regardless of the various forms of social mobility. The term needs to be supplemented by reference to the changing of occupation and residential area, which are closely related to social mobility. Furthermore, although upward mobility has attracted more of our attention, it should be remembered that social mobility has two directions: up and down, ascending and descending, social climbing and social sinking.

The members of the gentry who climbed to the top rung of the social ladder were men in motion. They moved from one occupation to another, from place to place, and from one position to another. There was "circulation of the elite" among the official positions of the local government. The gentry moved back and forth throughout the community. Above all, the sudden rise to wealth of some families meant some other houses were ruined. The aim of this chapter is to supplement the general conclusion reached by examining status mobility as a whole.

OCCUPATIONAL MOBILITY

The family and the school were the principal institutions to test the general biological, mental, and moral qualities of men and to determine only tentatively and in general in which of the fundamental strata an individual was to be placed and what kind of activity he was to follow. Such decisions, even for those who had successfully passed these "sieves" were, however, not final. They were further retested and reconsidered among those occupational organizations in which the individuals engaged. This process was of even greater importance for those who had not passed through all stages of the general agencies or who had failed. This group was tested principally by the occupational machinery. The decisions of the general agencies were close to being final in the sense that a series of privileged occupations was closed for a great majority of the "failures" in the family and school tests; and a great many men who successfully passed these tests were directed principally toward the privileged occupational groups. Even in those fields, however, there were exceptional revisions and alterations of the decisions in the general agencies by an occupational group. These organizations were especially important in testing the specific abilities of individuals necessary for successful performance of given forms of work. From all these points of view the testing and selecting role of an occupational organization was enormous.[1]

The occupational structure was so important a factor in the social system that a "job" could serve very largely to determine a man's general social status. His occupation had direct effects on factors like income, possessions, place of residence, associates, leisure, expenditures, and, in general, the kind of privileges and disadvantages that made up his daily experiences.[2] Furthermore, occupation was not so important for the salary as it was as a symbol of other goals, at least once a rather moderate level of income and assets had been reached. Money was not everything. Recognition of achievement and dignity of position were sometimes more valuable than pecuniary rewards. Money was an expression of various forms of personal assertion like prestige, power, honor, ascendancy, and domination. It is perhaps not so much to say that only in a very exceptional case could an adult man be genuinely self-respecting and enjoy a respected status in the eyes of others if he did not "earn a living" in an approved occupational role. Not only was a matter of his own economic support involved, but also, generally speaking, his occupational status was the primary source of the income and class status of his wife and children.[3]

Certain types of occupation had almost always composed the upper social layers, while other occupational groups had almost always been at the bottom. The principal occupational classes were not situated horizontally on the social level, but they were, so to speak, superimposed upon one another.[4] Definite changes of occupation were therefore almost always connected with changes in the social status of individuals, the reason why interoccupational mobility was considered a form of social mobility. The struggle for power and prestige in the occupational sphere was the most direct path to a sense of superiority and importance.

Occupational mobility not only included moves from one occupation to another during the lifetime of an individual, but it may also include changes from generation to generation. The general advance in the occupational levels of the sons as compared with the fathers in each generation frequently also involved rises in social status.

In China it was traditionally supposed that society had, from time immemorial, been divided into four ranks: the scholars, the farmers, the artisans, and the merchants. In the rural community of Kunyang, the official and literary classes occupied the highest positions. To these classes the intelligent and able members of the community had usually been drawn. They were not only among the renowned but also among the powerful. From ancient days to the present the teacher has continued to command respect. Learning was always held in high esteem, and the educated person, if not superior to the official, usually claimed equality in social status, and the physician was also appreciated by the community. Reaching down to the bulk of population, the craftsman supplied the needs of the people with articles of many kinds. True, manufactured goods had been imported, but articles for personal and family use were mainly made by hand labor at the guilds and in the homes. As commerce was carried on in the market towns, real merchants in the village were few. Numerically, however, the most important group was the farmers. Robust in health, simple in manner, however lowly in social status, the farmer constituted the backbone of the population. His counterpart in the towns was the common laborer, who earned his livelihood more by muscular exertion than by brain power. Although present in enormous numbers, the common workmen formed perhaps the lowest stratum of the society. Still, when choosing an occupation, the average man frequently weighed one element against another, the income an occupation might bring him against the social status it occupied in the hierarchy of occupations. Often the consideration of earnings was subordinated to that of social prestige.[5]

Occupations were not hereditary, though the conditioned facility of a boy for learning his father's trade tended to fix each generation into the same line. Freedom of occupational choice prevailed. Everyone was free to change his occupation as he preferred. In the village, however, change of occupation was very difficult. Villagers could change their occupations only by leaving the village. In other words, occupational mobility meant migration from village to town. For those who had been reared in the village, the change from being a farmer to being a merchant was very great. Nevertheless, the ambitious landowner, as soon as his wealth was great enough, moved his family into the town and opened a store, in the hope of satisfying his ambition and achieving status. But moving from village to town and changing from farmer to merchant necessitated a process of learning and adjustment. The life history of Commander Chu's great-grandfather is illustrative:

Commander Chu's great-grandfather, Chu Yuan, resided originally at a village named Wang Sien, which was situated at the edge of Kunming Lake five kilometers east of the City of Kunyang. He was a farmer. Though illiterate, he was intelligent and upright. His family was well-to-do at that time, but the village was filled with ne'er-do-wells, gamblers, and loafers who created many disturbances. Chu Yuan often overzealously urged them to be industrious. As a result, he was bitterly hated by the rascals and was shunned by the villagers. The location of the village was also unfortunate; as it was close to the lake, it was flooded every two or three years. When there was no flood, there would be drought instead. Chu Yuan felt that there was no future for him in the village.

Because of the difficulty of living and his isolation in the village, he decided to move into the city with his family. Before he left he sold five *kung* of land, mortgaged ten *kung,* and rented the remaining twenty-five *kung* to others. Once in the city he rented a room facing the street and opened a grocery store to sell such items as salt, wine, tobacco, bean oil, sugar, and soap. The first two years in this venture were dull, for he lacked experience in business. During these years, the family still depended for its living on the rents from their farm. Chu Yuan wished to return to the village but feared the ridicule of the people. He found it very difficult to find a solution.

One day an old woman came to Chu Yuan's shop to buy some bean oil with an earthen pot, which held a litle more than one *ching.* Usually one *ching* from other shops did not fill the container, but this time the container was filled to the brim. The woman was so happy that not only did she become a regular customer at Chu Yuan's shop but she also told of this generosity to others. As a result, his business improved gradually. He learned from the old woman that a person is always glad to receive a little more than the amount he has bargained for. Furthermore, Chu Yuan noticed that it was wise to have a pleasant disposition and to acknowledge that the customer was always right. If the customer had received a good impression, he would come again. His business prospered by leaps and bounds.

As he had become admirably successful, he continued to enlarge the business. When he needed capital, he would go to his village and sell farmland. He rented two more rooms at the back of his shop for a residence and after ten years was able to buy them. Chu Yuan thus became quite a rich merchant in the city. He felt satisfied with his successful change from farmer to merchant. Many people who had despised him before had changed their attitudes and come to admire him. He continued in his business until his death at the age of seventy-five.

The case history of Chu Yuan illustrates the process of learning and adjustment involved in moving from village to town and changing from farmer to merchant. Such change involved alteration of one's way of life. One who was able to achieve success gained much satisfaction and enviable social status.

A city dweller had a better opportunity than did a villager to change his occupation, especially to find a governmental position. But slow and painful learning was also essential as he drove toward power and esteem. The life history of Chief Ting provides an excellent illustration:

Ting had been anxious to achieve a position in the local government for a long time. In 1939 Mr. Hsu, a relative of Ting's father-in-law, was first appointed head of the first *chu* government of the county. Ting thought it wise to approach Mr. Hsu. Consequently, Ting was appointed clerk of the district government. Because of his lack of training, this job was fairly difficult for him. His handwriting was bad. When he was assigned to write a public letter, he held the brush-pen in his hand and did not know what to write. He felt hard pressed and uneasy, with his back covered with sweat. At that time he often sighed deeply and recited the popular couplet, "When books are being diligently used, there is self-reproach for having read little; if an affair is not passed through, you do not know the difficulty of it."

As he felt his lack of training, Ting tried to make up for his deficiency by being diligent and enthusiastic in doing every kind of work. If any question occurred to him, he would immediately ask Mr. Hsu to advise him. After half a year, Ting was promoted to an assistantship. During that time he learned many things like entertainment of superior officials, social etiquette in general, and the technique of grafting. At the same time he associated intimately with Chief Chang and other influential members of the gentry. After two years, when he was twenty-nine years old, the *chu* system was changed to the *hsiang-chên* system, and he was appointed *chên chang,* chief of the urban district. He rejoiced in his success.

For the poor but ambitious peasant, mercenary soldiering was the convenient way of changing occupations. As the life of a soldier was rough, he would usually quit the army after acquiring some fortune by looting or plundering. Regardless of whether an individual was rich or poor, when he left the village he would be separated from his farmland and would give up farming. He usually picked some kind of business for his next occupation. The life history of Yao's father, Yao Kuang-tsu, is a revealing case:

After the division of family with his brothers, Mr. Yao's grandfather, Yao Ta-sung, had sixteen *kung* of farmland and a house with two rooms. Ta-sung tried his best to let his only son, Kuang-tsu, go to school, though the economic condition of their family was not so good.

Kuang-tsu started to study at seven years of age. He had a good memory, studied very hard, and made fast progress. Unfortunately, he had to quit school at twelve and hired himself to a landowner as a cattle tender. His yearly wage was forty catties of rice, two suits of clothes, one pair of shoes, and a cap. He was clever and industrious. His master liked him very much. Kuang-tsu usually tended his cattle on the hill with a young companion. His companion recognized more characters than he and liked to read such popular novels as *The Romance of the Three Kingdoms, All Men Are Brothers, The Romance of Feudal States, The Record of a Journey to the West,* and the like. Kuang-tsu thus had an opportunity to learn from this fellow. After several years, he had read many novels, and his mind had been gradually enlightened. He talked expressively and elegantly.

When he was twenty-two years old, Kuang-tsu felt that there was no future for a farm laborer and that a man should be ambitious if he wanted to be prominent. He persuaded eight friends to go to Kwangsi Province to join the army voluntarily and to fight against the Manchu government. He was ingenious and eloquent. He often told stories that he had read from novels when he and his colleagues were off duty. His stories amused and encouraged his colleagues to forget fatigue, minor hardships, and danger. He was therefore liked by his superior officers and promoted to captain in a few years. After being in the army for eight years, he resigned his post and came home with six loads of silver and other precious articles. These loads were carried by six mules.

After returning home, he engaged in opium trading. Because he had been an officer, all the people highly respected him. He was wealthy and well known. He bought opium in Kunyang and transported it to Kunming once a month. Each trip he transported 10,000 *liang*. He was shrewd and energetic. After two years, he had accumulated about $200,-000. He bought 150 *kung* of farmland and built a magnificent large house.

Yao Kuang-tsu's case history shows us that, for the poor and ambitious peasants, a convenient way of changing occupations was to become mercenary soldiers. As the peasants usually had little formal education, if they could win some fortune by looting or plundering, their next convenient occupation would be some kind of business.

The traditional socially approved change of occupation was, of course, from agriculture to teaching and from teaching to public service. As a landowner, one had the essential leisure and was able to acquire a literary education. Through study one was able to master the arts deemed essential to administrative competence and would become eventually eligible to become an official. An official was popularly regarded as a ruler. His status commanded special privileges, power, ascendancy, and favorable prospects in every other way. The long process of occupational change might take several generations, which meant that most men did not jump suddenly from lower occupations to higher ones but moved gradually from one step to another. The life history of Chief Liao is illustrative:

Chief Liao, then head of the Department of Public Granary of the county government, was born in a village named Hsia Ho Pu, which was situated in a valley of one square mile about eight miles southeast of Kunyang. The village had a population of 582 persons on March 1, 1942. The most important occupation of the villagers was agriculture. Their supplementary occupations were gathering firewood in the mountains and raising sheep and pigs. A few either engaged in teaching or joined the army.

Chief Liao's great-grandfather, Liao Han-jo, had been a poor farmer. He had only eight *kung* of farmland. The harvest of his land could not support his family. He and his wife had to gather firewood to sell in the town to increase their income. When they went to the market town, they never bought anything to eat and would stay there for a long time. When Liao Han-jo was thirty years old, he was able to buy seven *kung* of farmland and thirty sheep. The sheep could produce at least ten lambs a year. The product of his farmland also increased because of the availability of fertilizer. He was therefore nicknamed Hsiao K'ung-ming, "Little K'ung-ming"* for his excellent reckoning. But he was still despised by his village fellows for his extreme stinginess and frugality. When he was thirty-six years of age, he bought two horses for the transporting of his firewood. Thereafter, the economic condition of his family improved day after day.

Chief Liao's grandfather, Liao Shan-tien, studied in a private school for two years. He recognized some simple characters but could not write. He was tall and energetic. He spoke in a loud voice and was quick in action. Though he was an industrious farmer, he was fond of participating in village affairs and frank to voice the villagers' grievances. He was therefore supported by the young villagers in an effort to take charge of

* K'ung-ming was the Prime Minister of Cho during the time of the Three Kingdoms and was famous for his many tricky calculations in the wars with other states.

the public affairs of the village. His family had then thirty-one *kung* of farmland.

When he was forty years old, his fortune was "smiling." The number of sheep had been doubled. Every year he could sell twenty sheep and three fat pigs. From these sales he could net twenty-four piculs of rice a year. He bought three mares and began producing two mules a year. He could earn annually another eight piculs of rice. He lent the rice to others and collected interest at twenty-four piculs of rice a year. After five years, he bought ten *kung* of farmland and repaired his house. As he watched over village affairs and participated in the community activities, he knew many noted men and had an insight into social affairs. His father had formerly advised him to be industrious and painstaking in farming. He therefore encouraged his own sons to study hard at school and to go to the outside world to look for fortune. He often said: "Distance is beauty. One cannot be held in esteem in his native place."

Chief Liao's father, Liao Fei-huang, was the younger of two brothers. When his father passed away, he was only eight years old. He never had the opportunity to enter school. He went into agriculture and always regretted his illiteracy. He admired the educated man who knew the affairs of the world and who was therefore never simply the creature of his own time and place and culture. He often said, "I tzŭ ch'ih ch'ieh chin."† One character is worthy of one *ching* of gold." He also liked to quote this story to prove it: "Once upon a time, a man assaulted another fellow with an ax. The family of the murdered man accused him to the Magistrate. The assailant bribed the head of the Department of Receiving and Sending Letters of the country government to help him out of the trouble. The head of the Department simply changed the character 'using' to 'wielding' in the petition.* The original meaning of 'maliciously using an ax to assault' the fellow was changed to 'wielding an ax accidentally to kill' the fellow. The magistrate therefore acquitted him of the crime.' Fei-huang was very clever and industrious. He was able to add twenty *kung* of farmland to his family property.

Chief Liao was the younger of two brothers. He entered a private school when he was seven years old. He had a very good memory and was one of the best students in the school. When he was sixteen years of age, he went to Kunming and entered the provincial normal school through competitive examination. His father was proud of him because in the village his son was the only one studying in Kunming, though many families were richer than his. Liao was thus greatly inspired by his father and studied very hard in the school.

After four years, he was graduated from the normal school. He came back home and taught in the primary school of his native district. After

† Under the Han Dynasty (200 B.C.-A.D. 222) *ch-ieh chin* meant one *ching* of gold or 10,000 copper coins.

* The Chinese symbol for "using" is 用 and that for "wielding" 用 . The difference between them is only a slight additional stroke in the character for "wielding."

teaching three years, he decided that the teaching job was too monotonous and the salary was too low. He resigned and became an assistant in the *chu* government. He was honest, careful, and enthusiastic and was therefore highly commended by the gentry and the people. After three years, he found that his great talent was employed in a small capacity. He wanted a position that had more power. He offered 1,000 silver dollars to Chu Hsin, Commander Chu's younger brother, to help him capture the position of chief in the sixth *chu* government of the county. Chu Hsin was then head of the Department of Finance of the county government and one of the most powerful members of the gentry. Liao's wish was fulfilled.

After obtaining the appointment, he spent several hundred silver dollars to entertain the top officials of the county government and the important gentry of the *chu*. Then he went to the district to take over the position. His plan was "reputation first, wealth accumulation next." After half a year, he had established his reputation in the district as a good administrator. Then he began to take advantage of every means possible to graft money. Within two years he had accumulated 10,000 silver dollars. His father bought eighty *kung* of farmland and repaired his house and rebuilt their ancestors' tomb.

In 1937, Magistrate Ho came to Kunyang. He found Liao able and sociable and appointed him head of the Department of Conscription of the county government. Within three years Liao had accumulated 60,000 silver dollars. To cover his grafting, he devoted himself to the buying and selling of iron and lumber. He gained 15,000 silver dollars more from this activity.

In 1943, he joined Chief Chang in accusing Magistrate Chao. He was dismissed by the Magistrate. In fact, he was happy over his dismissal because he was afraid of being involved in trouble over his having grafted for so long a time. In order to avoid the gossip of the people, he served as secretary to the army for two years.

In 1945, he returned home and devoted himself to buying and selling rice. In the next year, Magistrate Ma came to Kunyang and appointed him head of the Department of Public Granary of the county government. He was very active and always in high spirits.

Liao's life history indicates that a typical route of change for a peasant was from agriculture to teaching and from teaching to government service. The majority may have taken several generations to complete this long process of occupational change, however, whereas Liao achieved this goal in his lifetime.

We have gained the impression that the class of artisans and craftsmen had the smallest chances for upward mobility.[6] Indeed, the great Han historian, Ssŭ-ma Ch'ien, pointed out long ago that trade and commerce yielded much higher returns than did agriculture and crafts.[7] There were three factors limiting upward mobility for the artisans.

First, the full-time artisans do not appear to have been numerically and economically significant compared to the great mass of peasants. A large number of craftsmen in the villages was scattered in different occupations, as most farmers were engaged, during the slack seasons of winter and spring, in craftwork of one sort or another in order to obtain supplementary income. Among the 506 peasant households studied by Su, 243 or 48.2% had some sort of sideline occupations.[8] Craftsmen were also numerous in the cities, but, as modern influence spread, many found it difficult to adapt themselves to the changing social situation.[9]

Second, an industry adapted to using the slack period of agriculture and to earning some supplementary income for the family had to be on a small scale. Nor was there likely to be, among poor folks, a large amount of capital available for investing in tools; consequently labor and skill were the main elements in this sort of industry.

Finally, it could not acquire large amounts of material that had to be transported from afar. The types of article produced in such an industry had therefore to be limited to those made from local materials. For example, in a place where clay was produced, a pottery industry would develop.[10]

Although the craftsmen had the smallest chances for upward mobility, we did collect the case history of Pan Chin-pao, a successful shoemaker. Unfortunately, as he and his family had moved to Kunming City, we did not have a chance to obtain a direct interview with him. The following story was submitted by a member of his lineage:

Pan Chin-pao was born in a village named Ching Ku, five miles north of the City of Kunyang. The village had a population of 1,024 persons and was well known for its high educational level. It had eleven high-school students and one university graduate. The elementary school of the village had 140 students. The people of the village, especially those of the wealthy and powerful Pan lineage, were the most adventurous in business and trades. The assistant manager of the Farmers Bank in the City of Kunyang was also a member of Pan lineage.

Pan Chin-pao's ancestors had all been farmers. He started as an apprentice in a shoe shop when he was twelve years old. Before he entered his trade, he had been studying in a private school for four years. After working five years for his master without payment, he became a journeyman in the shop. After another eight years, he became a master and opened a shop himself in the City of Kunyang. His business was very successful.

In 1939, when he was forty years old, he was so prosperous that he was able to move with his family to Kunming and to open a fashionable leather-shoe shop on a main street in the city. After he established his store in Kunming City, his reputation became widespread in Kunyang. He was immediately called the "only industrialist" in Kunyang. The people praised him highly for his ingenuity, dexterity, and pleasant personality. His family was considered very promising because his first son was working in his shop and his second son was studying in a senior middle school in Kunming.

Pan Chin-pao's case history illustrates that there was upward social mobility for an artisan, not only within his trade, but also between his particular trade and other occupations.

Generally speaking, a village landowner moved up by one or more of several routes, but the direction was always the same. With wealth and leisure, he was able to acquire a literary education, eventually achieving scholarship and entry into officialdom. Or, though he may have possessed only a modicum of learning, the rich peasant might be used by bureaucrats to collect taxes and to draft conscriptions, and his sons might enter the gentry class by becoming full-fledged bureaucrats. Or such a man could join the army and become an officer to make common cause with various dissatisfied elements, become an outlaw leader, then a general, ruler of a province, and so on the way to ever greater power. Or he might succeed as a merchant, move to town, become the owner of a chain of related business enterprises, and provide his sons with enough leisure and education to move on into professional or official occupations.[11] The status of the gentry thus emerged in the rural society as the result of a slow and difficult occupational differentiation of the peasant population. The occupational mobility of the twenty-six gentry families of Kunyang is shown in Table 18.

It reveals that, of the twenty-six members of the gentry, seven were schoolteachers, seven bureaucrats, six merchants, five military men, and one a physician. It is noteworthy that the number of farmers among the forebears of gentry members had decreased from twenty-four among their great-great-grandfathers to ten among their fathers. No member of the county gentry was a farmer or an artisan.

ECOLOGICAL MOBILITY AS RELATED TO SOCIAL MOBILITY

In human society the phenomenon of struggling for livelihood and social status is everywhere manifest in ecological distribution. Territorial mobility is directly related to communication and contact and is therefore closely related to social mobility. It is a dimension

Table 18. Occupational Mobility of the Twenty-Six Upper
Gentry Families, Kunyang, 1946

Occupation	Gentry	Fathers	Grand-fathers	Great-Grand-fathers	Great-Great-Grand-fathers
Agriculture		10	15	21	24
Handicraft			1		
Commerce	6	4	6	3	2
Teaching	7	8	3	2	
Civil service	7	1	1		
Military service	5	1			
Medicine	1	2			
Total	26	26	26	26	26

of social life as functional as status. It is an integral part of the total process of social mobility. Many men would probably not have advanced so far in their careers if they had not been territorially mobile. Ecological mobility should therefore be considered inseparable from social mobility.

It should be stressed that spatial mobility, although in itself a nonsociological process, is nevertheless important because of its bearing upon the other aspects of social mobility being considered. When territorial mobility takes place, new contacts are made and new stimuli received, paving the way for changes in social relations, occupation, income, way of life, and social status. A man's contact with the experiences of other men broadens and develops him. As he enters a new world, he meets men whom he admires and respects, some of whom may become his friends or models for social advancement. He acquires new goals, new values, and a different way of life.

A large community is divided into a series of ecological areas regarded as having differential values, prestige, and advantages, both socially and economically. The relative size of a community affects the training, opportunities, perceptions of the occupational structure, and occupational aspirations of its citizens, and thus increases or decreases their chances for advantageous social mobility. Furthermore, since the growth of the cities, they have almost completely monopolized the function of social promotion among individuals. Unless he migrates to the city, a man of humble origins in the country has almost ceased to have any chance to climb, which explains why a permanent or temporary city dwelling becomes an inevitable step in climbing the social ladder. It also explains why the upper strata have been recruited almost exclusively from people who have either been born or, at any rate, have lived for substantial periods in cities. It is understandable that, for all who have been born in the country in humble conditions, migration to the city has been a necessary step toward social promotion.[12] When a man climbs higher and higher socially, he moves step by step from the village toward the town and from the small city toward the large city.

In China, the gentry and peasantry can be further contrasted by examining their ecological positions. To understand the rural economy of China up to recent times, one has to bear in mind the fact that life on the land offered no scope for ambition. The average farm in China was only a few acres. (In Yunnan a good-sized farm was only about one acre.) Small farming made accumulation of capital impossible. Villagers put it neatly, "Land breeds no land." In a community in which industry and commerce were not developed, in which land had already done its best, and in which pressure from the increasing population was felt, ambitious people had to seek their fortunes not through ordinary economic enterprises but through acquiring power, either legally or illegally. They had to leave their villages for good. When they obtained wealth, they might come back to their villages to acquire land, but if they retired to live in the villages, the pressure of population would bear down on them and soon wear them out—and after a few generations the big house would break up into a number of small holdings again. It was therefore essential for the rich to keep away from the villages. The place where they could maintain their power and wealth was the town.[13]

Towns in traditional China were not founded on manufacturing or commerce. In China the chief industries, like textiles, were mainly peasant occupations. Owing to the smallness of the farms, the peasants could not live entirely upon the land. It was a matter of necessity to have some additional income. As agriculture could not give full employment to the peasants, they had plenty of time to carry on industrial jobs in their homes. Peasants lived in a largely self-sufficient economy. The amount of goods they bought and sold was small. In most parts of China the periodical market took the place of the town. It took place only once in several days. Its size and frequency could be adjusted to temporary need. It seems clear that the permanent town had no place in the traditional rural economy.[14]

The traditional town was the seat of the gentry. The gentry class symbolized political and financial power. The *ch'eng,* the walled city, was the center of political power. The essential connection of the gentry with officialdom drew the former to the administrative center. The gentry in the city exercised authority in a still wider area. The town mainly consisted of residences of the gentry, rice stores, pawnshops, teahouses, wine restaurants, and private gardens. There was also a number of tailors, carpenters, blacksmiths, goldsmiths, and other craftsmen. The rice stores and the pawnshops were financial establishments. The peasants, when pressed for rents or taxes or involved in some other crises, had to sell their rice to the stores in town at low prices. When their reserves were eaten up, they would come to the stores to buy at high prices. The rice stores were therefore similar in nature to the pawnshops. Teahouses, wine restaurants, big gardens, and magnificent residences were also paraphernalia of the gentry. From morning until nightfall, the leisured gentlemen gathered in the teahouses to amuse themselves sipping tea, gambling, and smoking opium. Leisure meant prestige as well as privilege. By displaying the leisure at their disposal, they rose higher in the eyes of the lower classes. The professionals who lived in the town were dependent on the gentry for their employment.[15]

The mass of peasants did not live in the town. They looked at the seat of the gentry with mixed feelings of repulsion and admiration. They supported the minority by paying taxes, rents, and interests. The annual tribute was their burden. If this economic reason were not sufficient to arouse the ill will of the peasant toward the townsman, he would no longer remain undisturbed in the village when he found that his dissatisfied wife had run away from home to work as a maid in a gentleman's big house, which he himself dared not enter. The town remained the ideal, however, the dream and the incentive of the peasants. It seems that they were not antagonistic toward the town or the gentry as such. What they were against was their own inability to become one of those who exploited them. As long as they believed that paradise was not closed to them, they had no desire to deny that it was where their own hopes and wishes lay.[16]

The line of demarcation between town and country was clearly defined by the city wall. In the city there was an air of orderliness and cleanliness with wide paved streets and many large buildings. The country was littered with dirt and debris. It was obvious that the city was the symbol of greater security, comfort, and prosperity.

The gentry of Kunyang, as elsewhere, consisted of either city dwellers or countrymen more territorially mobile than were the farmer-peasants. Of the twenty-six gentry members, seven had been born and were living in the City of Kunyang. Most made frequent trips to Kunming, the provincial capital of Yunnan. For example, Chief Ting went to Kunming four or five times a month on business. The remaining nineteen gentry members had been mainly living in the city, though they had been born in the villages. On the average, they had dwelled in the city for 9.6 years. The shortest period was five years, and the longest was more than twenty-four years. The son of a peasant who became a member of the gentry had to leave his place of birth socially and territorially as part of the total process of upward mobility.

As a farmer who spent his life in the village, the peasant had little contact with the outside world. His world was, first of all, his own household. He ate and slept with other members of the household. He and his family members shared labor and recreation. The next most intimate group of which he was a member included his neighbors and his lineage members, with whom he cooperated in working. Most of the villages were lineage villages. Everyone in the village knew everyone else very well. Almost all the male inhabitants had been born there. All their connections and relationships were personal, face-to-face ones. The next wider acquaintance of the villager was in the neighboring market towns. With the towns he had occasional rather than everyday contacts. His contacts were largely economic. The farmer went there to buy tools or materials or to sell his products. The county seat was perhaps the farthest away he ever went. His visits to the county seat had rather the character of holiday trips. He went there as a spectator in search of amusement.

The range of the gentry's world was much wider than that of the peasants. Gentlemen did not stay at their homes and deal only with their own neighbors and relatives. Rather, they had to do business with people coming from a much larger area and with whom they had sometimes had no previous connections. They had traveled far and lived away from their native places for years, either while attending school or while building their careers. They had thus gained a wider perspective on the world. Of the twenty-six gentry members, twenty had traveled beyond the County of Kunyang, four outside the Province of Yunnan, and two out of China. On the average, a gentry member had traveled 10.2 years.

Most of the gentry members who had come from the countryside and moved above their parental statuses resided in the town or city. Of the twenty-six upper gentry members, the seven who were born in the county seat all remained in the city. Whereas nineteen of the twenty-six great-great-grandfathers lived in the villages, only two of the upper gentry members lived in the villages, five in towns, sixteen in the county seat, and three in the provincial capital. The gentry families had moved toward the town and city generation after generation.

The role of ecological mobility is consistent with that of upward social mobility. The gentry was both socially and territorially mobile. Territorial mobility may have been either a necessity of, or the pre-condition for, social and occupational mobility. Changes in residential area were an integral part of gentry lives and careers. The split between the gentry and the peasantry eventually became more marked through the tendency to separate into town- and country-dwellers. The gentry moved to the administrative centers for political power, economic advantage, and social status. The physical distance that separated the country from the city was at the same time a measure of the social distance between the peasantry and the gentry and a means by which this social distance could be maintained.

UPWARD AND DOWNWARD MOBILITY

The members of various status groups never consisted of the same individuals. There was constant turnover. Entries and exits occurred continually—the latter directed both upward and downward. The members of each status group were forever changing, to the point at which a group might consist of a completely new set of families. For the duration of its collective life or the time during which its identity might be assumed, each status group resembled a hotel or an omnibus, always full but always full of different people.[17]

Under normal conditions, the "ups" and "downs" took place gradually and in orderly fashion, being considerably controlled by a social mechanism of selection and distribution of individuals. The considerable ascending or descending displacement of a family or an individual demanded, several years in the quickest case and more often one, two, or three generations. This slowness was due to the fact that the ascending or descending displacements did not take place without the testing and training of individuals. A climber had to show his ability. Many years of training or work were necessary to acquire it. The "social promotion" of the climbers was therefore gradual and relatively slow. The same was true of the sinking men. Having been born to high positions, they automatically occupied places similar to those of their parents. With average ability and work, they might very easily keep them. Social inertia worked in their favor. Extraordinary moral or mental failures were necessary for such men to be ousted and displaced. Their first "failures" usually were not enough to produce their degradation. Persistent and recurring failures were necessary to call forth such effects, and they naturally took years and years. Social inertia explains partly why "ups" and "downs" came gradually.[18]

It must be added that there were many other factors that hindered sudden and quick ascents or descents. Most fundamental was the complex of social conditions styled briefly "juridical" or "factual" inheritance. Inheritance of wealth, the social position of a family, its traditions, its reputation all continued to play—juridically and psychologically—a very considerable part. In a democratic society, men boast that they judge other men only according to their personal qualities. This boast is true only to a degree. The social standing of a family, its titles, reputation, wealth, relatives, and so on still play a very great part in a man's reputation independent of his personal qualities. For these reasons, it is natural that in China a considerable proportion of the ascents and descents through considerable social distance demanded time spans of two or three generations. Other such displacements may have happened within single generations, but even they took considerable numbers of years.[19]

Chinese society, with its flexible social system, invited the individual to change his social status. Social mobility admitted of the possibility of transition from one social status to another either by promotion to a higher status or by degradation to a lower one. We have seen in the previous chapters that, through various channels and processes, a poor peasant could be elevated to the position of gentry member. We have not paid any attention to downward mobility. It should not be overlooked, however, that the sudden rise to wealth of the opium traders was correlated with the fact that so many houses in the village had been ruined by opium smoking. The area of cultivated land was comparatively fixed. If the rich families held their land too long, the consequences were that the candidates for land ownership had to wait that much longer and that the upward mobility of men was thus retarded. It is evident that upward mobility cannot be considered apart from downward mobility.

The rising and falling of families are facts. The only question we have to ask is, How does it happen that one family rises, while the other falls—quite apart from accidents, to which we may attribute a certain importance but not the crucial one? No matter which area we study, we always find that the relative positions of families in the status situation undergo change, not in such a way that the big ones grow bigger and the small ones smaller, but typically the other way around.[20]

Though downward mobility was extremely distasteful for everybody and was overtly condemned by the community in spite and ridicule, many families inevitably descended. Several causes were always found to be operating.

First, the principle of the local system of inheritance was the equal sharing of the father's estate by all the brothers. This principle had a disintegrating effect on the continuity of family landholding, for, however large the original estate might have been, it was broken up into small tracts as the male descendants multiplied.[21] Such a procedure fitted the traditional ideas of fairness and filial prosperity; the most humane course seemed to be to permit a certain amount of crowding on the limited quantity of land and to let the brothers share equally in the benefits or sacrifices.[22] As previously pointed out, from time to time, poorer homes rose in the world; but few held on. On the whole, the tendency to sink from big holdings to small holdings to landlessness was strong. The division of land among the sons was a factor in a family's social descent. As the population increased, wealthy houses could not be perpetuated. The life history of Captain Yang's family is illustrative:

Captain Yang's great-grandfather, Yang Ping-kan, had been an able, clever, strong man. Though he was illiterate, he spoke distinctly and eloquently. He was engaged in agriculture, and the family had ninety-five *kung* of farmland and a house of seven rooms. He was then the richest man in the village.

Yang Ping-kan wisely managed his farms. Every night he planned the work for the next day for his brothers and hired men. He himself worked only occasionally. Because of his clever management, all the members of his family inherited a good deal of money.

When Yang Ping-kan was forty years old, he divided the property of his family with his brothers and received twenty-five *kung* of farmland and two rooms for himself. As the harvest from the farms barely provided living expenses for his family, he had to work hard. Ten years later the economic condition of his family had greatly improved, and he bought ten *kung* of farmland.

Captain Yang's grandfather, Yang Hou-hsi, was the eldest of three brothers. He worked very hard as a farmer. During the winter lull in farming, he was accustomed to go to the mountains to gather firewood for his household for the whole next year. He rented ten *kung* of farmland from a landlord. In the busy period of the year the wages of a laborer were much higher than usual, and he therefore hurried to complete his own work so that he could hire out to others. After five years his family's economic condition was improved. Formerly it had had only one ox; now it had two. Formerly it had raised only two pigs; now the number had been doubled. After another five years, the family bought fifteen *kung* of farmland and built a house with two rooms. All the villagers admired Hou-hsi's ability.

When Hou-hsi was thirty-two, his father, Ping-kan, passed away. Two years later his mother died also. After the deaths of his parents, his wife's sisters-in-law began to quarrel, and his brothers became unhappy. The large family was divided into three small families.

Hou-hsi received ten *kung* of farmland and two rooms. Though the economic condition of the family was improving steadily during the first few years, Hou-hsi did not increase his property very much. The main reason for the decline of his family was that his only son, Yang Keng-ju, had been spoiled from boyhood and was very lazy. Keng-ju did nothing except eat and sleep. This laziness made Hou-hsi unhappy.

When Yang Keng-ju was thirty years old, he lost a great deal of money in gambling. As he had no way to repay his gambling debts, he had to leave home. He worked as a laborer in Anning and as a tin miner in Kuo Chiu. After one year of nomadic life, Yang Keng-ju temporarily changed his way of life. He worked very hard. He had then eight *kung* of farmland and two *kung* of truck garden. As the income was not enough for the expenses of his family, he had to work as a temporary laborer for others to increase his income. He was noted for his extraordinary strength. After three years, the economic condition of his family was improved, but, because of his habits of gambling and drinking, he did not save much money.

Yang Keng-ju married at the age of eighteen and had three sons and one daughter. Captain Yang was Keng-ju's first son.

This history shows that, through the increase of family members and the equal division of family property among the sons, after three generations Yang's family had dropped from a wealthy house to a poor one. Yang's great-grandfather had had ninety-five *kung* of farmland, whereas Yang's father had only eight *kung* of farmland and two *kung* of truck garden.

Rich people were proud of having big families and numerous sons and grandsons. Any family with comparatively large landholdings was likely to raise more children. It was impossible, however, to maintain the ideal of prosperity in both posterity and property at the same time. If a family with a large estate had several sons in each generation, after several generations, the large landholding will disappear. In this regard, the life history of Yuan Hsing-chao, who was an only son and held 160 *kung* of farmland through inheritance, may be taken for comparison:

Yuan Hsing-chao's ancestors had all been farmers. Hsing-chao's grandfather had been an only son and had had 125 *kung* of farmland. Hsing-chao's father had had two brothers. After the family was divided, each received about forty *kung* of farmland. Hsing-chao's elder uncle was married at seventeen years of age. His wife gave birth to four sons and two daughters. All of them died when they were young. The property of their family was therefore inherited by Hsing-chao.

Hsing-chao's younger uncle was married at twenty. His wife bore him two sons and four daughters. All of them died except a daughter. The daughter's husband lived with her family. Half of this uncle's property was also inherited by Hsing-chao.

Hsing-chao's father married at nineteen years of age. His mother gave birth to six sons and two daughters. Hsing-chao was the last. When he came along, all his brothers and sisters had died. Hsing-chao thus became an only son. He inherited not only his father's property but also his uncles' estates. His luck was well known in the district of Chiu Tu.

The difference between the cases of Captain Yang and Yuan Hsing-chao was ultimately a matter of population pressure. Hsing-chao became a landlord because all his brothers and cousins had died prematurely. Had they all lived and his 160 *kung* of farmland been divided into twelve portions accordingly, each would have become a petty landowner.

Second, the degenerating effect of wealth and power on the young was given full play among the gentry. The wealthy father felt proud to be able to say that his son did not have to work at all. If the youngster was in trouble, the father would do whatever he could to help his young ne'er-do-well. He would usually back the latter up, regardless of the issues involved, to the limit of his influence. Even when the youngster did not voluntarily react to his surroundings in that way, the people tended to force preference upon him because of his father's wealth and power, and they influenced his attitudes accordingly. Wealth and power, even in the hands of an adult who had prospered by hard and honest work and had originally had feelings of justice and humanity, could be detrimental in the long run. How much more dangerous were they in the hands of youngsters who had never worked for a single day and who firmly believed that whatever they desired in life would be forthcoming simply for the asking or the taking.[23]

Through the cultural patterns of a strong father-son tie and the big-family ideal, both of which were integrated under the ancestor's shadow, two different personality configurations were formed. The poor son shared his parents' hard-working habits and was trained to be an honest, hard-working man. The rich son shared his parents' power and glamor and began life in the firm belief that he was destined to command, rule, control, and be supplied with permanent good fortune.[24]

This difference in personality configuration between the two status groups helps to explain why family fortunes tended to rise and fall within periods of two or three generations. The hard-working child of a poor peasant might not succeed in raising his family fortune at once, but there was at least such a possibility. The easygoing child of a rich peasant might not bring about his family's immediate downfall, but his parasitic life would probably be the beginning of a downward trend.[25]

Every son had as much pocket money as his parents could afford to give him. The sons of the rich tended early in life to indulge in excessive spending. They were susceptible to the temptations of gambling and opium smoking. Unfortunately, in the monotonous rural community little else offered pleasure. Gambling and opium smoking were outstanding factors in bringing families to disaster. Conditions were at their worst when the head of the family was himself an opium smoker. Opium not only exhausted fortunes but destroyed physical strength as well. Opium addicts could not do really productive work.

In the wealthy downwardly mobile families it was more usual for the boys to go to school in a halfhearted manner or otherwise to idle away their time. A big house was a little empire in itself. The members, like subjects, lived under the rule and whim of the patriarch. They knew no initiative, originality, or independence until they themselves were promoted to the position of ruler. They depended upon their house for their livings. Their careers were determined by the house; for whatever they were worth the house was solely responsible. A boy reared in such an environment was detached from the life of the people. He lived in a large house devoid of sunshine. He grew up in reverence of the past, in the shadow of his ancestors, from whom his privileges were inherited. Mentally, he was resigned, conservative, and perhaps even cowardly. Physically, he was weak, slender, and sometimes even sterile.[26] The worst thing that could happen to a family was to have unworthy sons who could not maintain the family's glory and fortune. When the son failed, the failure was almost absolute. We cited in the last chapter the case history of Tang Sheng-kuang's great-grandfather, Tang Kao-hsun, to illustrate how governmental office served as an important route to fortune. The same life history offers a typical case of an unworthy son.

Tang Sheng-kuang's grandfather, Tang Heng-chuan, was the second of three brothers. His elder brother received the degree of *hsiu ts'ai* and then taught. His younger brother studied for five years and became a farmer. Heng-chuan also received the degree of *hsiu ts'ai*.

When their property was divided, Tang Heng-chuan received ninety *kung* of farmland and went into business. During the period of the Lolos' uprising, his childless elder brother was killed, leaving seventy *kung* of farmland. Heng-chuan's younger brother had no child either. Although this brother had squandered his property, he still had thirty-five *kung* of farmland. All the property was thus inherited by Heng-chuan, who then had three sons. Unfortunately, both his eldest and youngest sons died in their twenties.

Tang Sheng-kuang's father, Tang Su-hou, was the second of the three brothers. He entered a private school at eight and studied for twelve years. He was thin and weak, but he was intelligent.

When Tang Sheng-kuang was born, his father was already forty years old. Four years later, his father died. From then on Sheng-kuang was especially pampered by his mother. When Sheng-kuang was seven years of age, his elder brother also died. His mother then set all her hopes on him. The whole life of the family revolved around the only son. The large house had only three inhabitants—Sheng-kuang, his mother, and a maidservant. He would run out every day to play in the morning and not come back until the afternoon. If he was hungry, he would ask a rice-noodle seller to give him rice-noodles on credit. His mother would pay the money for him the next day. He learned to gamble and to smoke cigarettes. Sometimes he did not receive enough money from his mother; he would then steal from home. His mother was reluctant to restrain him.

He entered a private school when he was eight years of age. The schoolteacher was an old pedant who had failed to obtain any degree in the civil examinations. He had lost the sight of one eye. The classroom was located on the upper floor of a lineage hall, the walls of which were dark and dirty. The teacher's bedroom was situated upstairs in a neighboring building. Sheng-kuang was not in the least interested in his schoolwork. When the teacher was not in the classroom, he would persuade three or four schoolmates to go elsewhere to gamble or to smoke opium. He used a slim bamboo as a smoking pipe, and every day received money from his mother, which he spent on gambling and opium smoking. He was a constant truant. If the teacher asked him the reason for his absence, he would say that his mother needed his help at home. As his family had so few members, the teacher thought this explanation reasonable. If he stayed at home, he would tell his mother that the teacher had some other thing to do and that there was no school. Though he was in the school for seven years, he learned nothing.

Tang Sheng-kuang was married at the age of sixteen. His wife was three years younger than he. They slept together every night but never talked to each other. He wandered to the gambling house and opium den every day. As his wife was too young to understand him, he was unhappy and sometimes visited prostitutes.

From the time he became a gambler and an opium addict, he was despised by the local people. When he was eighteen years old, he resolved to change his environment and struggle for his future. As an officer was held in high esteem and was feared by the people, he decided to enlist in the army. This plan was reported to his mother. As he was an only son and the family's future was bound up in him, his mother tried to keep him from joining by every means she could. She cried and begged him every day to change his mind. She asked his friends to persuade him and hired several men to watch him. Still he eventually ran away and secretly enlisted in the army. After three months, he could neither bear the regimentation nor did he dare to run away. He wrote a letter to his mother, and she immediately sent $10,000* to him. He bribed the colonel to take him on as errand boy. He was thus free to gamble and visit prostitutes. When he needed money, he wrote to his mother. After five years, his mother had to sell fifteen *kung* of farmland to meet his debts.

He was urged by his friends to go to Ho Kou to be bodyguard of the Director-General. As he did not have much to do there, he resumed his practices of gambling and opium smoking. After one year he was dismissed and came back to Kunming, where he served as a policeman. Every month his mother sent him $2,000 for his expenses.

In 1926, when he was twenty-five years old, his mother personally went to Kunming and asked him to come back home. His mother had brought him two wool suits of clothes in Sun Yat-sen style, a fur hat, and a pair of leather shoes. He returned home with his mother. After three days, when he saw that a friend had lost all his money gambling and did not have the fare to go home, Tang sold one of his new suits and helped his friend with the money. He thus frittered away his family's money without any consideration.

By that time, his wife had become more mature. She served him carefully and hospitably and tried very hard to make him happy. He came to love her very much. They smoked opium together every night. In two years his wife had also become an opium addict. Tang consumed one *liang* of opium a day and his wife one-tenth of one *liang*. They usually went to the restaurant to eat instead of cooking at home. He also hired two gangsters to serve him. As he did not have any income except rent, he had to sell forty *kung* of farmland in another three years.

In 1930, he took a concubine because his wife had borne him no child. He sold twenty *kung* of farmland to meet this expense. She was young and pretty. They fell in love. Because she accompanied him to smoke opium every night, she also became an opium addict. But she bore him no child either. After two years, because she felt that the relationship was going to hell and because Tang's wife quarreled with her very often, she asked his permission to marry. Her husband paid Tang $8,000 for compensation.

In 1932, when he was thirty-one years old, Tang's mother died. He

* The money was in provincial notes of Yunnan; the exchange rate was ten provincial dollars for one national dollar.

sold fifteen *kung* of farmland and mortgaged two rooms of his six-room store to meet the expense of his mother's funeral.

In 1940, he and his wife moved to Kunming to open a grocery store. He sold thirty *kung* of farmland for capital. After one year, he returned to Kunyang because of the Japanese air raids.

In 1943, he sold fifteen *kung* of farmland and a room of his store for living expenses. He obtained $150,000 from the land sale and $30,-000 for the room. He suddenly discovered that he had sold almost all his farmland. If he did not try to be frugal, he would starve in his old age. So he cut off the opium. He found himself so uneasy that he was compelled to look for a substitute. He began drinking two *ching* of wine every night, and he played mah-jongg every day. After one year, however, he went back to opium smoking because of a serious cough.

In June, 1945, Tang sold his residence for $8,000,000 [equivalent to 1,460 silver dollars]. He received $800,000 in advance. After the surrender of Japan, the price dropped suddenly, and the buyer refused to pay the remaining money. Tang borrowed $2,000,000 to go to Kunming to hire a lawyer to help him. After one year the price went up again due to the outbreak of the civil war. The buyer then paid him $6,500,000. He paid $1,000,000 to the lawyer, gave $500,000 to his wife, and used $2,-000,000 for old debts. By that time, he had sold all his property except a one-room store.

In 1946, he entered on a long-term illness. He sold his last property —a store with one room—for $5,000,000 and then died. The money was used for quite a lavish funeral, which was managed by his wife and neighbors. The remaining $1,600,000 was allotted to his wife.

Tang had sold altogether 135 *kung* of farmland, a store with six rooms, a large house, and, in addition—some people said—a pretty concubine. His money was used mainly for gambling and opium smoking. He was criticized as "too lazy." The glory of Tang's family had vanished.

The history of Tang Sheng-kuang's family provides an ideal example of the son of a wealthy father who was a prisoner of his past. The family encouraged dependence and kept the youngster from participating in productive work. A child reared in such an environment was detached from the life of the people. He lacked initiative and aggressiveness through no fault of his own.

Third, the most competent social climber might slip down from a high rung of the ladder because of unexpected personal or natural calamities. If the descent had served as a means of natural selection, that is, the elimination of the unsuitable members from the higher rungs of the ladder, there would have been no reason to deplore it. The problem was that even the most competent climber might slip. It was destructive to prestige, which had, in its turn, much to do with the forfeiture of the relative social position of families. But we need not worry about such descents because the man or his family could rise again. The core of the problem lay in the chance or opportunity to climb.

By "chance or opportunity" we mean the occurrence of favorable or unfavorable events independent of the behavior of the family in question or of its position. Only in rare instances was an event of this nature significant enough to exert a critical and enduring effect on the fate of a family in a way that might not have happened otherwise. Even rarer were those cases in which not only the occurrences but also the effects of the events on families' positions were independent of their behavior—for even when chance operated, its effects were usually exploited or overcome. The significance of such accidents in the total family history was too slight to figure as more than aberrations, important only to an understanding of individual cases or groups of cases. We can also assess as quite insignificant the number of cases in which series of unrelated chances, individually unimportant but together carrying some weight, lifted up families or lowered them. For, by the law of probability, such events are bound to cancel each other out. Of course, the canceling out does not necessarily happen in the individual case, but no valid theory to account for social mobility can be built on foundations of chance.[27]

Human life takes its course like a current in the sea, sometimes peaceful and sometimes rough. No one can live a smooth, monotonous life. Life changes all the time. Even the most balanced life shifts under new stimuli or in new environments. Crises come and go. They are simple or prolonged, and each must be surmounted to establish once again a relatively stable state.[28] The history of Commander Chu's family furnishes an excellent illustration:

Commander Chu's father, Chu Kan, had a great deal of strength and could beat anyone in boxing and fencing. He could raise a square stone of sixty *ching* with one hand. He passed the civil-service examination of the county at twenty-six and passed the examination of the province and received the degree of *wu chü jen* at twenty-nine. Then he was chosen by the gentry and appointed by the Magistrate to be captain of the county guard. He collected a group of volunteers and trained them daily in the use of the sword and spear. He was adventurous and brave.

Chu Kan had the same personality traits as his father. He was very temperamental. In any argument he would never yield to others. He easily lost his temper and would knock others down. Once in a quarrel he grew angry and hit the other fellow with his hand so hard that the man died of a hemorrhage. The families, relatives, and members of the lineage of the deceased were furious and rushed into Chu's home in a body. They destroyed everything in sight and butchered his livestock for dinner. At the funeral everyone who walked by was invited in for a good meal and given a big piece of white cloth.* Monks and Taoists were invited to chant the canon of Buddhism and to go through rituals to keep off spirits or to recite dirges. The cost for Chu's family was incalculable. He was then the agent of the salt transportation station between Kunming and Yüchi for a company in Kunming. This job paid well, and it was not easy to come by such an occupation at that time. The manager of the company trusted him because he was an honest man of good repute. But after this incident the manager of the salt company had no more confidence in Chu Kan and fired him. Furthermore, Commander Chu's grandparents passed away in quick succession. Their funerals cost the house a great deal of money. The home became a mere shell of four walls. Chu Kan sold six *kung* of farmland to meet expenses. To his regret the fight had caused the family to lose half its property. Later, although Chu Kan became more controlled than before, his prestige decreased day by day and did not rise again until the third of his four sons became an officer.

The case of Commander Chu's father involved a personal incident. We shall take the case of Chief Ting's great-grandfather, whose calamity was caused by a social event, for another illustration:

Chief Ting's great-grandfather, Ting Nai-huan, was the richest man in Kunyang. His business was the transportation of salt from the mine to Kunyang. He employed at least thirty horses each time, and all the retail merchants of Kunyang bought salt from him. In fact, he monopolized the salt supply in the county.

Ting Nai-huan built a large, well-constructed house. There were three connected courts. The first court held the shops; the second was the residence; the third was the warehouse. This building was a well-known *ta fang tzŭ*, "large house."

Unfortunately, because of the revolt of the Governor of Yunnan against the Manchu government, there was a great battle in Kunyang, during which Nai-huan's house was used as a headquarters for one of the commanders. At that time Nai-huan's younger brother was killed and the house looted and badly damaged by the soldiers.

Fortunately, Nai-huan had buried his silver dollars in time. After the rebellion was suppressed, he used the money that remained to repair the house and resume his business. After five years, the family became prosperous again.

The case histories of Chu and Ting illustrate that a competent climber might slip from a high rung of the social ladder through unexpected personal or social calamities. He could rise again, but the significance of such accidents in the total picture of family history is important only to an understanding of individual cases.

Fourth, the process of upward mobility demanded enormous energies of able men. When the personality dynamics of the mobile

* The white cloth was used to symbolize mourning.

individual could not be adjusted to these demands, he became enervated and eventually stopped at a certain stage. The life history of
Brigadier-General Yeh furnishes an ideal case:

Yeh Lü-chang, Brigadier-General Yeh, was born in 1890 in a village
named Ching Kia Ho, which was located about ten miles south of the
City of Kunyang. According to the 1942 census, the village had a population of 495. There was a stream passing through the village. The land
was fertile, but the villagers were well known for their laziness.

Brigadier-General Yeh's great-grandfather, Yeh Chien-ken, had
studied for five years and was very clever. He was engaged in agriculture, for which his family had seventy-five *kung* of farmland. When he
was thirty years old, he was elected by his villagers to take charge of the
public affairs of the village. He was a careful and responsible official.

Brigadier-General Yeh's grandfather, Yeh Shu-hai, studied for three
years and became a carpenter and mason. The wage then was four *ching*
of rice for a working day. Upon dividing the property with his brother,
he received thirty-five *kung* of farmland.

Brigadier-General Yeh's father, Yeh Chi-hsiang, was the elder of
two brothers. He studied in a private school for four years and then
began farming. When the family property was divided, he received
eighteen *kung* of farmland. He was so strong and worked so hard that he
was nicknamed "Iron Man." He had been able to buy thirty-two *kung* of
farmland by the time he was fifty-five years old.

Brigadier-General Yeh was the youngest of four brothers. He entered a private school at the age of nine and studied for seven years.
When he was nineteen years old, his family was ordered to send one of
the four boys to the government on conscription. His parents decided to
let their third son be recruited. After his brother had been in the army
for three months, however, the brother's wife complained it was an unfair choice and threatened to commit suicide. This threat put Yeh's
parents in distress. He told his parents that he would join the army to
take his brother's place, but his own wife opposed this move. He advised
her to be obedient to his parents' decision.

After three months in the army, Yeh was promoted to sergeant. This
promotion gave him much encouragement and made him study hard. As
he had already studied seven years, he was chosen for officer-candidate
school. In six months he was promoted to third lieutenant in charge of
provision. He was an honest and careful officer.

In 1911, he was promoted to second lieutenant and ordered to lead
his troops to Tung Hai to suppress bandits. He successfully carried out
his first mission. In 1913, he was ordered to Yung Ch'ang again to suppress bandits. After successfully completing his task, he obtained a
promotion to captain.

In 1915, Yeh became a major colonel. His troops were praised by
the local people for their good discipline, and Yeh was on good terms
with the local gentry. In Yung Ch'ang he bought a house, took a concubine, and accumulated 15,000 silver dollars. At the same time, he bought

another house in Kunming. When this news was brought to Kunyang, his reputation rose greatly with the people, and his father was called Lao Tai Yeh, "Great Excellency."

After being promoted to major colonel, Yeh's social life expanded, and he became an opium addict. In 1925, when he was thirty-five years old, he was given a colonelcy and ordered to lead his troops to Szechwan to reinforce the army there. He took the advice of his concubine, however, and resigned his post. But he was reappointed with the rank of major colonel as a staff officer in the provincial government.

In 1926, he was made a superintendent of the training of the lower officers. After a year, he became commander of the First Regiment. In 1934, he was ordered to lead his troops to fight against the Communist army of Kiangsi Province on the border of Yunnan and Kweichow.

In 1936, he was made superintendent of militia training in Kuo Chiu, a tin mining area. His position was perfect to accumulate wealth. But he was very reasonable and interested in getting ahead.

He brought along a nephew with him, whom he appointed *aide-de-camp*. His nephew was a gambler and an opium addict and very corrupt. In a brawl he wounded the manager of the Provincial Bank of Mining. The local gentry resented the nephew and accused him to the Governor. As a result, Brigadier-General Yeh was dismissed. He was sad about this matter but had accumulated three loads of opium, four pistols, and 6,000 silver dollars.

In 1938, the Fifty-Eighth Army was ordered to move to the Province of Hunan to fight against the Japanese. Yeh was appointed to brigadier-general. He felt, however, that a long-distance march would be a hardship. Japanese soldiers had better arms, he was not familiar with the geography of foreign provinces, and, above all, it would be difficult to find opium. At the same time, his concubine was arguing that he should give up the appointment. In order to resign his post, he bribed a doctor with $20,-000 to say that he had serious stomach trouble. He came home without a job.

In 1939, General Sun, the commander of the Fifty-Eighth Army, wrote to him from the front. But he still refused to accept any position. From then on all his former colleagues and superior officers despised him for his cowardice. The gentry of Kunyang also scorned him for his lack of courage and determination. Nevertheless, he paid no attention to criticism and began buying and selling lumber and iron. During the first two years, he made a little money. Yeh then paid a great deal of money to an iron dealer in advance. The iron dealer went broke because of a price rise and refused to give him the goods he had ordered. He lost money. In 1941, his concubine died, and he took a new one. In the next year, he arranged a marriage for his younger son. He sold his house in Kunming for $600,000 [equivalent to 5,000 silver dollars] to meet these expenses. Both his sons had become opium addicts and gamblers.

He saw his future growing darker and darker. He became very pessimistic. He wanted to take a job, but there was no opportunity. The gentry of Kunyang elected him commander of the Corps of People's Self-

Defense of Kunyang, but he was not interested. In the next year, the local gentry elected him vice-chairman of the Citizens' Political Council of the County of Kunyang. Again he showed no enthusiasm. When the Association of Veteran Officers in Kunyang was organized, he was elected the chief staff officer. But he remained inactive. The gentry and the people lost all faith in him. He was often criticized as "too cowardly."

He rarely went out; he simply lay on his bed daydreaming and smoking opium, puffing his pipe and driving the worries from his mind. Sometimes he would stand by his upstairs window and look out for hours as though searching after his lost glory. Although he was a friendly man, he was unable to further himself socially. He had little involvement with anyone or anything. He became dull, flabby, and tired from this aimlessness. He always looked absent-minded. It seemed that he needed something to fill the void in his life.

The life history of Yeh illustrates that, when the personality dynamics of the mobile individual were not adjusted to the enormous energy demands of upward mobility, he became enervated and eventually stopped at a certain stage. The whole process of Yeh's career stopped, leaving an empty and regretful man, lonely and withdrawn. Yeh had maintained the steady upward curve of his career until he was thirty-five years old, but the curve suddenly dipped and seemed to be directed steadily downward. At last, he withdrew from his career world. Although he had acquired success and prestige for a period, his tenacity for higher achievement had melted away. Back in his home town, he became a rather sad figure. He was somewhat bitter over his lost status.

Yeh provides an important personality type to contrast to that of the mobile man whose career curve continued upward. We wonder what made him similar to, yet different from, the other upward mobile men. Three elements in his personality seem to provide the important clues:

First, men who move through long social distances must be able to separate themselves readily and easily from other people. They must direct themselves with total concentration toward their personal goals, with little attention and less concern for other objects or persons.[29] A successfully mobile man is able to leave other things and people behind without continuing emotional attachment or feelings of guilt and regret. Yeh was not able to forget his house, his concubine, and his comfortable home life. In other words, Yeh was not able to break away from his close and intimate ties. As a consequence, he was put into a situation that finally forced him to withdraw from his military career.

Second, the lives of mobile men have a theme that provides a basic rhythm to their life histories. This theme is recurrent departures and arrivals in every aspect of their lives. It is the common element, the necessary element, in this kind of career and life history. To achieve mobility each of these men has, as an underlying component of his personality, attitudes toward his world and the people in it that make these departures and arrivals possible.[30] The mobile man is that person who is able successfully to initiate and sustain this complex, interwoven series of changes. He must learn, rapidly and thoroughly, the new behavior appropriate to each new situation. He must be able to tolerate uprooting himself and to make use of, or create, opportunities to move to new positions. He must be able to leave his past behind as he moves into each new present.[31] When Yeh was appointed Brigadier-General of the Fifty-Eighth Army and ordered to move to the Province of Hunan to fight against the Japanese, he rationalized that the long-distance march would be a hardship, the Japanese soldiers had better arms, he was not familiar with the geography of foreign provinces, and it would be difficult to find opium. He was unable to sustain this series of changes.

Third, in general a mobile man is a determined and realistic man who sets goals consistent with his abilities at a given point in time and then drives hard to reach them.[32] Yeh seems not to have had full self-assurance in his career and social position. He appeared tired, isolated, and passive. He had little insight into his more basic motivations and was not able to set clearly for himself the goals of his life. Although he was a friendly person, he was without the ability to further himself socially. It was not likely that he could easily relate himself to the highly ambitious men who were constantly changing their life situations and continually learning what had to be known to live in the new environments they invaded.

Personality thus played an important part in the careers of the gentry. This point should not, however, be taken to indicate that personality is in any sense the only cause of a man's social mobility or that it controls his social mobility. The process of social mobility is complex; it must not be assumed that any single factor causes or maintains it. The cases of Yeh and Tang constitute an analysis of the process in terms of the individual. The role of individual personality and individual differences has been emphasized, but the social system and its operations played the crucial role in the process. The closed economy and the increase in population certainly played major parts in making men mobile in Chinese rural society. The school, the government, the army, commerce, medical practice, marriage, the "dynastic cycle," and socially and culturally given beliefs and "hopes of reward" facilitated upward mobility. At the same time, the equal division generation after generation of family property among the sons, the increase of population, and the sons' parasitic living off the wealthy house paved the way for downward mobility. Each of these factors played its part, and all came together to make social mobility comprehensible as well as operable. In this interacting system of various causes, personality was but one of many factors.

NOTES

1. Pitirim A. Sorokin, *Social and Cultural Mobility* (New York: The Free Press, 1959), p. 202.
2. E. T. Hiller, *Social Relations and Structures: A Study in Principles of Sociology* (New York: Harper & Row, Publishers, 1947), p. 339.
3. Talcott Parsons, "Age and Sex in the Social Structure of the United States," in Clyde Kluckhohn and Henry A. Murray, eds., *Personality in Nature, Society, and Culture* (New York: Alfred A. Knopf, Inc., 1948), p. 273.
4. Sorokin, *op. cit.,* p. 99.
5. Cf. Ta Chen, *Population in Modern China,* with an introduction by William F. Ogburn (Chicago: The University of Chicago Press, 1946), p. 44.
6. Wolfram Eberhard, *Social Mobility in Traditional China* (Leiden: E. J. Brill, 1962), p. 238.
7. Ping-ti Ho, *The Ladder of Success in Imperial China: Aspects of Social Mobility, 1368–1911* (New York: Columbia University Press, 1962), p. 77.
8. Ru-chiang Su, *Studies in Rural Economy in the County of Kunyang, Yunnan* (Kunyang: The Institute for Census Research, National Tsing Hua University, 1943), pp. 114–5.
9. Chen, *op. cit.,* p. 49.
10. Hsiao-tung Fei and Chih-i Chang, *Earthbound China: A Study of Rural Economy in Yunnan* (Chicago: The University of Chicago Press, 1945), p. 173.
11. The author is indebted to the late Bruno Lasker of the Institute of Pacific Relations for his discussion of the occupational mobility, among other things, in personal correspondence (September 13, 1954).
12. Sorokin, *op. cit.,* pp. 494–5.
13. Fei, "Peasantry and Gentry: An Interpretation of Chinese Social Structure and Its Changes," *American Journal of Sociology,* 52 (July, 1946), 1–17.
14. *Ibid.*
15. *Cf. ibid.*
16. *Ibid.*
17. *Cf.* Joseph A. Schumpeter, *Imperialism and Social Classes,* trans-

lated by Heinz Norden and edited by Paul M. Sweezy (New York: Augustus M. Kelly, Inc., 1951), p. 165.

18. Sorokin, *op. cit.*, p. 449.
19. *Ibid.*, pp. 449–50.
20. Schumpeter, *op. cit.*, p. 154.
21. Fei and Chang, *op. cit.*, p. 114.
22. *Ibid.*, p. 118.
23. Francis L. K. Hsu, *Under the Ancestors' Shadow: Chinese Culture and Personality* (New York: Columbia University Press, 1948), pp. 273–4.
24. *Ibid.*, p. 274.
25. *Ibid.*, p. 275.
26. *Cf.* Fei, "Peasantry and Gentry."
27. Schumpeter, *op. cit.*, pp. 149–50.
28. Lin Yueh-hwa, *The Golden Wing: A Sociological Study of Chinese Familism* (London: Routledge & Kegan Paul, 1947), p. 168.
29. W. Lloyd Warner and James C. Abegglen, *Big Business Leaders in America* (New York: Harper & Row, Publishers, 1955), p. 169.
30. *Ibid.*, p. 103.
31. *Ibid.*, p. 63.
32. *Ibid.*, p. 82.

9

Social Reform and
Class Mobility

Social status can be changed either
through individual social mobility or through social reform. Through
social reform the submerged group or class seizes power and raises
its own status. In the previous five chapters, we have analyzed upward
changes in status through the individual struggle for wealth, prestige,
and power, as well as the types and forms of social mobility. If we
view social mobility in the perspective of certain institutional factors
and contrast the institutional factors with individual factors, we see
that the former are functions of mass mobility and that the latter are
comparatively minimal. We have laid stress on individual talent,
intelligence, energy, efforts, enthusiasm, will, aggressiveness, and
ambition; and we have cited various examples. But we left out the
ninety-nine million others who did not make the grade.[1] Social mobility through the avenue of social reform may therefore be more
important than the other social avenues and should perhaps attract
our closer attention.

By "social reform" we mean the improvement or the salvation
of the social order or both, accomplished through the alteration of
some particular institution, activity, or condition. Reformers may be,
in their general social attitudes, either conservative or liberal, but
they are not exponents of social reform unless they hold that some
limited and specific rectification, betterment, or restoration of social

structure or associative relations will bring about a general improvement of society. To the reformer and the revolutionist, society is
essentially structural rather than confluent, and they regard the social
order as a necessary pattern composed of parts, each and all of which
may be more or less successfully set, remodeled, and maintained.
Reformers seek the construction of the patterns necessary for the
right form for this or that situation. "Reform" schools are postulated
with the purpose of redirecting human habits. Some ostensibly revolutionary movements may have reformist programs, and many reformist movements may bear revolutionary implications. Within the
context of aggregate social life, reformers and revolutionists are
simply different names for those with various focuses on the rectification or improvement of the process of social interaction.[2]

The status structure of a society changes by virtue of the fact
that the relative social positions of the classes undergo shifts. We see
such shifts most plainly when they occur because of a single historical
event. The most important instance is the forcible subjugation of one
social entity by another that is politically alien—usually nationally
alien as well, though that is not essential to us now. What interests us
in such an upheaval is the fact that classes that appear as "upper" or
"ruling" even to superficial observation—especially *the* "ruling class"
—are much more deeply affected than the "lower" classes and in altogether different ways. True, even the lower classes may often—
though not always or necessarily—be put in a worse economic plight,
but their positions as classes, their relative social ratings, are affected
only slightly or not at all, usually remaining essentially unchanged
under new overlords. The upper classes, on the other hand, are likely
to lose the very core of their positions—the more so, the nearer they
have been to the top of the social pyramid.[3]

There is another kind of shift in relative positions of the classes.
It results from a slow, organic process. As we have said, each class
is always linked to a special function, which it must fulfill according
to its whole concept and orientation and which it actually does discharge as a class and through the class conduct of its members. The
position of each class in the total social structure depends, on one
hand, on the significance that it attributes to that function and, on
the other hand, on the degree to which it successfully performs the
function. Changes in relative class position are always explained by
changes along these two lines and in no other way.[4]

A society differs from an organism in that, during the course of
history, it can and does change its structural type without any breach

of continuity. We recognize that an organism may function more or less efficiently. In relation to organic structures we can find strictly objective criteria by which to distinguish disease from health, the pathological from the normal, for disease is what either threatens the organism with death (the dissolution of its structure) or interferes with the activities characteristic of its organic type. Whereas an organism that is attacked by a virulent disease will react to it and, if its reaction fails, will die, a society thrown into a condition of functional disunity or inconsistency (which we shall provisionally identify with *dysnomia*) will not die but will continue to struggle toward some sort of *eunomia,* some kind of social health, and may in the process change its structural type.[5] This function is that of social reform.

SOCIAL REVOLUTION AS A SOCIAL AVENUE

After the Opium War (1839–1842) a hurricane began to blow through China. The hurricane was to continue to blow for more than 100 years.[6] Western influences served increasingly as a catalyst, intensifying indigenous weaknesses in the political, economic, and social structure and transforming them into dry rot. In the midst of doubt and uncertainty the Ch'ing Dynasty crumbled, and a large part of the Confucian value system fell into disrepute. What replaced the old empire and the beliefs pervading it was something akin to chaos, with one warlord group succeeding another after the rejection of the Emperor and with thousands of thoughtful Chinese groping for something to believe in.[7] In the absence of a powerful and effective leadership in any stratum of the social structure, there was no route to national modernization except the long and arduous path of revolution.[8]

The challenge coming from both the outside and inside had thrown the traditional social structure out of balance. In the long run it meant general impoverishment and social unrest. If the society was to survive at all, it had to seek a new equilibrium, a social system that would take advantage of modern technical advancement, on one hand, and would preserve the social integrity, on the other hand. The future of China depended upon the degree to which a stable modern industrialized society could be achieved. This conclusion was clear. The problem was how it could be more quickly realized.

In the community of Kunyang before 1949, although the old pattern was predominant, new trends were being felt too. After receiving modern educations, some of the younger gentry members put their duty toward society above their duty toward their families. They emphasized loyalty to the nation rather than to the community. As they had been reared in rural areas, they could not easily forget the sufferings of the peasantry, and they wanted to bring about social welfare. As they consciously flouted existing traditions and conventions and fought for progress, they were filled with zeal and militant self-confidence. These personalities were the symbols of a new age with a vision of a new society. Indeed, they were no longer a "lost generation," in the sense that they knew what they intended to do and where they aimed to go.

The life history of Lin Kuo-ying may give us some fresh suggestion as to how the general social situation brought the young educated people into the revolutionary camp. They were in desperate straits, felt utterly deserted by their society, and had nowhere else to turn. Lin's case serves to illustrate the tendency to break away from the old traditions and to take over elements from the social values of the West. Lin Kuo-ying expressed a feeling of dissatisfaction with his own civilization, waged a bitter struggle against the old society, and correctly characterized the sentiment of his time as an eager search for progress. Indeed, Lin appears to have utilized a social pole vault rather than a social ladder.

The Life History of Lin Kuo-ying

Lin Kuo-ying was born in 1920 in a village named Tieh Kwan Ts'un. According to the 1942 census the village had a population of 949 persons and was the largest village of Jen Teh Hsiang. It was located in a wide plain and surrounded by fertile fields. There was a stream passing through the outskirts of the village, which was convenient for washing, irrigation, and husking rice by water power. The village was therefore considered prosperous. There were seven or eight households with more than 100 *kung* of farmland each.

Lin Kuo-ying's foremost ancestors had immigrated to the village from the County of Chinning. They had started as agricultural laborers in the village. His great-grandfather had been industrious and painstaking. He had bought fifteen *kung* of farmland when he was thirty years old.

Lin Kuo-ying's grandfather had been the eldest of three brothers. He had studied in a private school only one year because the family needed his labor. He was very clever and learned very fast. He not only could read *The Romance of the Three Kingdoms, The Ghost and Love Stories in a Studio,* and *Liang Shan Pai and Chu Ying*

Tai but had also learned to do carpentry, masonry, and bamboo splitting for making baskets. His proper calling was agriculture. When he was forty years old, he bought twenty *kung* of farmland. His family had become well-to-do in the village.

Lin Kuo-ying's father was the second of five brothers. He had studied seven years in a private school and had then taken up farming. After he was thirty, he also established a business performing religious services and chanting liturgies for others. At the beginning, he worked as a helper of other Taoists. As the work was light and the pay good, he later became a full-time Taoist. He bought a set of musical instruments and made himself the manager of a group. He could earn eighty *ching* of rice for one engagement. When he divided the large family property with his brothers, he received twenty-five *kung* of farmland and a house of two rooms. After five years, he was able to buy thirty-five *kung* of farmland. When he was fifty years old, his elder brother died without a son. One of his own sons had been adopted as a stepson by his elder brother. Lin therefore inherited his elder brother's forty *kung* of farmland and a house of seven rooms. He had altogether 100 *kung* of farmland, and his family became one of the wealthiest families in the village.

Lin Kuo-ying was the youngest of four brothers. His eldest brother had been graduated from the normal school at Kunyang and was the principal of the central elementary school of his native district. Both his second and third elder brothers were engaged in agriculture. All four brothers had married, and each had several children. The large family was managed by their parents.

Lin Kuo-ying entered a private school at the age of six. He had a very good memory and was willing to work. When he was twelve years old, he could recite the Four Books fluently. Next he entered the elementary school in the city of Kunyang when he was thirteen years of age. He had a very good record, and, after graduation, he entered the normal school of the county. As he came from the country, he was proud of his new role and studied diligently.

After four years, he was graduated from the normal school and entered the Provincial Kun-hua Senior Normal School in Kunming. He was then especially interested in Chinese history and geography. At school he was very sociable and popular.

After three years, he was graduated from the normal school and returned to Kunyang. He was immediately appointed general inspector of education by the county government. He was enthusiastic and responsible in his job. During his year in that position, he twice visited the country and personally surveyed the village schools. He reported to the Magistrate what had happened in the villages. His report included four parts: the conditions of the schools he had visited; the economic depression in rural areas; the causes of the deterioration of the village schools; suggestions for the selection and training of teachers, increasing finances, and emphasizing adult education. He encouraged two villages to set up night schools. The Magistrate was pleased and had faith in him.

In 1944, Lin was sent by the county government to attend the advanced-study class for normal-school teachers at the Teachers College of Southwest Associated University in Kunming. As his expenses were paid by the county government, he felt very lucky.

After one year, right before graduation, he wrote a letter to the Magistrate of Kunyang and expressed his willingness to come back to the county to offer his service. He wished to be appointed principal of the normal school and junior middle school of Kunyang. About the same time, however, Wang Wen-hua, the youngest son of Chairman Wang, who was also studying at the Teachers College of Southwest Associated University, had been invited by the Magistrate to return to Kunyang as principal. Lin Kuo-ying wrote letters to the director of the Bureau of Education of the county government and some other influential gentry members to request them to help him win the position. As a result, the Magistrate appointed him principal of the school and asked Wen-hua to serve as head of a division in the Tax Department of the county government. Wen-hua was disappointed and hated Lin.

After assuming the position, Lin requested the Magistrate to increase the essential funds of the school and invited several teachers from Kunming. He announced various new regulations for the school and advocated "democratization." He invited teachers to hold free discussion sessions and encouraged the students to organize various study groups. Every morning he himself arose very early and went to the outskirts of the city to read for two hours. Consequently, the students of the school all followed his example and studied diligently. When the school bell rang, he was there, posted in the front of the school gate. If he caught a student lagging, he would punish him by standing him at the gate for fifteen minutes. He was impartial in administering reward and punishment. The atmosphere of the campus was completely changed. There was vitality in the school. All the parents of the students were pleased and praised Lin highly as a good principal.

In 1946 many of the gentry members of Kunyang reported the corruption of the Magistrate of Kunyang to the Governor. Wang Wen-hua took this opportunity to attack him for his inefficiency and dictatorialness. The Magistrate was dismissed, and Lin Kuo-ying was dismissed by the new Magistrate. Wen-hua took the position of principal.

During the short period of chaos, many students criticized Lin in the students' wall newspapers. Though many people admired his enthusiasm for his office, his resolution in action, and his interest in study, many others felt that he was arrogant, irritable, and conceited. He asked some of his faithful students to transcribe the criticisms from the wall newspapers for him. He took them to heart and kept the criticisms on his desk as reminders to himself. He had taken beatings previously, yet he had never felt so bitter. He knew that his losing his position was not because of his own lack of ability but because of the general rottenness of the society. He said: "In such a society everybody devotes his life to his own wealth, power, and prestige. All of us compete fiercely for recognition. No one is going to take care of the common good of the whole society. Our country is helpless." Lin believed that there was nobody else in Kunyang who could offer better service in the field of education than he and that his efforts of the previous year and a half should not be futile. His only unhappiness was that the gentry and the people did not distinguish right from wrong.

Before leaving, he gathered the students and gave them a farewell speech that lasted two hours. He left the school without formally passing over the property of the school to his successor. He asked a faithful staff member to take care of the remaining business. Lin took away the important documents of the school in order purposely to make things difficult for his successor.

After leaving the school, he went to Lin An to teach at the middle school of the county. He decided to concern himself no longer with education in Kunyang. When occasionally he came back to Kunyang, he did not even want to stop off in the city, and he avoided his acquaintances. Nevertheless, he still inquired secretly about the condition of the school. He was informed that, after taking over the position, Wang Wen-hua had found that the salary was not enough to live on and that it was not paid regularly. The teachers could not support themselves by their salaries and therefore did not take their jobs seriously. Wang was disappointed and showed no more interest in his position. He did not care much for the affairs of the school. Many of the students were encouraged to create disturbances by gentry members who were against the principal. Although he said, "Disturbances can make a strong school,"[9] Wang Wen-hua did nothing to improve its condition. In reality, the difficulties were beyond his ability to solve. When Lin heard these remarks, although he said nothing, he was pleased.

While Lin taught at the middle school of Lin An, he still did not change his arrogant attitude. He felt unhappy that he should have to take orders from other people. He was dissatisfied with the administration of the school, finding it backward and conservative. He made some suggestions for improvement, but the principal ignored them. He found that everywhere the social condition was the same. A person who had some sense of justice could not feel easy. He therefore resolved to draw consolation from the friendship of women. He began associating with the girl students. Soon his colleagues considered his conduct damaging to the reputation of the school. He resigned his position and left the school.

After leaving Lin An, Lin went to Lu Hsi and taught at the county normal school. There he was respected by his colleagues. The principal had faith in him and agreed to whatever he suggested. He was happy and enthusiastic in his job. After a semester, he was promoted to dean of the school. He became so zealous that he often interfered with the other teachers, whom he considered irresponsible. There was a rumor that he aimed to take over the position of principal. It was reported to the principal, and he was offended. At the same time, the students were encouraged by several of the teachers to stir up a disturbance against Lin. The disturbance soon changed into political agitation, however. The school's instructor of military science and tactics led a group of students to the mountains to wage guerrilla warfare against the government. Their watchword was "to plunder the rich to give to the poor." They claimed to be the troops of the "Democratic Front."[10] As a consequence, the government closed the school to prevent the remaining students from joining the "bandits."

During the disturbance at the Lu Hsi normal school, Lin secretly left the school for Chên Nan and taught at the normal school of the county. The more frustration he suffered, the more courageous he became. He often said, "Failure is the mother of success."

My assistant wrote to me in April, 1948:

A former colleague of Lin Kuo-ying at the normal school of Lu Hsi said that the county government considered Lin a Communist and had ordered his arrest. But he fled. The rumor might have been a pretext to implicate him in trouble. It might also have been true, however, because he was a man with radical ideas. He hated conservatism and selfishness. He wanted progress for the prosperity of society. Furthermore, he had been much frustrated and deeply dissatisfied with the backwardness of society and the inefficiency of the government.

Lin Kuo-ying was energetic and an avid reader. He was often criticized, however, as "too proud, too conceited." He was fond of discussion, debating, and making speeches. When he talked, he liked to quote phrases from the Four Books and the writings of Lu Hsün to support his points.

INSURRECTION AS A SOCIAL AVENUE

If the case history of Lin Kuo-ying represents the line of the modern functional revolution, the life history of Liu Tsung-tao symbolizes the traditional way of insurrection. The former is not limited to gaining political rule over the country but also attempts to change the socioeconomic system by the coordinated and conscious planning of a newly established government. Such revolutionists must have insights into national issues. The latter is limited to seizing political power under the same socioeconomic order. It does not produce any immediate change in the traditional social structure or set in motion any conscious movement toward a new social system. The insurrectionists, without any accompanying new ideology, are merely individuals involved in a struggle for power—and often none too effectively—with little support except from unorganized popular feeling for doing away with what their consciences feel to be wrong and unjust. After the overthrow of the old regime, the founder of the new dynasty may initiate changes in organization, policy, measures, and personnel. For example, Ts'ao Ts'ao (155–220) of the Wei Dynasty and T'ai-tsu (during 1368–1398 under his regime) of the Ming Dynasty both brought about some political, economic, and social reforms. In the 2000 years of recurring dynastic cycles, there had been a general continuity and consistent development of the institutional framework of Chinese society.

In traditional China, political power was attained by violence and imposed the relationship of conqueror to conquered. Insurrection or banditry openly challenged the rulers and aimed at seizing power. For harshly oppressed and dispossessed persons, the capacity to revolt and to form bands with military organizations to seek their fortunes through banditry had always been an important element of political transition in China. When the exploitation of the peasantry had resulted in the dispossession of a large number of farmers, bandit groups would spring up in many parts of the country. At times the government would legalize a group of bandits, and some bandit chiefs would become ranking military officers. When a bandit group felt strong enough to challenge the central government for control of a region, it would take the designation of *i-chun,* "righteous troops." The prestige a group of outlaws might enjoy was portrayed in an idealized way in the novel *All Men Are Brothers,* in which 108 heroes are all fugitives in their stronghold at Liang Shan, or Liang Hills, from the injustices of corrupt officialdom. Several of the military heroes of this novel are described as having originally been scholars and graduates.[11] Those few who emerged victorious in this struggle became rulers. For example, Liu Pang, the first Emperor of the Han Dynasty, and Chu Yuan-chang, the founder of the Ming Dynasty, both attained the throne in this way.

The gamble involved an extremely long chance, for if a man did succeed in the struggle for political power by violence, he might become Emperor; but, if he were to lose he would be killed and with him his family and lineage. When he challenged the established Emperor, he was called "bandit," and the might of the army would be directed against him.[12] One who started a career as an outlaw was therefore usually in an extremely desperate situation. The old popular saying, *pi shang liang shan,* "being compelled to go up Liang Hills," turns out to have had great modern implications. The life history of Liu Tsung-tao is at least a good example, if not a typical case.

Liu's case history portrays a kind of Chinese intellectual rebel of the past, who took up the cause of the people against the corrupt and oppressive government. It reveals the desperate mood that had been forced upon him and shows us how Liu was compelled to become a "bandit" by the Magistrate. Less characteristic of the traditional order than was Chairman Wang, he nevertheless represented a form of the "scholar's conscience" that, throughout Chinese history, has from time to time led to direct action against the abuses of authority.

The Life History of Liu Tsung-tao

Liu Tsung-tao was born in 1910 in a small village west of Kunyang. It was thirty-five miles from his native place to the City of Kunyang. The village was at the foot of a mountain, and communication with the outside world was very difficult. Most of the villagers were Lolos. Everyone engaged in agriculture except for a few rich people who had a lumber business. The farms, which were on the slopes of the mountains, were called *ti tien,* "ladder farms." The mountains, covered with thick forests, offered a safe refuge for many bandits.

Liu Tsung-tao's great-grandfather, Liu Shang-kuei, had been clever, energetic, and eloquent. Because the economic condition of his family was then quite good and he was an only son, he had been rather spoiled by his parents. From boyhood on, he liked to dress well and make friends, roam about, and gamble or drink in the market town. Between the ages of twenty and thirty, Liu Shang-kuei became a true good-for-nothing.

Liu Tsung-tao's grandfather, Liu Chen-lo, suffered a great deal when he was a young boy. Because his father did nothing good for his family, the boy had to assist his mother with chores around the farm when he was only seven years old. He did everything according to his mother's direction and became old for his years. He felt that, although his father was no good, he himself should have the determination to struggle for fame and wealth. If he did not strive when he was young, he would have no future. His mother also felt hopeful for him.

The improvement of his family's finances encouraged him to work harder still. He bought twenty goats for eight piculs of rice in order to obtain fertilizer. As a result, the harvest from his farm was greatly increased. The star of his family was in the ascendant during those years; his production of various kinds of grain rose greatly, and his domestic animals flourished. When he was forty-four, he bought the ten *kung* of farmland that he had rented from Hsieh Pao-hsin. His family were able to save eight piculs of rice aside from that used by themselves. He lent the eight piculs of rice to the villagers at a yearly interest of 70%. Although he was a rich man in his village, he and his family were so frugal that he would never spend a penny carelessly. When he was sixty, he had bought fifteen *kung* of farmland. His family thus had forty-five *kung* altogether.

Liu Tsung-tao's father, Liu Yen-tau, was an only son. His parents loved him "as though he were a pearl." He had to do nothing in the family. Although not well educated, Yen-tau was talented and careful, and everything he did was well planned. The fortunes of his family improved steadily. Every year he stored his rice until the following spring and then sold it at high prices. He was always ready to buy more farms.

By the time he was fifty, Liu Yen-tau had bought twenty *kung* of farmland. He had altogether sixty-five *kung* and was the richest farmer in the village. But, as he became richer, he became more frugal. He wore shabby clothes, and those who did not know him would have thought him a poor man. His only extravagance was wine drinking. Every morning he would go to the fields to see his farm and then return to look after his children. He did not do any heavy work.

Liu Tsung-tao was the elder son of Liu Yen-tau. When he was born, his father was very happy and loved him very much. Tsung-tao's self-centered and domineering tendencies were obvious when he was four or five years old. He claimed as his own everything that happened to please him. He threw away anything he had in his hand and cried all day when he lost his temper. His parents and others in the family acceded to his every wish in order to prevent his tantrums. When he played with other children, all his fellow players had to be under his command. If anyone did not obey his orders, he would knock him down or drive him away. When he wanted to do something, his action could not be checked.

Liu Tsung-tao started to study at age nine. He boarded at a private school located five miles from his home. He had a good memory and was an outstanding student.

After eight years in the private school, Liu Tsung-tao went to Kunyang to study in the junior normal school of the county. He felt proud of himself—although he had been born in the mountainous region, he had come to the city to study with the city boys. He had a strong sense of justice. If someone offended him, he would fight with him to the end. But his classmates liked him because he was eloquent and had fresh ideas. His Chinese composition was often praised by his teachers.

After four years he was graduated from the normal school. Before being graduated, he went to Kunming to compete in the examination given by the Department of Education of the provincial government. He stayed in Kunming for ten days. The contrast between the social life of Kunming and that of his native community greatly puzzled him. He could not help wondering, "Why is the city so rich, while the country is so poor?"

After returning to his home, Tsung-tao became a schoolteacher in an elementary school in a market town. After a year he went to Kunming to attend the elementary schoolteachers' advanced practice class during the summer vacation. Later he told his friends: "High officials and rich merchants live in the large cities. The country becomes poor because the wealth is concentrated in the city."

During his year of teaching, Tsung-tao visited the *chu* officials very often. He became friends with the head of the district government and with members of the local gentry. His ability, knowledge, sense of responsibility, and politeness were highly appreciated.

In 1938, when he came back from Kunming, Liu Tsung-tao was immediately asked by the head of the *chu* government to become a staff assistant. He felt much more interest in administrative work than in teaching. Little by little, he became an outstanding figure in the district.

Though he won the faith of the people and many members of the gentry, he stirred up the jealousies of the other staff members. He often openly criticized their corruption, their irresponsibility, and their hypocrisy, and he won many enemies among his colleagues. At last he was compelled to resign his position. The intrigues of the local administration impressed him deeply.

After leaving the *chu* government, Liu Tsung-tao won the warm sympathy of many common people and gentry members. He stood up bravely and told the people what he wanted to do for their benefit and for his native place. Simultaneously, the provincial government ordered the Magistrate to do away with the system of *chu* government and enlarge the original *hsiang-chên* instead. As Liu Tsung-tao found that public opinion was on his side, he took advantage of the opportunity to urge the people to divide their *chu* into two *hsiang*. He encouraged the people to present a petition to the county government. The Magistrate, finding that the district was too large and that there were bandits in that *chu,* promised to divide it into two *hsiang* for convenience in administration. The eastern part was named Nei Tien Hsiang, and the western part Chiu Tu Hsiang. Liu Tsung-tao was chosen head of Chiu Tu Hsiang. He was then twenty-seven.

After he was appointed head of the *hsiang,* Liu Tsung-tao immediately set up the machinery of the district administrative office. He decided that his staff members should include both able youths and older men of the gentry class. The former would be responsible for action and the latter for supervision. He took as his most important principles honesty and justice. First of all, the government should avoid doing harm to the people. Then it should try to do some welfare work in the district. He had no desire for wealth but only for a good reputation. He often said, "Chun tzŭ mou tao pu mou shih"

("The superior man searches after truth, not after food," a Confucian saying).

Liu Tsung-tao was an able youth. Both his character and his deeds were admired by the gentry and the people. After the establishment of the *hsiang,* taxes were suddenly decreased. The government was the center of activity of the people of the district. They knew what the government had done and would continue to do. Furthermore, Tsung-tao asked his staff members to make public the government expenses once a month. He himself did not charge fees. If he received orders from the county government, he explained them to the people. As a consequence, conditions in Chiu Tu Hsiang became much better than those in Nei Tien Hsiang.

After putting the affairs of the *hsiang* in order, Liu Tsung-tao turned his attention to popular education. There had formerly been a central elementary school under the *chu* government. When the *chu* was divided into two *hsiang,* Chiu Tu Hsiang had no central elementary school. Furthermore, there were no junior primary schools in most of the villages. He ordered every *pao* to build a junior primary school and made the head of the *pao* responsible for a compulsory education program. After one year the number of students was greatly increased. Then he suggested the establishment of a new central elementary school for his own *hsiang.*

Liu Tsung-tao's most outstanding achievement was the suppression of bandits. Formerly, bandits had been so common that persons were being looted or killed almost daily. People dared not walk freely in the daytime and could not sleep in peace at night. At first, Liu Tsung-tao secretly befriended the rascally element. He often invited them to drink wine and asked about the conditions of the bandits. At last he organized one group as a corps for bandit prevention and asked its leaders to be corps leaders. He divided his *hsiang* into three districts and distributed the districts to different leaders and organized still another group under his own command. He often led his corps in fights with the remaining bandits. Because of his bravery and strategy, he was very much feared. Recognizing his determination to be rid of them, the bandits fled. He thus kept public order in the whole *hsiang* and won the admiration and support of all the people.

As he was in a rather dangerous position, Liu carried a pistol and a knife with him at all times. He was always on the alert; if someone came to visit him, he would ask his identity before receiving him. Occasionally, he went out to a teashop or a restaurant, but he did not stay very long. When he left the *hsiang* offices, he usually rode a big horse and was guarded by four or five attendants. He was grand and very polite to the people.

Liu Tsung-tao had complete control of his *hsiang*. When he went to county-government meetings, he usually said exactly what he thought. Among the heads of the various *hsiang-chên* administrative offices, he was the only one who dared to offend the influential and to speak for the people. If he regarded something as unjust, he would fight it to the end. He often criticized the other officials: "They work merely for their own interest. Fighting for the correct principle means offending the influential. Who wants to take this risk? They are wise men." He was frequently criticized for being "too straightforward."

In 1943 Magistrate Chao came to Kunyang. A man from Liu Tsung-tao's native district who was a clerk in the county government and had wanted Liu Tsung-tao's position for a long time bribed the Magistrate to appoint him to office. Magistrate Chao dismissed Liu Tsung-tao without any reason. This greatly bewildered the gentry and people of the district. They petitioned the Magistrate to rescind the order and simultaneously asked Liu Tsung-tao to hold on to his office under any circumstances. At last the clerk led a group of armed men to the *hsiang* offices to take over the position by force. When they arrived, Liu Tsung-tao ordered his guards to fight them. In the ensuing battle, two of the clerk's men were killed, and four were wounded.

After the incident, Magistrate Chao tried to put a quick end to the matter because he feared that it would influence his prestige and position. He sent a group of armed policemen to arrest Liu Tsung-tao and had him thrown in irons. The people of the *hsiang* were greatly stirred up and refused to allow the clerk to become head of the *hsiang* government. In order to appease the anger of the people, Magistrate Chao was compelled to choose someone else to take the position. The matter was thus solved peacefully. But Liu Tsung-tao was still in jail. Though the people petitioned the Magistrate several times for his release, Magistrate Chao turned a deaf ear to their requests.

The Magistrate hoped that Liu Tsung-tao would bail himself out and bargained with him every night. But Liu Tsung-tao was an honest man and had not accumulated money, though he had been head of the *hsiang* for more than four years. He did not wish to ask his family for money.

He thought that he would be unable to face his parents and brother if he dissipated the fortunes of his family for himself. He said: "If I had grafted lots of money without considering the people, it would not have mattered if I gave a part of the money to Magistrate Chao. But I have never done anything that was harmful to the people." He decided not to give a single cent to Magistrate Chao. Nevertheless, life in jail was ugly. It was so dark that one could not see beyond five feet, even in the daytime. It had a filthy smell and was infested with bugs and lice. The prisoners sat by themselves on the wet ground. They did not receive enough food. At last Liu Tsung-tao had to ask his family to raise $25,000 (equivalent to 185 silver dollars in March, 1943) for bail. His family sold five *kung* of farmland in order to do so. Then Liu was released.

During his stay in jail for two and a half months, Liu Tsung-tao had become frail and weak. He was full of anger at and hatred for the government. He wrote in his diary: "How dark is our society. How absolute is our government. The tyrannous official distorts the truth. Barbarous institutions suppress justice. Money exterminates human nature." He hugged his anger and complained bitterly of the incapability, corruption, and meanness of the Magistrate and vowed vengeance against him.

Informed of Liu Tsung-tao's bitterness toward him, Magistrate Chao ordered him arrested again. When he heard this news, Tsung-tao immediately fled in desperation, thinking it was time to go to Liang Shan, the Liang Hills. It was a critical moment in the war against Japan. Because Japan had occupied Indochina and Burma, Yunnan was then threatened. Liu Tsung-tao followed the lead of certain Yunnanese bandits into the mountains and joined in fighting a guerrilla war against Japan. He instilled political ideas into the bandits and persuaded them to cooperate with the people. As guerrilla war could not be carried on without the support of the people, his first motto was "never do any harm to the people." But he considered it all right to loot the officials, opium dealers, and other rich people whose wealth was ill gotten. After he had joined the bandits, many of his intimate friends and youths inspired by him offered their services.

When Liu Tsung-tao had been with the bandits for a year and a half, Japan surrendered. Liu felt that, as the war was over, he should not continue in guerrilla warfare. As there was no longer any function for him in the mountains, he returned home in December,

1945. (Magistrate Chao had been dismissed, and a new magistrate had come to Kunyang.)

After his return, Liu Tsung-tao engaged in agriculture. He no longer concerned himself with the local government, became very silent, and only associated with his bosom friends. But the people thought well of him and were respectful to him. When he came to a teashop or a restaurant, the proprietors would not charge him anything. His intelligence, courage, and sense of justice were highly admired by the people. In the district even women and children knew the name of Liu Tsung-tao. Nobody considered him a "bandit."

After remaining home for half a year, Liu Tsung-tao was elected by the people to the Citizens' Political Council of the county. They found that he knew what was going on and also dared to speak for them. He was therefore considered qualified to represent them. At first he dared not attend meetings in the city. But, as the people had put their trust in him, he felt he must pluck up courage to go. He knew, however, that the Citizens' Political Council had no power to carry out what its members suggested. He often said: "The Nationalist government has been in power for twenty years. During these years they have said all the good words and done all the bad things. Endless talk will result in nothing." After the first term of the Citizens' Political Council, he was re-elected.

Liu Tsung-tao was tall and vigorous with a dark complexion and piercing eyes. He was clever in mind and quick in action. Although he was friendly with every kind of person, he often said, "A perfect gentleman finds it difficult to make friends with a mean man." He was ambitious for his future and liked to associate with energetic youths. He was always ready to fight against evil and looking for chances to realize his ideals. His life was very plain and unadorned. He liked to ride and hunt and could shoot accurately. He also liked to play the Chinese violin and the three-stringed guitar.

NOTES

1. The author is indebted to the late Professor Louis Wirth for his lectures on Social Organization during 1950–1951 at the University of Chicago.
2. Horace M. Kallen, "Reformism," *Encyclopaedia of the Social Sciences,* edited by Edwin R. A. Seligman and Alvin Johnson (New York: The Macmillan Company, 1934), vol. 13, pp. 194–5.
3. Joseph A. Schumpeter, *Imperialism and Social Classes,* translated by Heinz Norden, edited by Paul M. Sweezy (New York: Augustus M. Kelley, Inc., 1951), pp. 176–7.

4. *Ibid.*
5. A. R. Radcliffe-Brown, *Structure and Function in Primitive Society: Essays and Addresses* (New York: The Free Press, 1952), pp. 181–3.
6. Robert Payne, *Mao Tse-tung, Ruler of Red China* (New York: Henry Schuman, Inc., 1950), p. 3.
7. Robert C. North, *Moscow and Chinese Communists* (Stanford: Stanford University Press, 1953), p. 33. Regrettably, as the title suggests, the basic idea of this book is misleading. It devotes more space to the less important period (1921–1927) and less to the more important (1937–1949). It therefore fails to delineate the significance of successive periods in the development of the Chinese Communist Party. Furthermore, the book fails to relate the Communist protest movement to the larger pattern of Chinese political life since the May Fourth Movement in 1919, and thus it lacks a thoroughgoing appraisal of the underlying reasons for Mao Tse-tung's victory in China.
8. Hu Shih, *The Chinese Renaissance: The Haskell Lectures, 1933* (Chicago: The University of Chicago Press, 1934), p. 13.
9. This statement was adapted from the popular saying, "Disturbances can make the country prosperous," which was itself derived from Mencius: "When Heaven is about to confer a great office on any man, it first exercises his mind with suffering, and his sinews and bones with toil." (James Legge, "The Works of Mencius," in *The Chinese Classics,* II [2nd ed.; Oxford: Clarendon Press, 1895], p. 929.)
10. The political activity was basically anarchistic, antigovernment, unidentified leftist, and libertarian.
11. *Cf.* Morton H. Fried, "Military Status in Chinese Society," *American Journal of Sociology,* 57 (January, 1952), 347–55.
12. Hsiao-tung Fei, *China's Gentry: Essays in Rural-Urban Relations,* revised and edited by Margaret Park Redfield, with six life histories of Chinese gentry families collected by Yung-teh Chow and an introduction by Robert Redfield (Chicago: The University of Chicago Press, 1953), p. 20.

10

Conclusions and General Remarks

Γhe study presented in the preceding chapters was designed to test a conceptual framework of social mobility and the methods of empirical research associated with it. The status system and mobility in a Chinese county of 69,231 inhabitants provided the necessary social laboratory for testing both framework and methods. It proved best to distinguish social mobility from general social and cultural changes; to restrict the definition of social mobility to the shifting in positions of individuals, families, and status groups; and to conceive the transition of "social object or value" as the effects of social mobility. It turned out to be essential to distinguish between migration and social mobility. Ecological mobility may be either a necessity of, or the precondition for, social and occupational mobility. A "horizontal" movement in territorial space is not, as such, a "social phenomenon," and it is not necessarily identical with a change in social position.

This work therefore was concentrated on the social status and social mobility of the Chinese gentry and included three parts: First, we examined the status system of Chinese society and the social functions of the gentry; second, we investigated the social characteristics of the gentry; third, we inquired into the social mobility of the gentry. These three factors, the place of the gentry in the status system, the gentry's social personality, and the pattern of social mobility, were seen as functionally interdependent in the totality of social life.

China was a densely populated country. Farm implements were crude and simple. Labor was cheap, and work was actually toil. The gentry class, living on the rents collected from tenants, could pursue a high culture if so inclined. Chinese society, ruled mainly by tradition, gave high prestige to those who had access to the source of classical teachings. The propertied class therefore became also the prestige class. The gentry constituted an indispensable part of the local government and acted as a medium between the government and the common people. In a peasant society it constituted the local elite, the upholders of convention, and formed the numerous tentacles of the great power hierarchy. The continuous domination of the peasantry by the gentry had been maintained through centuries by the single fact that officials had been chosen from Confucian scholars in the past and from school graduates after the establishment of the modern educational system and that such scholars were chiefly recruited from the wealthy families. Generally, it was through education that the people found opportunities to rise into officialdom. It usually took several generations for a farmer-peasant's family to climb. A poor but ambitious peasant might climb up the social hierarchy within his lifetime through such channels as mercenary soldiering, but these shortcuts were the most hazardous and uncertain routes.

The source of material for this study was social statistics and life histories of the Chinese gentry families. The career histories included scholars, active or retired officials, rich merchants, wealthy landlords, and others. Among these gentry members were some who had not climbed successfully to the top. Some had stopped part way, whereas others had reverted to obscurity. The life histories were familistic and genealogical. In order to place the case histories of the gentry in perspective against the whole population of the community, social statistics were cited. The statistics of the gentry families were singled out for comparison with those of the population in general, and many such characteristics of the gentry as family size, education, occupation, land ownership, and life chance were shown by means of contrast.

As the main body of the material for this study was the life histories of the Chinese gentry families, intensive interviewing was the most important field method. Because interviewing was an arduous task and required special training and skill, our experience and tested methods proved valuable.

My findings verify these hypotheses. Several conclusions may be drawn.

THE GENTRY AS A STATUS GROUP

A social system implies order among the interacting units of the system. When a society has a large number of individuals, when the division of labor increases, and when the social units become more diverse, the need for coordination and integration also grows. As some of the roles and functions are considered more important or socially more valuable to the survival and development of the whole society, individual positions are evaluated and ranked. In every complex society there is a hierarchy of power and prestige. The positions of leadership and responsibility and those requiring superior intelligence and particular abilities or talents are usually ranked at the top of a social system. Status is thus created by evaluations or judgments of the relative worth of the members of a society.

Traditional Chinese society had two major groups: the peasantry and the gentry. But the gentry had been differentiated into two subgroups within a community—officialdom and the local gentry. Each group had its definite functions. Members of officialdom were the rulers and masters within the territory. They imposed the governmental power upon the people. They were too high up to be approached by the common people. The peasants were the ruled. They paid taxes to support the government and the ruling class. The gentry was made up of the families of prestige and power. They allied themselves with officialdom, from which their honors and rewards came, and served as a medium between the government and the common people.

The gentry at one time had operated well in fulfilling the basic functions of promoting the welfare of the people, but the group had proved unadaptable to the new social needs brought about by the impact of industrialization, with its agricultural mechanization and Western social values. Under the impact of Western social values like nationalism and democracy, science and technology, industry and commerce, the gentry as a status group no longer served as social prop in a changing world. The gentry, which had greatly affected the history of Chinese society, had been doomed for a long time.

After the Communist victory in 1949, the gentry as a status group was eradicated. If the gentry group has disintegrated, however, its functions must have been taken over by some other group. As C. K. Yang has pointed out, in surveying the changing relationship between the village and the national political order, it is worth observing that the members of the Communist Party and the Communist Youth League are functionally comparable to the traditional gentry, in the sense that both Communist membership and the gentry had national political consciousness based upon a single ideology, both were intimately related to the national bureaucracy, and both served as the extended arm of the formal national political power.[1] Here the past offers a clue to the future.

LEISURE AS A MODE OF LIFE

Each society has a series of ideal social personalities that correspond to the various statuses it recognizes. The style of life is the observable symbol of income and prestige. Veblen has characterized the motivations of upper-class behavior as "conspicuous leisure" and "conspicuous consumption." The members of different social classes in a society usually have distinctive habits, attitudes, ideas, and values. We may say that these classes have distinct subcultures.

The gentry was a status group that expressed a common heritage, a store of common traditions and sentiments. Its style of life, aspirations, and notions of family indicated its outlook on life and values. Conspicuous leisure was the very core of existence. Gentry members who had emancipated themselves from daily work had plenty of time to extend social contacts, to form beneficial friendships, to travel to famous places and foreign lands, to enjoy games and recreations, to devote themselves to reading and learning, to value objects associated with tradition and antiquity, and to cultivate religion and morality. It was mainly members of the gentry class who made great achievements in such fields as public administration, literature, philosophy, and the arts.

The gentry as a leisure class had its own standards and ideals. It might also encourage its members to be diligent, but a perfect gentleman worked with his brain rather than with his hands. He was supported by the labor of others and had no appreciation of productive work. He sought only wealth and high position. He drained capital from productive sources and hoarded it for private enjoyment. The best brains in the nation had little or no interest in technological improvement. This situation appears to have been in pointed conflict with the needs of modern society.

To be sure, the gentry constituted an educated class that was free to pursue knowledge as an end in itself. Those who had emancipated themselves from toil could enjoy classical literacy. But this freedom did not mean that all those who were supported by others and did no work with their hands necessarily were able and willing to work with their minds. Rural life was so boring that it easily enervated intellectual people. Gentry members might simply pass their days in indolence, roaming among the teashops, gambling houses, liquor restaurants, and opium dens. The opportunity of leisure was used for the mere killing of time, one basic reason for so many declining and declined families.

Leisure means the freedom to choose one's activities according to one's own preferences and one's own standards. It is not possible unless it has a durable and solid foundation of living. If we grasp the meaning of leisure, therefore, there will be a great subterranean change in our scale of values about the notion of "labor" and "laborer." A new and changing conception of the nature of human existence will come to light.

The Chinese Communists have introduced a set of new social values. The "new morality," which provides "love of the fatherland, love of the people, love of labor, love of science, and love of public property," is considered the highest value of citizenship.[2] These changes seem a pointed rectification of the old thoughts and conducts.

SOCIAL MOBILITY AS A CHARACTERISTIC OF CHINESE SOCIETY

Social mobility is the most conspicuous characteristic of all class societies. Although there is unequal rank and status, the status barriers are always surmountable and are, in fact, surmounted through various social channels. It is social mobility that transforms lower-class people into upper-class people. We may think of social mobility as the remaking of men, in which men triumph over the fate of their class and drive onward to attain desired goals. The principle of the status system provides the motives for the maximal use of the individual's energies, for the orderly functioning of institutions, and for responsible leadership hierarchies. If one is endowed with sufficient ability, skill, intelligence, and motivation, he may climb to the highest positions in the society. These two principles, social status and social mobility, though apparently antithetical, are yet mutually dependent.

The Chinese status system was flexible. The poor but talented young could rise on their merits, both in the lifetime of a single man and from one generation to another. Admittedly, only a small percentage climbed from the bottom to the top, and the process of social mobility was usually slow, yet hereditary and aristocratic principles that held families at the top did not operate in Chinese society.

In any class society there are many social objects associated with social status. The most important are prestige, power, and wealth. They are the goals of upward mobility, which the people seek. These goals can be reached via the various social ladders. The social ladders we have identified in China were the school, medical practice, the army, government, commerce, and marriage. Revolution and insurrection also served as two important routes during periods of social change.

Mobile people are set in motion by needs and drives. Ambition, aggressiveness, and the desire for prestige, wealth, and power give them no rest, and the situation may reach a breaking point. No matter how high they already are, they cannot be secure or satisfied and want to climb higher to outshine their peers. Everyone feels honor is at stake. Rivalry, frustration, and oppression make the environment potentially hostile so long as a man wants to get on top of others. The most militant is willing to shove, certainly, and even to cut an occasional throat. He climbs at the expense of others.

The aim of many ambitious young men is not to raise the lower class but to escape it. The rising young man strikes out for wealth, power, and fame. He fixes his eyes on those who already have these things and from whose example he may learn how to gain them; he tends to accept the ideals and standards of the actual upper class as he looks forward to sharing its status. In any class society, anywhere in the world, the deadly serious drama of competition and succession is forever being played. Sometimes the competition is in the form of open conflict, but more characteristically it is a silent struggle. It is a struggle with elbows rather than with fists.

Like everything else that has power in human life, the social climber represents, in some sense, the survival of the fittest—not necessarily the best or the ablest in other regards. When each individual is constantly trying to raise himself in the social scale—one by good conduct and steady and energetic exertion of his moral and intellectual qualities, another by injustice and wrong, by violence and illegality—the fittest may be persons without a sense of responsibility or any moral obligation or faith. Once the unscrupulous is selected on the top, once shrewdness replaces wisdom, as with Gresham's Law for money the bad character with inferior training will drive out the good. As a consequence, the conditions will become morally iniquitous and socially destructive.

Unless the principle that all men can live and work together harmoniously for the common good is embraced, a society can never realize its own immense potential of strength for building a better world. The principle of a new society lies not only in a new system but also in a new vision.

The Chinese Communists have always been proud of their "mass line." They speak of *fan-shen,* "turning over the body," of the common people. They say that the downtrodden and the oppressed are now able to "stand up" and "raise their heads." Labor has a new status. Students, teachers, and governmental officials are urged to learn from "the masses." The old class barrier between those who work with their minds and those who work with their strength is being torn down. In place of individualism, collectivism is now promoted. Instead of each person minding his own business, people are now asked to practice criticism and self-criticism in public meetings.[3] It would be interesting to learn what the new pattern of social mobility under the Communist system is becoming. The present regime in China has certainly removed the old elite from its position; but where does the new elite come from? Is there now greater mobility than before? Is the process of social mobility now basically different from what it was? It is greatly to be hoped that more research can be done in this field.

In short, although this study was confined to a single community and the phenomena observed in this restricted area undoubtedly were of a local character, it is of a good deal more than local interest. To be sure, a country is not merely the sum of its local communities. Many features that appear on the local scene may have no counterpart on the national scene, and we have to explain them by tracing threads that bind one community to another. In Yunnan, the local gentry acquired certain characteristics that may or may not have stood out clearly in its members' careers as national figures. Most of them never attained national reputations. It would be a mistake, therefore, to regard the local community as a microcosm of a corresponding macrocosm that was the nation. It is well to remember, however, that a great many, if not most, members of the gentry who became national figures were born and brought up in small communities and bore the cultural stamp of their earlier environments. They retained a peculiar character, a conditioning; they were rooted in local communities long after they had established themselves on the national scene. The gentry was but one facet of Chinese social life, and Kunyang was only one of about 2,000 counties in China.

Yet aside from the fact that investigation of such a community is worthwhile in itself, the data emerging from it have much wider significance that makes them interesting to students of sociology. This particular sample serves as a close reflection of the broad problems existing on the eve of Communist Revolution and throws light on changing social structure in China today.

NOTES

1. C. K. Yang, *A Chinese Village in Early Communist Transition* (Cambridge: The Technology Press, distributed by Harvard University Press, 1959), p. 255.
2. Theodore Hsi-en Chen, "The Marxist Remolding of Chinese Society," *The American Journal of Sociology,* 58 (January 1953), 340–6.
3. *Ibid.*

Selected
Bibliography

THEORETICAL AND METHODOLOGICAL REFERENCES
ON SOCIAL STRATIFICATION AND MOBILITY

Theoretical References

Bendix, R., and Lipset, S. M., eds. *Class, Status and Power: A Reader in Social Stratification.* New York: The Free Press, 1953.

Carlson, Gösta. *Social Mobility and Class Structure.* CWK Gleerup/ Lund: Häkan Ohlssons Boktrycheri, 1958.

Centers, Richard. *The Psychology of Social Classes: A Study of Class Consciousness.* Princeton: Princeton University Press, 1949.

Cooley, C. H. *Social Organization.* New York: Charles Scribner's Sons, 1925.

Cox, Oliver Cromwell. *Caste, Class, and Race: A Study in Social Dynamics.* Garden City: Doubleday & Company, Inc., 1948.

Davis, Kingsley. *Human Society.* New York: The Macmillan Company, 1949.

Durkheim, Emile. *The Division of Labor in Society,* translated from the French by George Simpson. New York: The Free Press, 1947.

Eggan, Fred. *Social Organization of the Western Pueblos.* Chicago: The University of Chicago Press, 1950.

Glass, D. V., ed. *Social Mobility in Britain.* New York: The Free Press, 1954.

Gordon, Milton M. *Social Class in American Sociology.* Durham: Duke University Press, 1958.

Hiller, E. T. *Social Relations and Structures: A Study in Principles of Sociology.* New York: Harper & Row, Publishers, 1947.

Hsu, F. L. K. *Clan, Caste, and Club.* Princeton: D. Van Nostrand Company, Inc., 1963.

Hughes, Everett C., and Hughes, Helen M. *Where People Meet: Racial and Ethnic Frontiers*. New York: The Free Press, 1952.

Landtman, Gunnar. *The Origin of the Inequality of the Social Classes*. Chicago: The University of Chicago Press, 1938.

Levy, Marion J., Jr. *The Structure of Society*. Princeton: Princeton University Press, 1952.

Linton, Ralph. *The Study of Man*. New York: Appleton-Century-Crofts, 1936.

Lipset, S. M., and Bendix, R. *Social Mobility in Industrial Society*. Berkeley: University of California Press, 1959.

Mannheim, Karl. *Man and Society in an Age of Reconstruction: Studies in Social Structure*. New York: Harcourt, Brace & World, Inc., 1951.

Marshall, T. H. *Citizenship and Social Class and other Essays*. London: Cambridge University Press, 1950.

Merton, Robert K. *Social Theory and Social Structure*. Revised and enlarged edition. New York: The Free Press, 1957.

Nadel, S. F. *The Theory of Social Structure*. New York: The Free Press, 1957.

North, C. C. *Social Differentiation*. Chapel Hill: The University of North Carolina Press, 1926.

Pieper, Josef. *Leisure—The Basis of Culture*. Translated by Alexander Dru, with an Introduction by T. S. Eliot. New York: Pantheon Books, Inc., 1952.

Radcliffe-Brown, A. R. *Structure and Function in Primitive Society: Essays and Addresses*. New York: The Free Press, 1952.

Russell, Bertrand. *Power: A New Social Analysis*. London: George Allen & Unwin Ltd., 1948.

Schumpeter, Joseph A. *Imperialism and Social Classes*. Translated by Heinz Norden and edited by Paul M. Sweezy. New York: Augustus M. Kelley, Inc., 1951.

Smelser, Neil J., and Smelser, William T., eds. *Personality and Social Systems*. New York: John Wiley & Sons, Inc., 1963.

Sorokin, Pitirim A. *Social and Cultural Mobility*. New York: The Free Press, 1959.

Tawney, R. H. *The Acquisitive Society*. New York: Harcourt, Brace & World, Inc., 1920.

Veblen, Thorstein. *The Theory of the Leisure Class: An Economic Study of Institutions*. New York: The Modern Library, 1934.

Warner, W. Lloyd, and Abegglen, James C. *Big Business Leaders in America*. New York: Harper & Row, Publishers, 1955.

————, and Associates. *Democracy in Jonesville: A Study of Quality and Inequality*. New York: Harper & Row, Publishers, 1949.

————, and Lunt, Paul S. *The Social Life of a Modern Community*. New Haven: Yale University Press, 1941.

Weber, Max. *Essays in Sociology*. Translated and edited by H. H. Gerth and C. Wright Mills. New York: Oxford University Press, Inc., 1946.

————. *The Theory of Social and Economic Organization*. Translated by A. M. Henderson and Talcott Parsons, edited with an introduction by Talcott Parsons. New York: Oxford University Press, Inc., 1947.

Wirth, Louis. *Community Life and Social Policy*. Edited by Elizabeth Wirth Marvick and Albert J. Reiss, Jr. Chicago: The University of Chicago Press, 1956.

Wolff, Kurt H., trans. and ed. *The Sociology of Georg Simmel*. New York: The Free Press, 1950.

Methodological References

Allport, Gordon W. *The Use of Personal Documents in Psychological Science*. Prepared for the Committee on Appraisal of Research. New York: Social Science Research Council, 1947.

Blumer, Herbert. *Critiques of Research in the Social Sciences: I. An Appraisal of Thomas and Znaniecki's The Polish Peasant in Europe and America*. New York: Social Science Research Council, 1946.

Dollard, John. *Criteria for the Life History, with Analysis of Six Notable Documents*. New York: Peter Smith, 1949.

Eisenstadt, S. N. *From Generation to Generation: Age Groups and Social Structure*. New York: The Free Press, 1956.

Garrett, Annette. *Interviewing: Its Principles and Methods*. New York: Family Service Association of America, 1950.

Goode, William J., and Hatt, Paul K. *Methods in Social Research*. New York: McGraw-Hill Book Co., Inc., 1952.

Gottschalk, Louis, Kluckhohn, Clyde, and Angell, Robert. *The Use of Personal Documents in History, Anthropology, and Sociology*. Prepared for the Committee on Appraisal of Research. New York: Social Science Research Council, 1947.

Hamilton, Gordon. *Principles of Social Case Recording*. New York: Columbia University Press, 1946.

Junker, Buford H. *Field Work: An Introduction to the Social Sciences*. With an Introduction by Everett C. Hughes. Chicago: The University of Chicago Press, 1962.

Murray, Henry A., *Explorations in Personality: A Clinical and Experimental Study of Fifty Men of College Age*. New York: Oxford University Press, Inc., 1938.

————, *Thematic Apperception Test*. Cambridge: Harvard University Press, 1943.

Redfield, Robert. *The Little Community: Viewpoints for the Study of a Human Whole*. Chicago: The University of Chicago Press, 1955.

Richardson, Stephen A., Dohrenwend, Barbara Snell, and Klein, David. *Interviewing, Its Forms and Functions*. New York: Basic Books, Inc., 1965.

Roethlisberger, F. J., and Dickson, William J. "The Interviewing Method" (Chapter 13), *Management and the Worker*. Cambridge: Harvard University Press, 1943.

Thomas, W. I., and Znaniecki, F. *The Polish Peasant in Europe and America*. 2 vols. New York: Alfred A. Knopf, Inc., 1927.

Warner, W. Lloyd, Meeker, Marchia, and Eells, Kenneth. *Social Class in America: A Manual of Procedure for the Measurement of Social Status*. Chicago: Science Research Associates, Inc., 1949.

Young, Pauline V. *Scientific Social Surveys and Research: An Introduc-*

tion to the Background, Content, Methods, and Analysis of Social Studies. With chapters on Statistics, Graphic Presentation, and Ecology by Calvin F. Schmid, and a foreword by Stuart A. Rice. New York: Prentice-Hall, Inc., 1947.

SPECIFIC REFERENCES ON CHINA

Belden, Jack. *China Shakes the World.* New York: Harper & Row, Publishers, 1949.

Chandrasekhar, S. *China's Population: Census and Vital Statistics.* Hong Kong: Hong Kong University Press, 1960.

Chang, Chung-li. *The Chinese Gentry: Studies on Their Role in Nineteenth-Century Chinese Society.* With an introduction by Franz Michael. Seattle: University of Washington Press, 1955.

————. *The Income of the Chinese Gentry: A Sequel to the Chinese Gentry. Studies on Their Role in Nineteenth-Century Chinese Society.* Seattle: University of Washington Press, 1962.

Chang, Kia-ngau, *The Inflationary Spiral: The Experience in China, 1939–1950.* New York: John Wiley & Sons, Inc., 1958.

Chen Kung-po. *The Communist Movement in China.* Edited by C. Martin Wilbur. New York: Columbia University Press, 1960.

Chen, Ta. *Population in Modern China.* With an introduction by William F. Ogburn. Chicago: The University of Chicago Press, 1946.

Chen, Theodore H. E. *Thought Reform of the Chinese Intellectuals.* Hong Kong: Hong Kong University Press, 1960.

Chou, Shun-hsin. *The Chinese Inflation, 1937–1949.* New York: Columbia University Press, 1963.

Chow, Tse-tsung. *The May Fourth Movement: Intellectual Revolution in Modern China.* Cambridge: Harvard University Press, 1960.

Chu, Tung-tsu. *Law and Society in Traditional China.* The Hague: Mouton and Co., 1961.

————. *Local Government in China Under the Ch'ing.* Cambridge: Harvard University Press, 1962.

Clark, Gerald. *Impatient Giant: Red China Today.* New York: David McKay Company, Inc., 1959.

Eberhard, Wolfram. *Conquerors and Rulers: Social Forces in Medieval China.* Leiden: E. J. Brill, 1952.

————. *Social Mobility in Traditional China.* Leiden: E. J. Brill, 1962.

Elegant, Robert S. *The Center of the World: Communism and the Mind of China.* Garden City: Doubleday & Company, Inc., 1964.

————. *China's Red Masters: Political Biographies of the Chinese Communist Leaders.* New York: Twayne Publishers, 1951.

Epstein, Israel. *Notes on Labor Problems in Nationalist China.* New York: Institute of Pacific Relations, 1949.

Fairbank, John K., ed. *Chinese Thought and Institutions.* Chicago: The University of Chicago Press, 1957.

————. *The United States and China.* Cambridge: Harvard University Press, 1949.

Giles, Herbert A. *A History of Chinese Literature.* New York: Appleton-Century-Crofts, 1937.

Hightower, J. R. *Topics in Chinese Literature: Outline and Bibliographies.* Revised edition. Cambridge: Harvard University Press, 1953.

Ho, Ping-ti. *The Ladder of Success in Imperial China: Aspects of Social Mobility, 1368–1911.* New York: Columbia University Press, 1962.
———. *Studies on the Population of China, 1368–1953.* Cambridge: Harvard University Press, 1959.

Hsia, C. T. *A History of Modern Chinese Fiction, 1917–1957.* With an appendix on Taiwan by Tsi-an Hsia. New Haven: Yale University Press, 1961.

Hsiao, Kung-chuan. *Rural China, Imperial Control in the Nineteenth Century.* Seattle: University of Washington Press, 1960.

Hsieh, Pao-chao. *The Government of China (1644–1911).* Baltimore: The Johns Hopkins Press, 1925.

Hsu, Cho-yun. *Ancient China in Transition: An Analysis of Social Mobility, 722–222 B. C.* Stanford: Stanford University Press, 1965.

Hu, Shih. *The Chinese Renaissance: The Haskell Lectures, 1933.* Chicago: The University of Chicago Press, 1934.

Hughes, E. R. *The Invasion of China by the Western World.* London: A. and C. Black, 1937.

Institute of Pacific Relations. *Agrarian China: Selected Source Materials from Chinese Authors.* Translated and edited by the research staff of the Chinese Secretariat. London: George Allen & Unwin, Ltd., 1939.

Kiang, Wen-han. *The Chinese Student Movement.* New York: King's Crown Press, 1948.

Kracke, E. A., Jr. *Civil Service in Early Sung China, 960–1067.* Cambridge: Harvard University Press, 1953.

Lang, Olga. *Chinese Family and Society.* New Haven: Yale University Press, 1946.

Lattimore, Owen, *China—A Short History.* New York: W. W. Norton & Company, Inc., 1947.

Levy, Marion J., Jr. *The Family Revolution in Modern China.* Cambridge: Harvard University Press, 1949.

Li, Choh-ming. *Economic Development of Communist China: An Appraisal of the First Five Years of Industrialization.* Berkeley: University of California Press, 1959.

Lin Yü-tang. *The Importance of Living.* New York: John Day Company, Inc., 1937.
———. *The Wisdom of China and India.* New York: Random House, Inc., 1942.

Liu, Hui-chen Wang. The Traditional Chinese Clan Rules. Locust Valley, N.Y.: J. J. Augustin Inc., 1959.

Lusin. *Ah Q and Others: Selected Stories of Lusin.* Translated by Chi-chen Wang. New York: Columbia University Press, 1941.

Marsh, Robert M. *The Mandarins: The Circulation of Elites in China, 1600–1900.* New York: The Free Press, 1961.

Milbank Memorial Fund. *Population Trends in Eastern Europe: The U.S.S.R. and Mainland China.* Proceedings of the thirty-sixth annual conference of the Milbank Memorial Fund, November 4–5, 1959, at the Carnegie Endowment International Center. New York: Milbank Memorial Fund, 1960.

Nibison, David S., and Wright, Arthur F., eds. *Confucianism in Action*. Stanford: Stanford University Press, 1959.

North, Robert C. *Kuomintang and Chinese Communist Elites*. With the collaboration of Ithiel de Sola Pool and an introduction by John K. Fairbank. Stanford: Stanford University Press, 1952.

————. *Moscow and Chinese Communists*. Stanford: Stanford University Press, 1953.

Payne, Robert. *Mao Tse-tung: Ruler of Red China*. New York: Henry Schuman, Inc., 1950.

Redfield, Margaret Park (Rev. and ed.). *China's Gentry: Essays in Rural-Urban Relations* by Hsiao-tung Fei, with six life histories of Chinese gentry families collected by Yung-teh Chow and an introduction by Robert Redfield. Chicago: The University of Chicago Press, 1953.

Rostow, W. W., in collaboration with Richard W. Hatch, Frank A. Kierman, Jr., and Alexander Eckstein. *The Prospects for Communist China*. New York: John Wiley & Sons, Inc., 1954.

Shih, Kuo-heng. *China Enters the Machine Age: A Study of Labor in Chinese War Industry*. With a supplementary chapter by Ju-kang Tien, edited and translated by Hsiao-tung Fei and Francis L. K. Hsu. Cambridge: Harvard University Press, 1944.

Smedley, Agnes. *The Great Road: The Life and Times of Chu Teh*. New York: Monthly Review Press, 1956.

Snow, Edgar. *The Other Side of the River: Red China Today*. New York: Random House, 1962.

Sun, E-tu Zen, and De Francis, John. *Chinese Social History: Translations of Selected Studies*. Washington, D.C.: American Council of Learned Societies, 1956.

Tawney, R. H. *Land and Labour in China*. London: George Allen & Unwin, Ltd., 1932.

Tung, Chi-ming. *An Outline History of China*. Peking: Foreign Languages Press, 1959.

Wales, Nym. *Red Dust: Autobiographies of Chinese Communists*. Stanford: Stanford University Press, 1952.

Williams, S. W. *The Middle Kingdom*. Revised edition. 2 vols. New York: Charles Scribner's Sons, 1904.

Wu, Han, and Fei, Hsiao-tung, *et al. Huang Chuan Yü Shên Chuan (The Emperor's Power and the Gentry's Power)*. Shanghai: Kuan Ch'a Press, 1948.

Yang, C. K. *The Chinese Family in the Communist Revolution*. With a foreword by Talcott Parsons. Cambridge: The Technology Press, Massachusetts Institute of Technology, distributed by Harvard University Press, 1959.

————. *Religion in Chinese Society: A Study of Contemporary Social Functions of Religion and Some of Their Historical Facts*. Berkeley: University of California Press, 1961.

Community Studies in China

Chen, Ta. *Emigrant Communities in South China: A Study of Overseas Migration and Its Influence on Standard of Living and Social Change.* English version edited by Bruno Lasker. New York: Secretariat, Institute of Pacific Relations, 1940.

Crook, Isabel, and Crook, David. *Revolution in a Chinese Village: Ten Mile Inn.* New York: Humanities Press, 1960.

Fei, Hsiao-tung. *Peasant Life in China: A Field Study of Country Life in the Yangtze Valley.* London: Routledge & Kegan Paul, Ltd., 1939.

————, and Chang, Chih-i. *Earthbound China: A Study of Rural Economy in Yunnan.* Chicago: The University of Chicago Press, 1945.

Fitzgerald, C. P. *The Tower of Five Glories: A Study of the Min Chia of Ta Li, Yunnan.* London: The Cresset Press, 1941.

Fried, Morton H. *Fabric of Chinese Society: A Study of the Social Life of a Chinese County Seat.* New York: Frederick A. Praeger, Inc., Publishers, 1953.

Gambles, Sidney D. *North China Villages: Social, Political and Economic Activities Before 1933.* Berkeley: University of California Press, 1963.

————. *Ting Hsien: A North Chinese Rural Community.* Introduction by Y. C. James Yen. New York: Institute of Pacific Relations, 1954.

Geddes, W. R. *Peasant Life in Communist China.* Ithaca: The Society for Applied Anthropology, 1963.

Hsu, Francis L. K. *Religion, Science and Human Crises: A Study of China in Transition and Its Implication for the West.* London: Routledge & Kegan Paul Ltd., 1952.

————. *Under the Ancestors' Shadow: Chinese Culture and Personality.* New York: Columbia University Press, 1948.

Kulp, D. H. *Country Life in South China: The Sociology of Familism.* New York: Bureau of Publication, Teachers College, Columbia University, 1925.

Lin, Yueh-hwa. *The Golden Wing: A Sociological Study of Chinese Familism.* London: Routledge & Kegan Paul, Ltd., 1947.

————. *The Lolo of Liang Shan (Liang-Shan I-Chia).* Translated by Ju-shu Pan. New Haven: HRAF Press, 1961.

Myrdal, Jan. *Report from a Chinese Village,* translated from the Swedish by Maurice Michael. New York: Pantheon Books, 1965. Illustrations and photographs by Gun Kessle. Original title: *Rapport fran Kinesisk,* 1963.

Osgood, Cornelius. *Village Life in Old China: A Community Study of Kao Yao, Yunnan.* New York: The Ronald Press Company, 1963.

Yang, C. K. *A Chinese Village in Early Communist Transition.* Cambridge: The Technology Press, distributed by Harvard University Press, 1959.

Yang, Martin C. *A Chinese Village: Taitou, Shantung Province.* New York: Columbia University Press, 1945.

ARTICLES

Bierstedt, Robert. "An Analysis of Social Power," *American Sociological Review,* 15 (1950), 730–8.

Bodde, Derk. "Feudalism in China," in *Feudalism in History,* edited by Rushton Coulborn. Princeton: Princeton University Press, 1956, pp. 49–92.

Carr-Saunders, A. M., and Wilson, P. A. "Professions," *Encyclopaedia of The Social Sciences,* edited by Edwin R. A. Seligman and Alvin Johnson (New York: The Macmillan Co., 1934), Vol. XII, pp. 476–80.

Chen, Theodore Hsi-en, "The Marxist Remolding of Chinese Society," *The American Journal of Sociology,* 58, no. 4 (January, 1953), 340–6.

————, and Chen, Wen-hui C. "The 'Three-Anti' and 'Five-Anti' Movements in Communist China," *Pacific Affairs,* 26, no. 1 (March, 1953), 3–23.

Davis, Allison. "American Status Systems and the Socialization of the Children," in Clyde Kluckhohn and Henry A. Murray, eds., *Personality in Nature, Society, and Culture.* New York: Alfred A. Knopf, Inc., 1948, pp. 459–68.

Fei, Hsiao-tung. "Peasantry and Gentry: An Interpretation of Chinese Social Structure and Its Changes," *American Journal of Sociology,* 52 (July, 1946), 1–17.

Fried, Morton H. "Community Studies in China," *The Far Eastern Quarterly,* 14 (November, 1954), 11–36.

————. "Review of the Chinese Gentry by Chung-Li Chang," *American Anthropologist,* 59 (1957), 560–1.

————. "Military Status in Chinese Society," *American Journal of Sociology,* 57 (January, 1952), 347–55.

Goldhammer, Herbert, and Shils, Edward A. "Types of Power and Status," *American Journal of Sociology,* 45 (September, 1939), 171–82.

Hatt, Paul K. "Stratification in the Mass Society," *American Sociological Review,* 15 (April, 1950), 216–22.

Heberle, Rudolf. "A Review of *Social Mobility* by Pitirim Sorokin," *American Journal of Sociology,* 34 (July, 1928), 219–25.

Hermann, Heller. "Political Power," *Encyclopaedia of the Social Sciences,* Edited by Edwin R. A. Seligman and Alvin Johnson (New York: The Macmillan Company, 1934), Vol. XII, pp. 300–5.

Ho, Ping-ti. "Aspects of Social Mobility in China, 1368–1911," *Comparative Studies in Society and History,* 1 (June, 1959), 330–59.

Hsu, Francis L. K. "Social Mobility in China," *American Sociological Review,* 14 (December, 1949), 764–71.

Hughes, Everett C. "Institutional Office and the Person," *American Journal of Sociology,* 43 (November, 1937), 365–76.

Kallen, Horace M. "Reformism," *Encyclopaedia of the Social Sciences,* Edited by Edwin R. A. Seligman and Alvin Johnson (New York: The Macmillan Company, 1934), Vol. XIII, pp. 194–5.

Kracke, E. A. "Family *vs.* Merit in Chinese Civil Service Examinations under the Empire," *Harvard Journal of Asiatic Studies,* 10 (1947), 103–23.

———. "Region, Family, and Individual in the Chinese Examination System," in John K. Fairbank, ed., *Chinese Thought and Institutions* (Chicago: The University of Chicago Press, 1957), pp. 251–68.

Lee, Shu-ching. "Intelligentsia of China," *American Journal of Sociology,* 52 (May, 1947), 489–97.

Mombert, Paul. "Class," *Encyclopaedia of The Social Sciences,* Edited by Edwin R. A. Seligman and Alvin Johnson (New York: The Macmillan Co., 1930), Vol. III, pp. 531–6.

Pan, Quentin, and Fei, Hsiao-tung. "K'o-chü yü She-hui Liu-tung" ("The Civil Service Examination and Social Mobility"), *She-hui K'o-hsueh (The Social Sciences),* 4, No. 1 (1947), 1–21.

Parsons, Talcott. "Age and Sex in the Social Structure of the United States," in *Personality in Nature, Society, and Culture.* Edited by Clyde Kluckhohn and Henry A. Murray (New York: Alfred A. Knopf, Inc., 1948), pp. 269–81.

———. "An Analytical Approach to the Theory of Social Stratification," *American Journal of Sociology,* 45 (May, 1940), 841–62.

Pfautz, Harold W., and Duncan, Otis Dudley. "A Critical Evaluation of Warner's Work in Community Stratification." *American Sociological Review,* 15 (April, 1950), 205–15.

Quesnay, François. "Le despotisme de la Chine," translated in Lewis A. Maverick, *China: A Model for Europe* (San Antonio: Paul Anderson Co., 1946), pp. 139–304.

Radin, Max. "Status," *Encyclopaedia of The Social Sciences,* Edited by Edwin R. A. Seligman and Alvin Johnson (New York: The Macmillan Co., 1934), Vol. XIV, pp. 373–7.

Riessman, Leonard. "Levels of Aspiration and Social Class," *American Sociological Review,* 18 (June, 1953), 233–42.

Shih, Ching. "Shên Chüan Ti Chi-Ti" ("The Continuity of the Gentry's Power"), *Kuan Ch'a (The Observation),* 4, No. 17 (June 19, 1948), 12, 13, 19.

———. "Shên Chüan Ti Pên-Chih" ("The Essentials of the Gentry's Power"), *Chung-kuo Chien-shih (China's Reconstruction),* 6, No. 6 (1948), 46–9.

Simmel, Georg. "Superiority and Subordination as Subject-Matter of Sociology," *American Journal of Sociology,* 2 (September and November, 1896), 167–89; 392–415.

Tawney, R. H. "The Rise of the Gentry, 1558–1640," *Economic History Review,* 11 (1941), 1–38.

Teng, Ssŭ-Yü. "Chinese Influence on the Western Examination," *Harvard Journal of Asiatic Studies,* 7 (September, 1943), 267–312.

Wang, Yi Chu. "The Intelligentsia in Changing China," *Foreign Affairs,* 36, No. 2 (January, 1958), 315–29.

———. "Western Impact and Social Mobility in China," *American Sociological Review,* 25 (December, 1960), 843–55.

Wang, Yu-ch'uan. "The Rise of the Land Tax and the Fall of Dynasties in Chinese History," *Pacific Affairs,* 9 (1936), 201–20.

Wittfogel, Karl A. "Public Office in the Liao Dynasty and the Chinese Examination System," *Harvard Journal of Asiatic Studies,* 10 (1949), 13–40.

REPORTS AND UNPUBLISHED MATERIALS

Institute for Census Research, National Tsing Hua University. "Experimental Population Census and Vital Registration in Kunming Lake Region, Yunnan Province." Kunming: Committee on Experimental Census and Vital Registration for Kunming Lake Region, 1944.

————. "A Report on Experimental Population Census in Kunming Lake Region, Yunnan Province." Appendix 10 (B). Kunming: Committee on Experimental Census and Vital Registration for Kunming Lake Region, 1944.

————. "A Report on the Registration of Vital Statistics in Chengkung and Kunyang, Yunnan Province." Kunming: Committee on Experimental Census and Vital Registration for Kunming Lake Region, 1946.

Kuo, Pao. "The Power Structure in a Rural Community in Yunnan," Chengkung: Station for Sociological Research, National Yunnan University, 1943.

Levy, Marion, J., Jr., and Shih, Kuo-heng. "The Rise of the Modern Chinese Business Class." New York: Institute of Pacific Relations, 1949.

Su, Ru-chiang. "Studies in Rural Economy in The County of Kunyang, Yunnan." Kunyang: Kunyang Research Station, The Institute for Census Research, National Tsing Hua University, 1943.

Taylor, Burton Wakeman. "Status Mobility; An Aspect of Social Mobility." New York: Columbia University (Doctoral Dissertation), 1936.

Index

Abegglen, James C., 29, 44, 225, 258
Adoption of children, 118–19, 156
Agriculture. *See* Farmers; Land; Peasants
Alcohol. *See* Drinking
All Men Are Brothers (Shih Nai-an), 102, 268
Ancestral cult; ancestor worship, 13, 14, 15, 78, 117; tombs, 123–24, 178
Animism, 14, 15
Army, the, 4, 39, 158, 161, 162, 181–82, 237, 253; mobility through, 57, 107, 117, 157, 158–72, 231–32, 238; way to wealth through, 220
Artisans; craftsmen, 229, 235–37, 238

Bandits; banditry, 68–73, 82–83, 162, 163, 170–71, 184; political transition and, 267–75
Birth, 111–13; ceremony, 90, 120, 121; elite by, 204–13; naming infants, 90; rates, 13, 112–13
Bodde, Derk, 42
Bribery, 65, 179, 219. *See also* Corruption
Buddhism, 14, 15
Bureaucracy, 2–7, 39, 60, 65, 87, 129 (*See also* Government; Officialdom); mobility through, 157, 172–86, 214, 237, 238
Burial. *See* Funerals; Tombs
Business; businessmen (merchants), 12, 39, 40, 41, 99, 229; and mobility, 157–58, 186–94, 220–22, 237, 238

Calligraphy, 97, 98, 138, 176. *See also* Writing
Ceremonies; ceremonialism, 90, 93–94, 120–27. *See also* Birth; Funerals; Weddings
Chan, Yang, 18, 20–21
Chance (opportunity), mobility and, 251–57, 278
Chang, Chief, 25–26, 53–54, 55, 61–63, 132, 135, 208, 210, 211; and community service, 86–87, 91; and extended family system, 119–20; and government, 173–82; and housebuilding ceremony, 123; Ting and, 201, 202, 203
Chang, Major, 60–61, 208, 210; and army, 165–69; and education, 106, 107
Chang, Chih-I, 31, 33, 93, 145, 194, 226, 257, 258
Chang, Chung-li, 41, 42, 43, 45
Chang Wei-lung, 119, 173–75
Chao, Magistrate, 47–48, 50, 62–63, 135, 190; Liu Tsung-tao and, 273–

75; Chief Chang and, 168, 180–81, 202; Shen and, 147–48; Ting and, 132–33
Chen, Magistrate, 86–87, 177
Chen, Ta, 9, 31, 43, 257
Chen, Theodore Hsi-en, 284
Ch'eng (walled city), 239–40
Chengkung, 9, 14, 15, 16
Chien, Mr., 87
Chien-shêng (academic title), 3–4
Chien Tsai-wan, 198–99
Children, 13, 108–20, 121, 156, 246–47; adoption of, 118–19, 156; education of, 107 (*See also* Education); extended family system and, 108–20; mobility and, 246–47 (*See also* Generations, mobility and)
Chin-shih (academic degree), 3, 4, 35–38
China's Gentry . . . (Fei). *See* Fei, Hsiao-tung
Chinese Village . . ., A (Martin C. Yang), 31, 33–34, 44, 225
Chinese Village in Early Communist Transition, A (C. K. Yang), 31, 33, 43, 284
Ch'ing Dynasty, 35, 36, 41, 124, 261
Chou, Shun-hsin, 43
Chow, Yung-teh, 42, 93, 276
Chu, Commander, 25, 50, 51, 53, 61, 74, 76, 129, 153, 181; and ceremonial display, 122, 123–24; and community service, 88, 91; daily life of, 99; defense of community by, 83–85; and education, 107; family of, 205, 211–12, 230–31, 251–52; and the military, 117, 159–65, 220
Chu Erh Lao Yeh, 73–75
Chu Fu, 164, 211
Chu Hsin, 85–86, 129, 163, 212, 235
Chu Hun, 160–61
Chu-jen (academic degree), 3, 4, 36–38
Chu Kan, 84, 160–61, 211–12, 251–52
Chu Lung, 54–55, 107, 135, 168; as birth elite, 205–6, 210; entertainment display by, 128
Chu Yuan, 124, 159–60, 230–31
Chu Yuan-chang, 268
Cities (towns), ecological mobility and, 238–42
Civil service, 35–39, 41, 101, 124. *See also* Bureaucracy; Government; Officialdom
Class mobility, social reform and, 259–75
Class status. *See* Status system

295

DATE DUE
